Responding Voices:

A Reader for Emerging Writers

Responding Voices:
A Reader for Emerging Writers

Jon Ford

College of Alameda

Elaine Hughes

Nassau Community College

The McGraw-Hill Companies, Inc.

New York   St. Louis   San Francisco   Auckland   Bogotá   Caracas   Lisbon
London   Madrid   Mexico City   Milan   Montreal   New Delhi   San Juan
Singapore   Sydney   Tokyo   Toronto

McGraw-Hill

A Division of The McGraw·Hill Companies

RESPONDING VOICES:
A Reader For Emerging Writers

Acknowledgments appear on pages 403-405, and on this page by reference.

This book is printed on acid-free paper.

1 2 3 4 5 6 7 8 9 0 DOC DOC 9 0 9 8 7 6

ISBN 0-07-021526-X

This book was set in Palatino by ComCom, Inc.

The editor was Tim Julet;

the designer was Joan Greenfield; the production supervisor was Leroy A. Young.

Project supervision was done by Hockett Editorial Service.

R. R. Donnelley & Sons Company was printer and binder.

Library of Congress Cataloging-in-Publication Data

Ford, Jon.
    Responding voices: a reader for emerging writers / Jon Ford,
Elaine Hughes.
        p.   cm.
    Includes bibliographical references and index.
    ISBN 0-07-021526-X
    1. College readers.   2. English language--Rhetoric.   3. English
language--Grammar.   I. Hughes, Elaine   II. Title
PE1417.F59   1997
808'.0427--dc20   96-19889

About the Authors

JON FORD studied comparative literature at the University of Texas and the University of Wisconsin, where he was a Woodrow Wilson Fellow. He was founding editor of *Poetryflash,* a San Francisco Bay Area review of poetry books and events. Since 1970, he has taught English at the College of Alameda, where he coordinates the English program and works in a computerized writing center that he helped develop. He has coauthored a number of readers for college writing classes, including *Dreams and Inward Journeys, Writing as Revelation, Coming from Home,* and *Imagining Worlds.*

ELAINE HUGHES taught at Hinds Community College in Raymond, Mississippi, for a number of years before coming to New York in 1979 to teach at Nassau Community College on Long Island. Since retiring from Nassau College in 1994, she has lectured and conducted writing workshops for many organizations, including the Esalen Institute in California. Elaine Hughes is the author of *Writing from the Inner Self* and coauthor of *Rules of Thumb* and *Finding Answers: A Guide to Conducting and Reporting Research.*

Contents

RHETORICAL TABLE OF CONTENTS xiii

PREFACE TO THE INSTRUCTOR xix

TO THE STUDENT xxiii

THE READING AND WRITING PROCESS

Chapter 1 Responding as a Reader   3

Chapter 2 Responding as a Writer   15

READINGS

Chapter 3 Education   37

 Introduction 38

  Isaac Asimov: *What Is Intelligence, Anyway?* 40
  John Holt: *How Teachers Make Children Hate Reading* 43
  Tin Le: *An Immigrant in a New School (student essay)* 49
  Jayme Plunkett: *He Couldn't Get Off the Ground*
   (student essay) 52

Merle Woo: *Poem for the Creative Writing Class, Spring 1982*
(*poem*) 55
Shirley Jackson: *Charles (short story)* 58
Jonathan Kozol: *Corla Hawkins* 64
Deborah Tannen: *How Male and Female Students Use Language
Differently* 70
Mike Rose: *I Just Wanna Be Average* 77
Rainbow Schwartz: *I Just Wanna Be Challenged
(student essay)* 88
Richard Carrillo: *Surviving Adolescence (student essay)* 92

Making Connections 96

Chapter 4 Family 99

Introduction 100

Ellen Goodman: *Our Kids Are Not Just Copies of Us* 102
Lawrence Wright: *Reunion* 105
Amy Marx: *My Grandfather's Memories (student essay)* 109
Charlie Wu: *Family Friends: A Process of Growth
(student essay)* 112
Alberto Alvaro Rios: *Nani (poem)* 116
Tillie Olsen: *I Stand Here Ironing (short story)* 119
Amy Tan: *Snapshot: Lost Lives of Women* 128
Joan Didion: *On Going Home* 132
Alice Walker: *Father* 136
Beverley Skinner: *My Dad and Walker's "Father"
(student essay)* 143
Shu Fan Lee: *Alice Walker's "Father": A Process of Understanding
and Acceptance (student essay)* 146

Making Connections 149

Chapter 5 Gender 151

Introduction 152

Elizabeth Cady Stanton: *You Should Have Been a Boy!* 154
Scott Russell Sanders: *The Men We Carry in Our Minds . . . and How
They Differ from the Real Lives of Most Men* 158

Quynhchau Tran: *The Battle between Men and Women*
   (student essay)   163
Greg Matthews: *Indiscriminate Discrimination*
   (student essay)   166
Marge Piercy: *A Work of Artifice (poem)*   169
Wakako Yamauchi: *And the Soul Shall Dance*
   (short story)   171
Rick Cary: *Coming Out*   179
Julius Lester: *Being a Boy*   184
Nina Woodle: *On Being Female (student essay)*   189
Magnolia Tse: *What about Being a Girl? (student essay)*   192

Making Connections   194

Chapter 6   Nature   197

Introduction   198

Lewis Thomas: *On Embryology*   200
Linda Hogan: *Walking*   203
David Kerr: *Strawberry Creek: A Search for Origins*
   (student essay)   207
Jeff Hunze: *Lessons from the Earth (student essay)*   211
William Stafford: *Traveling through the Dark (poem)*   214
Peter Taylor: *A Walled Garden (short story)*   216
John T. Nichols: *What Is a Naturalist, Anyway?*   221
Annie Dillard: *Sojourner*   227
Elizabeth Marshall Thomas: *Do Dogs Have Thoughts and
   Feelings?*   231
Kirsten Simon: *Dogs in Transition (student essay)*   235
Lori Pascerella: *Dogs and Empathetic Observation*
   (student essay)   238

Making Connections   240

Chapter 7   Health   243

Introduction   244

Donald M. Murray: *Reflections from a Sick Bed*   246
Geoffrey Kurland: *A Doctor's Case*   251

Dickon Chan: *The Health Care Plan I Favor (student essay)*   255
Kirsten Simon: *Massage-Message (student essay)*   258
Robin Becker: *Medical Science (poem)*   261
William Carlos Williams: *The Use of Force (short story)*   263
Perri Klass: *Learning the Language*   268
Anna Quindlen: *The War on Drinks*   273
Bill Moyers: *The Art of Healing*   276
Katherine Razum: *Doctor, Do You Care? (student essay)*   282
Derek Collins: *Responding to "The Art of Healing"*
  (student essay)   286

Making Connections   289

Chapter 8   WORK   291

Introduction   292

Richard Rodriguez: *Labor*   294
Nancy K. Austin: *Workable Ethics*   299
Jennifer Holmes: *The Work Ethic and Me (student essay)*   305
Kevin (Wing Kuen) Hip: *Why I Hate Work (student essay)*   308
Laureen Mar: *My Mother, Who Came from China, Where She Never
  Saw Snow (poem)*   311
Heinrich Böll: *The Laugher (short story)*   313
Maya Angelou: *Cotton Pickers*   317
Mickey Kaus: *Yes, Something Will Work: Work*   321
Barbara Ehrenreich: *A Step Back to the Workhouse?*   325
Nikki Corbin: *Why Workfare? (student essay)*   331
Deirdre Mena: *Welfare versus Workfare (student essay)*   334

Making Connections   337

Chapter 9   Community   339

Introduction   340

P. W. Alexander: *Christmas at Home*   342
Arthur Ashe: *Can a New "Army" Save Our Cities?*   347
Julian Castro: *Politics . . . Maybe (student essay)*   351
Jeremy Taylor: *A Call to Service (student essay)*   354
Tess Gallagher: *The Hug (poem)*   361
Toni Cade Bambara: *My Man Bovanne (short story)*   364

David Morris: *Rootlessness*   371

Kathryn McCamant and Charles Durrett: *Cohousing and the American Dream*   376

Evan McKenzie: *Trouble in Privatopia*   382

Cecilia Fairley: *Whatever Happened to the Neighborhood?* *(student essay)*   389

Kimberly Curtis: *Modern America: Metropolis or Necropolis?* *(student essay)*   394

Making Connections   399

Bringing Ideas Together: Making Further Connections   400

Acknowledgments   403

INDEX   407

Rhetorical Table of Contents

Narration

P. W. Alexander: *Christmas at Home*   342
Henrich Böll: *The Laugher*   313
Toni Cade Bambara: *My Man Bovanne*   364
Richard Carrillo: *Surviving Adolescence*   92
Rick Cary: *Coming Out*   179
Joan Didion: *On Going Home*   132
Tess Gallagher: *The Hug*   361
Shirley Jackson: *Charles*   58
Jonathan Kozol: *Corla Hawkins*   64
Tin Le: *An Immigrant in a New School*   49
Julius Lester: *Being a Boy*   184
Amy Marx: *My Grandfather's Memories*   109
Tillie Olsen: *I Stand Here Ironing*   119
Lori Pascerella: *Dogs and Empathetic Observation*   238
Mike Rose: *I Just Wanna Be Average*   77
William Stafford: *Traveling through the Dark*   214
Amy Tan *Snapshot: Lost Lives of Women*   128
Peter Taylor: *A Walled Garden*   216
Alice Walker: *Father*   136
William Carlos Williams: *The Use of Force*   263
Wakako Yamauchi: *And the Soul Shall Dance*   171

Description

Maya Angelou: *Cotton Pickers*   317
Robin Becker: *Medical Science*   261

Joan Didion: *On Going Home*   132
Annie Dillard: *Sojourner*   227
Linda Hogan: *Walking*   203
Jeff Hunze: *Lessons from the Earth*   211
David Kerr: *Strawberry Creek: A Search for Origins*   207
Tillie Olsen: *I Stand Here Ironing*   119
Jayme Plunckett: *He Couldn't Get Off the Ground*   52
Lewis Thomas: *On Embryology*   200
Merle Woo: *Poem for the Creative Writing Class,
     Spring 1982*   55
Charlie Wu: *Family Friends: A Process of Growth*   112

Examples and Illustration

Nancy K. Austin: *Workable Ethics*   299
Julian Castro: *Politics . . . Maybe*   351
Ellen Goodman: *Our Kids Are Not Just Copies of Us*   102
Kevin (Wing Kuen) Hip: *Why I Hate Work*   308
Jennifer Holmes: *The Work Ethic and Me*   305
Jeff Hunze: *Lessons from the Earth*   211
Perri Klass: *Learning the Language*   268
Greg Matthews: *Indiscriminate Discrimination*   166
Bill Moyers: *The Art of Healing*   276
Marge Piercy: *A Work of Artifice*   169
Kirsten Simon: *Dogs in Transition*   235
Nina Woodle: *On Being Female*   189

Comparison and Contrast

Richard Carrillo: *Surviving Adolescence*   92
Kimberly Curtis: *Modern America:
     Metropolis or Necropolis?*   394
Cecilia Fairley: *Whatever Happened to the Neighborhood?*   389
Ellen Goodman: *Our Kids Are Not Just Copies of Us*   102
Shu Fan Lee: *Alice Walker's "Father": A Process of Understanding
     and Acceptance*   146
Julius Lester: *Being a Boy*   184
Laureen Mar: *My Mother, Who Came from China, Where She Never
     Saw Snow*   311
Donald M. Murray: *Reflections from a Sick Bed*   246
Alberto Alvaro Rios: *Nani*   116
Richard Rodriguez: *Labor*   294
Scott Russell Sanders: *The Men We Carry in Our Minds . . . and How*

They Differ from the Real Lives of Most Men   158
Rainbow Schwartz: *I Just Wanna Be Challenged*   88
Deborah Tannen: *How Male and Female Students Use Language
    Differently*   70
Peter Taylor: *A Walled Garden*   216
William Carlos Williams: *The Use of Force*   263
Wakako Yamauchi: *And the Soul Shall Dance*   171

Definition

Isaac Asimov: *What Is Intelligence, Anyway?*   40
Nancy K. Austin: *Workable Ethics*   299
Henrich Böll: *The Laugher*   313
Rick Cary: *Coming Out*   179
Annie Dillard: *Sojourner*   227
Kathryn McCamant and Charles Durrett: *Cohousing and the American
    Dream*   376
Linda Hogan: *Walking*   203
John Holt: *How Teachers Make Children Hate Reading*   43
Perri Klass: *Learning the Language*   268
Evan McKenzie: *Trouble in Privatopia*   382
David Morris: *Rootlessness*   371
John T. Nichols: *What Is a Naturalist, Anyway?*   221
Richard Rodriguez: *Labor*   294
Deborah Tannen: *How Male and Female Students Use Language
    Differently*   70
Elizabeth Marshall Thomas: *Do Dogs Have Thoughts and
    Feelings?*   231
Lewis Thomas: *On Embryology*   200

Process

Rick Cary: *Coming Out*   179
John Holt: *How Teachers Make Children Hate Reading*   43
John T. Nichols: *What Is a Naturalist, Anyway?*   221
Beverley Skinner: *My Dad and Walker's "Father"*   143
Elizabeth Cady Stanton: *You Should Have Been
    a Boy!*   154
Lawrence Wright: *Reunion*   105

Classification and Division

Cecilia Fairley: *Whatever Happened to the Neighborhood?*   389
Jeff Hunze: *Lessons from the Earth*   211

Perri Klass: *Learning the Language*   268
Bill Moyers *The Art of Healing*   276
Deborah Tannen *How Male and Female Students Use Language
  Differently*   70

Cause and Effect

Julian Castro: *Politics . . . Maybe*   351
Ellen Goodman: *Our Kids Are Not Just Copies of Us*   102
John Holt: *How Teachers Make Children Hate Reading*   43
Geoffrey: Kurland *A Doctor's Case*   251
Kathryn McCamant and Charles Durrett: *Cohousing and the American
  Dream*   376
Evan McKenzie: *Trouble in Privatopia*   382
David Morris: *Rootlessness*   371
Bill Moyers: *The Art of Healing*   276
Marge Piercy: *A Work of Artifice*   169
Anna Quindlen: *The War on Drinks*   273
Katherine Razum: *Doctor, Do You Care?*   282
Quynhchau Tran: *The Battle between
  Men and Women*   163
Alice Walker: *Father*   136
Wakako Yamauchi: *And the Soul Shall Dance*   171

Argument

Arthur Ashe: *Can a New "Army" Save Our Cities?*   347
Dickon Chan: *The Health Care Plan I Favor*   255
Derek Collins: *Responding to "The Art of Healing"*   286
Nikki Corbin: *Why Workfare?*   331
Kimberly Curtis: *Modern America: Metropolis or
Necropolis?*   394
Barbara Ehrenreich: *A Step Back to the Workhouse?*   325
Kevin (Wing Kuen) Hip: *Why I Hate Work
  (student essay)*   308
John Holt: *How Teachers Make Students Hate Reading*   43
Mickey Kaus: *Yes, Something Will Work: Work*   321
Greg Matthews: *Indiscriminate Discrimination*   166
Kathryn McCamant and Charles Durrett: *Cohousing and the American
  Dream*   376
Evan McKenzie: *Trouble in Privatopia*   382
Deirdre Mena: *Welfare versus Workfare*   334
David Morris: *Rootlessness*   371

Bill Moyers: *The Art of Healing*   276
Anna Quindlen: *The War on Drinks*   273
Katherine Razum: *Doctor, Do You Care?*   282
Scott Russell Sanders: *The Men We Carry in Our Minds . . . and How
    They Differ from the Real Lives of Most Men*   158
Kirsten Simon: *Dogs in Transition*   235
Kirsten Simon: *Massage-Message*   258
Deborah Tannen: *How Male and Female Students Use Language
    Differently*   70
Jeremy Taylor: *A Call to Service*   354
Quynhchau Tran: *The Battle between Men and Women*   163
Magnolia Tse: *What about Being a Girl?*   192

Poetry
Robin Becker: *Medical Science*   261
Tess Gallagher: *The Hug*   361
Laureen Mar: *My Mother, Who Came from China, Where She Never
    Saw Snow*   311
Marge Piercy: *A Work of Artifice*   169
Alberto Alvaro Rios: *Nani*   116
William Stafford: *Traveling through the Dark*   214
Merle Woo: *Poem for the Creative Writing Class,
    Spring 1982*   55

Preface to the Instructor

OVERVIEW

Responding Voices is a thematic anthology designed to bridge the gap between the developmental and transfer-level composition course through motivating the student to produce writing that is powerful and committed in its voice, ideas, support, and structure. The book encourages students to write in response to a range of essays, stories, and poems, as well as take strong positions on controversial contemporary issues related to the major themes of the text: education, family, gender, health, nature, work, and community. Although the essays and fictional texts are fairly short, ranging from one to four pages, both the professional and the student readings in each chapter will challenge students' comprehension and engage their critical thinking abilities.

HIGHLIGHTS OF THE BOOK

• Warm, engaging tone that invites student involvement
• Two full-length introductory chapters, one on the reading process and the reading journal; one on the writing process, collaboration, and peer editing
• A total of forty-seven professional writings, including essays developed using narration, description, illustration, process, definition, comparison, classification, causal reasoning, and argument, as well as seven poems and seven short stories
• Twenty-eight student essays, four per chapter, written in response to the chapter themes and to the professional writings in the chapter

- Special emphasis on journal-keeping, with numerous journal writing suggestions throughout the book.
- Consistent organization pattern that makes the book easier to use and helps keep focus on student writing
- Apparatus that invites critical thinking, close reading, small-group discussions, and strong written response
- Rich mixture of different types of writing represented: shorter argumentative pieces, some from current periodicals, mixed with quality memoir, fiction, and poetry
- Longer end-of-chapter activities that help students make connections among readings and develop longer, independent projects

APPARATUS

The apparatus for *Responding Voices* focuses on close reading, critical thinking, and group work, inviting informal written responses in the reader's journal as well as more formal essay responses. The same apparatus is used for the student essays as for the professional writings. Each selection in the text begins with a brief headnote that gives information about the author's background, themes, and concerns. After the reading selection there is a suggestion for freewriting in response to the major issue of the story; often a personal response is asked for. The freewriting is followed by three "Responding through Interpretation" questions; these call for doing a close reading of the selection and for drawing some conclusions about the writer's ideas. The "Responding through Discussion" questions, which come next, focus on evaluation and further study of the text. Many of these questions are designed for collaborative, small-group work. Finally, two options are provided under "Responding through Writing" for either longer journal responses or essays. Our suggestions give students a wide range of writing types to practice, from stories and narratives to formal argumentation. Another aspect of our apparatus that instructors and students should find helpful is the use of initial journal writings in response to the chapter theme in each of the seven chapter introductions. In addition, each chapter ends with several suggestions for longer projects that involve either doing outside research or creating connections among the themes and issues raised by several of the writers in the chapter.

PROFESSIONAL READINGS

In preparing this book we tried to select and arrange thematically what we felt to be the most stimulating and enjoyable readings we could find, regardless of period and genre limitations. We let ourselves be guided by our tastes as well as by what we have received in feedback from students. Rather than including only recent selections, we have tried for a balance between newer essays that probe often controversial issues and more familiar fictional works with strong thematic concerns, such as Tillie Olsen's "I Stand There Ironing," Shirley Jackson's "Charles," and William Carlos Williams's classic story, "The Use of Force." We have included texts from writers from a wide range of cultural backgrounds—Amy Tan, Richard Rodriguez, Roberto Alvaro Rios, Alice Walker, and Maya Angelou, among others—trying to create a reader that is both multicultural as well as universal in its concerns. We hope that the works we have selected will make reading a pleasure for students in the course, as well as a valuable learning experience.

FOCUS ON STUDENT WRITING

Perhaps the most unusual feature of *Responding Voices* is its emphasis on student writings: Twenty-eight student essays are included in the book, four for each chapter. We have never particularly liked the way student essays are presented in textbooks, which usually treat student works simply as examples of correct or incorrect writing, as necessary stages in the writing process. In contrast, we have designed our entire book to focus on students as "voiced" authors writing *in response* to other authors and to ideas; thus each chapter is arranged as a kind of conversation among the student and professional writers included. We begin with two short professional pieces on the theme of the chapter and then provide two student essays that comment on the chapter issues from their own perspective, often disagreeing with one another as in a typical energized class discussion. At the end of each chapter, two student essays respond to a professional writing immediately preceding. These student writers take diverse perspectives, some agreeing with the professional author's perspective, some dissenting, each one bringing unique experiences to enrich the discussion. Although we think the quality of the essays we have included is generally high, the essays certainly are not flawless; thus we invite your class to debate the ideas and writing strategies used in the student essays, not to perceive them simply as models to imitate.

INSTRUCTOR'S MANUAL

An instructor's manual will be available for use with *Responding Voices*. It will provide possible responses to the interpretation and discussion questions in the book, additional suggestions for writing and discussion, and some helpful ideas for working with students both individually and in groups to enhance their reading skills and to develop strong student essays. Computer tips will also be available for instructors working in electronic classrooms or in colleges with strong computer support.

ACKNOWLEDGMENTS

We would like to thank all the people at McGraw-Hill who encouraged us with this book: Lesley Denton, who urged us to submit the original proposal; Allison Husting, who helped us develop the concept; Phil Butcher, who worked out the contractual issues; and English editor Tim Julet, whose patience and flexibility were invaluable assets as we revised and shaped the book. We would also like to thank David Damstra for his assistance in production and design, Judy Duguid for her copy editing, as well as Santi Buscemi and Marjorie Ford for their suggestions in the early stages. Special thanks is also due to the students whose work is featured in *Responding Voices:* All of them worked hard on their essays, and this book wouldn't have been possible without their efforts.

Finally, we would like to thank our reviewers for their insightful comments and observations: Judith Branzberg, Pasadena City College; Alan Brown, University of West Alabama; Liz Buckley, East Texas State University; Sandra Stefani Comerford, College of San Mateo; Jo Devine, University of Alaska; Jack Halligan, Johnson Community College; Chris Hayes, University of Georgia; Ellen King, Vincennes University; Janet Marting, University of Akron; Suzanne Norton, Norwalk Community Technical College; Peggy Porter, Houston Community College; Richard Prystowsky, Irvine Valley College; Christie Rubio, American River College; Stephen Straight, Manchester Community-Technical College; Joseph Ugoretz, Borough of Manhattan Community College.

To the Student

We have based *Responding Voices* on three concepts that have helped guide us in the writing of this book, and we encourage you to keep these concepts in mind as you go through the book, both as a reader and as a writer:

First, becoming the writer you want to be involves writing often—not just when you are in class or when you have a particular assignment due. Because we know firsthand the value of writing regularly, we have asked you to keep a journal in order to develop your potential as a writer.

Second, reading can become one of your most inspiring teachers. Through reading a wide variety of writers and thoughtfully relating what you read to your own life, you will find enrichment, both in content and in style, for your writing. Your journal, in which we've asked you to record your responses to the readings, can serve as a permanent resource of ideas for pieces you might want to write.

Third, becoming a writer means having something to say and believing in your right to say it. You are a unique individual with a wealth of experiences and observations from which to write. You already have something worthwhile to say, and you need to believe in yourself as someone who deserves to be heard.

Responding Voices is primarily a sourcebook of readings that we have organized around seven topics: *education, family, gender, nature, health, work,* and *community.* We have chosen these topics because we feel that they have particular relevance for you at this stage of your life when you are enrolled in college and possibly making decisions about your future. We hope that the readings we've selected will give you information and ideas that will become important to you as you go along your current path.

Each of the seven chapters of readings contains eleven selections: five professional essays, four student essays, one short story, and one poem. Some of the professional pieces are complete essays, chapters from a book, or magazine or newspaper articles. Others are excerpts from books. In the headnotes to each section, we've indicated which pieces are excerpted from a longer work and give you the title of the book in case you would like to find it and read further. We've also included one poem and one short story in each of the units.

The four student essays in each chapter are of two types: Two are general essays about the topic, and two are student responses to one or more of the professional essays in the chapter. We've included them for your analysis to illustrate the wide range of possibilities for student essays. We think you can learn something about writing your own papers by looking at both the strengths and the weaknesses of the student papers.

After each reading a freewriting assignment gives you an opportunity to respond quickly to the piece. Then three short groups of questions and suggestions follow:

Responding through Interpretation

Responding through Discussion

Responding through Writing

These questions should help you in responding more fully to the piece. At the end of each chapter (and also at the end of the book) a section entitled "Making Connections" gives you an opportunity to look at several of the pieces in the unit and make connections among them through writing.

Although *Responding Voices* is primarily a reader, we have included two general chapters at the front of the book—one to help you with your reading and one to help you with your writing. You may find that your instructor will assign the chapters in a different sequence from the way we have ordered them; each set of readings can stand on its own. We hope you and your instructor will select from *Responding Voices* what you need, when you need it. Beyond that—and most of all—we hope that you will have an enjoyable time with both your reading and your writing as you study this book and practice the writing activities we have included.

Responding Voices:

A Reader for Emerging Writers

CHAPTER 1

Responding as a Reader

Reading opens the door to many worlds and ideas. Through reading, you come in contact with other minds, other cultures, and age-old questions and problems that make up the universal experience of being human. Reading gives you the opportunity to learn about yourself and to create meaning through your response to what you read. Everything you read and respond to deeply has the potential to influence and inspire you, to become your own, intertwined with your life and experiences.

Responding personally to what you read happens almost involuntarily. A dialogue between your inner self—your ideas, feelings, and experiences—and the voice of the text goes on nearly all the time that you are actively engaged in the reading process. This dialogue between your imaginative mind and the text you are reading helps you develop and clarify your personal ideas and values. In fact, you become a co-creator with the author of every text you read. Thus, staying aware of your inner responses as you read will, with practice, help you to become a better reader. You will find yourself becoming more active, able to make deeper connections and better evaluations as you read.

KEEPING A READING/WRITING JOURNAL

When you were younger, you might have kept a journal or diary to record your personal insights and feelings. Maybe you were once asked to keep a journal by a teacher. We invite and encourage you to keep a journal as you go through the selections in this book. Your journal will serve a dual purpose during the course you're now taking: (1) It will serve as a place to keep your responses to the reading selections; and (2) it will serve as a good place to record your observations and ideas for essays you will later write.

Keeping a reading/writing journal gives you a chance to keep your personal writing voice alive and growing, as well as an opportunity to write frequently and to reflect on your writing process—not just to make your writing more "correct," but also to understand more about your motivations for writing and about how your inner world of feelings and sensations can be translated into words. The process of putting thoughts and feelings into words and onto paper helps to clarify your ideas. Later, you can turn to your journal entries as a source of ideas for longer, more sustained writing projects. The following entry from a student's journal explores what keeping a journal has meant to her and how the journal has helped her to develop her talents as a writer:

> *I write in my journal about class readings and try to relate them to memories, values, morals, or thoughts and ideas which have taken me by surprise and have stayed with me. Some thoughts stay at the back of my mind and continue to grow until I write them down and fully explore them. I feel my responses to readings, thoughts and ideas becoming organized as I am writing in my journal. When I write journal entries in a free-flowing style, I often discover in the finished entry new ideas and viewpoints.*

Writers keep many types of journals, depending on their goals and interests. Some writers use their journal simply as a way of reflecting on their private feelings and ideas, while others see it as a place to record ideas and early drafts for essays, stories, and poems—as well as for short observations that may later find their way into finished works of fiction or nonfiction. We ask you to develop your journal as both a *writer's* journal and a *reader's* journal. Both approaches will help you to increase your understanding of yourself as a writer *and* a reader. The questions and suggestions following each reading selection in *Responding Voices* offer you many opportunities for responding in different ways to what you have read. In fact, now would be a good time to begin your reading/writing journal, as you will find a number of suggested activities for journal entries in the pages that follow.

YOUR RELATIONSHIP WITH READING

Take a few moments to think about your relationship with reading. What kind of reader are you? What have been some of the most influential readings for you? If you feel you have problems with reading, think briefly about what they are and what you feel have caused them. Now write a journal entry that traces your earliest recollections of yourself as a reader, thinking back to one of your earliest reading experiences. As you explore your memories, you might remember many times when someone read aloud to you; those are a good place to begin. Then travel through time and recollect a moment in your childhood when you actually held a book in your hands and understood some of the words on the page. What were your feelings about the story in the book? Do you recall the physical aspects of the book—the illustrations, the paper, the words? What were your favorite books when you were a child? How did they influence your life? Write down as much as you can remember about your reading when you were a child and compare how you felt about reading then and how you feel about it now.

After writing about yourself as a reader, you may have uncovered some important moments in your life which still have an effect on your reading today. Are you satisfied with your progress as a reader? If not, why not? What changes would you like to make in your reading habits? Add a final paragraph to your journal entry which sums up what you learned from writing the journal entry and how you feel about what you wrote.

Perhaps the most important ingredient in becoming a responsive reader is *interest*. If you practice reading things that really interest you, then you'll develop the skills you need when you have to read things that don't appeal to you very much. For instance, sometimes it's necessary to read strictly for information—to take exams, to fulfill assignments, to hold down your job. Think about such reading as a sport: If you practice doing it often enough, you'll be able to do it under pressure when you have to perform. But, above all, reading should be fun, so try to find something enjoyable in all the reading you do, and in the reading process itself.

Here is what one student had to say about her pleasure in reading. She explains why she reads and also gives some personal details about the way she reads.

> *I read for two different reasons—to relax and to learn. Most of the "leisure" reading that I do is pretty heavy stuff. I enjoy reading history texts and classic novels. When I have to read, I read mostly nonfiction history books. My books are full of notes, and I try to retain as much of the information as possible. I also enjoy reading novels that were written during the turn of the century. Often I will read a novel that was written during a certain time period before I read a history about that time. If I find a book particularly interesting, I will usually read it a second time to catch anything I might have missed. Whatever it is that I'm reading, I like to spend at least one hour on it at each sitting—usually more. I don't feel that I can really concentrate and get the most out of any book in less than an hour. I have a hard time reading assigned material at times because a lot of it is not information I would normally be interested in, so I will usually read it right before I go to sleep. In fact I always read something for at least thirty minutes before I go to sleep at night.*

Whatever your feelings are about reading, or about yourself as a reader, we hope that the selections in *Responding Voices* will be a pleasurable reading experience for you. We have chosen the selections for this book carefully with the intention of helping you become a better reader and a better writer in several ways: (1) The selections are short enough to be read quickly so that you can then read them through several times; in this way, you can increase your ability to comprehend what you read more fully. (2) The selections can give you new ideas and insights to draw on in making future choices about your life—especially around the issues of education, family, gender, health, work, and community. (3) The selections can also be used as a springboard for your writing by providing interesting content that will evoke meaningful responses. Furthermore, the different types of selections—complete essays, excerpts from books and longer works, short stories, and poems—can inspire you to experiment with different kinds of writing.

FOUR STAGES IN READING

Below we have outlined four stages of reading that we hope will guide you both in understanding yourself further as a reader and in helping you to become a more active and accurate reader. These stages are ones used primarily for close and thoughtful reading. You don't need to go through all these stages for everything you read. Obviously you don't read the ingredients on a box of cereal as intensely as you read a detective novel, and you probably don't read a detective novel as closely as you read a play by Shakespeare. There are, of course, many different levels of reading, and you almost automatically adjust your reading techniques to the level of the material you're reading. The four stages listed below are the steps you generally go through when you want to give a piece of writing a close reading, evaluate the piece, and then respond to it.

The four stages are:

1. Pre-reading
2. Skimming
3. Studying
4. Post-reading response

Stage 1: Pre-reading

The pre-reading stage gives you an opportunity to get a quick overview of what you will be reading. This overview can save you time and energy in

your reading, so it's usually worth taking the five or ten minutes necessary
to go through this stage. Pre-reading primarily involves glancing over the
selection to see what the title is, who the author is, what type of piece it is
(in the case of the readings in this book, whether the piece is an essay, an
excerpt, a short story, or a poem), as well as when it was written, and to discover any other preliminary information you need before beginning to read.
For example, before beginning a reading selection in this book, take time
to read the headnote that precedes each piece; these headnotes will quickly
give you necessary information. Next look over the selection to determine
its approximate length and notice any subheads or sentences that stand out
at a glance. As you go through the pre-reading stage, you might want to jot
down a few items, such as title, author, dates, and perhaps one or two questions or observations that strike you during this initial browsing.

The following checklist of questions will help guide you through the
pre-reading stage:

- *Is the work primarily factual or literary?* Your first activity should
  be to determine whether you will be reading a piece based on the
  writer's imagination—as in the case of short stories and poems—or
  one based on the writer's actual experiences and research—as in the
  case of essays and excerpts.
- *When was the piece written?* Consider the historical framework of
  what you will be reading. Whether the piece was written a century
  ago, four decades ago, twenty-five years ago, or two years ago, you
  will want to note that and write down what you know about that particular time—or will need to know, if anything, in order to fully appreciate the piece.
- *Are the author's background and experiences similar to your own?*
  You might want to consider if the writer is male or female, if the writer
  is from a different cultural background from your own, and if he or
  she is writing about a subject that is familiar or unfamiliar to you.
- *What is the author's purpose?* Is the author's purpose to explain
  something? To persuade you of something? To entertain you? Understanding the writer's purpose will affect your approach to reading
  the text. If, for example, you see in the overview that the writer will
  be explaining something complex, you will want to read more slowly
  so that you can grasp the information; if the author is trying to persuade you of a point of view, you will want to read more critically.
- *Which audience was this selection originally intended for?* Was the
  piece originally aimed at student readers? Mass newspaper or maga-

zine audiences? A specialized audience in a certain field or social class? Most of the selections in this book, while written for different audiences, are directed at general readers like yourself; however, if you feel that you are not among a targeted audience for a particular piece, try to put yourself in the position of the intended audience so you will get the full impact of the piece.

A quick notation during the pre-reading stage for one of the selections in this book might look like this:

"You Should Have Been a Boy!"—Elizabeth Cady Stanton
excerpt from her autobiography
she was born in 1815; this piece must be over 100 years old
early leader in women's rights movement
her brother died
who wants her to be a boy?—oh, her father; don't fathers still get pretty fixated on having boys?
poor girls; I'm the only boy out of six children. My sisters have it kind of rough; I'm sort of spoiled

An overview with brief notes such as these takes only a few minutes and gives you immediate access to the piece you later will be reading more closely.

Stage 2: Skimming

After previewing the work and considering the questions given above, read the entire text for the first time. At this stage, you simply plunge in and read the work quickly to get an overall sense of its meaning. Move rapidly through the material, keeping your mind mentally relaxed but alert, jotting down a quick question or putting a few checks in the margins to remind yourself that you want to pay special attention to those spots later. Don't stop to look up words you don't understand; instead try to get a fuller sense of the purpose and main concepts behind the reading. After you've skimmed the material, write a quick response in your journal without worrying about what you missed or didn't fully understand. Here are a few questions to keep in mind during the skimming stage and the writing of an initial response:

- Does the piece touch on any previous experiences I have had?
- Is the piece what I expected it to be after I did the overview? If not, what did I expect it to be like?

- Which specific thoughts and feelings did it evoke in me?
- Did it challenge my thinking in any way during the initial reading?
- What are some of the things I want to understand better when I read over it again?

After the skimming stage, in which you've gone through the piece rapidly, you then can write a brief initial response, incorporating some of the ideas that occurred to you based on some of the above questions. Following is a sample of the kind of brief written response you might make after you finish skimming:

"The Use of Force" by William Carlos Williams

I liked this story but it seems more like something that really happened rather than a short story. I was surprised to find out that Williams was a doctor—I'll bet this really happened to him. One thing I noticed immediately is that Williams doesn't use any quotation marks around what the people are saying; looks strange on the page. At first I felt mad at the doctor for treating the little girl so harshly but now I realize that he probably saved her life. Makes me think about how much I hated doctors when I was little, especially Dr. Harmer who used to hurt my ears with those long needles. I still remember how much it hurt. When I read this story again, I want to try to understand the doctor more and figure out if this was really a life-and-death situation or if the doctor was just angry. Wonder if a lot of doctors don't get angry at patients?

Stage 3: Studying

After pre-reading and skimming a selection to get an overall response to it, you will need to go back to read and study it more thoroughly in order to draw the entire reading together for yourself. Studying a piece involves slowing down and asking yourself at different intervals whether you understand fully what the author is saying. You might stop to make notes that sum up what you think the author means or to write down a question about something you want to explore later. In the studying stage, pay attention to words that seem to have special meaning, looking them up in a dictionary if you aren't sure what they mean or if you suspect the author is implying multiple levels of meaning for the word. In this stage, look closely at the way the author has put together sentences and paragraphs, and re-read the introduction and the conclusion several times to see how they serve to unify the piece.

You might also study the author's style and make special notes of particular sentences that you think are very well written, or that surprised you with an unusual comparison or detail.

Several strategies will help you more fully understand the text at this stage in the reading process:

1. *Reading aloud.* You might have been taught to read silently without moving your lips because this is a more rapid way to read. However, during the studying stage, reading aloud gives you the chance to really appreciate the voice, the structure, and the language of a given work. If you don't want to read aloud, you might try whispering some of the key passages to yourself. Read with an awareness of the sounds of the words and the rhythms of the sentences to help you gain the full meaning of the text. This "voicing" strategy is very important when you are studying thoughtful personal essays, fiction, poetry, and other imaginative and philosophical writings.

2. *Marking the text.* Marking your text is an essential part of the process of studying closely and perceptively. Cultivate the habit of writing questions and comments in the margin of your text. Circle words and phrases that are confusing or ones you want to remember. Underline key ideas, passages, topic sentences. All these activities will help you to understand the main points of your text. You can also make margin notes to yourself—notes that have personal meaning for you and help you create connections beyond the piece itself. For borrowed books, copy key passages into your journal or photocopy pages that you can then mark up.

3. *Using the dictionary.* The dictionary can be a valuable source of information. You might naturally turn to a dictionary to find the definitions of words you don't know or have never seen in print. But you will also find it helpful to look up words that you recognize but aren't sure of how they are being used in a particular context. The various levels of meaning can give you additional information you might not be aware of. In addition to the meaning of the words, study also the etymology—the origins of the words. Whenever you study, use a substantial, longer dictionary rather than an abbreviated paperback.

4. *Paraphrasing and summarizing.* Writing paraphrases and summaries of passages and even of entire texts will help you pay close attention to what you are reading and will help you be certain you thoroughly understand what you have read. To *paraphrase,* you put the main ideas of the text into your own words and sentence structure.

You take someone else's words and literally *reword* them in your
own voice and style. If you're able to paraphrase an idea, you can
be pretty certain that you understand it. To *summarize,* you restate
the text's main idea and overall perspective in a much shorter form.
You can summarize a paragraph or an entire book in a sentence or
two. Use paraphrase and summary at important points during your
reading in order to remind yourself of the major highlights of what
you've read.

In order to be certain that you understand thoroughly the material you
have read, there are several good strategies for taking yourself through the
piece step by step and making sure that you have grasped both the content
and the form of the reading. *Outlining* is one technique you can use. You
can outline as you go, taking time to paraphrase and summarize each paragraph. Another technique is *mapping*—creating a visual map of the piece
you've read. The fun part of mapping is that you really get to use your creativity in figuring out the best way to map a particular piece; mapping is
like high-level doodling. Here is a sample of how mapping might be done.

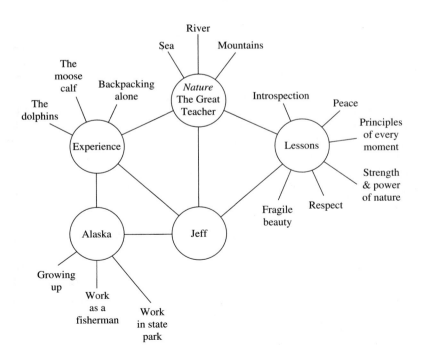

After you finish your map, you can then study it and analyze why you mapped the piece the way you did. At that point you can write a response to the piece in your reading journal, which might be similar to the following journal entry written in response to an essay included in the "Nature" chapter of *Responding voices:*

"Lessons from the Earth" by Jeff Hunze

Hunze's essay made me yearn to be out in nature again. Nature has been Jeff's greatest teacher, and he has spent most of his life out in nature. He worked as a commercial salmon fisherman in Alaska when he was 15 and worked in a state park when he was 17. He spends a great deal of time backpacking and camping out—most of the time alone. The major lessons he says he has learned from nature are (1) the beauty and tenacity of life; (2) respect, especially for the power of nature; (3) appreciation for beauty and strength; (4) how precious and fleeting every moment is; and (5)— above all, "peace in the great silence of nature . . . I have learned the art of introspection." Hunze uses the examples of watching the dolphins, saving the moose calf, and sitting on a mountain alone at midnight to illustrate the lessons nature has taught him. "Lessons from the Earth" is full of beautiful, vivid details which made me feel that I was there with Hunze. He says "I never tire of watching the daily miracle of life on our small planet" and then throughout the rest of the essay, he shows you he means what he has said.

Stage 4: Post-reading Response

This stage is the one in which you begin to make your own decisions about the piece you have read, using such strategies as interpretation, evaluation, comparison, and counterargument. Here is where you take a stand in relation to a selection that you have studied carefully. To develop an evaluative response to a selection, read it over again rapidly, after reviewing your previously written comments and notes. Consider how this final reading confirms, expands upon, or causes you to doubt or revise your earlier responses to the piece. Using specific elements in the text as evidence, draw some broader evaluative conclusions about the work and your response to it. Consider the following points in making your post-reading response:

- What is my overall response to the values and ideas in the work?
- How does this piece of writing connect with my own life experiences, my ideas, feelings, etc.?

- What do I think about the quality of writing in this piece? Do I feel the author effectively presented the material?
- Was there anything new or special about the experience of reading this piece? Did it make me think of any other pieces I've read?
- After reading this work, would I want to read anything else by this writer? Would I want to read any other related works? Would I recommend this piece to other readers?

Evaluative responses can range in length from a short paragraph to a one-page journal entry to a full-length paper. Most of the time, however, we ask you in the follow-up questions to make brief responses in your reading journal. Even if you plan to write an essay on a particular piece, it's still a good idea to write a short journal entry, or a full paragraph, to get yourself started. Here's an example of what a brief evaluation might be like:

"Cotton Pickers" by Maya Angelou

This brief excerpt from Angelou's autobiography, I Know Why the Caged Bird Sings, *showed me an aspect of life I've never known much about. I've lived all my life in the East and have never been down to the rural South. I knew nothing about cotton picking until I read this piece, and I must say that Angelou's writing about the hard, simple life these people lived really moved me. Imagine getting up at daybreak and walking miles to get to a job of tough labor in the hot sun with almost no food in your stomach. Then at the end of the day to face certain disappointment because no matter how much you picked, it was never enough to even pay for the basic necessities. And all you had to look forward to that night was sewing the tough cotton sack by the light of a coal-oil lamp—probably on an empty stomach. Angelou somehow makes the lives of these people beautiful. Maybe it's because of her ability to create great images through her descriptive writing; but it's really more than that—maybe it's deep love or a reverence for the lives of these people . . . I don't know exactly. I just know that right now I feel many different things I can't yet express. I definitely want to get a copy of Angelou's book and read the whole thing soon.*

We hope that as you go through the different readings and assignments in this book, you will find several comfortable reading levels for yourself. Becoming a truly responsive reader can open up a multitude of new worlds for you, both as a reader and as a writer. The more you read, the more you will discover about yourself and others. And you will discover that the more deeply you read what someone else has written, the more you become a collaborator with that author. *You* are the audience that author was hoping would show up. Your reading brings to life what otherwise would remain a static page of printed words.

CHAPTER 2

Responding as a Writer

You might consider yourself a "beginner" in the world of writing, but you have already been a writer for a long time. No matter what language you grew up speaking, you have been writing words, sentences, and paragraphs in that language almost without realizing it. Think about all the times and places you have had to take on the role of "writer," even when you were very young. You may have written birthday cards to your family before you started school, and by now you've probably written dozens of cards and letters in your lifetime to friends and relatives. You've no doubt had to fill out many kinds of applications over the years, possibly even writing paragraphs to justify your application. And if you've been enrolled in school, it's pretty safe to say you've had to write numerous required papers for different courses. There's also a good possibility that you write for the pleasure of it—keeping a journal on your own, writing stories or poems—or, at the least, perhaps you've had a few experiences when writing came out of you almost unexpectedly in response to some deep thought, feeling, or experience.

Before we go further into this chapter about writing, think back on all the kinds of writing you have done so far. Make a list of everything you can remember, starting with your early childhood and ending with the present. Keep on with the list until you feel you've thought of nearly everything. Put a star by the writings you enjoyed the most or felt best about. Then circle the ones you didn't like or didn't feel comfortable with. Study your list closely before beginning the following journal entry:

Journal Entry

Write about your relationship with writing, tracing this relationship from your earliest memories up until the present. What do you feel best about in your writing? What kinds of writing have you enjoyed the most? What do you feel most

15

frustrated about as a writer? What do you think you need in order to become happy with yourself as a writer? Refer to specific events in your life that you feel have influenced your relationship with writing.

After writing this journal entry and re-reading it, what new information did you discover about yourself? How can this writing class be used to gain the qualities you think you might like to have as a writer? Add your response to these questions to your journal entry.

As textbook writers and longtime English teachers, we believe in the importance of teaching skills that will help you to succeed in your academic writing, but we also believe in the importance of helping you to write in an authentic voice about subjects that are deeply important to you. We think of writing as one way to respond to your life and to the world around you. This dual response will happen almost naturally if you keep alive a connection between what is *inside* you as a unique human being and what is *outside* you in the world around you and in the reading you do for pleasure and for learning. The last thing we want to happen to you as a writer is to come out of a writing class having learned writing skills but sounding less genuine and less committed to what you are writing than you are now. That would be a real loss.

Here is the way two students wrote about what writing is like for them:

Writing is like learning to speak all over again. Your brain knows what you mean but somehow the words never seem to come out right. You have to keep trying, practicing, and eventually it starts to work. Little by little you're getting it. All the wrong words disappear and the right ones take their place. It's finally coming together. All it takes is time and determination. Eventually you'll get it right. When you're tired of being silent, then you'll be heard. Your voice will soar.

Writing's a lot like painting. You cannot be sure of where your imagination will lead you, but the final output of both is your creation—a product of your imagination and your knowledge of the subject. Both writing and painting communicate with images. Writing uses creative words just like painting utilizes vivid colors to produce a masterpiece so strong that it could move people to action, make them feel, and make them see the beauty of something previously unknown. Writing, like painting, brings out the artistic imagination of the one who creates.

A BRIEF PROCESS FOR WRITING

In the section that follows, we have outlined for you some of the ingredients that we feel will guide you along the path of writing. We think that writing gets done more easily and with more pleasure if you take it in small, manageable steps. After you have gained some experience as a writer, you will no doubt find your own method for how you want to proceed step-by-step through any writing experience. In the meantime, here's a method that many people, including the authors of this book, still find workable. This method breaks the process of writing down into four stages:

Prewriting

Drafting

Revising

Proofreading

Stage 1: Prewriting

Prewriting is the stage in which you experiment with what you really want to do. This stage is usually exciting because your creativity can soar and your mind can buzz with endless possibilities. This is the stage in which to play with ideas and find out which ones work best for you. Don't be in too big a hurry. Here's your chance to daydream, to doodle, to make lists, to dash off unrelated questions, ideas, emotions, etc. Below we explain three easy and productive strategies—*brainstorming, clustering,* and *freewriting*—for doing your prewriting work. One strategy may appeal to you more than the other, but we urge you to try them all and even to use all three of them during one prewriting session.

Brainstorming

Brainstorming is a high-energy activity that involves writing down—as rapidly as possible—in list form all the words, phrases, ideas, descriptions, thoughts, or questions that come to your mind in response to a particular topic or idea. Brainstorming will bring up new ideas and associations that can build on each other, and very often you will see connections between ideas that previously had seemed unconnected. It's essential in brainstorming not to stop to censor, judge, or correct anything that comes up. Put everything on the paper and decide later whether or not you want to use it. When the listing process seems complete, go back and find the relationships between the different items on the list. Which ones belong together? Which ones can be contrasted? Which ones lead to other ideas?

Look, for example, at one student's list when he brainstormed on the topic of health:

bacteria   pollutants

asthma   new diseases

public health   slimy lake

eczema   breathing difficulties

recent article in the paper—local pollutions

the new water purification system

heartburn   Dr. Lucassi

chlorine—awful smell and taste

Jefferson's drinking water—it's changed

polluted water unsafe

public is unaware

many dangers (get more info on this)

After doing further work with his brainstorming, this student decided that his real interest lay in writing a paper on the dangers of the polluted drinking water in his town.

Clustering

Clustering is similar to the mapping strategy that we illustrated for you in Chapter 1.

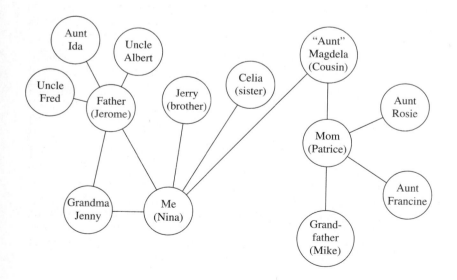

The difference between the two techniques is that mapping is used when you are analyzing someone else's writing and ideas. Clustering is used when you want to organize your own ideas. A cluster begins with a single word—the topic you think you want to explore in your writing. After placing this word in the center of the page, draw a circle around it. On the same page, jot down words and phrases related to your topic. Circle them and draw lines to connect them to the main circle—and to one another when appropriate. As with brainstorming, clustering should be done quickly and without stopping. You can usually come up with a very complex cluster in less than ten minutes. Once a cluster feels complete, study it and decide where you feel you want to go with it. Write a couple of sentences to serve as an "anchor" to the clustering.

The diagram on page 18 shows how a student clustered around the topic of "family."

> *Doing this clustering on "family" showed me how exceptionally close I feel to my father's mother, Grandma Jenny, and also to my mother's favorite cousin, "Aunt" Magdela. I was surprised to realize that I feel closer to Aunt Magdela than I do to any of my real aunts on either side of the family. I think a possible idea for a paper is what strong role models these two women have been for me. They are both fire-crackers! They taught me early in life to speak up for myself in any situation. That's why I have the reputation in my family of being "the mouth."*

Freewriting

Freewriting, like brainstorming and clustering, is a way to tap into your creative process. Sometimes you will do general freewrites, say when you just pick up your journal and start to write with no particular idea in mind. Other times, you will do a focused freewrite around a particular topic. Most of the journal entries we ask you to write after each reading selection are focused freewrites because we give you a specific topic with which to start.

Freewriting means writing as quickly as you can without stopping to think. You keep the pen moving on the paper and don't stop to search for the perfect word, or to correct grammar, or to polish sentences. You work against stopping yourself the whole time and push yourself to keep going as rapidly as possible in a given length of time—usually 10 to 20 minutes. A freewrite is a great way to begin any writing task because even a short freewrite can become the nucleus for a full-length paper. When you freewrite as we suggest—rapidly without censoring yourself—you are never quite sure what will come out on the page. Freewriting is a way to find out what is important to you about the topic and is equally valuable in showing you what you already know that you might not have been aware of. Here is a sample of a freewrite made by a student on the topic "nature."

Nature. Funny word. Makes me think of natural, naturopath, nayture, mother nature, human nature, doing what comes naturally. I guess I'm supposed to do this freewrite on nature—the great outdoors. What great outdoors? I live in a 12-story apartment complex on the 7th fl. in an apartment that's one room—. an "efficiency" they call it but it's sure not that. Nature . . . hummm I'm getting off the track . . . well, there are a few grassy spots and some trees in fact i like to lie under the one in the back and read when it's not too hot. hot boy Montgomery was sweltering last summer. never go back down there again. I couldn't breathe but there was lots of "nature" there—trees everywhere, lakes, fields. i just remembered the park over in Brentwood that my sister and i use to go to when we were little. What ever happened to that park? Had the greatest merry-go-round you could push with your feet and a huge slide that looped around. Really dusty too—dirt with no grass. I guess "nature" for me is a thing of the past. Playing outside when I was little. Nothing nature about my life now. busy busy busy.

Looking back over the freewrite, you can see several threads that the writer might pursue further: living out of touch with nature, playing outdoors as a child, the lushness of nature in a sweltering climate, even perhaps lying under a tree and reading a book. Any of these ideas could be developed further into a full-length paper.

Stage 2: Drafting

Drafting is simply the process of writing early versions of what you hope will become a finished product. The nice thing about considering most of your early versions as drafts is that you don't have to worry about perfection. The whole idea of "drafting" is that you're working on a fluid piece of writing that is changing and becoming something else. This open-ended attitude can make writing far less stressful and much more exciting. There are a number of different ways to draft a paper, ranging from simply "plunging in," with only an idea of what you want to say, all the way to developing a meticulous plan and/or outline of all the ideas you want to include in your paper. As you get deeper into your writing, you will discover your own personal preferences in how to create your first few drafts. For now, we will present two different approaches to drafting to help you get started.

Tentative Thesis and Scratch Outline

If you practice the prewriting activities that we discussed above, you will nearly always have key material that will serve as the beginnings of your first draft. Look over your prewriting material and circle or mark in the margins any key ideas you want to use in your paper. Then try to state what you think you would like most to emphasize or develop. Write one or two sentences stating this main idea, and this will serve as your thesis statement. For example, the student who did the freewrite about nature might decide to write about lying under a tree and reading a book: "I feel that, because of my busy schedule, I have been living out of touch with nature for over a year and feel that doing so has been detrimental to my health and well-being. Writing this paper will be my discovery of ways I—and others—can 'get back to nature,' even though I am overworked and live in a rather unnatural and ugly environment." Once you do a first draft, you are likely to uncover new ideas, and these new ideas might lead you in another direction. In that case, you would modify your thesis statement to help you create a new focus for your next draft.

After you've looked over your thesis statement, you might then want to create a "scratch outline," a list of points you would like to cover, in reasonable order, to support your central idea. Although the outline doesn't need to be elaborate and you should feel free to revise it as you go along, many writers like to work with a brief outline because it provides them with a ready guide for where to go next. The student writing about nature, for example, might make this tentative scratch outline:

Why has "nature" disappeared from my life this past year?

The adverse effects on me

Way I used to be in nature—reading under trees, playing in parks, camping

Present environment—uninspiring, detrimental to my health

Remedies:

join a health club

move to a "greener" apartment complex

seek out neighborhood parks

work in a neighborhood beautification project once a month

locate the state parks; plan a weekend at one

join a bikers group

Discovery Drafting

Although some writers like to do some organizing before they begin a draft, other writers prefer to start more intuitively, using each successive draft to discover ideas. Discovery drafting usually begins with a key concept or with an image that grabs the writer's attention and seems to contain special meaning. This key concept or image will usually lead to discovering further ideas. With this discovery approach, you may find your real thesis sentence in the second, third, or even the concluding paragraph. At that point, you can use new revelations from the first draft to shape another central statement that can guide the second draft—and so on. After two or three drafts, you might find that you want to take the time to outline and reshape your material for better effectiveness.

Drafting requires concentration. This means you must set aside periods of an hour or more when all you will do is concentrate on each draft. Drafting can be a pleasurable activity, one through which you will learn a great deal about how your mind works. In order to discover thoughts while you are drafting, you must remember not to edit or censor your ideas. Don't stop at the end of each sentence you produce to reread or correct; simply try to keep your thoughts flowing during the times you've set aside for drafting. At this stage of the writing process, keep in mind that the final order of your thoughts is yet to be determined. There will be plenty of time to move sections of the paper around, to experiment with different examples, to refine sentences, and to try out different introductions and conclusions. In fact, unless the opening and closing paragraphs just occur to you naturally, it's often better not to worry about them until you get to the revision stage. Your primary goal during the drafting stage is to get your ideas down on paper. The refinements will—and should—come later.

Stage 3: Revising

A natural place to begin the process of revision is by reading over your last draft. Think about what you intended to do and what you actually did do. Check your last draft against the other drafts to be certain that you didn't accidentally drop something. Now is the time to fill in the gaps: Check word usage and spelling, grapple with awkward sentences, gather missing information. This is also the time to ask yourself some specific questions—and it helps if you write down the answers:

- Who is the audience for this piece of writing?
- Have I adopted the right tone of voice for this audience?
- What is my main purpose in writing this?
- Do I have a strong opinion I am trying to persuade others to agree with? If so, what is that opinion?
- Have I restated my main point in several different ways throughout?

After you've read over your draft and have thought about the changes that you want to make, it can be helpful to create an outline of your thesis, main ideas, and supporting details. You will probably, at this point, have to make changes, rearrangements, deletions, or additions. To check the unity and flow of your ideas, you might summarize each paragraph in a single sentence and then rearrange the sentences until you feel that you have found the strongest organization.

After becoming better acquainted with your draft through outlining it, you can then begin the process of rewriting—a process that will probably result in at least two subsequent drafts. Here is a suggested process you might follow in taking your paper through the final drafts.

Whole Essay Revision

In this stage, you look at the paper as a whole, concentrating first on the overall content, development, and order of your paper. You might begin this first phase by examining your outline of the draft and seeing where you might want to add or better develop some topics. Go over your thesis to be certain that it is clearly worded and directed to a strong purpose. Next, go through and slim down your paper by deleting any parts that seem irrelevant, overwritten, or repetitious. Finally, expand certain sections of your essay with examples or further details to be certain that your abstract ideas are developed concretely. The more complex the thought, the more examples you will need to illustrate it.

Paragraph Revision

After thinking about how your paper works as a whole, you can concentrate more specifically on the form and structure of your paragraphs. Paragraphing is used to call attention to a turn or shift of ideas in your paper. How many paragraphs your paper has, or how long the individual paragraph should be, is a matter of choice, but you want to look at each paragraph to be sure that some balance is present. Most student papers tend to have paragraphs averaging from four to seven sentences, a length adequate enough to support a single idea with examples and clarification. In general, avoid extra-long paragraphs or too-short ones—although sometimes one- or two-sentence paragraphs can be very effective. Go through and assess how your paragraphs look visually: Are they similar in length?

Once you have decided that your paragraphs are satisfactory in length, you can begin to examine them more closely to strengthen and focus them. Does each paragraph have a topic sentence? Do all the other sentences in that one paragraph relate to or support the topic sentence? If a paragraph lacks this kind of unity, you will want to add or remove certain sentences or rearrange them for better focus.

This is the stage where you now rethink your introduction and your conclusion. Go back and look them over. If you were a reader skimming through a magazine, would the introduction snag your interest? Your first concern in the introduction should be to catch the reader's attention and pull him or her into reading the essay. There are numerous examples of good introductory paragraphs in the selections in this anthology. Some of them tell a brief story; others provide an intriguing fact or idea; still others ask a leading question. There are many possibilities for creating good, strong opening paragraphs. Here's the way two students, whose essays are printed in this collection, chose to begin their papers:

> *A major problem in American schools is the excessive amount of attention devoted to sports programs, especially among colleges where much money can be made from sports. Although such programs may begin with the intention of giving students increased physical discipline, energy, and commitment, many schools encourage coaches and athletes to devote so much energy to sports programs that the education needs of students are neglected.*
>> *"He Couldn't Get Off the Ground" by Jayme Plunkett*

> *As I stand in the doorway of the store, the familiar rush of anxiety overwhelms me. How can another year have flown by so quickly? Is it possible that it is birthday time, and I am yet again faced with the task of choosing "anything," while my grandfather waits impatiently to pay? Shuffling his feet and chewing a toothpick, my grandfather presents himself as a dominant figure of stubbornness and will.*
>> *"My Grandfather's Memories" by Amy Marx*

Every paper needs a conclusion as well as a beginning. In a very short essay, your conclusion may be only a sentence or so, although most of the time you will want to include a full paragraph to complete your ideas and leave the reader with a strong and convincing impression. Some students feel it is enough to simply sum up or restate the main points made in the thesis, but this is a routine method that may not inspire your readers to take you seriously.

Strategies for conclusions that leave a more lasting impression include a reemphasis of the importance of the paper's central issue or a repetition of a key line or brief passage from the introduction. The conclusion can also include a prediction for the future, give suggestions for solutions to a problem, or raise further questions. Most of all, don't settle for a weak ending that just limps away, leaving the reader wondering what the purpose of your essay was. Play around with your conclusion until it actually says something—until it adds a strong final note to your composition.

Here are the concluding paragraphs for the papers that were excerpted above:

The saddest part of this story is that no one seems to care. The high schools and the majority of colleges around the country are acting as though nothing is wrong. They sit back, mind their own businesses, and ignore the needs of the students. They should realize that they are responsible for shaping the minds of the men and women of the future and should start advising students about the decisions they make. Without a radical change in the educational system in the U.S., students will not receive the education needed, and the nation will lag behind the rest of the world in nearly everything except sports. Change and reform in the schools are the keys to stopping more tragedies like Mark Munns'.

"He Couldn't Get Off the Ground"

Although I can never internalize the pain that my grandfather harbors, I can be more understanding toward our differences. I can appreciate his compassionate soul, while still coming to terms with our contrasting personalities. In addition, I can recognize my own identity, realizing that I had the privilege to develop under the canopy of a loving and supportive family.

"My Grandfather's Memories"

Fine-Tuning Revision

Fine-tuning revision focuses on writing problems at the level of the sentence and the individual word. At this stage, you are working to improve your writing style, the rhythm and sense of your sentences, your choice of words. This stage is highly important, and a close discussion of all that is involved is beyond the scope of this book. We encourage you to use a student handbook throughout this course and to consult it for further help and information. Briefly, however, here are some of the strategies you will want to be aware of as you fine-tune your paper.

Sentences: At the sentence level, you want first of all to be certain that your sentences are complete (not fragments or run-ons) and that they make sense. Next you want to be certain that they sound "musical" and that you have included a variety of different rhythms. In order to achieve the goal of musical sentences, it's necessary for you to read your essay aloud several times and listen closely to how the sentences flow from one to the other and from paragraph to paragraph. It's easy to fix that unwanted "singsong" sound by adjusting your sentences so there is a mix of short and long sentences as well as a variety of different sentence patterns.

Punctuation: Integral to effective sentence structure is punctuation. You will need to know the punctuation for correct sentences and how and when to use commas. Equally as important, you will want to familiarize yourself with the most common punctuation marks—*periods, question marks, exclamation points, commas, semicolons, colons, parentheses, dashes,* and *quotation marks*—to give yourself many different options in putting your sentences together. Punctuation is an aid to adding clear and precise meaning to what you write, and the way you use punctuation is also part of your style and self-expression. For instance, formal, academic writing tends to rely on punctuation marks such as the semicolon, colon, and parenthesis, whereas less formal papers and personal correspondence use punctuation such as the dash and the exclamation point. Your writer's handbook or even a good dictionary will define for you the major rules of punctuation, but look for those areas where punctuation is "optional"—this is where you have the choice to slow down and formalize your writing with a peppering of varied forms of punctuation, or to speed things up a bit and get more conversational by using fewer marks and less formal punctuation.

Words: Finally, you come to the smallest unit of language in your paper—words. When you revise individual words and phrases, you are using language in its most fundamental form. The words you choose are what ultimately brings your writing to life. Therefore, try to go beyond thinking of the "proper" or the "correct" words to use. Using words correctly is essential to getting your meaning across, but you will want to consider also the importance of variety in word use and the various levels of meanings suggested by certain words. Here's where a dictionary and a thesaurus can come to your aid. Even more importantly, reading good writing can dramatically improve your ability to select vibrant words that move on the page.

Stage 4: Proofreading

This is the final stage in completing your paper, and it's the stage that students are most apt to give less effort to. By now you might be worn-out and sick of working with your paper. However, if you don't do a good job at this stage, you could make all your hard work impossible to read. The final "look" of your paper is an important part of making a good impression on your reader. Proofreading is extremely important because *everybody* has errors—professional writers, editors, doctors, printers, all have to proofread to correct errors. And so must students. The fact is, many student "errors" aren't errors at all but oversights, lapses in attention, or typing errors—all of which can be fixed through adequate proofreading.

After you have performed some major revisions of your paper, you should now be ready to do a final proofreading prior to either retyping or entering changes in your computer. If you're using a computer, be certain to run your paper through the spelling check to catch typos and misspelled words. However, the spelling check will not catch spacing problems, re-peated words, words frequently confused (such as *there* for *their*), omitted words, and other glitches. That's why it's imperative that you read your hard copy several times after you have printed it out. Reading it aloud will also help you catch errors. If you find small errors, such as omitted words or a repeated word, it is usually acceptable to make small corrections neatly in pen. This shows your reader that you followed your paper all the way to the finish line.

You will want especially to catch errors that commonly occur in such areas as capital and lowercase letters; spelling, especially of proper names; figures; punctuation; subject-verb agreement; verb endings; consistent pro-nouns; and all types of typographical errors such as switched letters, illeg-ible or omitted or repeated words, and blank spaces. Also, make certain that your paper is typed in proper manuscript form—double-spaced and with suf-ficient margins. Again, a good student handbook for correct usage will be your best source for calling your attention to specific problems you might have.

Following are a few tips to keep in mind when you get ready to proof-read:

- Take a break between finishing your paper and then typing it.
- Also take a break between typing your paper and proofreading it.
- When you proofread, slow down considerably. Read at a much slower pace than you usually do.
- When you proofread a second or third time, try reading back to front and look hard at each word.
- Check all the shifts from paragraph to paragraph and from page to page to be sure nothing was dropped.
- Make final, minor corrections neatly with a black pen.

Finally the time will arrive when you have run out of time and energy for a particular writing project. You've gone as far with it as you can go. With the ending of each new project, it's a good idea to assess how well you met your own goals. If you are still not entirely satisfied with a project even after finishing it, remember that no paper is ever really finished; it is always a work in progress. And there's always the possibility that one day you might decide to return to it and write it a different way.

PURPOSES AND STRATEGIES FOR WRITING

The student and professional essays in this book serve a range of writing purposes and use appropriate, effective overall strategies to achieve their ends. As in most writing courses, many of the student essays respond to a specific piece of writing; this puts a particular burden on students to understand the purpose and stategies of the original piece of writing as part of their reading and prewriting process. You'll find also that the assignments following the selections are designed to give you an opportunity to write for a variety of purposes. Some of the different purposes and related strategies you might find helpful in responding to the selections in this book are *description, narration, interpretation, comparison, evaluation,* and *persuasive argument.* In the following sections you will find examples of all these methods, defined so that you can both recognize them in the readings you will come across later in the book and make more conscious and effective use of them in your own writing, at the level of the paragraph and, in some cases, as strategies for organizing and developing entire essays.

Description

Description is one of the techniques that you find in most works of fiction and nonfiction. You can incorporate description into almost anything you write, both the essays you write in response to vivid works of others and in the essays you write to share your own experiences and ideas. Descriptions, if they are vivid, create memorable pictures and leave a strong impression on the reader's mind. They can be extended, like a film, or be brief, like snapshots that help to "illustrate" the points in an essay. To create vivid descriptions, you need only to use your own observations, memories, and imagination. Rather than settling for an "idea" of what you want to describe, try closing your eyes and getting a concrete picture of it in your mind. Invite your five senses—sight, sound, smell, touch, and taste—to collaborate with you and contribute specific details for you to use. David Kerr's paper "Strawberry Creek: A Search for Origins" depends mostly on description for its development. Here is a descriptive paragraph from the paper:

> *Entering the tunnel, we tried to balance ourselves on any flat rocks we could find, some of which were covered with a fine green moss from the occasional flow of water that passed over them. We tried our best to stay dry, something that was to be a losing battle. Inside the tunnel, we discovered that there was a small dry ledge upon which we could walk. Our strange mixture of lights created long and short dancing shadows on the walls and rushing water. The rocks in the creek seemed almost alive as our flashlight beams crossed over them. The whole scene was straight out of some old horror movie—which made us all a little nervous.*

Narration

Most people love to tell stories—and to listen to them. Thus, you will generally find that narration (telling stories) is included in most of the pieces you read in this anthology. In your own writing, you will want to make a conscious effort to include narration, as you do with description, both to serve as concrete examples of the points you are making and to attract and hold the reader's attention. When you use narration, pare down the stories so that they don't become boring. Use strong, descriptive details and keep the pace moving swiftly. Don't let a story bog down your own piece or possibly even take it in another direction. In his narrative essay, "Politics . . . *Maybe,"* Julian Castro keeps the pace moving with short and vivid stories from beginning to end. Here is a paragraph from the middle of his essay. Notice the variety of vivid details he uses in a relatively brief paragraph:

> *I remember buttons and pens, posters, stickers, and pictures: "Viva La Raza!" "Black and Brown United!" "Accept me for who I am—Chicano." These and many other powerful slogans rang in my ears like war cries. And I remember my mother during that time. She worked for what seemed like an infinite number of nonprofit organizations. She sat on this committee and that board. There was the YWCA, Leadership 2000, and others that drift in and out of my memory. She got involved in the PTA at my school because she was the first to show up at a first-of-the-year meeting. Her list of things to do was miles long I thought. At seven or eight years old, I did not understand why my mother worked so diligently for these nonprofit organizations and political causes. I did not see what profit she gained from her work, and I wondered why she would give so much of herself. The slogans and discussions of this and that "ism" meant nothing to me either.*

Interpretation

You will find interpretation useful when you want to redefine or explain what an author has said, often adding your own ideas and comments as you do so, and indicating how strategies the author uses help to reveal meaning. Interpretation is somewhat different from paraphrase, in which you simply repeat what the author is saying in your own words. When you interpret a reading, you are thinking about it critically and revealing your own thought processes as you write. The questions that follow immediately after each selection are specifically designed to encourage you to write and interpret thoughtfully. In order to write effective interpretations, you must be certain that you fully understand what the author has said and demonstrate your understanding in what you write. In a paragraph from his essay "Alice Walker's 'Father': A Process of Understanding and Acceptance" (included in the "Family" chapter of this book), student writer Shu Fan Lee begins with several paragraphs of interpretation of Walker's narrative essay. Notice how Lee comments on Walker's statement that "writing about people helps us to understand them." He then goes on to say that this claim "reveals her intention" and follows by remarking on how her use of description, contrast, and questioning of her own experience helps to clarify and justify her initial claim:

> Walker claims in the beginning of her essay that "writing about people helps us to understand them." This shows her intention to recount the parent-child relationship she had with her father, even though reliving the relationship might be a bitter process. With the help of a description of her father from her older siblings that contrasted vividly with her own memories, Walker begins to question her initial impression of him. This is a common reevaluation process for adults who have become more mature as they grow older and gain more life experience. A person's own experience with his or her children might act as the catalyst to motivate a person to review the relationship with parents during his or her childhood.

Comparison

A major activity that goes on when we read is comparison. We contrast the writer's world and experiences with our own, almost without realizing it. Many of the student writers included in *Responding Voices* structure their responses to an essay through comparing their experiences with those of the professional writer. You'll find numerous comparison questions and assignments throughout this book because we feel that comparing is a natural way of responding to reading. Whenever you use comparison, you will want to select only a few areas to compare; choose them ahead of time and develop them around your own topics. You don't need to go through the writer's piece step-by-step and cover every major point; in fact, your essay will be more interesting if you select ideas or statements for comparison from the piece you have read and then organize them in a way that fulfills the aims of your own paper. Magnolia Tse in her paper "What about Being a Girl?" compares her experiences of being a girl with those described by Julius Lester in his essay "Being a Boy" in order to make the point that girls have a hard time growing up, just as boys do.

> Lester believed that girls led the easy life: "Throughout the day as my blood was let . . . I thought of girls sitting in the shade of porches, playing with their dolls, toy refrigerators and stoves." However, in many cases, girls are forced to help set the table for dinner or to go grocery shopping with their mothers. When I was a child, I always wanted to walk around or to stay after school with my friends or even go to their houses to play video games. I hated to clean the house, let alone my room. Nevertheless, I always ended up having to go home to be trained by my mother

to be a successful housewife. I only knew back then that if I didn't do well, nobody would want me. Compared to this, guys' efforts to prove themselves by setting fire to a garage seem far less stressful.

Evaluation

Evaluation plays a very important role in life. Whether you are selecting things to buy, finding movies to see, or getting to know new people, you are constantly evaluating, making judgments. When reading, you also are evaluating—reacting, questioning, judging the text. We introduced evaluation in the previous chapter on reading, and presented an example of an evaluative entry from a student's reading journal on Maya Angelou's "Cotton Pickers." However, in order for your written evaluations to be effective, you must go beyond the immediate response stage, taking the time to enter the author's world and understand both the information given and the author's intention in writing the piece. You might also combine evaluation with comparison, showing how a particular piece of writing is superior to another on the same subject. Be sure whenever you evaluate to use fair, reasonable standards: How much is it reasonable to expect a writer to accomplish in a short newspaper editorial, for instance, as opposed to an entire book on the same subject? Here is how Rainbow Schwartz in her paper "I Just Wanna Be Challenged" evaluates Mike Rose's essay "I Just Wanna Be Average":

The times have changed a lot since Mike Rose was in high school, but his essay "I Just Wanna Be Average" is still relevant. While drugs, teen pregnancy, and violence have changed the atmosphere of many high schools, I think these problems are just a symptom of a bigger problem: uninspired, encouraging teachers. An encouraging teacher can help build a student's self-confidence. Believing in the student's abilities to create and learn will result in a happier student, one who will get better grades and a more complete education. Mike Rose's essay embodies this theory. "I Just Wanna Be Average" is more than a sign of hope for all students; it's a clear message that teachers can make a huge difference in the lives of their pupils.

Persuasive Argument

Most writing could be thought of as a persuasive argument, a way to convince the reader that what the writer has to say is worth listening to, a valid way of seeing and understanding the world. Most of the pieces of writing in this book set forth a point of view and try to convince the reader to agree with this point of view. When you have a strong point of view and want to get it across to someone else, you should find it relatively easy to adopt a strong writing voice and style. However, to be convincing, you must carefully build your case as logically as possible, relying on facts and using emotion in an honest way, not as your only means of support. Following are two paragraphs from Greg Matthew's essay "Indiscriminate Discrimination," included in the "Gender" chapter. Notice how Matthews begins his paper by establishing an issue of concern: Are men discriminated against? He then clarifies his position and indicates what he will examine and criticize in his paper: three examples that are often given to support the argument that antimale discrimination on the job exists, but that Matthews believes are unconvincing. Notice how he uses an imaginary, but logical and well-developed, example of his own to support his view and persuade his readers.

> *[T]oday some men are making their own claims of sexual discrimination. In the workplace some men argue that they are being denied promotions so that some women may be promoted to meet quotas for gender equality. In physically demanding jobs, such as those of police officers and firefighters, some men feel that less qualified women are given hiring preferences for reasons of gender-based quotas. Male athletes in high school and college also complain about the way that some men's sports have been cut back or discontinued, while new women's athletic programs have been added at many schools. Although the three examples mentioned above may appear to be cases of male gender discrimination, in practice, the examples are not as simple and clear-cut as they might appear. . . .*
>
> *Let's take [an] . . . imaginary example. In this case, some men feel they are unfairly discriminated against in the hiring of new police and firefighter cadets. In these two professions, individuals who try out for the available positions are subjected to rigorous physical tests and are given oral examinations as well. The men lodge a complaint because they are certain that they outperformed the female candidates on the physical tests because of superior strength and endurance. However, equality quotas may not have been the only reason some women were chosen over male applicants; the women may have done substantially better on the oral examinations, making them stand out despite somewhat lower performance on physical-based tests. In the life and death situations modern police and firefighters must face, intelligence, mastery of technology, resourcefulness, and empathy are sometimes more important than sheer muscle power.*

COLLABORATION: WORKING WITH OTHER WRITERS AND READERS

If you've ever been part of any group—for example, a sports team, a work group, or a club, you know the value of sharing your ideas and abilities with others. This simple sharing often provides the inspiration that will carry you into new territory. The same holds true with writing and with reading: The more you share with others what you've written, the stronger sense you will gain of yourself as a real writer with important feelings and ideas to express. Thus, throughout this book following each selection, we've asked you to participate with a small group of your peers in order to experience the value of being part of a community of readers and writers. Such groups can help you to understand the reading assignments better, to express your responses to them verbally, to get started on writing projects, and to work through the revising and editing process; but you need to take the opportunity of group work seriously to get the most out of it, seeing yourself as a responsible and committed participant. Here's what two students have to say about peer collaboration:

> *I feel that doing the peer sharing is a great part of our lesson. Knowing my classmates would read my essay made me really focus on what I was writing. It made me look for a way to project my own voice into the work. Since I usually don't talk much in my classes, it was a mandatory way for me to express verbally what I normally would not. I enjoyed hearing outside interpretations—how my work could be looked at by an audience and how my writing was received by those in my group. Although I was extremely nervous before reading it to the group, I appreciated the opportunity and the experience.*

> *I've never really worked much in groups before, and I have found it quite helpful. My group has turned out to be a great sounding board for my ideas. I also get help with my writing blocks and with my rough drafts. It seems like one thought or comment automatically triggers more ideas and often sparks a discussion and then the discussions will often help me to choose a topic for a paper when I'm having problems thinking of what to write. I like hearing the different viewpoints and opinions that our discussions encourage. Sometimes after my group has discussed a work, I'll go back over it and find things I missed before. Hearing other people's interpretations makes me realize how a single word can make a big difference in understanding a particular reading.*

CONCLUSION: BECOMING THE BEST WRITER YOU CAN

Before we move on to the readings in the book, we want to remind you that you can return to this chapter whenever you need help with structuring your papers or when you need inspiration. We also want to leave you with some words from one of our favorite books on writing, a book by Brenda Ueland entitled *If You Want to Write* (1938). We hope you will find Ueland's words as encouraging as we do, a constant reminder that you are entitled to become the very best writer that you can.

I have been writing a long time and have learned some things, not only from my own long hard work, but from a writing class I had for three years. In this class were all kinds of people: prosperous and poor, stenographers, housewives, salesmen, cultivated people and little servant girls who had never been to high school, timid people and bold ones, slow and quick ones. This is what I learned: that everybody is talented, original and has something important to say.

With every sentence you write, you have learned something. It has done you good. It has stretched your understanding. I know that. Even if I knew for certain that I would never have anything published again, and would never make another cent from it, I would still keep on writing.

Readings

CHAPTER 3

Education

Introduction

ISAAC ASIMOV	What Is Intelligence, Anyway?
JOHN HOLT	How Teachers Make Children Hate Reading
TIN LE	An Immigrant in a New School
JAYME PLUNCKETT	He Couldn't Get Off the Ground
MERLE WOO	Poem for the Creative Writing Class, Spring 1982
SHIRLEY JACKSON	Charles
JONATHAN KOZOL	Corla Hawkins
DEBORAH TANNEN	How Male and Female Students Use Language Differently
MIKE ROSE	I Just Wanna Be Average
RAINBOW SCHWARTZ	I Just Wanna Be Challenged
RICHARD CARRILLO	Surviving Adolescence

Making Connections

INTRODUCTION

Journal Entry

Think back over your education. What memories immediately come to mind when you think about your years in school until now? Think through a number of events—both positive and negative—and what you learned from some of these events. Freewrite in your journal about what education means to you.

If you feel critical about some aspects of your education, you're certainly not alone. Almost everyone feels that there is something wrong with American education, but few people agree on how to solve the various problems. There seems to be a constant debate about the need for making classes smaller, getting more funding, hiring more and better qualified teachers, increasing parental involvement, achieving better discipline in the classroom, giving more homework, adding multicultural content into the curriculum, going back to the basics, offering courses that have more relevancy to students' lives, and so on.

You have probably had many varied experiences throughout your years of education. Some of these experiences may have stimulated you and caused you to want to learn a great deal more; some of them might have caused you to have a negative feeling about teachers or education and caused you not to want to learn or study further. However, the fact that you are in school probably indicates that obtaining an education is important to you. Keep in mind, though, that "getting an education" doesn't always mean that significant learning has taken place. It's possible for someone to take a class, pass it with a good grade, and still know very little about the subject that was studied.

After you've examined some of your own experiences in education, you might find interesting similarities and differences between yourself and others through reading the selections in this section. Some of the student and professional essays we have included in this chapter criticize public education for failing to address the needs of the individual student. For example, Mike Rose dramatically illustrates this failure in "I Just Wanna Be Average." Rose was misdiagnosed as a "slow learner" because his records were mixed up with those of another boy. In Deborah Tannen's "How Male and Female Students Use Language Differently," Tannen shows how her female students seem to respond differently to traditional classroom techniques designed with the male learner in mind and suggests some ideas for change. John Holt argues strongly against classroom practices that make students hate to read, while students Richard Carrillo, Rainbow Schwartz, Tin Le, and Jayme Plunckett all offer evidence of how education has failed students.

Although many of the readings in this chapter are critical of education, there is room for hope. Educational critic Jonathan Kozol presents in "Corla Hawkins" a portrait of a brilliant teacher working effectively with limited resources in an impoverished school environment. In "What Is Intelligence, Anyway?" Isaac Asimov provides a humorous look at practical sense versus book sense. Shirley Jackson's short story "Charles" and Merle Woo's poem "Poem for the Creative Writing Class" will evoke an even wider range of ideas for you to ponder regarding the meaning of education.

We hope the selections in this chapter will set you thinking about yourself as a student and what you want out of your education—now and in the future.

What Is Intelligence, Anyway?

Isaac Asimov

Isaac Asimov immigrated to the United States from Russia; he was a bio-
chemist and professor who was best known for his many science fiction
stories and novels, such as *I, Robot* (1950) and *The Gods Themselves*
(1973). In addition to his fiction, Asimov wrote many articles on a variety of subjects, including the way people think and understand the world.
In the following essay, Asimov draws on his everyday experiences to develop a reflection on the nature of intelligence.

What is intelligence, anyway? When I was in the Army, I received a kind   1
of aptitude test that all soldiers took and, against a normal of 100, scored
160. No one at the base had ever seen a figure like that, and for two hours
they made a big fuss over me. (It didn't mean anything. The next day I
was still a buck private with KP as my highest duty.)

All my life I've been registering scores like that, so that I have the   2
complacent feeling that I'm highly intelligent, and I expect other people
to think so, too. Actually, though, don't such scores simply mean that I
am very good at answering the type of academic questions that are considered worthy of answers by the people who make up the intelligence
tests—people with intellectual bents similar to mine?

For instance, I had an auto repairman once, who, on these intelli-   3
gence tests, could not possibly have scored more than 80, by my estimate.
I always took it for granted that I was far more intelligent than he was.
Yet, when anything went wrong with my car, I hastened to him with it,
watched him anxiously as he explored its vitals, and listened to his pro-
nouncements as though they were divine oracles—and he always fixed
my car.

Well then, suppose my auto repairman devised questions for an in-   4
telligence test. Or suppose a carpenter did, or a farmer, or, indeed, almost anyone but an academician. By every one of those tests, I'd prove
myself a moron. And I'd *be* a moron, too. In a world where I could not
use my academic training and my verbal talents but had to do something
intricate or hard, working with my hands, I would do poorly. My intelligence, then, is not absolute but is a function of the society I live in and
of the fact that a small subsection of that society has managed to foist itself on the rest as an arbiter of such matters.

Consider my auto repairman, again. He had a habit of telling me   5
jokes whenever he saw me. One time he raised his head from under the
automobile hood to say, "Doc, a deaf-and-dumb guy went into a hardware store to ask for some nails. He put two fingers together on the
counter and made hammering motions with the other hand. The clerk
brought him a hammer. He shook his head and pointed to the two fingers he was hammering. The clerk brought him nails. He picked out the
sizes he wanted, and left. Well, doc, the next guy who came in was a
blind man. He wanted scissors. How do you suppose he asked for
them?"

Indulgently, I lifted my right hand and made scissoring motions   6
with my first two fingers. Whereupon my auto repairman laughed
raucously and said, "Why, you dumb jerk, he used his *voice* and asked
for them." Then he said, smugly, "I've been trying that on all my customers today." "Did you catch many?" I asked. "Quite a few," he said,
"but I knew for sure I'd catch *you*." "Why is that?" I asked. "Because
you're so goddamned educated, doc, I *knew* you couldn't be very
smart."

And I have an uneasy feeling he had something there.

RESPONDING TO "WHAT IS INTELLIGENCE, ANYWAY?"

Freewrite about what you think is true "intelligence."

Responding through Interpretation

1. In what sense was Asimov's mechanic intelligent, even though he probably scored low on intelligence tests? If he were to devise questions for
   an intelligence test, what kind might they be?
2. What do you think is Asimov's opinion of intelligence tests? Find specific sentences where he expresses his opinion.
3. Asimov uses two short anecdotes in order to make his point about intelligence testing. What do you think each anecdote contributes specifically
   to the essay?

Responding through Discussion

1. With a group of classmates, discuss your experiences with and your
   opinions of IQ testing. Make a group list of pros and cons which you can
   later share with the whole class.

2. Tell about a time when you were tested and felt that the test results were unfair. Be specific about why you felt you were unfairly tested and explain how this situation affected your life and/or future education.

Responding through Writing

1. In your journal, relate a story in which you illustrate the difference between "educated" intelligence and "practical" intelligence.
2. Write an essay in which you explore your ideas and beliefs about intelligence testing or other academic achievement tests you have taken in the past. Do you believe such tests are fair or unfair? What purposes do these tests serve? What kinds of tests do you think give the best measure of a person's intelligence? Make your position clear. If possible, incorporate the story you wrote in your journal as an example to support your point of view.

How Teachers Make Children Hate Reading

John Holt

John Holt went to Yale University and spent fourteen years as an elementary school teacher. Based on his experiences, he wrote two influential books on education in the 1960s: *How Children Fail* (1964) and *How Children Learn* (1967). As can be seen from the essay "How Teachers Make Children Hate Reading," first published November 1967 in *Redbook*, Holt believed that drills and other traditional, structured classroom activities tend to destroy a student's creativity and desire to learn. Holt's writings encouraged the growth of the alternative school movement. In his later years Holt came to the conclusion that parents would do better to keep their children out of school and educate them at community learning centers or at home.

When I was teaching English at the Colorado Rocky Mountain School,   1
I used to ask my students the kinds of questions that English teachers usually ask about reading assignments—questions designed to bring out the points that *I* had decided *they* should know. They, on their part, would try to get me to give them hints and clues as to what I wanted. It was a game of wits. I never gave my students an opportunity to say what they really thought about a book.

I gave vocabulary drills and quizzes too. I told my students that   2
every time they came upon a word in their book they did not understand, they were to look it up in the dictionary. I even devised special kinds of vocabulary tests, allowing them to use their books to see how the words were used. But looking back, I realize that these tests, along with many of my methods, were foolish.

My sister was the first person who made me question my conven-   3
tional ideas about teaching English. She had a son in the seventh grade in a fairly good public school. His teacher had asked the class to read Cooper's *The Deerslayer*. The choice was bad enough in itself; whether looking at man or nature, Cooper was superficial, inaccurate and sentimental, and his writing is ponderous and ornate. But to make matters worse, this teacher had decided to give the book the microscope and x-ray treatment. He made the students look up and memorize not only the definitions but the derivations of every big word that came along—and

there were plenty. Every chapter was followed by close questioning and testing to make sure the students "understood" everything.

Being then, as I said, conventional, I began to defend the teacher, 4 who was a good friend of mine, against my sister's criticisms. The argument soon grew hot. What was wrong with making sure that children understood every thing they read? My sister answered that until this year her boy had always loved reading, and had read a lot on his own; now he had stopped. (He was not really to start again for many years.)

Still I persisted. If children didn't look up the word they didn't 5 know, how would they ever learn them? My sister said, "Don't be silly! When you were little you had a huge vocabulary, and were always reading very grown-up books. When did you ever look up a word in a dictionary?"

She had me. I don't know that we had a dictionary at home; if we 6 did, I didn't use it. I don't use one today. In my life I doubt that I have looked up as many as fifty words, perhaps not even half that.

Since then I have talked about this with a number of teachers. More 7 than once I have said, "According to tests, educated and literate people like you have a vocabulary of about twenty-five thousand words. How many of these did you learn by looking them up in a dictionary?" They usually are startled. Few claim to have looked up even as many as a thousand. How did they learn the rest?

They learned them just as they learned to talk—by meeting words 8 over and over again, in different contexts, until they saw how they fitted.

Unfortunately, we English teachers are easily hung up on this matter 9 of understanding. Why should children understand everything they read? Why should anyone? Does anyone? I don't, and I never did. I was always reading books that teachers would have said were "too hard" for me, books full of words I didn't know. That's how I got to be a good reader. When about ten, I read all the D'Artagnan stories and loved them. It didn't trouble me in the least that I didn't know why France was at war with England or who was quarreling with whom in the French court or why the Musketeers should always be at odds with Cardinal Richelieu's men. I didn't even know who the Cardinal was, except that he was a dangerous and powerful man that my friends had to watch out for. This was all I needed to know.

Having said this, I will now say that I think a big, unabridged dic- 10 tionary is a fine thing to have in any home or classroom. No book is more fun to browse around in—*if* you're not made to. Children, depending on their age, will find many pleasant and interesting things to do with a big dictionary. They can look up funny-sounding words which they like, or long words, which they like, or forbidden words, which they like best of all. At a certain age, and particularly with a little encouragement from parents or teachers, they may become very interested in where words came from and when they came into the language and how their meanings have changed over the years. But exploring for the fun of it is very different from looking up words out of your reading because you're going to get into trouble with your teacher if you don't.

While teaching fifth grade two years or so after the argument with   11
my sister, I began to think again about reading. The children in my class were supposed to fill out a card—just the title and author and a one-sentence summary—for every book they read. I was not running a competition to see which child could read the most books, a competition that almost always leads to cheating. I just wanted to know what the children were reading. After a while it became clear that many of these very bright kids, from highly literate and even literary backgrounds, read very few books and deeply disliked reading. Why should this be?

At this time I was coming to realize, as I described in my book *How*   12
Children Fail, that for most children school was a place of danger, and their main business in school was staying out of danger as much as possible. I now began to see also that books were among the most dangerous things in school.

From the very beginning of school we make books and reading a   13
constant source of possible failure and public humiliation. When children are little we make them read aloud, before the teacher and other children, so that we can be sure they "know" all the words they are reading. This means that when they don't know a word, they are going to make a mistake, right in front of everyone. Instantly they are made to realize that they have done something wrong. Perhaps some of the other children will begin to wave their hands and say, "Ooooh! O-o-o-oh!" Perhaps they will just giggle, or nudge each other, or make a face. Perhaps the teacher will say, "Are you sure?" or ask someone else what he thinks. Or perhaps, if the teacher is kindly, she will just smile a sweet, sad smile—often one of the most painful punishments a child can suffer in school. In any case, the child who has made the mistake knows he has made it, and feels foolish, stupid, and ashamed, just as any of us would in his shoes.

Before long many children associate books and reading with mis-   14
takes, real or feared, and penalties and humiliation. This may not seem sensible, but it is natural. Mark Twain once said that a cat that sat on a hot stove lid would never sit on one again—but it would never sit on a

cold one either. As true of children as of cats. If they, so to speak, sit on a hot book a few times, if books cause them humiliation and pain, they are likely to decide that the safest thing to do is to leave all books alone.

After having taught fifth-grade classes for four years I felt quite sure   15
of this theory. In my next class were many children who had had great trouble with schoolwork, particularly reading. I decided to try at all costs to rid them of their fear and dislike of books, and to get them to read oftener and more adventurously.

One day soon after school had started, I said to them, "Now I'm   16
going to say something about reading that you have probably never heard a teacher say before. I would like you to read a lot of books this year, but I want you to read them only for pleasure. I am not going to ask you questions to find out whether you understand the books or not. If you understand enough of a book to enjoy it and want to go on read-ing it, that's enough for me. Also I'm not going to ask you what words mean.

"Finally," I said, "I don't want you to feel that just because you start   17
a book, you have to finish it. Give an author thirty or forty pages or so to get his story going. Then if you don't like the characters and don't care what happens to them, close the book, put it away, and get another. I don't care whether the books are easy or hard, short or long, as long as you enjoy them. Furthermore I'm putting all this in a letter to your par-ents, so they won't feel they have to quiz and heckle you about books at home."

The children sat stunned and silent. Was this a teacher talking? One   18
girl, who had just come to us from a school where she had had a very hard time, and who proved to be one of the most interesting, lively, and intelligent children I have ever known, looked at me steadily for a long time after I had finished. Then, still looking at me, she said slowly and solemnly, "Mr. Holt, do you really mean that?" I said just as solemnly, "I mean every word of it."

Apparently she decided to believe me. The first book she read was   19
Dr. Seuss's *How the Grinch Stole Christmas,* not a hard book even for most third graders. For a while she read a number of books on this level. Per-haps she was clearing up some confusion about reading that her teach-ers, in their hurry to get her up to "grade level," had never given her enough time to clear up. After she had been in the class six weeks or so and we had become good friends, I very tentatively suggested that, since she was a skillful rider and loved horses, she might like to read *National Velvet.* I made my sell as soft as possible, saying only that it was about a girl who loved and rode horses, and that if she didn't like it, she could

put it back. She tried it, and though she must have found it quite a bit harder than what she had been reading, finished it and liked it very much.

During the spring she really astonished me, however. One day, in one of our many free periods, she was reading at her desk. From a glimpse of the illustrations I thought I knew what the book was. I said to myself, "It can't be," and went to take a closer look. Sure enough, she was reading *Moby Dick*, in the edition with woodcuts by Rockwell Kent. When I came close to her desk she looked up. I said, "Are you really reading that?" She said she was. I said, "Do you like it?" She said, "Oh, yes, it's neat!" I said, "Don't you find parts of it rather heavy going?" She answered, "Oh, sure, but I just skip over those parts and go on to the next good part." 20

This is exactly what reading should be and in school so seldom is— an exciting, joyous adventure. Find something, dive into it, take the good parts, skip the bad parts, get what you can out of it, go on to something else. How different is our mean-spirited, picky insistence that every child get every last little scrap of "understanding" that can be dug out of a book. 21

RESPONDING TO "HOW TEACHERS MAKE CHILDREN HATE READING"

Freewrite on your thoughts and feelings about reading.

Responding through Interpretation

1. Holt argues against the way that reading is usually taught in the early grades. What are his main arguments, and how well does he back them up?
2. How does Holt use stories, such as the story told by his sister and the stories of his own students, to get his ideas across? Which story did you like best?
3. At one point Holt asks some teachers how they learned to read. What did his questioning of English teachers reveal, and how did what he learned help his presentation of ideas in the essay?

Responding through Discussion

1. Discuss with your group how you believe reading should be taught to young children. Pretend you are concerned parents and write a community letter to a local school board stating your beliefs and suggestions for

change. Choose a member from each group to read the letters to the entire class.
2. Working with your group members, develop a brief skit based on Holt's essay, and assign each group member a part. You can use Holt's anecdotes, but also create your own dramatic situations which could include a variety of viewpoints.

Responding through Writing

1. Write a journal entry about your earliest memories of learning to read. What influence did your different teachers have on your enjoyment of or displeasure with reading?
2. Based on some of your past experiences, what do you think is the best way for young people to learn reading skills? Write a paper in which you argue strongly for how reading should be taught in schools. Incorporate some of the ideas from your group discussions as well as some of the information used in your journal entries.

An Immigrant in a New School

Tin Le

Tin Le was born in Vietnam, and in 1985 his family reunited in the United States after six years of separation. Tin Le grew up with the love of nature and wild animals. He enjoys taking photographs and looking at landscape pictures taken by professional photographers, and hopes someday to have a chance to travel to Africa and photograph animals. In the following essay, notice how Tin Le uses fantasy to help him cope with the abuse from his classmates.

Have you ever been harassed or even physically abused by your schoolmates or other people you encountered just because you were different from the "average" person in your school or community? This happened to me when I came to America in 1985, an immigrant from Vietnam, and was placed in a seventh-grade classroom in Redwood City. It was a small school in a quiet community, but also a place where I had a stormy life for about a year. It was the most horrible experience that I ever had in my life. Kids at that age can be very mean to each other, and I was unfortunate to be on the receiving end of the cruelty.

I went to a school that did not have a lot of Asians. Because I was Asian, my schoolmates often teased me. Some of them, influenced by Japanese ninjas and Chinese martial arts fighters in movies, often challenged me to fight with them because they thought that I was one of "them," the Asian martial arts fighters. When I refused to fight, they taunted me, calling me chicken. They also called me weak and a nerd because I wore glasses. For a whole year in seventh grade I suffered from their harassment.

I especially remember one day when a classmate came to me on the playground and asked if I knew karate. When I answered, "No," he acted surprised and remarked, "All Chinese know Kung Fu; aren't you one of them? You're supposed to know some karate. Let's fight and see who is better." Although I ignored him and walked away, he followed me and started to push me around. The more I yielded, the more he attacked me, yet I could do nothing because he was so much bigger than I was. Eventually he seemed to achieve his goal because other students started to gather around us and cheer for him. He became the hero, the macho guy, and I became the laughing-stock of the school. From then on, they labeled me chicken and a weak Chinese, even though I am actually Vietnamese. In my classmates' eyes, all Asians were the same; there were no distinctions.

After this episode many students hit me or pushed me around when-   4
ever they felt like it, because they knew that I would not fight back. For example, often at lunchtime, several of them would pretend that they did not see me and would walk right into me, spilling my milk or any-thing else on my tray; then they would say "Sorry." However, saying sorry solved nothing and did not replace my lunch.

The worst part about this experience was that I did not have any-   5
one to turn to for help. I did not have the courage to share my problem with my parents, for I was afraid that worrying about my problem would just contribute to their own burdens. My parents had to work long hours every day so that they could provide for my brother and me a happy life. Once they came home, they were very tired and they needed to rest. Furthermore, I wanted them to feel proud of me as they always had. Fortunately, I found a way to resolve my problem by developing a fantasy to endure the pain. I fantasized that I had Bruce Lee's fighting skill, for he was the greatest movie star martial arts fighter; his skill even surpassed that of Chuck Norris. I imagined that I fixed up a date after school to settle my unfinished business with the guy who started my nightmare. The moment for our showdown came, and with just one roundhouse kick, I knocked him down to the ground in front of hun-dreds of schoolmate spectators. He begged me to let him go and promised that he would not pick on anyone else anymore. In my fan-tasy world, from that point on, my friends began to respect me and even to move aside wherever I went. I also imagined that I would disguise myself in black clothes like those of the ninjas and rescue other victims from bullies in the school, disappearing from the scene as soon as every-thing was over.

Even though the fantasy did not actually solve my problem, it   6
helped me to escape and forget about the bitter reality that I was in, al-lowing me to enter a world of my own. The fantasy was very helpful to me because it brought joy and a feeling of victory into my harsh expe-rience at school. As a recent immigrant, it was hard enough for me to try to cope with the language and cultural barriers, and, at the same time, to deal with the bullying and abuse from the students at my school. I still cannot understand how human beings could be so cruel to one an-other. I realize now that we use fantasies all the time as defense mecha-nisms to release us from the stress and abuse we must endure in daily life. I wish that we could get to a stage where we would not have to use these compensatory fantasies, a stage in which people could accept one

another for who they are, despite differences in physical character, race, and culture.

RESPONDING TO "AN IMMIGRANT IN A NEW SCHOOL"

Freewrite about a fantasy or daydream that you have had at school.

Responding through Interpretation

1. What do you think of the technique Tin Le used in order to cope with his problems with his schoolmates? Discuss the content or nature of his fantasies. What caused them?
2. Le develops his story through the use of examples and descriptive details. Which details stand out the most for you? Can you think of others he might have added or expanded? At the ending of the essay, how might Le have expanded his argument more fully to emphasize his point?

Responding through Discussion

1. Tin Le ends his essay with the wish that people could accept one another for who they are, "despite differences in physical character, race, and culture." With your group, brainstorm about how such a large ideal might be realized in today's world. Make a list of specific actions that students might take in order to bring about more acceptance of each others' cultural differences.

Responding through Writing

1. Write a response to Tin Le's essay in which you discuss your reactions to his writing. Tell him why you enjoyed and/or didn't particularly like specific parts of this essay.
2. Write an essay about a time that you were the target of someone else's prejudices.

He Couldn't Get Off the Ground

Jayme Plunckett

Jayme Plunckett wrote the following essay in his English class after reading about college athletes who drop out or accomplish little in school because they have been trained for sports rather than academics. Notice how
Plunckett develops his criticism of college athletics around an extended
case history of an athlete who had been poorly prepared for college.

A major problem in American schools is the excessive amount of   1
attention devoted to sports programs, especially among colleges where
much money can be made from sports. Although such programs may
begin with the intention of giving students increased physical discipline,
energy, and commitment, many schools encourage coaches and athletes
to devote so much energy to sports programs that the educational needs
of students are neglected.

This was the case of Mark Munns, a young athletic star from   2
Spokane, Washington. After ending his senior year with a state cham-
pionship in basketball and in the high jump, Munns turned down four-
year scholarship offers from Notre Dame, Duke, and USC to attend
Moses Lake Community College. Why would a young athlete turn down
a chance to attend a prestigious university and settle for a community
college? The answer is simple. Mark knew he didn't have the educational
preparation to survive at a university.

When Mark first arrived at high school, he focused on a well-   3
balanced program of education and sports. As Mark's coaches began to
notice his potential to become a great athlete, they involved him in the
rigorous training they felt he needed to succeed. However, Mark's ded-
ication was so strong that he soon neglected his educational goals and
focused solely on sports. By his senior year in high school, Mark was a
fantastic athlete; however, his academic skills had declined. The way the
faculty at Mark's school allowed his neglect of classroom learning further intensified his problems. The faculty neither took notice of Mark's
declining interest in education, nor did they seem to realize that Mark's
future depended on their guidance. Instead, the faculty praised him for
his athletic achievements. Mark is a prime example of how an intelligent
person preoccupied with athletics can float through the high school educational system without developing real intellectual skills.

Eventually Mark ended up in the vocational track where he enrolled   4
in English, accounting, keyboarding, work release, and two PE classes. Because of his athletic abilities, his PE teacher allowed him to practice on his own during scheduled class times and to use the gymnasium during his work release. Mark's high school counselor saw that Mark was spending nearly half his time practicing in school. Did the counselor confront Mark about his decisions? No. Instead, she sat by, watching Mark make his own decisions rather than trying to persuade him to consider the consequences of his decision. Even when Mark nearly failed his two "academic" classes—English and accounting—his counselor ignored the importance of his education because she was struck dumb by his athletic talent.

Academic neglect of athletes doesn't stop after high school. Many   5
colleges neglect the academic interests of their students because of the money-making opportunities sports programs bring. Many faculty overlook the academic quality of work produced by those students who contribute to the college's sports programs. Because of greed, Mark may once again slip through the educational system without learning anything valuable that he can apply toward a career in the future. Once again, he will be treated as a hero and will be led to believe that he is on the right course for success. If he succeeds in his dream to play in the NBA, he will be in good shape, and, with luck, will be able to retire from professional sports with enough money invested to live on for many years. However, if his dream doesn't become reality, he will have to struggle through the inadequacies in his education in order to succeed in life after sports.

The saddest part of this story is that no one seems to care. The high   6
schools and the majority of colleges around the country are acting as though nothing is wrong. They sit back, mind their own businesses, and ignore the needs of students. They should realize that they are responsible for shaping the minds of the men and women of the future and should start advising students about the decisions they make. Without a radical change in the educational system in the U.S., students will not receive the education needed, and the nation will lag behind the rest of the world in nearly everything except sports. Change and reform in the schools are the keys to stopping more tragedies like Mark Munns'.

RESPONDING TO "HE COULDN'T GET OFF THE GROUND"

Freewrite about some of your experiences with and attitudes concerning high school athletics.

Responding through Interpretation

1. What are some of the specific ways that high schools and colleges give support to athletics? When does this support seem excessive and when does it seem justifiable?
2. Look more closely at Plunckett's ending idea. He doesn't give any concrete solutions to the abuses in high school and college athletics. What are some of the solutions you think would be effective?

Responding through Discussion

1. With your group, discuss whether you agree or disagree with Plunckett's ideas about how schools neglect their athletes' academic achievement. Develop a list of possible solutions to this problem.

Responding through Writing

1. In your journal, write an account of either your own or someone else's experience which is similar to Mark Munns' story.
2. Using the list of solutions generated in your group discussion, choose one solution and write a paper that argues how this solution would help alleviate the problem of academic neglect of athletes.

Poem for the Creative Writing Class, Spring 1982

Merle Woo

Merle Woo is the daughter of Chinese-Korean immigrants. Her essays, stories, and poems have been included in anthologies such as *This Bridge
Called My Back: Writings by Radical Women of Color* (1981) and in her
own poetry collection, *Yellow Woman Speaks* (1986). Woo talks about
combining her work as teacher, activist, and poet: "We poets who are outspoken as Asian Americans, women, lesbians/gays, workers, cannot separate ourselves from the reality in which we live. We are freedom fighters with words as our weapons—on the page or on the picket sign."

The silence in the classroom
of people I've grown to respect—
seems like so much potential here:
men and women
brown black yellow jewish white   5
gay and straight.

Classrooms are ugly,
cages with beautiful birds in them.
scraped, peeling walls

empty bookcases   10
an empty blackboard—
no ideas here.

And one window.
One writer comes in
from sitting on the sill,   15
three stories up.
We all want to fly
and feel the sun on the backs of our wings—

Inhale the breath
pulling in the energy of   20
seventeen people around me

and exhale
putting out my ideas, ideas, ideas.
We all want to fly out that window.
A breeze comes in once in a while,   25
we want to go out with it
to where the birds are.

To take flight
using the words
that give us wings.   30

What is language after all
but the touching and uplifting
one to the others:
scenes
poems   35
dreams
our own natural imagery:
coins
a train to El Salvador
sleeping, pregnant mothers   40
menacing garages/a fist pounding/voices yelling
a yogi
cops being the bowery boys
roller coasters
blood   45
a girl on a swing
roses
water, streams, rivers, oceans
rise. rise.

Who can keep us caged?   50

RESPONDING TO "POEM FOR THE CREATIVE WRITING CLASS, SPRING 1982"

Freewrite about an exciting and creative classroom learning experience that stands out vividly in your memory.

Responding through Interpretation

1. The poem compares ordinary classrooms to "cages with beautiful birds in them." What attitude toward school and students does this comparison reveal? Do you agree?
2. As the poem continues, how does the poem go beyond this original comparison? What final view of the potential of education does the poem leave us with?
3. Point out specific powerful words and details that the poet uses to contrast the ugliness and sterility of the classroom to the creative spirit and vital ideas of the students in the room.

Responding through Discussion

1. Get together with a small group of perhaps two or three other classmates. Have each member of the group read the poem aloud slowly. Reserve comments until the poem has been read aloud by each person. Then discuss what new insights, ideas, understandings you gained by hearing the poem read aloud several times and by different readers.
2. Discuss among the group any feelings of being caged or imprisoned which your group members have experienced during their years of your education. How can students cope with such feelings?

Responding through Writing

1. Study the poem carefully, going through it several times and looking at how it is physically structured on the page. Now put the poem away and write a short piece in which you tell the story of the poem as if it were your own experience. Don't look back at the poem to check out words; just allow your memory of the poem to shape your own imagination and writing.
2. Write an essay about ways that teachers can help make classrooms freer, more expressive environments, more like the creative writing class described in Woo's poem.

Charles

Shirley Jackson

A prolific and compelling writer, Shirley Jackson is most famous for her short story "The Lottery" and other similar stories, which often contain elements of horror and mystery. Jackson has also written numerous books, most notably *The Haunting of Hill House* (1959) and *We Have Always Lived in the Castle* (1962). The following selection, "Charles," was first published in *Mademoiselle* in 1948 and was reprinted in *The Lottery and Other Stories* (1949), the only collection of Jackson's stories to appear during her lifetime.

The day my son Laurie started kindergarten he renounced corduroy   1
overalls with bibs and began wearing blue jeans with a belt; I watched
him go off the first morning with the older girl next door, seeing clearly
that an era of my life was ended, my sweet-voiced nursery-school tot
replaced by a long-trousered, swaggering character who forgot to stop
at the corner and wave good-bye to me.

He came home the same way, the front door slamming open, his cap   2
on the floor, and the voice suddenly become raucous shouting, "Isn't
anybody *here?*"

At lunch he spoke insolently to his father, spilled his baby sister's   3
milk, and remarked that his teacher said we were not to take the name
of the Lord in vain.

"How *was* school today?" I asked, elaborately casual.   4

"All right," he said.   5

"Did you learn anything?" his father asked.   6

Laurie regarded his father coldly. "I didn't learn nothing," he said.   7

"Anything," I said. "Didn't learn anything."   8

"The teacher spanked a boy, though," Laurie said, addressing his   9
bread and butter. "For being fresh," he added, with his mouth full.

"What did he do?" I asked. "Who was it?"   10

Laurie thought. "It was Charles," he said. "He was fresh. The teacher   11
spanked him and made him stand in a corner. He was awfully fresh."

"What did he do?" I asked again, but Laurie slid off his chair, took a   12
cookie, and left, while his father was still saying, "See here, young man."

The next day Laurie remarked at lunch, as soon as he sat down,   13
"Well, Charles was bad again today." He grinned enormously and said,
"Today Charles hit the teacher."

"Good heavens," I said, mindful of the Lord's name, "I suppose he   14
got spanked again?"

"He sure did," Laurie said. "Look up," he said to his father.   15

"What?" his father said, looking up.   16

"Look down," Laurie said. "Look at my thumb. Gee, you're dumb."   17
He began to laugh insanely.

"Why did Charles hit the teacher?" I asked quickly.   18

"Because she tried to make him color with red crayons," Laurie   19
said. "Charles wanted to color with green crayons so he hit the teacher
and she spanked him and said nobody play with Charles but everybody
did."

The third day—it was Wednesday of the first week—Charles   20
bounced a see-saw on to the head of a little girl and made her bleed, and
the teacher made him stay inside all during recess. Thursday Charles had
to stand in a corner during story-time because he kept pounding his feet
on the floor. Friday Charles was deprived of blackboard privileges because he threw chalk.

On Saturday I remarked to my husband, "Do you think kinder-   21
garten is too unsettling for Laurie? All this toughness, and bad grammar, and this Charles boy sounds like such a bad influence."

"It'll be all right," my husband said reassuringly. "Bound to be   22
people like Charles in the world. Might as well meet them now as
later."

On Monday Laurie came home late, full of news. "Charles," he   23
shouted as he came up the hill; I was waiting anxiously on the front steps.
"Charles," Laurie yelled all the way up the hill, "Charles was bad again."

"Come right in," I said, as soon as he came close enough. "Lunch is   24
waiting."

"You know what Charles did?" he demanded, following me through   25
the door. "Charles yelled so in school they sent a boy in from first grade
to tell the teacher she had to make Charles keep quiet, and so Charles
had to stay after school. And so all the children stayed to watch him."

"What did he do?" I asked.   26

"He just sat there," Laurie said, climbing into his chair at the table.   27
"Hi, Pop, y'old dust mop."

"Charles had to stay after school today," I told my husband. "Every-   28
one stayed with him."

"What does this Charles look like?" my husband asked Laurie.   29
"What's his other name?"

"He's bigger than me," Laurie said. "And he doesn't have any rub-   30
bers and he doesn't ever wear a jacket."

Monday night was the first Parent-Teachers meeting, and only the   31
fact that the baby had a cold kept me from going; I wanted passionately
to meet Charles's mother. On Tuesday Laurie remarked suddenly, "Our
teacher had a friend come to see her in school today."

"Charles's mother?" my husband and I asked simultaneously.   32

"Naaah," Laurie said scornfully. "It was a man who came and made   33
us do exercises, we had to touch our toes. Look." He climbed down from
his chair and squatted down and touched his toes. "Like this," he said.
He got solemnly back into his chair and said, picking up his fork,
"Charles didn't even *do* exercises."

"That's fine," I said heartily. "Didn't Charles want to do exercises?"   34

"Naaah," Laurie said. "Charles was so fresh to the teacher's friend   35
he wasn't *let* do exercises."

"Fresh again?" I said.   36

"He kicked the teacher's friend," Laurie said. "The teacher's friend   37
told Charles to touch his toes like I just did and Charles kicked
him."

"What are they going to do about Charles, do you suppose?" Lau-   38
rie's father asked him.

Laurie shrugged elaborately. "Throw him out of school, I guess," he   39
said.

Wednesday and Thursday were routine; Charles yelled during story   40
hour and hit a boy in the stomach and made him cry. On Friday Charles
stayed after school again and so did all the other children.

With the third week of kindergarten Charles was an institution   41
in our family; the baby was being a Charles when she cried all afternoon; Laurie did a Charles when he filled his wagon full of mud and
pulled it through the kitchen; even my husband, when he caught his
elbow in the telephone cord and pulled telephone, ashtray, and a
bowl of flowers off the table, said, after the first minute, "Looks like
Charles."

During the third and fourth weeks it looked like a reformation in   42
Charles; Laurie reported grimly at lunch on Thursday of the third week,
"Charles was so good today the teacher gave him an apple."

"What?" I said, and my husband added warily, "You mean   43
Charles?"

"Charles," Laurie said. "He gave the crayons around and he picked   44
up the books afterward and the teacher said he was her helper."

"What happened?" I asked incredulously.   45

"He was her helper, that's all," Laurie said, and shrugged.   46

"Can this be true, about Charles?" I asked my husband that night.   47
"Can something like this happen?"

"Wait and see," my husband said cynically. "When you've got a   48
Charles to deal with, this may mean he's only plotting."

He seemed to be wrong. For over a week Charles was the teacher's   49
helper; each day he handed things out and he picked things up; no one
had to stay after school.

"The P.T.A. meeting's next week again," I told my husband one   50
evening. "I'm going to find Charles's mother there."

"Ask her what happened to Charles," my husband said. "I'd like to   51
know."

"I'd like to know myself," I said.   52

On Friday of that week things were back to normal. "You know what   53
Charles did today?" Laurie demanded at the lunch table, in a voice
slightly awed. "He told a little girl to say a word and she said it and the
teacher washed her mouth out with soap and Charles laughed."

"What word?" his father asked unwisely, and Laurie said, "I'll have   54
to whisper it to you, it's so bad." He got down off his chair and went
around to his father. His father bent his head down and Laurie whis-
pered joyfully. His father's eyes widened.

"Did Charles tell the little girl to say *that?*" he asked respectfully.   55

"She said it *twice*," Laurie said. "Charles told her to say it *twice*."   56

"What happened to Charles?" my husband asked.   57

"Nothing," Laurie said. "He was passing out the crayons."   58

Monday morning Charles abandoned the little girl and said the evil   59
word himself three or four times, getting his mouth washed out with
soap each time. He also threw chalk.

My husband came to the door with me that evening as I set out for   60
the P.T.A. meeting. "Invite her over for a cup of tea after the meeting,"
he said. "I want to get a look at her."

"If only she's there," I said prayerfully.   61

"She'll be there," my husband said. "I don't see how they could hold   62
a P.T.A. meeting without Charles's mother."

At the meeting I sat restlessly, scanning each comfortable matronly   63
face, trying to determine which one hid the secret of Charles. None of
them looked to me haggard enough. No one stood up in the meeting and
apologized for the way her son had been acting. No one mentioned
Charles.

After the meeting I identified and sought out Laurie's kindergarten   64
teacher. She had a plate with a cup of tea and a piece of chocolate cake;

I had a plate with a cup of tea and a piece of marshmallow cake. We maneuvered up to one another cautiously, and smiled.

"I've been so anxious to meet you," I said. "I'm Laurie's mother."   65

"We're all so interested in Laurie," she said.   66

"Well, he certainly likes kindergarten," I said. "He talks about it all   67
the time."

"We had a little trouble adjusting, the first week or so," she said   68
primly, "but now he's a fine little helper. With occasional lapses, of
course."

"Laurie usually adjusts very quickly," I said. "I suppose this time   69
it's Charles's influence."

"Charles?"   70

"Yes," I said, laughing, "you must have your hands full in that   71
kindergarten, with Charles."

"Charles?" she said. "We don't have any Charles in the kinder-   72
garten."

RESPONDING TO "CHARLES"

Freewrite about a memory of yourself in kindergarten or first grade. How
did you feel about school? What was your teacher like?

Responding through Interpretation

1. What motivates Laurie to make up the story of Charles? Does Laurie
   seem to be having a normal response to the pressures of kindergarten,
   or should his parents be worried?
2. Were you surprised at the outcome of the story, or did you guess the ending? Why was it so hard for Laurie's parents to understand the real identity of Charles?
3. Based on the evidence provided in the story, what do you think Laurie's
   parents will say to him after the PTA meeting?

Responding through Discussion

1. In a group of four classmates, give each person a role and read the story
   aloud as if it were a play. Afterward, discuss what you think of the story
   and its characters.
2. With your group, discuss some of the ways each of you coped with
   the pressures of school in your early years. How did you feel about
   school? How did you act? What are some of the events you still remember?

Responding through Writing

1. Part of the fun of this story lies in the surprise at the end. Write a narrative account of some humorous event that ended with a big surprise. Incorporate dialogue into your narrative (study Jackson's dialogue for punctuation and style).
2. Write a brief evaluation of "Charles," explaining what happens and how Jackson makes the reader believe such a story. Use evidence from the story to support your ideas.

Corla Hawkins

Jonathan Kozol

Jonathan Kozol has worked as a writer and social critic all of his adult life. He is best known for his nonfiction that reveals the corruption and inequality of opportunity within the public schools system. He won the National Book Award in 1967 for *Death at an Early Age*. Another of his books is *Prisoner of Silence: Breaking the Bonds of Adult Illiteracy in the United States* (1980). His most recent book is *Amazing Grace: The Lives of Children and the Conscience of a Nation* (1995). The selection we have included, "Corla Hawkins," is excerpted from his *Savage Inequalities* (1992), in which Kozol exposes the failure of public education in inner-city schools.

Even in the most unhappy schools there are certain classes that stand   1
out like little islands of excitement, energy and hope. One of these classes
is a combination fifth and sixth grade at Bethune, taught by a woman,
maybe 40 years of age, named Corla Hawkins.

The classroom is full of lively voices when I enter. The children are   2
at work, surrounded by a clutter of big dictionaries, picture books and
gadgets, science games and plants and colorful milk cartons, which the
teacher purchased out of her own salary. An oversized Van Gogh collection, open to a print of a sunflower, is balanced on a table-ledge next
to a fish tank and a turtle tank. Next to the table is a rocking chair. Handwritten signs are on all sides: "Getting to know you," "Keeping you safe"
and, over a wall that holds some artwork by the children, "Mrs.
Hawkins's Academy of Fine Arts." Near the windows, the oversized
leaves of several wild-looking plants partially cover rows of novels,
math books, and a new World Book Encyclopedia. In the opposite corner is a "Science Learning Board" that holds small packets which contain bulb sockets, bulbs and wires, lenses, magnets, balance scales and
pliers. In front of the learning board is a microscope. Several rugs are
thrown around the floor. On another table are a dozen soda bottles
sealed with glue and lying sideways, filled with colored water.

The room looks like a cheerful circus tent. In the center of it all,   3
within the rocking chair, and cradling a newborn in her arms, is Mrs.
Hawkins.

The 30 children in the class are seated in groups of six at five of what   4
she calls "departments." Each department is composed of six desks

pushed together to create a table. One of the groups is doing math, another something that they call "math strategy." A third is doing reading. Of the other two groups, one is doing something they describe as "mathematics art"—painting composites of geometric shapes—and the other is studying "careers," which on this morning is a writing exercise about successful business leaders who began their lives in poverty. Near the science learning board a young-looking woman is preparing a new lesson that involves a lot of gadgets she has taken from a closet.

"This woman," Mrs. Hawkins tells me, "is a parent. She wanted to help me. So I told her, 'If you don't have somebody to keep your baby, bring the baby here. I'll be the mother. I can do it.' " 5

As we talk, a boy who wears big glasses brings his book to her and asks her what the word *salvation* means. She shows him how to sound it out, then tells him, "Use your dictionary if you don't know what it means." When a boy at the reading table argues with the boy beside him, she yells out, "You ought to be ashamed. You woke my baby." 6

After 15 minutes she calls out that it is time to change their tables. The children get up and move to new departments. As each group gets up to move to the next table, one child stays behind to introduce the next group to the lesson. 7

"This is the point of it," she says. "I'm teaching them three things. Number one: self-motivation. Number two: self-esteem. Number three: you help your sister and your brother. I tell them they're responsible for one another. I give no grades in the first marking period because I do not want them to be too competitive. Second marking period, you get your grade on what you've taught your neighbors at your table. Third marking period, I team them two-and-two. You get the same grade as your partner. Fourth marking period, I tell them, 'Every fish swims on its own.' But I wait a while for that. The most important thing for me is that they teach each other. . . . 8

"All this stuff"—she gestures at the clutter in the room—"I bought myself because it never works to order things through the school system. I bought the VCR. I bought the rocking chair at a flea market. I got these books here for ten cents apiece at a flea market. I bought that encyclopedia—"she points at the row of World Books—"so that they can do their research right here in this room." 9

I ask her if the class reads well enough to handle these materials. "Most of them can read some of these books. What they cannot read, another child can read to them," she says. 10

"I tell the parents, 'Any time your child says, "I don't have no homework," call me up. Call me at home.' Because I give them homework 11 every night and weekends too. Holidays I give them extra. Every child in this classroom has my phone."

Cradling the infant in her lap, she says, "I got to buy a playpen." 12

The bottles of colored water, she explains, are called "wave 13 bottles." The children make them out of plastic soda bottles which they clean and fill with water and food coloring and seal with glue. She takes one in her hand and rolls it slowly to and fro. "It shows them how waves form," she says. "I let them keep them at their desks. Some of them hold them in their hands while they're at work. It seems to calm them: seeing the water cloud up like a storm and then grow clear. . . .

"I take them outside every day during my teacher-break. On Satur- 14 days we go to places like the art museum. Tuesdays, after school, I coach the drill team. Friday afternoons I tutor parents for their GED [high school equivalency exam]. If you're here this afternoon, I do the gospel choir."

When I ask about her own upbringing, she replies, "I went to 15 school here in Chicago. My mother believed I was a 'gifted' child, but the system did not challenge me and I was bored at school. Fortunately one of my mother's neighbors was a teacher and she used to talk to me and help me after school. If it were not for her I doubt that I'd have thought that I could go to college. I promised myself I would return that favor."

At the end of class I go downstairs to see the principal, and then re- 16 turn to a second-floor room to see the gospel choir in rehearsal. When I arrive, they've already begun. Thirty-five children, ten of whom are boys, are standing in rows before a piano player. Next to the piano, Mrs. Hawkins stands and leads them through the words. The children range in age from sixth and seventh graders to three second graders and three tiny children, one of whom is Mrs. Hawkins's daughter, who are kindergarten pupils in the school.

They sing a number of gospel songs with Mrs. Hawkins pointing to 17 each group—soprano, alto, bass—when it is their turn to join in. When they sing, "I love you, Lord," their voices lack the energy she wants. She interrupts and shouts at them, "Do you love Him? Do you?" They sing louder. The children look as if they're riveted to her directions.

"This next song," she says, "I dreamed about this. This song is my 18 favorite."

The piano begins. The children start to clap their hands. When she 19 gives the signal they begin to sing:

Clap your hands!
Stamp your feet!
Get on up
Out of your seats!
Help me
Lift 'em up, Lord!
Help me
Lift 'em up!

When a child she calls "Reverend Joe" does not come in at the right   21
note, Mrs. Hawkins stops and says to him: "I thought you told me you
were saved!"
The children smile. The boy called "Reverend Joe" stands up a lit-   22
tle straighter. Then the piano starts again. The sound of children clap-
ping and then stamping with the music fills the room. Mrs. Hawkins
waves her arms. Then, as the children start, she also starts to sing.

Help me lift 'em up, Lord!
Help me lift 'em up!

There are wonderful teachers such as Corla Hawkins almost every-   23
where in urban schools, and sometimes a number of such teachers in a
single school. It is tempting to focus on these teachers and, by doing this,
to paint a hopeful portrait of the good things that go on under adverse
conditions. There is, indeed, a growing body of such writing; and these
books are sometimes very popular, because they are consoling.
The rationale behind much of this writing is that pedagogic prob-   24
lems in our cities are not chiefly matters of injustice, inequality or segregation, but of insufficient information about teaching strategies: If we
could simply learn "what works" in Corla Hawkins's room, we'd then
be in a position to repeat this all over Chicago and in every other system.
But what is unique in Mrs. Hawkins's classroom is not what she   25
does but who she is. Warmth and humor and contagious energy cannot be replicated and cannot be written into any standardized curriculum. If they could, it would have happened long ago; for wonderful teachers have been heroized in books and movies for at least three
decades. And the problems of Chicago are, in any case, not those of insufficient information. If Mrs. Hawkins's fellow fifth grade teachers
simply needed information, they could get it easily by walking 20 steps

across the hall and visiting her room. The problems are systemic: The number of teachers over 60 years of age in the Chicago system is twice that of the teachers under 30. The salary scale, too low to keep exciting, youthful teachers in the system, leads the city to rely on low-paid subs, who represent more than a quarter of Chicago's teaching force. "We have teachers," Mrs. Hawkins says, "who only bother to come in three days a week. One of these teachers comes in usually around nine-thirty. You ask her how she can expect the kids to care about their education if the teacher doesn't even come until nine-thirty. She answers you, 'It makes no difference. Kids like these aren't going anywhere.' The school board thinks it's saving money on the subs. I tell them, 'Pay now or pay later.' "

RESPONDING TO "CORLA HAWKINS"

Freewrite about the qualities you think make a teacher outstanding.

Responding through Interpretation

1. What is the meaning of Corla Hawkins' statement, "The most important thing for me is that they teach each other"? How does Hawkins attempt to make her statement a reality in her classroom?
2. How does Kozol define a gifted teacher? Do you think Corla Hawkins is a gifted teacher?
3. Point out some instances of the ongoing dialogue between Corla Hawkins and her students. What is revealed about Corla Hawkins, her values, and her relationship with her students through the use of dialogue in the essay?

Responding through Discussion

1. Discuss with your group some of the things you think could be done to reverse some of the problems in public schools today.
2. Let each member describe to the group some of the most gifted teachers he or she has had. Come up with a group list of the qualities of a great teacher.

Responding through Writing

1. Write a journal entry in which you describe the elementary or junior high school teacher from whom you learned the most. What did his or her

classroom look like? What were some of the learning activities that took place in the classroom? What is your most vivid memory of this teacher?

2. Expand your journal entry into a paper by using the teacher you described to illustrate a definite point you wish to make about education. Use your teacher as an example by giving specific details and descriptions throughout your paper.

How Male and Female Students Use Language Differently

Deborah Tannen

Deborah Tannen, a professor of linguistics at Georgetown University, is the author of *You Just Don't Understand: Women and Men in Conversation* (1990), *Talking from 9 to 5* (1994), and other books about communication between the sexes. Tannen believes that teachers need to find diverse ways to organize the classroom so that both male and female students feel comfortable and participate fully in class discussions, a point she makes in the following article from the *Chronicle of Higher Education* (June 1991).

When I researched and wrote my latest book, *You Just Don't Understand: Women and Men in Conversation,* the furthest thing from my mind was reevaluating my teaching strategies. But that has been one of the direct benefits of having written the book.   1

The primary focus of my linguistic research always has been the language of everyday conversation. One facet of this is conversational style: how different regional, ethnic, and class backgrounds, as well as age and gender, result in different ways of using language to communicate. *You Just Don't Understand* is about the conversational styles of women and men. As I gained more insight into typically male and female ways of using language, I began to suspect some of the causes of the troubling facts that women who go to single-sex schools do better in later life, and that when young women sit next to young men in classrooms, the males talk more. This is not to say that all men talk in class, nor that no women do. It is simply that a greater percentage of discussion time is taken by men's voices.   2

The research of sociologists and anthropologists such as Janet Lever, Marjorie Harness Goodwin, and Donna Eder has shown that girls and boys learn to use language differently in their sex-separate peer groups. Typically, a girl has a best friend with whom she sits and talks, frequently telling secrets. It's the telling of secrets, the fact and the way that they talk to each other, that makes them best friends. For boys, activities are central: their best friends are the ones they do things with. Boys also tend to play in larger groups that are hierarchical. High-status boys give orders and push low-status boys around. So boys are expected to   3 use language to seize center stage: by exhibiting their skill, displaying their knowledge, and challenging and resisting challenges.

These patterns have stunning implications for classroom interaction.   4
Most faculty members assume that participating in class discussion is a necessary part of successful performance. Yet speaking in a classroom is more congenial to boys' language experience than to girls', since it entails putting oneself forward in front of a large group of people, many of whom are strangers and at least one of whom is sure to judge speakers' knowledge and intelligence by their verbal display.

Another aspect of many classrooms that makes them more hos-   5
pitable to most men than to most women is the use of debate-like formats as a learning tool. Our educational system, as Walter Ong argues persuasively in his book *Fighting for Life* (Cornell University Press, 1981), is fundamentally male in that the pursuit of knowledge is believed to be achieved by ritual opposition: public display followed by argument and challenge. Father Ong demonstrates that ritual opposition—what he calls "adversativeness" or "agonism"—is fundamental to the way most males approach almost any activity. (Consider, for example, the little boy who shows he likes a little girl by pulling her braids and shoving her.) But ritual opposition is antithetical to the way most females learn and like to interact. It is not that females don't fight, but that they don't fight for fun. They don't *ritualize* opposition.

Anthropologists working in widely disparate parts of the world   6
have found contrasting verbal rituals for women and men. Women in completely unrelated cultures (for example, Greece and Bali) engage in ritual laments: spontaneously produced rhyming couplets that express their pain, for example, over the loss of loved ones. Men do not take part in laments. They have their own, very different verbal ritual: a contest, a war of words in which they vie with each other to devise clever insults.

When discussing these phenomena with a colleague, I commented   7
that I see these two styles in American conversation: many women bond by talking about troubles, and many men bond by exchanging playful insults and put-downs, and other sorts of verbal sparring. He exclaimed: "I never thought of this, but that's the way I teach: I have students read an article, and then I invite them to tear it apart. After we've torn it to shreds, we talk about how to build a better model."

This contrasts sharply with the way I teach: I open the discussion of   8
readings by asking, "What did you find useful in this? What can we use in our own theory building and our own methods?" I note what I see as weaknesses in the author's approach, but I also point out that the writer's discipline and purposes might be different from ours. Finally, I offer per-

sonal anecdotes illustrating the phenomena under discussion and praise students' anecdotes as well as their critical acumen.

These different teaching styles must make our classrooms wildly dif-   9
ferent places and hospitable to different students. Male students are more likely to be comfortable attacking the readings and might find the inclusion of personal anecdotes irrelevant and "soft." Women are more likely to resist discussion they perceive as hostile, and, indeed, it is women in my classes who are most likely to offer personal anecdotes.

A colleague who read my book commented that he had always   10
taken for granted that the best way to deal with students' comments is to challenge them; this, he felt it was self-evident, sharpens their minds and helps them develop debating skills. But he had noticed that women were relatively silent in his classes, so he decided to try beginning discussion with relatively open-ended questions and letting comments go unchallenged. He found, to his amazement and satisfaction, that more women began to speak up.

Though some of the women in his class clearly liked this better, per-   11
haps some of the men liked it less. One young man in my class wrote in a questionnaire about a history professor who gave students questions to think about and called on people to answer them: "He would then play devil's advocate . . . *i.e.,* he debated us. . . . That class *really* sharp-ened me intellectually. . . . We as students do need to know how to de-fend ourselves." This young man valued the experience of being at-tacked and challenged publicly. Many, if not most, women would shrink from such "challenge," experiencing it as public humiliation.

A professor at Hamilton College told me of a young man who was   12
upset because he felt his class presentation had been a failure. The pro-fessor was puzzled because he had observed that class members had lis-tened attentively and agreed with the student's observations. It turned out that it was this very agreement that the student interpreted as fail-ure: since no one had engaged his ideas by arguing with him, he felt they had found them unworthy of attention.

So one reason men speak in class more than women is that many of   13
them find the "public" classroom setting more conducive to speaking, whereas most women are more comfortable speaking in private to a small group of people they know well. A second reason is that men are more likely to be comfortable with the debate-like form that discussion may take. Yet another reason is the different attitudes toward speaking in class that typify women and men.

Students who speak frequently in class, many of whom are men, as-   14
sume that it is their job to think of contributions and try to get the floor

to express them. But many women monitor their participation not only to get the floor but to avoid getting it. Women students in my class tell me that if they have spoken up once or twice, they hold back for the rest of the class because they don't want to dominate. If they have spoken a lot one week, they will remain silent the next. These different ethics of participation are, of course, unstated, so those who speak freely assume that those who remain silent have nothing to say, and those who are reining themselves in assume that the big talkers are selfish and hoggish.

When I looked around my classes, I could see these differing ethics   15
and habits at work. For example, my graduate class in analyzing conversation had twenty students, eleven women and nine men. Of the men, four were foreign students: two Japanese, one Chinese, and one Syrian. With the exception of the three Asian men, all the men spoke in class at least occasionally. The biggest talker in the class was a woman, but there were also five women who never spoke at all, only one of whom was Japanese. I decided to try something different.

I broke the class into small groups to discuss the issues raised in the   16
readings and to analyze their own conversational transcripts. I devised three ways of dividing the students into groups: one by the degree program they were in, one by gender, and one by conversational style, as closely as I could guess it. This meant that when the class was grouped according to conversational style, I put Asian students together, fast talkers together, and quiet students together. The class split into groups six times during the semester, so they met in each grouping twice. I told students to regard the groups as examples of interactional data and to note the different ways they participated in the different groups. Toward the end of the term, I gave them a questionnaire asking about their class and group participation.

I could see plainly from my observation of the groups at work that   17
women who never opened their mouths in class were talking away in the small groups. In fact, the Japanese woman commented that she found it particularly hard to contribute to the all-woman group she was in because "I was overwhelmed by how talkative the female students were in the female-only group." This is particularly revealing because it highlights that the same person who can be "oppressed" into silence in one context can become the talkative "oppressor" in another. No one's conversational style is absolute; everyone's style changes in response to the context and others' styles.

Some of the students (seven) said they preferred the same-gender   18
groups; others preferred the same-style groups. In answer to the question "Would you have liked to speak in class more than you did?" six

of the seven who said yes were women; the one man was Japanese. Most startlingly, this response did not come only from quiet women; it came from women who had indicated they had spoken in class never, rarely, sometimes, and often. Of the eleven students who said the amount they had spoken was fine, seven were men. Of the four women who checked "fine," two added qualifications indicating it wasn't completely fine: One wrote in "maybe more," and one wrote, "I have an urge to participate but often feel I should have something more interesting/relevant/wonderful/intelligent to say!!"

I counted my experiment a success. Everyone in the class found the small groups interesting, and no one indicated he or she would have preferred that the class not break into groups. Perhaps most instructive, however, was the fact that the experience of breaking into groups, and of talking about participation in class, raised everyone's awareness about classroom participation. After we had talked about it, some of the quietest women in the class made a few voluntary contributions, though sometimes I had to ensure their participation by interrupting the students who were exuberantly speaking out.   19

Americans are often proud that they discount the significance of cultural differences: "We are all individuals," many people boast. Ignoring such issues as gender and ethnicity becomes a source of pride: "I treat everyone the same." But treating people the same is not equal treatment if they are not the same.   20

The classroom is a different environment for those who feel comfortable putting themselves forward in a group than it is for those who find the prospect of doing so chastening, or even terrifying. When a professor asks, "Are there any questions?" students who can formulate statements the fastest have the greatest opportunity to respond. Those who need significant time to do so have not really been given a chance at all, since by the time they are ready to speak, someone else has the floor.   21

In a class where some students speak out without raising hands, those who feel they must raise their hands and wait to be recognized do not have equal opportunity to speak. Telling them to feel free to jump in will not make them feel free; one's sense of timing, of one's rights and obligations in a classroom, are automatic, learned over years of interaction. They may be changed over time, with motivation and effort, but they cannot be changed on the spot. And everyone assumes his or her own way is best. When I asked my students how the class could be changed to make it easier for them to speak more, the most talkative woman said she would prefer it if no one had to raise hands, and a for-   22 eign student said he wished people would raise their hands and wait to be recognized.

My experience in this class has convinced me that small-group interaction should be part of any class that is not a small seminar. I also am convinced that having the students become observers of their own interaction is a crucial part of their education. Talking about ways of talking in class makes students aware that their ways of talking affect other students, that the motivations they impute to others may not truly reflect others' motives, and that the behaviors they assume to be self-evidently right are not universal norms. 23

The goal of complete equal opportunity in class may not be attainable, but realizing that one monolithic classroom-participation structure is not equal opportunity is itself a powerful motivation to find more-diverse methods to serve diverse students—and every classroom is diverse. 24

RESPONDING TO "HOW MALE AND FEMALE STUDENTS USE LANGUAGE DIFFERENTLY"

Freewrite on how you think class discussions should be handled in order to assure that both male and female students have the opportunity to fully participate.

Responding through Interpretation

1. How does Tannen define the basic male/female differences in classroom style? What are some of the underlying reasons for male dominance in class discussion given in her essay? Could you think of others?
2. Explain what Tannen means when she says in paragraph 20, "But treating people the same is not equal treatment if they are not the same." Do you agree?
3. Tannen uses a wide range of support for her ideas and solutions to the problems of male dominance in class discussions. Give examples of her use of her own classroom experience, the experiences of her colleagues, as well as more formal classroom research and theories.

Responding through Discussion

1. Form a small group to discuss Tannen's essay. The group should contain a balance of males and females and discuss the issue of gender dominance in class discussion. Appoint one member to make sure that all

members participate equally and to take notes on different communication styles and dominance of male and female group members. Report back to the class as a whole.

2. Form a small discussion group that is composed entirely of men or entirely of women. Proceed as in the previous group. Have one group member take notes on communication styles and report back to the class as a whoie.

Responding through Writing

1. In your journal, write about your own experiences in class discussions. Include examples of several situations you can remember and explain how you responded in each. How often did you feel that either male or female students dominated the discussion?

2. Write a paper in which you give examples of male or female instructors who you feel were either especially effective or particularly ineffective at bringing out and encouraging students of different genders and backgrounds to participate in class discussions. What conclusions would you draw from your observations?

I Just Wanna Be Average

Mike Rose

From an Italian immigrant family, Mike Rose grew up in South Los Angeles in an impoverished neighborhood. Hoping for a better life for their only son, his parents sent Rose to Our Lady of Mercy High, a large Catholic school with several different "tracks" of students. Rose began in the lowest track, but eventually went on to study at Loyola College and UCLA. Currently he is a poet, an English teacher, and a critic of modern education. His most recent book is *Possible Lives: The Promise of Public Education in America* (1995). The following excerpt is taken from his book, *Lives on the Boundary* (1989), in which he discusses some of the shortcomings of public education in America.

Entrance to school brings with it forms and releases and assessments. Mercy relied on a series of tests, mostly the Stanford-Binet, for placement, and somehow the results of my tests got confused with those of another student named Rose. The other Rose apparently didn't do very well, for I was placed in the vocational track, a euphemism for the bottom level. Neither I nor my parents realized what this meant. We had no sense that Business Math, Typing, and English-Level D were dead ends. The current spate of reports on the schools criticizes parents for not involving themselves in the education of their children. But how would someone like Tommy Rose, with his two years of Italian schooling, know what to ask? And what sort of pressure could an exhausted waitress apply? The error went undetected, and I remained in the vocational track for two years. What a place.

My homeroom was supervised by Brother Dill, a troubled and unstable man who also taught freshman English. When his class drifted away from him, which was often, his voice would rise in paranoid accusations, and occasionally he would lose control and shake or smack us. I hadn't been there two months when one of his brisk, face-turning slaps had my glasses sliding down the aisle. Physical education was also pretty harsh. Our teacher was a stubby ex-lineman who had played old-time pro ball in the Midwest. He routinely had us grabbing our ankles to receive his stinging paddle across our butts. He did that, he said, to make men of us. "Rose," he bellowed on our first encounter; me standing geeky in line in my baggy shorts. " 'Rose'? What the hell kind of name is that?"

"Italian, sir," I squeaked.   3
"Italian! Ho. Rose, do you know the sound a bag of shit makes when   4
it hits the wall?"
"No, sir."   5
"Wop!"   6
Sophomore English was taught by Mr. Mitropetros. He was a large,   7
bejeweled man who managed the parking lot at the Shrine Auditorium.
He would crow and preen and list for us the stars he'd brushed against.
We'd ask questions and glance knowingly and snicker, and all that fu-
eled the poor guy to brag some more. Parking cars was his night job. He
had little training in English, so his lesson plan for his day work had us
reading the district's required text, *Julius Caesar,* aloud for the semester.
We'd finish the play way before the twenty weeks was up, so he'd have
us switch parts again and again and start again: Dave Snyder, the fastest
guy at Mercy, muscling through Caesar to the breathless squeals of
Calpurnia, as interpreted by Steve Fusco, a surfer who owned the
school's most envied paneled wagon. Week ten and Dave and Steve
would take on new roles, as would we all, and render a water-logged
Cassius and a Brutus that are beyond my powers of description.
Spanish I—taken in the second year—fell into the hands of a new   8
recruit. Mr. Montez was a tiny man, slight, five foot six at the most, soft-
spoken and delicate. Spanish was a particularly rowdy class, and Mr.
Montez was as prepared for it as a doily maker at a hammer throw. He
would tap his pencil to a room in which Steve Fusco was propelling spit-
balls from his heavy lips, in which Mike Dweetz was taunting Billy
Hawk, a half-Indian, half-Spanish, reed-thin, quietly explosive boy. The
vocational track at Our Lady of Mercy mixed kids traveling in from
South L.A. with South Bay surfers and a few Slavs and Chicanos from
the harbors of San Pedro. This was a dangerous miscellany: surfers and
hodads and South-Central blacks all ablaze to the metronomic tapping
of Hector Montez's pencil.
One day Billy lost it. Out of the corner of my eye I saw him strike 9
out with his right arm and catch Dweetz across the neck. Quick as a
spasm, Dweetz was out of his seat, scattering desks, cracking Billy on
the side of the head, right behind the eye. Snyder and Fusco and others
broke it up, but the room felt hot and close and naked. Mr. Montez's ten-
uous authority was finally ripped to shreds, and I think everyone felt a
little strange about that. The charade was over, and when it came down
to it, I don't think any of the kids really wanted it to end this way. They
had pushed and pushed and bullied their way into a freedom that both
scared and embarrassed them.

Students will float to the mark you set. I and the others in the voca-   10
tional classes were bobbing in pretty shallow water. Vocational education has aimed at increasing the economic opportunities of students
who do not do well in our schools. Some serious programs succeed in
doing that, and through exceptional teachers—like Mr. Gross in *Ho-
race's Compromise*—students learn to develop hypotheses and trou-
bleshoot, reason through a problem, and communicate effectively—the
true job skills. The vocational track, however, is most often a place for
those who are just not making it, a dumping ground for the disaffected.
There were a few teachers who worked hard at education; young Brother
Slattery, for example, combined a stern voice with weekly quizzes to try
to pass along to us a skeletal outline of world history. But mostly the
teachers had no idea of how to engage the imaginations of us kids who
were scuttling along at the bottom of the pond.

And the teachers would have needed some inventiveness, for none of   11
us was groomed for the classroom. It wasn't just that I didn't know things—
didn't know how to simplify algebraic fractions, couldn't identify different kinds of clauses, bungled Spanish translations—but that I had developed various faulty and inadequate ways of doing algebra and making
sense of Spanish. Worse yet, the years of defensive tuning out in elementary school had given me a way to escape quickly while seeming at least
half alert. During my time in Voc. Ed., I developed further into a mediocre
student and a somnambulant problem solver, and that affected the subjects
I did have the wherewithal to handle: I detested Shakespeare; I got bored
with history. My attention flitted here and there. I fooled around in class
and read my books indifferently—the intellectual equivalent of playing
with your food. I did what I had to do to get by, and I did it with half a mind.

But I did learn things about people and eventually came into my   12
own socially. I liked the guys in Voc. Ed. Growing up where I did, I understood and admired physical prowess, and there was an abundance
of muscle here. There was Dave Snyder, a sprinter and halfback of true
quality. Dave's ability and his quick wit gave him a natural appeal, and
he was welcome in any clique, though he always kept a little independent. He enjoyed acting the fool and could care less about studies, but
he possessed a certain maturity and never caused the faculty much trouble. It was a testament to his independence that he included me among
his friends—I eventually went out for track, but I was no jock. Owing to
the Latin alphabet and a dearth of *R*s and *S*s, Snyder sat behind Rose,
and we started exchanging one-liners and became friends.

There was Ted Richard, a much-touted Little League pitcher. He was   13
chunky and had a baby face and came to Our Lady of Mercy as a sea-

soned street fighter. Ted was quick to laugh and he had a loud, jolly laugh, but when he got angry he'd smile a little smile, the kind that simply raises the corner of the mouth a quarter of an inch. For those who knew, it was an eerie signal. Those who didn't found themselves in big trouble, for Ted was very quick. He loved to carry on what we would come to call philosophical discussions: What is courage? Does God exist? He also loved words, enjoyed picking up big ones like *salubrious* and *equivocal* and using them in our conversations—laughing at himself as the word hit a chuckhole rolling off his tongue. Ted didn't do all that well in school—baseball and parties and testing the courage he'd speculated about took up his time. His textbooks were *Argosy* and *Field and Stream*, whatever newspapers he'd find on the bus stop—from the *Daily Worker* to pornography—conversations with uncles or hobos or businessmen he'd meet in a coffee shop, *The Old Man and the Sea*. With hindsight, I can see that Ted was developing into one of those rough-hewn intellectuals whose sources are a mix of the learned and the apocryphal, whose discussions are both assured and sad.

And then there was Ken Harvey. Ken was good-looking in a puffy   14 way and had a full and oily ducktail and was a car enthusiast . . . a hodad. One day in religion class, he said the sentence that turned out to be one of the most memorable of the hundreds of thousands I heard in those Voc. Ed. years. We were talking about the parable of the talents, about achievement, working hard, doing the best you can do, blah-blah-blah, when the teacher called on the restive Ken Harvey for an opinion. Ken thought about it, but just for a second, and said (with studied, minimal affect), "I just wanna be average." That woke me up. Average? Who wants to be average? Then the athletes chimed in with the clichés that make you want to laryngectomize them, and the exchange became a platitudinous melee. At the time, I thought Ken's assertion was stupid, and I wrote him off. But his sentence has stayed with me all these years, and I think I am finally coming to understand it.

Ken Harvey was gasping for air. School can be a tremendously dis-   15 orienting place. No matter how bad the school, you're going to encounter notions that don't fit with the assumptions and beliefs that you grew up with—maybe you'll hear these dissonant notions from teachers, maybe from the other students, and maybe you'll read them. You'll also be thrown in with all kinds of kids from all kinds of backgrounds, and that can be unsettling—this is especially true in places of rich ethnic and linguistic mix, like the L.A. basin. You'll see a handful of students far excel you in courses that sound exotic and that are only in the curriculum of the elite: French, physics, trigonometry. And all this is happening while you're trying to shape an identity, your body is changing, and your emotions are running wild. If you're a working-class kid in the vocational track, the options you'll have to deal with will be constrained in certain ways: you're defined by your school as "slow"; you're placed in a curriculum that isn't designed to liberate you but to occupy you, or, if you're lucky, train you, though the training is for work the society does not esteem; other students are picking up the cues from your school and your curriculum and interacting with you in particular ways. If you're a kid like Ted Richard, you turn your back on all this and let your mind roam where it may. But youngsters like Ted are rare. What Ken and so many others do is protect themselves from such suffocating madness by taking on with a vengeance the identity implied in the vocational track. Reject the confusion and frustration by openly defining yourself as the Common Joe. Champion the average. Rely on your own good sense. Fuck this bullshit. Bullshit, of course, is everything you—and the others—fear is beyond you: books, essays, tests, academic scrambling, complexity, scientific reasoning, philosophical inquiry.

The tragedy is that you have to twist the knife in your own gray matter to make this defense work. You'll have to shut down, have to reject intellectual stimuli or diffuse them with sarcasm, have to cultivate stupidity, have to convert boredom from a malady into a way of confronting the world. Keep your vocabulary simple, act stoned when you're not or act more stoned than you are, flaunt ignorance, materialize your dreams. It is a powerful and effective defense—it neutralizes the insult and the frustration of being a vocational kid and, when perfected, it drives teachers up the wall, a delightful secondary effect. But like all strong magic, it exacts a price.   16

My own deliverance from the Voc. Ed. world began with sophomore biology. Every student, college prep to vocational, had to take biology, and unlike the other courses, the same person taught all sections. When teaching the vocational group, Brother Clint probably slowed down a bit or omitted a little of the fundamental biochemistry, but he used the same book and more or less the same syllabus across the board. If one class got tough, he could get tougher. He was young and powerful and very handsome, and looks and physical strength were high currency. No one gave him any trouble.   17

I was pretty bad at the dissecting table, but the lectures and the textbook were interesting: plastic overlays that, with each turned page, peeled away skin, then veins and muscle, then organs, down to the very bones that Brother Clint, pointer in hand, would tap out on our hanging skeleton. Dave Snyder was in big trouble, for the study of life—ver-   18 sus the living of it—was sticking in his craw. We worked out a code for our multiple-choice exams. He'd poke me in the back: once for the answer under *A,* twice for *B,* and so on; and when he'd hit the right one, I'd look up to the ceiling as though I were lost in thought. Poke: cytoplasm. Poke, poke: methane. Poke, poke, poke: William Harvey. Poke, poke, poke, poke: islets of Langerhans. This didn't work out perfectly, but Dave passed the course, and I mastered the dreamy look of a guy on a record jacket. And something else happened. Brother Clint puzzled over this Voc. Ed. kid who was racking up 98s and 99s on his tests. He checked the school's records and discovered the error. He recommended that I begin my junior year in the College Prep program. According to all I've read since, such a shift, as one report put it, is virtually impossible. Kids at that level rarely cross tracks. The telling thing is how chancy both my placement into and exit from Voc. Ed. was; neither I nor my parents had anything to do with it. I lived in one world during spring semester, and when I came back to school in the fall, I was living in another.

Switching to College Prep was a mixed blessing. I was an erratic student. I was undisciplined. And I hadn't caught onto the rules of the game: why work hard in a class that didn't grab my fancy? I was also hopelessly behind in math. Chemistry was hard; toying with my chemistry set years before hadn't prepared me for the chemist's equations. Fortunately, the priest who taught both chemistry and second-year algebra was also the school's athletic director. Membership on the track team covered me; I knew I wouldn't get lower than a *C.* U.S. history was taught pretty well, and I did okay. But civics was taken over by a football coach who had trouble reading the textbook aloud—and reading aloud was the centerpiece of his pedagogy. College Prep at Mercy was certainly an improvement over the vocational program—at least it carried some status—but the social science curriculum was weak, and the mathematics and physical sciences were simply beyond me. I had a miserable quantitative background and ended up copying some assignments and finessing the rest as best I could. Let me try to explain how it feels to see again and again material you should once have learned but didn't.   19

You are given a problem. It requires you to simplify algebraic fractions or to multiply expressions containing square roots. You know this is pretty basic material because you've seen it for years. Once a teacher took some time with you, and you learned how to carry out these operations. Simple versions, anyway. But that was a year or two or more in the past, and these are more complex versions, and now you're not sure. And this, you keep telling yourself, is ninth- or even eighth-grade stuff.   20

Next it's a word problem. This is also old hat. The basic elements   21
are as familiar as story characters: trains speeding so many miles per
hour or shadows of buildings angling so many degrees. Maybe you
know enough, have sat through enough explanations, to be able to begin
setting up the problem: "If one train is going this fast . . ." or "This
shadow is really one line of a triangle . . ." Then: "Let's see . . ." "How
did Jones do this?" "Hmmmm." "No." "No, that won't work." Your attention wavers. You wonder about other things: a football game, a dance,
that cute new checker at the market. You try to focus on the problem
again. You scribble on paper for a while, but the tension wins out and
your attention flits elsewhere. You crumple the paper and begin day-
dreaming to ease the frustration.

The particulars will vary, but in essence this is what a number of stu-   22
dents go through, especially those in so-called remedial classes. They
open their textbooks and see once again the familiar and impenetrable
formulas and diagrams and terms that have stumped them for years.
There is no excitement here. *No* excitement. Regardless of what the
teacher says, this is not a new challenge. There is, rather, embarrassment
and frustration and, not surprisingly, some anger in being reminded
once again of long-standing inadequacies. No wonder so many students
finally attribute their difficulties to something inborn, organic: "That part
of my brain just doesn't work." Given the troubling histories many of
these students have, it's miraculous that any of them can lift the shroud
of hopelessness sufficiently to make deliverance from these classes possible. . . .

Jack MacFarland couldn't have come into my life at a better time.   23
My father was dead, and I had logged up too many years of scholastic
indifference. Mr. MacFarland had a master's degree from Columbia and
decided, at twenty-six, to find a little school and teach his heart out. He
never took any credentialing courses, couldn't bear to, he said, so he had
to find employment in a private system. He ended up at Our Lady of
Mercy teaching five sections of senior English. He was a beatnik who was
born too late. His teeth were stained, he tucked his sorry tie in between
the third and fourth buttons of his shirt, and his pants were chronically
wrinkled. At first, we couldn't believe this guy, thought he slept in his
car. But within no time, he had us so startled with work that we didn't
much worry about where he slept or if he slept at all. We wrote three or
four essays a month. We read a book every two to three weeks, starting
with the *Iliad* and ending up with Hemingway. He gave us a quiz on the
reading every other day. He brought a prep school curriculum to Mercy
High.

MacFarland's lectures were crafted, and as he delivered them he   24
would pace the room jiggling a piece of chalk in his cupped hand, using
it to scribble on the board the names of all the writers and philosophers
and plays and novels he was weaving into his discussion. He asked questions often, raised everything from Zeno's paradox to the repeated last
line of Frost's "Stopping by Woods on a Snowy Evening." He slowly and
carefully built up our knowledge of Western intellectual history—with
facts, with connections, with speculations. We learned about Greek philosophy, about Dante, the Elizabethan world view, the Age of Reason,
existentialism. He analyzed poems with us, had us reading sections
from John Ciardi's *How Does a Poem Mean?*, making a potentially difficult book accessible with his own explanations. We gave oral reports on
poems Ciardi didn't cover. We imitated the styles of Conrad, Hemingway, and *Time* magazine. We wrote and talked, wrote and talked. The
man immersed us in language.

Even MacFarland's barbs were literary. If Jim Fitzsimmons, hung   25
over and irritable, tried to smart-ass him, he'd rejoin with a flourish that
would spark the indomitable Skip Madison—who'd lost his front teeth
in a hapless tackle—to flick his tongue through the gap and opine, "good
chop," drawing out the single "o" in stinging indictment. Jack MacFarland, this tobacco-stained intellectual, brandished linguistic weapons of
a kind I hadn't encountered before. Here was this *egghead,* for God's sake,
keeping some pretty difficult people in line. And from what I heard,
Mike Dweetz and Steve Fusco and all the notorious Voc. Ed. crowd settled down as well when MacFarland took the podium. Though a lot of
guys groused in the schoolyard, it just seemed that giving trouble to this
particular teacher was a silly thing to do. Tomfoolery, not to mention assault, had no place in the world he was trying to create for us, and instinctively everyone knew that. If nothing else, we all recognized Mac-
Farland's considerable intelligence and respected the hours he put into
his work. It came to this: the troublemaker would look foolish rather than
daring. Even Jim Fitzsimmons was reading *On the Road* and turning his
incipient alcoholism to literary ends.

There were some lives that were already beyond Jack MacFarland's   26
ministrations, but mine was not. I started reading again as I hadn't since
elementary school. I would go into our gloomy little bedroom or sit at
the dinner table while, on the television, Danny McShane was paralyz-
ing Mr. Moto with the atomic drop, and work slowly back through *Heart
of Darkness,* trying to catch the words in Conrad's sentences. I certainly
was not MacFarland's best student; most of the other guys in College
Prep, even my fellow slackers, had better backgrounds than I did. But I

worked very hard, for MacFarland had hooked me. He tapped my old interest in reading and creating stories. He gave me a way to feel special by using my mind. And he provided a role model that wasn't shaped on physical prowess alone, and something inside me that I wasn't quite aware of responded to that. Jack MacFarland established a literacy club, to borrow a phrase of Frank Smith's, and invited me—invited all of us—to join.

There's been a good deal of research and speculation suggesting that the acknowledgement of school performance with extrinsic rewards—smiling faces, stars, numbers, grades—diminishes the intrinsic satisfaction children experience by engaging in reading or writing or problem solving. While it's certainly true that we've created an educational system that encourages our best and brightest to become cynical grade collectors and, in general, have developed an obsession with evaluation and assessment, I must tell you that venal though it may have been, I loved getting good grades from MacFarland. I now know how subjective grades can be, but then they came tucked in the back of essays like bits of scientific data, some sort of spectroscopic readout that said, objectively and publicly, that I had made something of value. I suppose I'd been mediocre for too long and enjoyed a public redefinition. And I suppose the workings of my mind, such as they were, had been private for too long. My linguistic play moved into the world; . . . these papers with their circled, red B-pluses and A-minuses linked my mind to something outside it. I carried them around like a club emblem.

One day in the December of my senior year, Mr. MacFarland asked me where I was going to go to college. I hadn't thought much about it. Many of the students I teach today spent their last year in high school with a physics text in one hand and the Stanford catalog in the other, but I wasn't even aware of what "entrance requirements" were. My folks would say that they wanted me to go to college and be a doctor, but I don't know how seriously I ever took that; it seemed a sweet thing to say, a bit of supportive family chatter, like telling a gangly daughter she's graceful. The reality of higher education wasn't in my scheme of things: no one in the family had gone to college; only two of my uncles had completed high school. I figured I'd get a night job and go to the local junior college because I knew that Snyder and Company were going there to play ball. But I hadn't even prepared for that. When I finally said, "I don't know," MacFarland looked down at me—I was seated in his office—and said, "Listen, you can write."

My grades stank. I had A's in biology and a handful of B's in a few English and social science classes. All the rest were C's—or worse. Mac-

86

Farland said I would do well in his class and laid down the law about doing well in the others. Still, the record for my first three years wouldn't have been acceptable to any four-year school. To nobody's surprise, I was turned down flat by USC and UCLA. But Jack MacFarland was on the case. He had received his bachelor's degree from Loyola University, so he made calls to old professors and talked to somebody in admissions and wrote me a strong letter. Loyola finally accepted me as a probationary student. I would be on trial for the first year, and if I did okay, I would be granted regular status. MacFarland also intervened to get me a loan, for I could never have afforded a private college without it. Four more years of religion classes and four more years of boys at one school, girls at another. But at least I was going to college. Amazing.

RESPONDING TO "I JUST WANNA BE AVERAGE"

Freewrite about what you think it means to be "average" in school.

Responding through Interpretation

1. What does Rose mean when he says that "Students will float to the mark you set" (paragraph 10)? How do many of the examples he uses in his essay help to emphasize this idea?
2. Rose contrasts the many examples he presents in his essay of weak or incompetent teachers with one strong example of a good teacher, Jack MacFarland, who had a powerful impact on Rose and his future. What qualities make MacFarland a "good teacher"? How does he differ from the average Mercy instructor?
3. In paragraph 15 the author uses the expression "Ken Harvey was gasping for air." What does Rose mean by this nonliteral expression or metaphor? Try to find other nonliteral expressions such as this in the essay. How do they contribute to the power of the writing and the picture of Mercy High and its students and teachers?

Responding through Discussion

1. Get together with your group and have all members read their freewrites about what it means to be average. Make note of the different attitudes and discuss these differences.

2. Spend about 10 minutes in silence while all the members of the group make a list of their individual educational goals. Afterward, let each member read his or her list and have someone in the group keep a tally of the ones most frequently mentioned. Choose several goals that seem important to the group as a whole and report your findings to the rest of the class.

Responding through Writing

1. Write a journal entry about a specific incident when a teacher taught you well. Keep your narrative to one event and describe it in detail, using strong and descriptive language as Mike Rose does.
2. Rose states in his essay that he "loved getting good grades from Mac-Farland." What is your attitude about grades? Are grades more important or less important to you now than they used to be? Do you think that grades promote or inhibit learning? Write a paper in which you take a position about grades, including as examples your own experiences throughout your years of education.

I Just Wanna Be Challenged

Rainbow Schwartz

Rainbow Schwartz grew up in Berkeley, California, and attended public schools there. She is taking courses in fashion design and English in evening school, and wrote the following essay about her educational experiences for her English class. Notice how she uses examples from different teachers and classes to support her points.

The times have changed a lot since Mike Rose was in high school, but   1
his essay "I Just Wanna Be Average" is still relevant. While drugs, teen pregnancy, and violence have changed the atmosphere of many high schools, I think these problems are just a symptom of a bigger problem: uninspired, unencouraging teachers. An encouraging teacher can help build a student's self-confidence. Believing in the student's abilities to create and learn will result in a happier student, one who will get better grades and a more complete education. Mike Rose's essay embodies this theory. "I Just Wanna Be Average" is more than a sign of hope for all students; it's a clear message that teachers can make a huge difference in the lives of their pupils.

Looking back on high school, I have many memories of uninterested   2
and even unintelligent teachers. It could be argued that the quality of teachers doesn't matter if the students are motivated and smart, but I feel that the intelligence and interest level of the teacher is connected in many ways to that of the student. In Rose's essay a familiar-sounding teacher is mentioned: "Civics was then taken over by a football coach who had trouble reading the textbook aloud—and reading aloud was the centerpiece of his pedagogy." In my junior year I had a similar experience with a track coach turned Spanish teacher. Apparently everyone assumed that because he had a Spanish name he was qualified to be a Spanish teacher. As a student in his class, I thought otherwise. The first month's syllabus was based solely on memorizing our Spanish names and the first one hundred numbers. From that experience and others with unqualified teachers, I learned that while it is possible to get A's in those teachers' classes, it is impossible to get an education. Students who have been in classes where A's are handed out like scratch paper know that while an A may look good on transcripts, it feels bad inside if it is undeserved. Like Rose, I too have felt "embarrassment and frustration . . ." when given "material [I] should have learned but didn't."

Grade inflation is a cop-out on the part of the teacher and an injustice to the students.

Although most of my junior high and high school teachers were lit-   3
tle better than average, one teacher rose high above the rest. She was my seventh-grade English teacher, Ms. Delp. In pinpointing the qualities that made her a good teacher, such adjectives as challenging, exciting, and versatile come to mind. She possessed all of these qualities, and used them daily in her teaching.

Boredom is often the enemy that attacks students in high school   4
classrooms. The teacher, being the leader of the troops, must come up with a counterattack to ward off the enemy. From years of sitting in class-rooms and letting boredom win the battle in my head, I know that a teacher who challenges the class to learn and dares students to create and revise is the teacher who will win the fight. Challenges bring excitement, excitement to try something new, to understand something never un-derstood before. For me the challenge was Shakespeare. In seventh grade we read *Romeo and Juliet* in Ms. Delp's class. The way she described the symbolism and hidden meaning made reading seem like a puzzle. I was fascinated by the many layers of meaning in the play to understand and study. Ms. Delp dared us to find meaning beyond the obvious—and we did so. She once said that she loved teaching because she felt like she al-ways learned something new from her students. Because she valued and respected our thoughts and revelations, we all followed in her path of excitement and willingness to learn.

Ms. Delp was also versatile. She not only had us read and write; she   5
also assigned maps and pictorial representations. Being a predominantly creative person, I responded well to her visual ways of mapping out es-says and books. This made learning more accessible to me. She reached many students with her not-so-traditional teaching ways. With such a wide range of ideas and assignments, she made learning a more tangi-ble process for everyone.

From my high school experience and that of Mike Rose, it is obvi-   6
ous that there are good teachers out there who can make positive changes in the lives of their students. But most of those teachers aren't teaching in the lower tracks. I have found that in classrooms in the lower tracks there are many unacceptable teachers, including many who are boring, worn out, or even ignorant. Most of the smart, exciting teachers are put in the college prep or AP tracks, because those classes are harder and need intelligent teachers. The flaw in the logic of this system is the assumption that ignorant teachers are acceptable for lower-level stu-dents. It is apparent to me that these teachers are not acceptable for any-

one. It is ridiculous to think that students with low grades or short attention spans deserve poor teachers. It is the exact opposite! These students in particular need teachers who will tantalize their imaginations and bring excitement to learning. These are the teachers I would like to see in the lower tracks, and when the lower tracks receive these teachers, that's when I will no longer condemn tracking.

While reading Rose's "I Just Wanna Be Average" I realized that my education was not a unique one. Many people go through twelve years of schooling encountering only a couple of outstanding teachers. Although the high schools of the nineties are different, and certainly more plagued with drugs and violence than the high schools of the past, teachers still do have an effect on their students. With so many poor teachers, students are looking elsewhere for guidance and fulfillment. Perhaps if classes were more stimulating and teachers more challenging and sincere, then violence and drug abuse wouldn't be so prevalent in schools. It may sound idealistic, but the cycle has to stop somewhere, and it is up to the adult administrators and teachers to do what they can to stop it. Success stories such as Rose's should not be a fluke. We have to work to make the exception the rule. 7

RESPONDING TO "I JUST WANNA BE CHALLENGED"

Freewrite about one of the most uninspiring or one of the most inspiring teachers you have ever had.

Responding through Interpretation

1. Compare Rainbow Schwartz's high school experiences with those of Mike Rose. Did her experiences and her attitude toward them seem more or less negative than the experiences described by Rose?
2. Like Rose, Schwartz uses a number of vivid details about memorable classroom experiences, positive and negative. Which details did you consider most effective? What do her details reveal about her attitude toward school and teachers?

Responding through Discussion

1. Schwartz argues that it is "ridiculous to think that students with low grades or short attention spans deserve poor teachers." Use this statement as a point of departure for a group discussion: Do group members agree with Schwartz that the worst teachers usually teach the students who have

the most problems with learning? If so, what could be done to improve the situation?

Responding through Writing

1. Write a short essay about your experiences with boring teachers. What advice would you have for other students for coping with classroom boredom?
2. At the end of her essay, Schwartz blames the failure of schools primarily on teachers. Does she ignore other factors that make it difficult for teachers to be effective in the classroom? Write a short paper in which you agree or disagree with Schwartz's views, supporting your ideas with specific examples.

Surviving Adolescence

Richard Carrillo

Born in Chicago to a working-class family, Richard Carrillo is the first
member of his family to complete high school. Carrillo worked as a steel-
worker, joined the Navy Seals, and worked as a sanitation worker for a
number of years after high school before returning to school at a community College in Alameda, California. Carrillo wrote the following essay to
compare his educational experiences with those of Mike Rose in "I Just
Wanna Be Average." Like Rose, Carrillo uses strongly narrated personal
memories to make his story vivid and alive.

"I Just Wanna Be Average" deals with Mike Rose's experiences in a   1
Catholic high school, where a mistake on his records placed him
incorrectly in a vocational track so that he was stigmatized for a while
as a "slow" student. When I read Mike Rose's essay, I discovered a
strong common link between his experiences as the child of Italian
immigrant parents lost in an urban high school environment and my
own experiences at a Catholic high school in Chicago in the early 1970s.

I came from a family whose grandparents were immigrants from   2
Mexico who settled in Chicago in the 1920s. I was the first of my nuclear
family to graduate from high school. After spending the last 17 years in
the military and working blue-collar jobs, I started back to school only
this year. Two of the resounding themes of my early life were the fear
of failure and the distrust of adults, particularly teachers. Both of these
themes were reinforced in my school experiences, both in primary and
in secondary school.

Although I was a better-than-average student in early elementary   3
school, I soon began to notice the negativity of many of my instructors.
I'll never forget how patronizing and cruel my fifth-grade math teacher
was, how he completely intimidated our whole class. I remember asking one or two questions in class that year, and feeling totally embarrassed and humiliated in front of my peers after asking what my teacher
termed "a dumb question." From that point on, I was silent in class, lost
and withdrawn.

The eighth grade was my first experience with Catholic schools,   4
and I rebelled against the overzealous discipline inflicted upon me by
the school nuns, referred to sarcastically behind their backs as "pen-

guins." As Mike Rose puts it, "I did what I had to do to get by, and I did it with half a mind." At the end of the school year, I was voted by my peers and Sister Grace, our teacher, as the student most likely to end up in prison. I wore that title like a badge of honor.

Like Mike Rose, I was sent to a Catholic high school (Leo High) that   5
had a respectable academic program. In my case I had the company of my brother, who had been awarded a football scholarship at Leo the year before. I was eager to join him there, but I was intimidated by the high school placement examinations. I was terrified about the math tests, certain that the school I had my heart set on going to was about to find out how dumb I really was.

Somehow I managed to pass most of my placement exams and en-   6
roll at Leo. Like Mike Rose, I had to be bused to school, traveling through several different neighborhoods in two long bus rides which took nearly an hour. Located in an all-black neighborhood, Leo had an integrated student body, 50 percent black, 45 percent white (bused in from the suburbs), and about 5 percent Hispanic and Asian students. It was a real melting pot of cultures, and the Franciscan brothers who ran the school maintained a strong sense of discipline.

In my freshman year, I had to attend remedial math classes in the   7
summer, prior to school's official opening in September. This is where I realized that the "penguins' " form of discipline in the eighth grade was mild compared to the hands-on style that the "brothers" employed. I, along with many other students who talked or acted up in class, experienced slaps across the face hard enough to make me feel as though my head would do a complete 360 degree turn like Linda Blair in the film "The Exorcist." This definitely gave me an incentive to get my work done quietly.

My first two years at Leo were academically bland and unchal-   8
lenging, probably due to the fact that I, like Mike Rose, was not taking any college prep courses. I did do well in the subjects I was studying, with the exception of math, where I usually just squeaked by. Near the end of my second year, I heard of a new curriculum that was going to be offered to junior and senior students interested in the humanities. I had heard that there would be less regimentation and no more math in the program. It seemed to be just what I wanted.

At this time in my life, as in Mike Rose's family, there was a great   9
deal of turmoil in my home. My oldest brother, an alcoholic, was coming to the house at all hours to fight and raise hell with everyone. He hated the world and himself, and it was very hard to deal with him. My

mother was going through her third divorce, and my other brother, who had the football scholarship to Leo's, was quitting school to join the Army. I remember feeling at that time that I was going to explode. These feelings of confusion and tension at home inevitably had an influence on my school life, making it more difficult for me to concentrate and to devote the time necessary to my studies.

When my junior year at Leo began, I was happy to be in a college-style atmosphere with less discipline involved. Nevertheless, unlike Mike Rose, I totally blew my chances to succeed in the program and to take advantage of the challenging, college-bound curriculum offered to me that year. We studied courses such as anthropology, television communications, and other humanities-related subjects, many of which I can no longer recall. For the first time, like Mike Rose after his experience with an inspiring teacher, I was taking courses designed to liberate me rather than simply to occupy me. If I had worked hard to apply myself, I believe that I could have received an academic scholarship somewhere, but I didn't.   10

In fairness to the instructors, I know they wanted to inspire me, for we were basically a test group for a new program. Because I've always been a good auditory learner, I was able to pass the tests without opening a textbook. Looking back on those days, I realize now that I was too busy feeling sorry for myself and angry about my chaotic home life to focus on the opportunity before me. I told myself that I just wanted to be left alone, concentrating all my negative energies into solitary athletic endeavors such as martial arts and weight-lifting. For many years, these activities would be the only positive release I would know. While I withdrew from what the academic world offered to me, Mike Rose reached out to take full advantage of the opportunities given to him, and achieved entry into a fine college and an eventual academic career of distinction. It takes a great deal of courage to be willing to step into the unknown and give fully of yourself, knowing that you still might fail. I did not have this type of courage in me when I was sixteen and seventeen years old. I was one of those kids Rose describes as saying, "Fuck this bullshit. Bullshit, of course, is everything you . . . fear is beyond you."   11

I only wish that I had been awakened by a caring teacher as Rose was through his contact with Mr. MacFarland, who really inspired Mike Rose to read, write, and believe in himself and his academic potential. In my case, the only adults I looked up to at that time in my life were two middle-aged men, Jerry Hirsch and Rich Levine, neither one of whom were schoolteachers. These guys were very tough blue-collar   12 workers who did weight training at the South Chicago YMCA after doing their shifts at the steel factory. I'd go to the Y after work, lift weights, and listen to their advice to me. They encouraged me to take responsibility for my own decisions and to make something out of life. They told me to stay in school, but they never made me feel bad when I chose not to. They were my chosen family at that time in my life, just as Mr. MacFarland and Rose's academically inclined friends were his. I loved them dearly.

Originally, I convinced myself not to pursue a college education be- 13
cause I wanted to become independent from my family more quickly by getting a job. Although I thought that high school was boring, I also was afraid of failing, like many of today's high school students. Teenagers need special counseling and encouragement, as they experience so many disrupting factors in their attempts to get an education—school violence, family pressures, economic needs. Just a few words of praise by a teacher like Mr. MacFarland can make a difference to a young adult who can't hear it at home. I've had a tough seventeen years out in the world, and have made accomplishments that give me great pride, so I no longer feel the sense of insecurity I had in high school. I am very happy at this time in my life to get a second chance at a college education which I know will improve the quality of my life. The encouragement and praise I have received from my teachers in the short time I have been back in college have helped to give me the hope and strength to succeed in my educational goals.

RESPONDING TO "SURVIVING ADOLESCENCE"

In a freewrite, explore your family's attitudes about the value of education.

Responding through Interpretation

1. What two experiences does Carrillo say underscored his early life? How did these two experiences affect his education?
2. Carrillo, like Rose, highlights several important problems that many students often carry with them into the classroom. Describe several of these problems and explain how they can interfere with a student's education.

Responding through Discussion

1. Look over Carrillo's paper with your group and decide among yourselves what you have learned from this essay that you could apply to your own

individual writing. Make a master list of all the techniques and ideas pointed out by each group member.

Responding through Writing

1. Write an open letter to Richard Carrillo in which you express your responses to his essay. Tell Carrillo how you feel about both his ideas and the way he has written his essay.
2. Using your own experiences, write an account of your journey along the paths of formal education. Highlight the most important steps you took which finally brought you to the college you are now attending.

MAKING CONNECTIONS

Look back through the selections you have read in this chapter and refresh your memory about each selection. Reading through your freewrites or your journal entries will help you remember details of the various selections. Some of the authors were critical of education, some gave examples of good learning experiences, and others introduced specific ideas about reading, gender differences in the classroom, and intelligence testing. Think about which of these authors excited your thinking. Following are several unifying themes that will help you to compare the selections in this unit.

1. *Teachers at work.* Several of the selections in this chapter provide examples of effective, even gifted, teachers at work. Drawing on the examples presented by writers such as Rose, Schwartz, and Kozol, as well as on your own experience, write a personal opinion essay about what you believe to be the characteristics of a good teacher.
2. *Student difficulties.* Some students don't do well in school because of difficulties they have in the classroom or at home. Write a short paper in which you discuss some of the examples Tannen, Carrillo, Rose, or Le provide of students who don't fit in or who have trouble communicating and expressing themselves in school. Make clear what factors you think lead to difficulties in student success.
3. *The current state of education.* Particularly if you have been out of school for a few years, the concerns expressed by the writers in this chapter about the current state of primary and secondary education may become more real to you through doing some firsthand classroom observations. Ask to observe in a school in your community; interview some instructors, administrators, and students. Write up your findings in the form of a short paper that evaluates the schools

and classes you observed. Include some direct quotations from your interviews as well as some narrative and descriptive detail.

4. *Recent films relating to education.* A number of recent films explore themes and issues related to education. *Stanley and Iris,* for instance, presents an adult learner's struggle to overcome illiteracy. *Mr. Holland's Opus, Stand and Deliver,* and *Dangerous Minds* focus on a dedicated teacher working in a school where there is little support and limited resources. *Little Man Tate* explores the world of a gifted child from a family of limited resources who must struggle to obtain an education that suits his needs, while *Hoop Dreams* examines the way sports provides both a hope and a distraction for student-athletes. Select a film or video for viewing that presents an issue related to education and to the themes of one or more of the selections in this chapter. After viewing the film and taking some notes on it, write a short review in which you explain what commentary the film seems to be making on education today.

CHAPTER 4

Family

Introduction

ELLEN GOODMAN	Our Kids Are Not Just Copies of Us
LAWRENCE WRIGHT	Reunion
AMY MARX	My Grandfather's Memories
CHARLIE WU	Family Friends: A Process of Growth
ALBERTO ALVARO RIOS	Nani
TILLIE OLSEN	I Stand Here Ironing
AMY TAN	Snapshot: Lost Lives of Women
JOAN DIDION	On Going Home
ALICE WALKER	Father
BEVERLEY SKINNER	My Dad and Walker's "Father"
SHU FAN LEE	Alice Walker's "Father": A Process of Understanding and Acceptance

Making Connections

INTRODUCTION

Journal Entry

Write a journal entry in which you explore how the kind of family you are likely to have will differ from or be similar to the one you grew up in.

What is a family? That used to be an easy question to answer, because not too long ago the average family consisted of a mother, a father, two or more children, and sometimes a couple of sets of grandparents. There also used to be aunts, uncles, and many cousins—at least that's our nostalgic view of what family was. How accurate that picture really was, no one knows for certain, but it hasn't been true for several decades, even though we still cling to the comfortable portrait of the "regular" family.

You probably know from your own observations or experiences that the family today is in the midst of great change and redefinition. When the writers of President Clinton's health plan sat down to try to define "family" for purposes of health coverage, it took an entire day to arrive at a suitable description. They had to consider many different configurations of what to now consider a family: Is a family just one's self and one's spouse and children? Does family include stepchildren from various previous marriages? Should unmarried persons living together or same-sex partners be considered a family? All these questions are debated today and have important implications for many people, both as individuals and as partners in relationships and certainly also for the children born into these relationships.

Regardless of how you define it, the family is without a doubt one of the most important influences, if not the most important influence, in our lives. It is an influence that we continually return to and frequently reevaluate as we mature. The selections in this chapter offer views of different kinds of families and different experiences in coming to terms with families. Columnist Ellen Goodman in her essay "Our Kids Are Not Just Copies of Us" looks at the way parents often create confusion and distrust among their children by trying too hard to make them conform to the parents' own sense of values and need for accomplishments. Lawrence Wright's autobiographical essay, "Reunion," explores the complicated love-hate relationship between fathers and sons, and Alice Walker's piece, "Father," explores the process through which she as a daughter comes to accept her father in later life and to realize the impact he has had on her values. All four of the student essays by Amy Marx, Charlie Wu, Beverley Skinner, and Shu Fan

Lee explore aspects of the process through which the writers came to understand and accept their family—or particular family members.

The deep interconnectedness of family, for better or worse, can be seen in several other works such as Alberto Alvaro Rios's poem "Nani," Tillie Olsen's short story "I Stand Here Ironing," and Amy Tan's "Snapshot: Lost Lives of Women." In "On Going Home," Joan Didion dramatically illustrates how we all eventually have to give up picture-postcard ideals about families as we change, expand our lives, and become more individual.

The readings in this chapter and the writing suggestions that follow will give you both questions to ponder concerning your relationship to your family members and, it is hoped, insight into the kinds of changes you may want to make in the family you have already created or will eventually create.

Our Kids Are Not Just Copies of Us

Ellen Goodman

Ellen Goodman graduated from Smith College and currently works for the *Boston Globe*. She is a nationally syndicated newspaper columnist whose columns frequently address women's issues. Her books include *Making Sense* (1989), and *Value Judgments* (1993). In the following essay, which originally appeared in the *Boston Globe* in 1993, Goodman discusses the accepting attitudes held by parents of adoptive children toward the "differences" of their children.

Some time ago, my friends adopted a baby and set about the business 1 of getting to know him. I watched this process from a distance of many miles and from a perspective of many parenting years. I saw them become familiar with their son, to become family in the slow way that other people become friends.

The boy had come from another continent at 6 months old. He trav- 2 eled here out of his own brief history on their passport, and they seemed to regard him from the very beginning as both their baby and his own person. They paid studious attention to this new subject of their affection—not just to their affection.

The boy woke up slowly in the morning, happy with some time alone. 3 Then, on some internal cue, he started a small lament that would, if untended, turn into a loud, raucous cry of need. He had a greed for breakfast, a taste for apricots, a temperament that was cheerful and careful.

Over the months, I saw them taking cues from this little boy. Peo- 4 ple who were, in their own lives, curious and impatient, were, in their son's life, curious and patient.

The father was a man who had, in youth, jumped onto racing bikes 5 and out of planes. The boy approached a new tricycle as if he had to memorize the driver's manual before he stepped on the pedals.

The mother was a woman who tore apart the pieces of a broken 6 toaster and reassembled them—usually—from memory. The son was one of those children who studied his toys before he played with them.

They noted these differences with amusement rather than surprise. 7 And let the boy set his own pace.

The point was that their parenting had come without a full genetic 8 set of assumptions. This son was no more different from his parents than many biological children. But they were different.

They didn't assume that their own strengths and weaknesses had   9
traveled along the DNA to their offspring. They didn't assume that he
had inherited his mother's nearsightedness or musical talent, his father's straight teeth or short attention span or mathphobia.

They didn't look for proof that he was just like them, or just like Aunt   10
Emily, or just like Grandpa Bill.

So they set out to know him as himself. And in the process let him   11
be himself.

I have been a parent for more than two decades, a biological mother,   12
a birth mother, a child-raising mother, an adult child's mother . . . the
works. And it seems to me that my friends started out in the parenting
business one step ahead of the rest of us.

Those of us who give our genes as well as our love to children set   13
out to reproduce . . . ourselves. We deliver unconscious expectations
in the birthing room. We think we know them—because they are
"ours."

During their early years, we often assume that they will be as much   14
like us in interests, in habits, in mindsets, in hopes, dreams, whatever,
as they are in biology.

The absolute cliché of parenting is surprise. It's the tennis coach   15
surprised to find that his son prefers to read. The down-to-earth parents
surprised at the fanciful inner life of their child.

Parents say, "I don't know where she gets it from." We say—if only   16
to ourselves—that nobody in our family ever played rugby or the cello.
Our people were always quick at languages or mechanics.

Only later, sometimes much later, are we forced to get to know our   17
children as they are, to stop assuming and start listening or watching.
In adolescence they begin to insist, noisily, sometimes angrily, on their
own identities. In their 20s we stop, finally, raising them, and start, finally, listening to them. Or else we lose them.

What I have learned from my friends and from their son is that our   18
children may be our own but we can't claim ownership. What I have
learned is that sooner—in their case—or later in mine, we must learn to
share children. We share them with the world. But most particularly, we
learn to share them with themselves.

RESPONDING TO "OUR KIDS ARE NOT JUST COPIES OF US"

Freewrite about a trait or quality you have that seems very different from
that of the rest of your family.

Responding through Interpretation

1. What is the meaning of Goodman's statement, "The absolute cliché of parenting is surprise"? How is this observation central to the meaning of the essay?
2. What faulty assumptions do birth parents often make about their children, and from where do such mistaken beliefs come?
3. Goodman uses a strong central example or case history to structure her essay and support her ideas. Does the example of the adoptive parents Goodman uses seem typical, or do you think that many adoptive parents have trouble adjusting to their children just as birth parents do?

Responding through Discussion

1. With your group, discuss your opinions of the ways parents or guardians show that they accept or reject a child as an individual. Share the results of your discussion with the rest of the class.
2. Discuss Goodman's statement, "In their 20s we stop, finally, raising them, and start, finally, listening to them. Or else we lose them." Have each group member interpret this statement and explain what Goodman means.

Responding through Writing

1. Write a journal entry as a letter to a parent who is having difficulty accepting the "difference" of one of his or her children. Without being judgmental or preachy, give the parent some suggestions for overcoming this difficulty.
2. Using the topic of adoption, write a paper that explores both the good side and the bad side of adopting children. When is adoption a positive action and when is it a negative one? Should parents who have children of their own be allowed to adopt others? If appropriate, use some of your own observations and experiences in writing the paper.

Reunion

Lawrence Wright

Lawrence Wright is a freelance writer who has written for many national periodicals. He also has completed several nonfiction works, including *Saints and Sinners* (1993) and *Remembering Satan* (1994), about false-memory syndrome. The following essay, "Reunion," which first appeared in the *Texas Monthly*, describes Wright's experiences as both a son and a father.

When my son, Gordon, was three, he saw his first gorilla. The gorilla cast   1
him an indifferent look and went back to watching "General Hospital" on the color TV just outside his cage. I was holding Gordon, and when we got outside, he wanted to walk alone.

That night Gordon had a nightmare. "Big monkey in the sky!" he   2
kept screaming as my wife tried to calm him. "Bang on my head with a hammer!"

He was, I realized, dreaming about me. All week I had been doing   3
carpentry work in the basement underneath Gordon's room. When I was a boy, my own father and I spent many hours in another basement re-finishing furniture, and it gave me a lifelong taste for woodworking. Those were the hours when I felt closest to my father, when I had him all to myself. It was an experience I was eager to pass along to my son. But he was afraid of power tools. Loud noises frightened him. In his room, safely away from the violence of my basement construction, he still complained about my hammering. I could see myself as he had imagined me in his dream: a menacing ape with a hammer in his hand, a creature of fear and punishment, a simian Jehovah. I knew then that Gordon would love me with the same fear and intensity with which I loved my father, for a boy's father is, after all, his first competitor and his eternal enemy.

I remember vividly my father's gait. He took giant strides, and I had   4
to run to stay in step. He was big; his voice was deep. I admired the way he sang in church. In the shower he would sing "Marie, the dawn is breaking" without knowing all the words and "K-K-K-Katie . . . I'll be waiting at the k-k-k-kitchen door" and all the wonderful songs of the big band, wartime era. He gave me "whisker kisses" when he needed a shave. He punished me when I misbehaved. He was strict, sometimes

harsh, usually merciful, always fair. I think it was his fairness that I feared most.

He was an infantry officer in World War II and came home eager to have children. I arrived in the first wave of the baby boom; two sisters quickly followed. I have often wondered why the urge to procreate, which was so pronounced in his generation, should be so stunted in my own. Perhaps it has something to do with the wars each generation has had to fight. All wars are horrible, but men who fight in a just cause become heroes. He was such a hero. I would never be.

We spent much of my childhood and all of my adolescence in a prolonged and canny combat—for that's how it is with fathers and sons; they are bound to grapple with each other, to test their wills, to compete. Boys naturally fear their fathers and envy them. The father sets limits; the son rebels. The father is stronger, but time and nature favor the son.

History—especially American history—is a long story of sons' overturning their progenitors. The battle of the generations began in our country with the American Revolution against "Papa" George III and continued in my generation with the reaction against Vietnam. By then my father and I were bloody veterans of my rebellion. We would stand in the living room blazing away at each other like the *Monitor* and the *Merrimack,* giving no quarter, asking none, both of us furious, inflexible, verbally skilled, and ruthless.

But neither of us was prepared for the savagery of the war at home—certainly the most divisive episode in the long saga of American families. One could feel the generations peeling apart. However angry my father and I might have been in the past, we were now irreconcilable. It was a subject we knew to avoid, and yet neither of us could leave it alone. All family gatherings deteriorated into the same grinding argument: duty versus conscience. Our ethics made us savage. On the day I graduated from college—the day I became eligible for the draft—we had a showdown in the hotel parking lot. It was a fight we had been expecting for quite a long time, and no weapon would fail to be used. What I remember most about the encounter is the cruel pleasure we took in this final bloodletting, as Mother wailed helplessly for us to stop, to leave some love in the family. But of course we couldn't stop; we had been building toward it since the moment of my conception. There was an Old Testament glory in our willingness to play out the tragedy of fathers and sons to its bitter conclusion. I left the U.S. soon after that, as a conscientious objector. By then my country and my father were one and the same to me.

It is one of the surprises of life that a son turns out to love his father   9
after all. Two years abroad took the heat out of our relationship. I was
married and on my own, but the preoccupations of my life gradually
took on a familiar character—they were my father's hobbies and en-
thusiasms, his traits, his failings, rubbed into my grain like an oil stain
on one of the cabinets we refinished in my youth, rubbed in, moreover,
with real force, with elbow grease, so that the stain would sink deeply
into my pores and my life would always be colored by his influence.

When Gordon was born, my father and I were reconciled, in a cau-   10
tious fashion. There is a time when all fathers must surrender, a time
when their sons no longer think of them and the battle becomes moot.
As for the sons, they grow up and get their own punishment.

Would I ever be as good a father to Gordon as my father was to me?   11
It was not a question I would have thought to ask myself some years earlier, although there was a time in my life (I now remembered) when I
believed I had the very best father in the world—the strongest, the
bravest, the fairest. The fear I had upon becoming a father myself was
that a man could be all those things to his son and still be his enemy. But
isn't that a father's highest, noblest duty to his son? To be his son's
friendly foe? To create the man who will better him? To teach him and
prod him and discipline him? To challenge him and make him work beyond himself? To beat him sometimes at his favorite games so that he
can feel the bite of competition? To make him stand up for what he believes in—even when, one day, what his son believes in may break his
heart? And finally, finally, to show him how to lose, as all fathers must
lose if they are successful, for what man wishes for a son who is not his
superior?

Just after Gordon was born, I stood looking at him through the glass   12
of the hospital nursery. He was red-faced and bawling. At nearly ten
pounds and 22 1/2 inches long, he was the biggest baby born all week
(he would certainly be bigger than me). We would play catch together.
We would fish. I would take him camping. We would build things together in the basement. I would give him the love and attention my father gave me, and no doubt he would give me in turn what I gave my
father.

At that moment I noticed my father's reflection in the glass. He had   13
come up behind me and was standing there watching his son. Almost
immediately I began boasting—the proud father myself now—about
Gordon's size, his obvious good looks, his brilliant future. My father
smiled. He recalled that his own son had been a big baby.

Not as big as my baby.   14

I said it aloud, a thought I let slip before I had fully handled its ab-   15
surdity. I was still competing, still comparing my accomplishments with
my father's, and I had thoroughly bested him this time. My baby is bigger than your baby, but your baby was . . . me.

And we laughed together, two wise old fathers in the presence of   16
life's new rebel.

RESPONDING TO "REUNION"

Freewrite about what you think are the causes of a particular conflict you
have had with a parent or other relative.

Responding through Interpretation

1. What meaning does Wright find for himself in his young son's dream?
   Does his interpretation seem justified?
2. Explain what Wright means when he says that "History . . . is a long story
   of sons' overturning their progenitors." Do you agree with Wright's idea
   of history? What support does he give?
3. Interpret the meaning of the final scene and line of the story. What hope
   is suggested? Does the story's ending contradict Wright's earlier comments about the war between fathers and sons?

Responding through Discussion

1. Before beginning your group discussion, allow time for members to
   make a brief list of feelings of rivalry they've either felt or observed in
   families. Then let each member choose the rivalry he or she feels is most
   significant and explain it.
2. Take quiet time within the group so that members can close their eyes
   briefly and remember a childhood nightmare they had. Rapidly write a
   summary of the dream. Have those members who would like to share
   their dreams read them aloud.

Responding through Writing

1. In your journal, write about a time when you became aware of a conflict
   that repeated itself from one generation in your family to another.
2. Using Wright's essay as a resource for ideas, write your own essay about
   a conflict between you and one of your parents. Trace the process of this
   conflict and, like Wright, add your own interpretations and analyses.

My Grandfather's Memories

Amy Marx

Amy Marx, a political science major, grew up in Lexington, Massachusetts. Writing the following essay about her grandfather was especially difficult for Marx because she had never before attempted to articulate her views about him. However, the essay turned out to be a positive experience for her, helping her to discover the real basis for the respect she holds for her grandfather. As you read her essay, notice how Marx first focuses on her own memories of her grandfather and then imagines what his memories might be like.

As I stand in the doorway of the store, the familiar rush of anxiety   1
overwhelms me. How can another year have flown by so quickly? Is it
possible that it is birthday time, and I am yet again faced with the task
of choosing "anything," while my grandfather waits impatiently to pay?
Shuffling his feet and chewing a toothpick, my grandfather presents
himself as a dominant figure of stubbornness and will.

A highly opinionated person, he "suggests" with the utmost au-   2
thority. Whether arguing with restaurant owners or making sarcastic
comments about the family inheritance, my grandfather represents the
archetype of conservative arrogance. Nevertheless, I view him with un-
matched respect and admiration. Despite his defensiveness, his soul
abounds with love, compassion, and kindness. Only insiders are provided a rare glimpse of the past which has shaped my grandfather's out-
ward personality.

Unlike my grandfather, I have never been totally helpless and com-   3
pletely alone. I cannot imagine the immense pain he must feel upon seeing a war memorial, reading a mourner's prayer, or viewing the only picture of his family. I will never be able to internalize the void that he feels
when the monthly reparation check arrives to compensate for his mother
and sister who were slaughtered by the Nazis. How can I say what my
personality would be like if I had lived through the nightmare that he
still lives?

At the age of eighteen, my grandfather joined the emerging Zionist   4
movement. After leaving Germany to build the state of Israel, he soon
discovered that his mother and sister were trapped under the Nazi
regime. Already deported, my great-aunt and great-grandmother wrote
desperate letters from the concentration camps. My grandfather was

helpless; heartbroken, he realized that any effort was futile. His mother and sister inevitably became numbers on the growing list of slaughtered Jews.

My grandfather seldom speaks of his tragic past. What I know of it 5 I have learned from my grandmother's stories, from the letters sent from the concentration camps, and from my grandfather's vague references. The slightest mention of his family's tragic past brings him to tears.

I caught a first glimpse at my grandfather's relationship with his 6 memories when we toured Yad Vashem, Israel's largest Holocaust museum. My grandfather entered the memorial with me at his side. As he scrutinized each picture, I began to consider his thoughts. I was hit head-on with the nightmare that had been my grandfather's reality. I looked at the pictures of emaciated prisoners and wondered if my grandfather recognized his sister. I grimaced at the sight of unmarked bodies, asking myself if my grandfather saw images of his mother.

Despite these stirrings of feelings within me, I have never ques- 7 tioned my grandfather on the subject of the Holocaust. I desperately want to know more, but I am equally afraid of bringing up the subject. For no apparent reason, my family has always abided by a tacit agreement never overtly to discuss the subject of the Holocaust. If only I had the courage to overstride these unmarked boundaries.

My grandfather's materialism may stem from a fear of losing things. 8 His home, family, and education were once swept from beneath him. As a result, his plate is always cleared, out of an unconscious fear that one day there may be no more food. Possessions, bought with hard-earned money, are meticulously maintained. My grandfather built his own life with no parent to send him to college, no sister to chat with on the phone, no house to go home to for Thanksgiving, and no inheritance with which to build a future.

My grandfather is not exactly a philanthropist. From an idealistic 9 point of view, I expect that a persecuted individual would want to turn around and root out all social injustices. After having seen the damage that hate can cause, I would expect him to reach out to all others. My grandfather, on the other hand, has a slightly different view. After all, if he fought the odds and "won," why are the hungry and the poor unable to help themselves?

This is not to say that my grandfather is not kind-hearted. Rather, 10 his compassion is reserved. He believes strongly in the ideals of family. He has rebuilt a life and is proud to be the foundation of our tightly knit family. I always feel slightly uneasy in his house, as I enter the rooms full of pictures of myself, my brother, and my sister. Likewise, I feel self-conscious as I meet all his friends who have "heard so much about me," for I know this is by no means an exaggeration.

Although I can never internalize the pain that my grandfather har-   11
bors, I can be more understanding toward our differences. I can appreciate his compassionate soul, while still coming to terms with our contrasting personalities. In addition, I can recognize my own identity, realizing that I had the privilege to develop under the canopy of a loving and supportive family.

RESPONDING TO "MY GRANDFATHER'S MEMORIES"

Freewrite about a family member who intrigues but perhaps also puzzles you.

Responding through Interpretation

1. What does this essay suggest about how the lives of grandparents may influence the lives of their grandchildren?
2. What do you think of the title of Marx's essay? How is it significant to the essay, especially to the ideas contained in the essay's final paragraph?

Responding through Discussion

1. With your group, think about a family member whose life you know something about. Let each group member tell a brief history of a relative's life. Leave time at the end to discuss the value of these family stories for your own lives. What have you learned from observing the lives of others in your family?

Responding through Writing

1. After your group discussion, write a journal entry that expands your relative's story.
2. Using your freewrite, the ideas you got from the group discussion, and your journal entry, write a paper about your relative. Even though this is a portrait of your relative, be certain to include yourself in the story—your relationship with the relative as well as your observations and reactions.

Family Friends: A Process of Growth

Charlie Wu

Charlie Wu grew up in Fremont, California, and remained there after his parents moved away in his senior year in high school. In his essay "Family Friends," Wu explores the changes in himself and in his relationship with his sister and other family members that began when his older sister moved back home to help him out after his parents' departure. Charlie Wu uses both narrative and process analysis to explain his evolving attitude toward his family and his awareness of his own growth.

As a growing teenager, I felt more comfortable with my friends than with   1
my own family. So many precious moments of teenage life were spent at school where friends were always willing to discuss personal and critical issues with me, such as girls and the difficulty in finding a unique personal identity. When I wasn't present at school, I spent the majority of my time just hanging out with close friends, or when that wasn't possible, I would "hang out" with them via a telephone conference line. The more time I spent with my friends, the less comfortable I became with my own family. Eventually I came to spend hardly any time with my family and totally failed to communicate with them. To me, every member of my family was just an acquaintance. It wasn't until my family moved away, leaving me with my sister as their sole representative, that I began to understand the importance of family and to discover who I really was in relation to my own family.

Halfway through my senior year in high school, my parents moved   2
to Texas in hopes that they could prosper in their hotel business venture in order to put my siblings and myself through college. My parents asked my sister, who had been pursuing her own educational goals at the University of California at Berkeley, to move down to Fremont (about a 40-minute commute from Berkeley) so that she could care for and watch over me in the absence of my parents.

Though my sister was very reluctant to move to Fremont because   3
of the college experience that she would miss out on, she agreed to move in order to provide the parental guidance and love that my parents would no longer be able to provide on a constant and daily basis. When she moved in, she made every effort to make me feel comfortable around her. Every night at the dinner table, she would briefly describe her day at school or work in hopes that it would lead to a full and lively con-

versation. Furthermore, she always made it a point to include me in her plans, and she always sincerely asked me how I was doing in school and in my personal life.

However, I simply did not want to include my sister in my life. Not   4 only did I feel she was as much a stranger to me as anyone off the streets, I also felt that I would be forced to deal with this living arrangement for only a few months before I would move away to college with my friends. No matter how hard she tried, I just couldn't seem to feel very comfortable when I was around her. I never made an effort to keep a conversation going, and was indifferent to everything she said. Often I would nod my head to give the impression that I was listening to her when I couldn't have cared less about the feelings she had just shared with me. At the moments when she would inquire about my academic performance or personal life, I would always coldly reply, acting annoyed, that everything was "just fine." I simply couldn't wait to move to San Diego to be at the University of California with my close friends.

Ironically, because of a simple letter I received from U.C. San Diego   5 just one month before I had planned to move there for my higher education, my relationship with my sister took a turn for the better. When I unfolded the letter, I almost broke down in tears. The academic evaluator wanted to inform me that my admission to the university had been canceled due to the grades I had received during my senior year. For days, I simply stared at the letter in disbelief. As I watched my close friends leave for college until I was the only one of our group left in Fremont, I felt very alone and detached, and began to realize the importance of having someone to talk to every day.

This loneliness soon began to make me value and respect the friend-   6 ship that my sister had so earnestly tried to create with me. I realized that my sister was the only person left in Fremont who truly cared about me. I began to see that I would need her friendship and guidance to help me through this rough period. With this in mind, I began to make an effort to give something back to the relationship that my sister had tried to build with me.

At first, my attempts to build a relationship with my sister made me   7 feel uncomfortable and awkward because she was still very much a stranger to me. However, little by little, our relationship started to blossom. Because of the childish attitude that I had during my senior year in high school, I had never really known that my sister was a very good and friendly person. When I finally began to join conversations that my sister would start at the dinner table, I discovered that she was full of feelings and ideas. The moments of silence and my constant head-nodding soon became conversations filled with laughter and compassion. Gradually, I began to see the friend within Jenny, not just our sibling tie.

As I began to build upon my relationship with my sister, I could   8
clearly see not only that the growing friendship was wonderful and refreshing, but that it was one of the best friendships I had ever experienced. Before long, just as she was always willing to share her innermost feelings with me, I became eager to share feelings with her that I would have otherwise kept hidden because I knew that her caring insight and knowledgeable advice would help me to find a solution to any problem that I encountered. As our relationship progressed, it got to the point where I no longer saw her just as my sister, but as one of my best friends.

Even though my sister/friend has since moved to Los Angeles to   9
pursue a pharmaceutical degree at USC, our friendship has not been affected. We call each other almost every night and talk just as if we were sitting at the dinner table. Her friendship means so much to me that I find myself trying harder than ever to make the most of our relationship because of the immaturity that caused me to take my sister for granted when she first moved in with me. I regret having lost time with my sister, and I make it a point to call her often to make up for lost time.

Because of the relationship I have built with my sister, I also have   10
begun to make up for lost times with other members of the family, including my parents, my second sister, and my brother. Jenny showed me that family members are human beings, and that with effort good friendships can be built between members of a family. Thanks to my sister, I now feel that my family is the closest group of friends I will ever have.

RESPONDING TO "FAMILY FRIENDS: A PROCESS OF GROWTH"

Freewrite about your relationship with one of your brothers or sisters or a close relative. How has it changed over the years?

Responding through Interpretation

1. Explain the steps Wu went through in the process of his becoming friends with his sister. Include the external events as well as his internal responses to all of the events.
2. In his very first sentence, Wu makes a strong statement that lets the reader know that this is an essay about change. Go through the essay and

note the transitions and sentences that indicate the major points of change.

Responding through Discussion

1. In his conclusion, Wu gives a definition of family which may be different from what some think of as family. Focus your group discussion on his final sentence: "Thanks to my sister, I now feel that my family is the closest group of friends I will ever have." Allow time for each group member to make a statement about his or her own experiences. Afterward, if time permits, discuss the ways that people in families can become good friends.

Responding through Writing

1. Write a journal entry about your relationship with your family as a whole. Do you consider them your friends? If so, explain how this has happened; if not, explore what you see that is different about family as opposed to friends.
2. Write a paper about a time when you went through a significant change in a relationship that was important to you.

Nani

Alberto Alvaro Rios

Born in the border town of Nogales, Arizona, Alberto Alvaro Rios currently teaches English at Arizona State University, Tempe. His books include *The Iguana Killer: Twelve Stories of the Heart* (1984) and *Five Indiscretions* (1985). In his poetry and stories Rios examines the culturally diverse stories of his family heritage. Notice how his poem "Nani," published in Rios's collection *Whispering to Fool the Wind* (1982), begins with an ordinary event in family life and explores its personal, cultural, and imaginative complexity on several levels.

Sitting at her table, she serves
the sopa de arroz[1] to me
instinctively, and I watch her,
the absolute mamá, and eat words
I might have had to say more   5
out of embarrassment. To speak,
now-foreign words I used to speak,
too, dribble down her mouth as she serves
me albóndigas.[2] No more
than a third are easy to me.   10
By the stove she does something with words
and looks at me only with her
back. I am full. I tell her
I taste the mint, and watch her speak

smiles at the stove. All my words   15
make her smile. Nani never serves
herself, she only watches me
with her skin, her hair. I ask for more.

I watch the mamá warming more
tortillas for me. I watch her   20
fingers in the flame for me.

[1]Rice soup.
[2]Meatballs.

Near her mouth, I see a wrinkle speak
of a man whose body serves
the ants like she serves me, then more words
from more wrinkles about children, words   25
about this and that, flowing more
easily from these other mouths. Each serves
as a tremendous string around her,
holding her together. They speak
nani was this and that to me   30
and I wonder just how much of me
will die with her, what were the words
I could have been, was. Her insides speak
through a hundred wrinkles, now, more
than she can bear, steel around her,   35
shouting, then, What is this thing she serves?

She asks me if I want more.
I own no words to stop her.
Even before I speak, she serves.

RESPONDING TO "NANI"

Freewrite about a special meal that you remember having with one or both
of your grandparents—or with some other family member.

Responding through Interpretation

1. What do you think the narrator means by his description of Nani as "The
   absolute mamá"? What does this reveal about his feelings toward her?
2. The narrator says that he sits silent at the table "out of embarrassment."
   About what is he embarrassed?
3. The narrator comments that Nani's abundant speech is full of "now-
   foreign words I used to speak." What is the significance of the "now-
   foreign" quality of Nani's Spanish? Why do you think the narrator has
   forgotten his childhood language?

Responding through Discussion

1. Discuss in your group the differences and similarities between the traditional grandmother in this poem and the lifestyles and values of your
   own grandmothers or mothers.

2. Study the poem together with your group, going through it by reading alternating lines and commenting on the imaginative comparisons in the poem such as the line about Nani's wrinkles: "Each serves/as a tremendous string around her."

Responding through Writing

1. Write about an older relative who has kept family traditions alive through ritual observations and stories. What are your feelings about your relative?
2. Write a paper in which you explore the changes in your family values and traditions over the years of your life. Evaluate the changes that have been made and make predictions or suggestions for members of the next generation.

I Stand Here Ironing

Tillie Olsen

Olsen was born in Nebraska in 1912, to a family who fled Russia after the revolution of 1905. She left high school to work, raise four children, and continue the family tradition of labor organizing. Her books include *Tell Me a Riddle* (1961) and *Silences* (1978). When her children were younger, Olsen could only write in "stolen moments . . . in the deep night hours for as long as I could stay awake, after the kids were in bed, after the household tasks were done, sometimes during. It is no accident that the first work I considered publishable began: 'I stand here ironing.' "

I stand here ironing, and what you asked me moves tormented back and forth with the iron.

"I wish you would manage the time to come in and talk with me about your daughter. I'm sure you can help me understand her. She's a youngster who needs help and whom I'm deeply interested in helping."

"Who needs help." Even if I came, what good would it do? You think because I am her mother I have a key, or that in some way you could use me as a key? She has lived for nineteen years. There is all that life that has happened outside of me, beyond me.

And when is there time to remember, to sift, to weigh, to estimate, to total? I will start and there will be an interruption and I will have to gather it all together again. Or I will become engulfed with all I did or did not do, with what should have been and what cannot be helped.

She was a beautiful baby. The first and only one of our five that was beautiful at birth. You do not guess how new and uneasy her tenancy in her now-loveliness. You did not know her all those years she was thought homely, or see her poring over her baby pictures, making me tell her over and over how beautiful she had been—and would be, I would tell her—and was now, to the seeing eye. But the seeing eyes were few or non-existent. Including mine.

I nursed her. They feel that's important nowadays. I nursed all the children, but with her, with all the fierce rigidity of first motherhood, I did like the books then said. Though her cries battered me to trembling and my breasts ached with swollenness, I waited till the clock decreed.

Why do I put that first? I do not even know if it matters, or if it explains anything.

She was a beautiful baby. She blew shining bubbles of sound. She   8
loved motion, loved light, loved color and music and textures. She would
lie on the floor in her blue overalls patting the surface so hard in ecstasy
her hands and feet would blur. She was a miracle to me, but when she
was eight months old I had to leave her daytimes with the woman downstairs to whom she was no miracle at all, for I worked or looked for work
and for Emily's father, who "could no longer endure" (he wrote in his
good-bye note) "sharing want with us."

I was nineteen. It was the pre-relief, pre-WPA world of the depres-   9
sion. I would start running as soon as I got off the streetcar, running up
the stairs, the place smelling sour, and awake or asleep to startle awake,
when she saw me she would break into a clogged weeping that could
not be comforted, a weeping I can hear yet.

After a while I found a job hashing at night so I could be with her   10
days, and it was better. But it came to where I had to bring her to his
family and leave her.

It took a long time to raise the money for her fare back. Then she got   11
chicken pox and I had to wait longer. When she finally came, I hardly
knew her, walking quick and nervous like her father, looking like her
father, thin, and dressed in a shoddy red that yellowed her skin and
glared at the pockmarks. All the baby loveliness gone.

She was two. Old enough for nursery school they said, and I did not   12
know then what I know now—the fatigue of the long day, and the lac-
erations of group life in the nurseries that are only parking places for children.

Except that it would have made no difference if I had known. It was   13
the only place there was. It was the only way we could be together, the
only way I could hold a job.

And even without knowing, I knew. I knew the teacher that was evil   14
because all these years it has curdled into my memory, the little boy
hunched in the corner, her rasp, "why aren't you outside, because Alvin
hits you? that's no reason, go out, scaredy." I knew Emily hated it even
if she did not clutch and implore "don't go Mommy" like the other children, mornings.

She always had a reason why she should stay home. Momma, you   15
look sick, Momma. I feel sick. Momma, the teachers aren't there today,
they're sick. Momma, we can't go, there was a fire there last night.
Momma, it's a holiday today, no school, they told me.

But never a direct protest, never rebellion. I think of our others in   16
their three-, four-year-oldness—the explosions, the tempers, the de-

nunciations, the demands—and I feel suddenly ill. I put the iron down. What in me demanded that goodness in her? And what was the cost, the cost to her of such goodness?

The old man living in the back once said in his gentle way: "You should smile at Emily more when you look at her." What *was* in my face when I looked at her? I loved her. There were all the acts of love. 17

It was only with the others I remembered what he said, and it was the face of joy, and not of care or tightness or worry I turned to them— too late for Emily. She does not smile easily, let alone almost always as her brothers and sisters do. Her face is closed and sombre, but when she wants, how fluid. You must have seen it in her pantomimes, you spoke of her rare gift for comedy on the stage that rouses a laughter out of the audience so dear they applaud and applaud and do not want to let her go. 18

Where does it come from, that comedy? There was none of it in her when she came back to me that second time, after I had had to send her away again. She had a new daddy now to learn to love, and I think per- haps it was a better time. 19

Except when we left her alone nights, telling ourselves she was old enough. 20

"Can't you go some other time, Mommy, like tomorrow?" she would ask. "Will it be just a little while you'll be gone? Do you promise?" 21

The time we came back, the front door open, the clock on the floor in the hall. She rigid awake. "It wasn't just a little while. I didn't cry. Three times I called you, just three times, and then I ran downstairs to open the door so you could come faster. The clock talked loud. I threw it away, it scared me what it talked." 22

She said the clock talked loud again that night I went to the hospi- tal to have Susan. She was delirious with the fever that comes before red measles, but she was fully conscious all the week I was gone and the week after we were home when she could not come near the new baby or me. 23

She did not get well. She stayed skeleton thin, not wanting to eat, and night after night she had nightmares. She would call for me, and I would rouse from exhaustion to sleepily call back: "You're all right, darling, go to sleep, it's just a dream," and if she still called, in a sterner voice, "now go to sleep, Emily, there's nothing to hurt you." Twice, only twice, when I had to get up for Susan anyhow, I went in to sit with her. 24

Now when it is too late (as if she would let me hold and comfort her like I do the others) I get up and go to her at once at her moan or rest- 25 less stirring. "Are you awake, Emily? Can I get you something?" And the answer is always the same: "No, I'm all right, go back to sleep. Mother."

They persuaded me at the clinic to send her away to a convalescent 26
home in the country where "she can have the kind of food and care you can't manage for her, and you'll be free to concentrate on the new baby." They still send children to that place. I see pictures on the society page of sleek young women planning affairs to raise money for it, or dancing at the affairs, or decorating Easter eggs or filling Christmas stockings for the children.

They never have a picture of the children so I do not know if the girls 27
still wear those gigantic red bows and the ravaged looks on the every other Sunday when parents can come to visit "unless otherwise noti-fied"—as we were notified the first six weeks.

Oh it is a handsome place, green lawns and tall trees and fluted 28
flower beds. High up on the balconies of each cottage the children stand, the girls in their red bows and white dresses, the boys in white suits and giant red ties. The parents stand below shrieking up to be heard and the children shriek down to be heard, and between them the invisible wall "Not To Be Contaminated by Parental Germs or Physical Affection."

There was a tiny girl who always stood hand in hand with Emily. 29
Her parents never came. One visit she was gone. "They moved her to Rose College," Emily shouted in explanation. "They don't like you to love anybody here."

She wrote once a week, the labored writing of a seven-year-old. "I 30
am fine. How is the baby. If I write my letter nicely I will have a star. Love." There never was a star. We wrote every other day, letters she could never hold or keep but only hear read—once. "We simply do not have room for children to keep any personal possessions," they pa-tiently explained when we pieced one Sunday's shrieking together to plead how much it would mean to Emily, who loved so to keep things, to be allowed to keep her letters and cards.

Each visit she looked frailer. "She isn't eating," they told us. 31

(They had runny eggs for breakfast or mush with lumps, Emily said 32
later, I'd hold it in my mouth and not swallow. Nothing ever tasted good, just when they had chicken.)

It took us eight months to get her released home, and only the fact 33
that she gained back so little of her seven lost pounds convinced the so-cial worker.

I used to try to hold and love her after she came back, but her body 34
would stay stiff, and after a while she'd push away. She ate little. Food

sickened her, and I think much of life too. Oh she had physical lightness and brightness, twinkling by on skates, bouncing like a ball up and down up and down over the jump rope, skimming over the hill; but these were momentary.

She fretted about her appearance, thin and dark and foreign-looking   35
at a time when every little girl was supposed to look or thought she should look a chubby blonde replica of Shirley Temple. The doorbell sometimes rang for her, but no one seemed to come and play in the house or be a best friend. Maybe because we moved so much.

There was a boy she loved painfully through two school semesters.   36
Months later she told me how she had taken pennies from my purse to buy him candy. "Licorice was his favorite and I brought him some every day, but he still liked Jennifer better'n me. Why, Mommy?" The kind of question for which there is no answer.

School was a worry to her. She was not glib or quick in a world   37
where glibness and quickness were easily confused with ability to learn. To her overworked and exasperated teachers she was an overconscientious "slow learner" who kept trying to catch up and was absent entirely too often.

I let her be absent, though sometimes the illness was imaginary.   38
How different from my now-strictness about attendance with the others. I wasn't working. We had a new baby, I was home anyhow. Sometimes, after Susan grew old enough, I would keep her home from school, too, to have them all together.

Mostly Emily had asthma, and her breathing, harsh and labored,   39
would fill the house with a curiously tranquil sound. I would bring the two old dresser mirrors and her boxes of collections to her bed. She would select beads and single earrings, bottle tops and shells, dried flowers and pebbles, old postcards and scraps, all sorts of oddments; then she and Susan would play Kingdom, setting up landscapes and furniture, peopling them with action.

Those were the only times of peaceful companionship between her   40
and Susan. I have edged away from it, that poisonous feeling between them, that terrible balancing of hurts and needs I had to do between the two, and did so badly, those earlier years.

Oh there are conflicts between the others too, each one human, need-   41
ing, demanding, hurting, taking—but only between Emily and Susan, no, Emily toward Susan that corroding resentment. It seems so obvious on the surface, yet it is not obvious. Susan, the second child, Susan, golden- and curly-haired and chubby, quick and articulate and assured, everything in appearance and manner Emily was not; Susan, not able to

resist Emily's precious things, losing or sometimes clumsily breaking them; Susan telling jokes and riddles to company for applause while Emily sat silent (to say to me later: that was *my* riddle, Mother, I told it to Susan); Susan, who for all the five years' difference in age was just a year behind Emily in developing physically.

I am glad for that slow physical development that widened the dif-   42
ference between her and her contemporaries, though she suffered over it. She was too vulnerable for that terrible world of youthful competition, of preening and parading, of constant measuring of yourself against every other, of envy, "If I had that copper hair," "If I had that skin. . . ." She tormented herself enough about not looking like the others, there was enough of the unsureness, the having to be conscious of words before you speak, the constant caring—what are they thinking of me? without having it all magnified by the merciless physical drives.

Ronnie is calling. He is wet and I change him. It is rare there is such   43
a cry now. That time of motherhood is almost behind me when the ear is not one's own but must always be racked and listening for the child cry, the child call. We sit for a while and I hold him, looking out over the city spread in charcoal with its soft aisles of light. *"Shoogily,"* he breathes and curls closer. I carry him back to bed, asleep. *Shoogily.* A funny word, a family word, inherited from Emily, invented by her to say: *comfort.*

In this and other ways she leaves her seal, I say aloud. And startle   44
at my saying it. What do I mean? What did I start to gather together, to try and make coherent? I was at the terrible, growing years. War years. I do not remember them well. I was working, there were four smaller ones now, there was not time for her. She had to help be a mother, and housekeeper, and shopper. She had to set her seal. Mornings of crisis and near hysteria trying to get lunches packed, hair combed, coats and shoes found, everyone to school or Child Care on time, the baby ready for transportation. And always the paper scribbled on by a smaller one, the book looked at by Susan then mislaid, the homework not done. Running out to that huge school where she was one, she was lost, she was a drop; suffering over the unpreparedness, stammering and unsure in her classes.

There was so little time left at night after the kids were bedded   45
down. She would struggle over books, always eating (it was in those years she developed her enormous appetite that is legendary in our family) and I would be ironing, or preparing food for the next day, or writing V-mail to Bill, or tending the baby. Sometimes, to make me

laugh, or out of her despair, she would imitate happenings or types at school.

I think I said once: "Why don't you do something like this in the   46 school amateur show?" One morning she phoned me at work, hardly understandable through the weeping: "Mother, I did it. I won, I won; they gave me first prize; they clapped and clapped and wouldn't let me go."

Now suddenly she was Somebody, and as imprisoned in her dif-   47 ference as she had been in anonymity.

She began to be asked to perform at other high schools, even in col-   48 leges, then at city and statewide affairs. The first one we went to, I only recognized her that first moment when thin, shy, she almost drowned herself into the curtains. Then: Was this Emily? The control, the command, the convulsing and deadly clowning, the spell, then the roaring, stamping audience, unwilling to let this rare and precious laughter out of their lives.

Afterwards: You ought to do something about her with a gift like   49 that—but without money or knowing how, what does one do? We have left it all to her, and the gift has as often eddied inside, clogged and clotted, as been used and growing.

She is coming. She runs up the stairs two at a time with her light   50 graceful step, and I know she is happy tonight. Whatever it was that occasioned your call did not happen today.

"Aren't you ever going to finish the ironing, Mother? Whistler   51 painted his mother in a rocker. I'd have to paint mine standing over an ironing board." This is one of her communicative nights and she tells me everything and nothing as she fixes herself a plate of food out of the icebox.

She is so lovely. Why did you want me to come in at all? Why were   52 you concerned? She will find her way.

She starts up the stairs to bed. "Don't get me up with the rest in the   53 morning." "But I thought you were having midterms." "Oh, those," she comes back in, kisses me, and says quite lightly, "in a couple of years when we'll all be atom-dead they won't matter a bit."

She has said it before. She *believes* it. But because I have been dredg-   54 ing the past, and all that compounds a human being is so heavy and meaningful in me, I cannot endure it tonight.

I will never total it all. I will never come in to say: She was a child   55 seldom smiled at. Her father left me before she was a year old. I had to work her first six years when there was work, or I sent her home and to his relatives. There were years she had care she hated. She was dark and thin and foreign-looking in a world where the prestige went to blondeness and curly hair and dimples, she was slow where glibness was prized. She was a child of anxious, not proud, love. We were poor and could not afford for her the soil of easy growth. I was a young mother, I was a distracted mother. There were the other children pushing up, demanding. Her younger sister seemed all that she was not. There were years she did not want me to touch her. She kept too much in herself, her life was such she had to keep too much in herself. My wisdom came too late. She has much to her and probably nothing will come of it. She is a child of her age, of depression, of war, of fear.

Let her be. So all that is in her will not bloom—but in how many does   56
it? There is still enough left to live by. Only help her to know—help make it so there is cause for her to know—that she is more than this dress on the ironing board, helpless before the iron.

RESPONDING TO "I STAND HERE IRONING"

Freewrite about some hardship or difficulty in your family that you've had to adjust to.

Responding through Interpretation

1. Although Emily "was a beautiful baby," her life hasn't turned out ideally. In your reading journal, write down some of the circumstances that had an impact on Emily's childhood.
2. Write a short portrait of Emily in your reading journal. Use your imagination, combined with the images and ideas that you got from reading the story, to write your portrait of Emily.
3. Look back through the story and note all the references to both ironing and the iron throughout the story. How do the images of the iron and ironing board underscore the meaning of the story?

Responding through Discussion

1. Discuss with your group whether or not you feel that the narrator in Olsen's story is a "good" mother. Give reasons why you feel she either is or is not. Look through the story and gather evidence before you make your decision and then use this evidence to support your opinion.

2. What makes this story different from most of the other autobiographical narratives you've read so far? As you discuss this idea in the group, have someone make a list of the similarities and differences between this story and the first-person narratives already read. Then discuss your ideas with the rest of the class.

Responding through Writing

1. How do you feel about the mother's comment about Emily when she says ". . . all that is in her [Emily] will not bloom"? Write your response to this comment.
2. Olsen's story covers a period of nineteen years. Imagine that another five years in Emily's life has passed and that she is now twenty-five years old. Write a story about *one day* in her life at this age. Where is she now? What has happened to her? You can write your story from Emily's point of view or her mother's, but keep the details of "I Stand Here Ironing" in mind as you write so that your story will seem possible in light of the information Olsen has given.

Snapshot: Lost Lives of Women

Amy Tan

Amy Tan was born in Oakland, California, in 1952, only 2 1/2 years after her parents emigrated from China. She earned her M.A. (1974) at San Jose State College before publishing her best-selling novel *The Joy Luck Club* (1989). Tan has completed two other novels, *The Kitchen God's Wife* (1991), and *The Hundred Secret Senses* (1995). *The Joy Luck Club* was made into a successful film in 1993. Tan has remarked that writing has helped her discover "how very Chinese I was. And how much had stayed with me that I had tried to deny." "Snapshot" appeared in *Life* magazine in April 1991.

When I first saw this photo as a child, I thought it was exotic and remote,   1
of a faraway time and place, with people who had no connection to my American life. Look at their bound feet! Look at that funny lady with the plucked forehead!

The solemn little girl is, in fact, my mother. And leaning against the   2
rock is my grandmother, Jingmei. "She called me Baobei," my mother told me. "It means Treasure."

The picture was taken in Hangzhou, and my mother believes the   3
year was 1922, possibly spring or fall, judging by the clothes. At first
glance, it appears the women are on a pleasure outing.

But see the white bands on their skirts? The white shoes? They are in   4
mourning. My mother's grandmother, known to the others as Divong,
"The Replacement Wife," has recently died. The women have come to this
place, a Buddhist retreat, to perform yet another ceremony for Divong.
Monks hired for the occasion have chanted the proper words. And the
women and little girl have walked in circles clutching smoky sticks of in-
cense. They knelt and prayed, then burned a huge pile of spirit money so
that Divong might ascend to a higher position in her new world.

This is also a picture of secrets and tragedies, the reasons that warn-   5
ings have been passed along in our family like heirlooms. Each of these
women suffered a terrible fate, my mother said. And they were not peasant women but big city people, very modern. They went to dance halls
and wore stylish clothes. They were supposed to be the lucky ones.

Look at the pretty woman with her finger on her cheek. She is my   6
mother's second cousin, Nunu Aiyi, "Precious Auntie." You cannot see
this, but Nunu Aiyi's entire face was scarred from smallpox. Lucky for
her, a year or so after this picture was taken, she received marriage proposals from two families. She turned down a lawyer and married another man. Later she divorced her husband, a daring thing for a woman
to do. But then, finding no means to support herself or her young daughter, Nunu eventually accepted the lawyer's second proposal—to become his number two concubine. "Where else could she go?" my mother
asked. "Some people said she was lucky the lawyer still wanted her."'

Now look at the small woman with a sour face (third from left).   7
There's a reason that Jyou Ma, "Uncle's Wife," looks this way. Her husband, my great-uncle often complained that his family had chosen an
ugly woman for his wife. To show his displeasure, he often insulted Jyou
Ma's cooking. One time Great-Uncle tipped over a pot of boiling soup,
which fell all over his niece's four-year-old neck and nearly killed her.
My mother was the little niece, and she still has that soup scar on her
neck. Great-Uncle's family eventually chose a pretty woman for his second wife. But the complaints about Jyou Ma's cooking did not stop.

Doomma, "Big Mother," is the regal-looking woman seated on a   8
rock. (The woman with the plucked forehead, far left, is a servant, remembered only as someone who cleaned but did not cook.) Doomma
was the daughter of my great-grandfather and Nu-pei, "The Original
Wife." She was shunned by Divong, "The Replacement Wife," for being
"too strong," and loved by Divong's daughter, my grandmother.

Doomma's first daughter was born with a hunchback—a sign, some said, of Doomma's own crooked nature. Why else did she remarry, disobeying her family's orders to remain a widow forever? And why did Doomma later kill herself, using some mysterious means that caused her to die slowly over three days? "Doomma died the same way she lived," my mother said, "strong, suffering lots."

Jingmei, my own grandmother, lived only a few more years after this picture was taken. She was the widow of a poor scholar, a man who had the misfortune of dying from influenza when he was about to be appointed a vice-magistrate. In 1924 or so, a rich man, who liked to collect pretty women, raped my grandmother and thereby forced her into becoming one of his concubines. My grandmother, now an outcast, took her young daughter to live with her on an island outside of Shanghai. She left her son behind, to save his face. After she gave birth to another son she killed herself by swallowing raw opium buried in the New Year's rice cakes. The young daughter who wept at her deathbed was my mother. 9

At my grandmother's funeral, monks tied chains to my mother's ankles so she would not fly away with her mother's ghost. "I tried to take them off," my mother said. "I was her treasure. I was her life." 10

My mother could never talk about any of this, even with her closest friends. "Don't tell anyone," she once said to me. "People don't understand. A concubine was like some kind prostitute. My mother was a good woman, high-class. She had no choice." 11

I told her I understood. 12

"How can you understand?" she said, suddenly angry. "You did not live in China then. You do not know what it's like to have no position in life. I was her daughter. We had no face! We belonged to nobody! This is a shame I can never push off my back." By the end of the outburst, she was crying. 13

On a recent trip with my mother to Beijing, I learned that my uncle found a way to push the shame off his back. He was the son my grandmother left behind. In 1936 he joined the Communist party—in large part, he told me, to overthrow the society that forced his mother into concubinage. He published a story about his mother. I told him I had written about my grandmother in a book of fiction. We agreed that my grandmother is the source of strength running through our family. My mother cried to hear this. 14

My mother believes my grandmother is also my muse, that she helps me write. "Does she still visit you often?" she asked while I was writing my second book. And then she added shyly, "Does she say anything about me?" 15

"Yes," I told her. "She has lots to say. I am writing it down."   16

This is the picture I see when I write. These are the secrets I was sup-   17
posed to keep. These are the women who never let me forget why stories need to be told.

RESPONDING TO "SNAPSHOT: LOST LIVES OF WOMEN"

Freewrite: Think of an old family photograph that you have seen. Write
down a description of all you remember about it. Later try to locate the photograph to see if your memory of it is accurate.

Responding through Interpretation

1. To be sure you understand the relationships of the women in the photograph to each other, draw a family tree or diagram and place each of the
women in relationship to all the others.
2. Explain why Tan sees the picture as one of "secrets and tragedies."
3. Write a brief statement about the meaning of the essay's title. What does
the title add to the essay?

Responding through Discussion

1. In a small group, tell stories about the lives of your ancestors—your great-
grandparents, your grandparents, your aunts and uncles, your parents. Be
certain each person has an opportunity to tell at least one story. If time permits, the group can tell a second family story. After the discussion, write
a summary in your reading journal of the most interesting story you heard.
2. Discuss with your group some of the ways your lives differ from those
of your parents and/or grandparents.

Responding through Writing

1. Find an old family photograph that seems to hold special meaning for
you. Spend time looking at it closely. If possible, ask your relatives
questions about the photograph—when it was taken, where, who the people are, what their lives were like back then. In your journal, describe
the photograph, using some of the same techniques as Tan has done in
analyzing her photograph.
2. Write an essay that explores the impact, if any, that your family history
and family values have had on you. Use some of the information you
have gained through the freewriting, journal entry, and group discussion
for this selection. If you would like to include a photograph, do so and
explain why it is significant to your essay.

On Going Home

Joan Didion

Joan Didion was born in Sacramento, California, in 1934, and has worked as an editor, journalist, essayist, and novelist. With her husband, John Gregory Dunne, she has also collaborated on a number of screenplays. Didion is a prolific writer who is well known for her clear and detailed style. She has published novels, essays, and books on current affairs. Her most widely known works are two essay collections: *Slouching toward Bethlehem* (1968), from which "On Going Home" is taken, and *The White Album* (1979). As you read the following essay, notice how Didion struggles to find a part of her own heritage to give to her daughter.

I am home for my daughter's first birthday. By "home" I do not mean   1
the house in Los Angeles where my husband and I and the baby live,
but the place where my family is, in the Central Valley of California. It
is a vital although troublesome distinction. My husband likes my family
but is uneasy in their house, because once there I fall into their ways,
which are difficult, oblique, deliberately inarticulate, not my husband's
ways. We live in dusty houses ("D-U-S-T," he once wrote with his finger
on surfaces all over the house, but no one noticed it) filled with
mementos quite without value to him (what could the Canton dessert
plates mean to him? how could he have known about the assay scales,
why should he care if he did know?), and we appear to talk exclusively
about people we know who have been committed to mental hospitals,
about people we know who have been booked on drunk-driving
charges, and about property, particularly about property, land, price per
acre and C-2 zoning and assessments and freeway access. My brother
does not understand my husband's inability to perceive the advantage
in the rather common real-estate transaction known as "sale-leaseback,"
and my husband in turn does not understand why so many of the people
he hears about in my father's house have recently been committed to
mental hospitals or booked on drunk-driving charges. Nor does he
understand that when we talk about sale-leasebacks and right-of-way
condemnations we are talking in code about the things we like best, the
yellow fields and the cottonwoods and the rivers rising and falling and
the mountain roads closing when the heavy snow comes in. We miss
each other's points, have another drink and regard the fire. My brother

refers to my husband, in his presence, as "Joan's husband." Marriage is the classic betrayal.

Or perhaps it is not any more. Sometimes I think that those of us who are now in our thirties were born into the last generation to carry the burden of "home," to find in family life the source of all tension and drama. I had by all objective accounts a "normal" and a "happy" family situation, and yet I was almost thirty years old before I could talk to my family on the telephone without crying after I had hung up. We did not fight. Nothing was wrong. And yet some nameless anxiety colored the emotional charges between me and the place that I came from. The question of whether or not you could go home again was a very real part of the sentimental and largely literary baggage with which we left home in the fifties; I suspect that it is irrelevant to the children born of the fragmentation after World War II. A few weeks ago in a San Francisco bar I saw a pretty young girl on crystal take off her clothes and dance for the cash prize in an "amateur-topless" contest. There was no particular sense of moment about this, none of the effect of romantic degradation, of "dark journey," for which my generation strived so assiduously. What sense could that girl possibly make of, say, *Long Day's Journey into Night?* Who is beside the point?

That I am trapped in this particular irrelevancy is never more apparent to me than when I am home. Paralyzed by the neurotic lassitude engendered by meeting one's past at every turn, around every corner, inside every cupboard, I go aimlessly from room to room. I decide to meet it head-on and clean out a drawer, and I spread the contents on the bed. A bathing suit I wore the summer I was seventeen. A letter of rejection from *The Nation,* an aerial photograph of the site for a shopping center my father did not build in 1954. Three teacups hand-painted with cabbage roses and signed "E.M.," my grandmother's initials. There is no final solution for letters of rejection from *The Nation* and teacups hand-painted in 1900. Nor is there any answer to snapshots of one's grandfather as a young man on skis, surveying around Donner Pass in the year 1910. I smooth out the snapshot and look into his face, and do and do not see my own. I close the drawer, and have another cup of coffee with my mother. We get along very well, veterans of a guerrilla war we never understood.

Days pass. I see no one. I come to dread my husband's evening call, not only because he is full of news of what by now seems to me our remote life in Los Angeles, people he has seen, letters which require attention, but because he asks what I have been doing, suggests uneasily that I get out, drive to San Francisco or Berkeley. Instead I drive across the river to a family graveyard. It has been vandalized since my last visit and the monuments are broken, overturned in the dry grass. Because I once saw a rattlesnake in the grass I stay in the car and listen to a country-and-Western station. Later I drive with my father to a ranch he has in the foothills. The man who runs his cattle on it asks us to the roundup, a week from Sunday, and although I know that I will be in Los Angeles I say, in the oblique way my family talks, that I will come. Once home I mention the broken monuments in the graveyard. My mother shrugs.

I go to visit my great-aunts. A few of them think now that I am my   5
cousin, or their daughter who died young. We recall an anecdote about a relative last seen in 1948, and they ask if I still like living in New York City. I have lived in Los Angeles for three years, but I say that I do. The baby is offered a horehound drop, and I am slipped a dollar bill "to buy a treat." Questions trail off, answers are abandoned, the baby plays with the dust motes in a shaft of afternoon sun.

It is time for the baby's birthday party: a white cake, strawberry-   6
marshmallow ice cream, a bottle of champagne saved from another party. In the evening, after she has gone to sleep, I kneel beside the crib and touch her face, where it is pressed against the slats, with mine. She is an open and trusting child, unprepared for and unaccustomed to the ambushes of family life, and perhaps it is just as well that I can offer her little of that life. I would like to give her more. I would like to promise her that she will grow up with a sense of her cousins and of rivers and of her great-grandmother's teacups, would like to pledge her a picnic on a river with fried chicken and her hair uncombed, would like to give her *home* for her birthday, but we live differently now and I can promise her nothing like that. I give her a xylophone and a sundress from Madeira, and promise to tell her a funny story.

RESPONDING TO "ON GOING HOME"

Freewrite about a time when you went back home for a visit to family or other relatives.

Responding through Interpretation

1. Why do you think it is difficult for Didion to go home? How does Didion's difficulty in going home parallel with the "You can't go home again" dilemma most people face at times?

2. What items does Didion finally give her daughter for her first birthday? What do you think these three items symbolize? Take each item and write about what it suggests in your own mind.
3. Notice that Didion writes her essay in the present tense, even though it is an event that has taken place in the past. What do you think she accomplishes by using the present tense? Experiment with present tense by writing a paragraph first in past tense and then in present tense. How does the shift in tenses affect the way your paragraph sounds?

Responding through Discussion

1. Before beginning the discussion, let the members of the group brainstorm to come up with a list of words they associate with *home* and another list of words they associate with *house*. Then discuss the differences and similarities between the two words and try to come up with a group definition for each word. Bring these definitions back to the classroom for a large-group discussion.
2. Didion says, "I was almost thirty years old before I could talk to my family on the telephone without crying after I had hung up." Discuss what she means by that statement. Is this an experience any of the group members have ever had? If so, those members might want to share these experiences with the group.

Responding by Writing

1. Write a journal entry in which you describe and define the possessions, the feelings, the ideas, and the values that were part of your home—or homes—when you were growing up.
2. Write a paper in which you set forth your expectations of and goals for your ideal home. Then describe the process by which you plan to create this ideal home. Keep in mind that a home is more than a house.

Father

Alice Walker

Alice Walker was born in a small town in Georgia and graduated from Sarah Lawrence College. She currently lives in Northern California. Her fictional works include *The Color Purple* (1982), *In Love and Trouble: Stories of Black Women* (1973), and *The Temple of My Familiar* (1989). As you read the following selection, "Father" (1984), which is taken from her collection of essays, *Living by the Word: Selected Writings (1973–1987)*, notice how Walker explores through images and memories the enduring impact that her father has had on both her life as a woman and on her career as a writer.

Though it is more difficult to write about my father than about my mother, since I spent less time with him and knew him less well, it is equally as liberating. Partly this is because writing about people helps us to understand them, and understanding them helps us to accept them as part of ourselves. Since I share so many of my father's characteristics, physical and otherwise, coming to terms with what he has meant to my life is crucial to a full acceptance and love of myself. 1

I'm positive my father never understood why I wrote. I wonder sometimes if the appearance, in 1968, of my first book, *Once,* poems largely about my experiences in the Civil Rights movement and in other countries, notably African and Eastern European, surprised him. It is frustrating that, because he is now dead, I will never know. 2

In fact, what I regret most about my relationship with my father is that it did not improve until after his death. For a long time I felt so shut off from him that we were unable to talk. I hadn't the experience, as a younger woman, to ask the questions I would ask now. These days I feel we are on good terms, spiritually (my dreams of him are deeply loving and comforting ones), and that we both understand our relationship was a casualty of exhaustion and circumstances. My birth, the eighth child, unplanned, must have elicited more anxiety than joy. It hurts me to think that for both my parents, poor people, my arrival represented many more years of backbreaking and spirit-crushing toil. 3

I grew up to marry someone very unlike my father, as I knew him— though I feel sure he had these qualities himself as a younger man— someone warm, openly and spontaneously affectionate, who loved to talk to me about everything, including my work. I now share my life with 4 another man who has these qualities. But I would give a lot to be able to talk grownup to grownup with Daddy. I'd like to tell him how hard I am working to understand. And about the humor and solace I occasionally find (while writing *The Color Purple*, for instance, in which some of his early life is imagined) in the work.

> My father
> (back blistered)
> beat me
> because I
> could not
> stop crying.
> He'd had
> enough "fuss"
> he said
> for one damn
> voting day.

In my heart, I have never wanted to be at odds with my father, but ⁵ I have felt, over the years, especially when I was younger, that he gave me no choice. Perhaps if I could have relaxed and been content to be his favorite, there would have been a chance for closeness, but because a sister whom I loved was clearly not favorite material I did not want to be either. When I look back over my life, I see a pattern in my relationships going back to this, and in my love relationships I have refused men who loved me (at least for a time) if they in turn were loved by another woman but did not love her in return. I am the kind of woman who could positively forbid a married lover to leave his wife.

The poem above is one of my earliest as an adult, written after an ⁶ abortion of which my father would not have approved, in which I felt that visceral understanding of a situation that for a poet can mean a poem. My father far away in the South, me in college in the North—how far away from each other! Yet in the pain of the moment and the illumination of some of what was wrong between us, how close. If he ever read the poem, I wonder what he thought. We never discussed my work, though I thought he tended to become more like some of my worst characters the older he got. I remember going home once and being told by my mother of some of the curses he was capable of, and hardly believing her, since the most I'd ever heard my father say was "God damn!" and I could count the number of times on toes and fingers. (In fact, his favorite curse, when a nail refused to go in straight or he dropped the hammer on his sore corn was "God damn the goddam luck to the devil!" which always sounded rather ineffectual and humorous to me, and which, thinking of it, I hear him say and see his perspiring dark face.)

Did he actually beat me on voting day? Probably not. I suppose the illegal abortion caused me to understand what living under other people's politics can force us to do. The only time I remember his beating me was one day after he'd come home tired and hungry from the dairy (where he and my brothers milked a large herd of cows morning and afternoon), and my brother Bobby, three years older than me and a lover of chaos, and I were fighting. He had started it, of course. My mother, sick of our noise, spoke to my father about it, and without asking questions he took off his belt and flailed away, indiscriminately, at the two of us. 7

Why do certain things stick in the mind? I recall a scene, much earlier, when I was only three or so, in which my father questioned me about a fruit jar I had accidentally broken. I felt he knew I had broken it; at the same time, I couldn't be sure. Apparently breaking it was, in any event, the wrong thing to have done. I could say, Yes, I broke the jar, and risk a whipping for breaking something valuable, or, No, I did not break it, and perhaps bluff my way through. 8

I've never forgotten my feeling that he really wanted me to tell the truth. And because he seemed to desire it—and the moments during which he waited for my reply seemed quite out of time, so much so I can still feel them, and, as I said, I was only three, if that—I confessed. I broke the jar, I said. I think he hugged me. He probably didn't, but I still feel as if he did, so embraced did I feel by the happy relief I noted on his face and by the fact that he didn't punish me at all, but seemed, instead, pleased with me. I think it was at that moment that I resolved to take my chances with the truth, although as the years rolled on I was to break more serious things in his scheme of things than fruit jars. 9

It was the unfairness of the beating that keeps it fresh in my mind. (And this was thirty-seven years ago!) And my disappointment at the deterioration of my father's ethics. And yet, since I am never happy in my heart when estranged from my father, any more than I would be happy shut off from sunlight, in writing this particular poem I tried to see my father's behavior in a context larger than our personal relationship. 10

Actually, my father was two fathers. 11

To the first four of his children he was one kind of father, to the second set of four he was another kind. Whenever I talk to the elder set I 12 am astonished at the picture they draw, for the man they describe bears little resemblance to the man I knew. For one thing, the man they knew was physically healthy, whereas the man I knew was almost always sick; not sick enough to be in bed, or perhaps he was but with so many children to feed he couldn't afford to lie down, but "dragging-around" sick, in the manner of the very poor. Overweight, high blood pressure, diabetes, or, as it was called, "sugar," rotten teeth. There are certain *facts*, however, that identify our father as the same man; one of which is that, in the 1930s, my father was one of the first black men to vote in Eatonton, Georgia, among a group of men like himself he helped organize, mainly poor sharecroppers with large families, totally at the mercy of the white landlords. He voted for Roosevelt. He was one of the leading supporters of the local one-room black school, and according to everyone who knew him then, including my older brothers and sister, believed in education above all else. Years later, when I knew him, he seemed fearful of both education and politics and disappointed and resentful as well.

And why not? Though he risked his life and livelihood to vote more than once, nothing much changed in his world. Cotton prices continued low. Dairying was hard. White men and women continued to run things, badly. In his whole life my father never had a vacation. (Of course my mother had less of one: she could not even get in the car and drive off to town, as he could.) Education merely seemed to make his children more critical of him. When I went south in the mid-sixties to help register voters, I stopped by our house to say hello but never told either of my parents what I planned to do. I didn't want them to worry about my safety, and it never occurred to me that they cared much about the vote. My father was visibly ill, paranoid, complaining the whole time of my mother's religious activities (she had become a Jehovah's Witness). Then, for no apparent reason, he would come out with one of those startlingly intelligent comments about world affairs or some absolutely clear insight into the deficiencies of national leaders, and I would be reminded of the father I didn't know. 13

For years I have held on to another early memory of my life between the ages of two and four. Every afternoon a tired but jolly very black man came up to me with arms outstretched. I flew into them to be carried, to be hugged, to be kissed. For years I thought this black man was my father. But no. He was my oldest brother, Fred, whose memories of my father are, surprisingly, as painful as *my* memories of him, because as my father's first child, and a son, he was subjected to my father's very confused notions of what constituted behavior suitable for a male. And of course my father himself didn't really know. He was in his late teens, a 14 child himself, when he married. His mother had been murdered, by a man who claimed to love her, when he was eleven. His father, to put it very politely, drank, and terrorized his children.

My father was so confused that when my sister Ruth appeared in   15
the world and physically resembled his mother, and sounded like his mother, and had similar expressions, he rejected her and missed no opportunity that I ever saw to put her down. I, of course, took the side of my sister, forfeiting my chance to be my father's favorite among the second set of children, as my oldest sister, Mamie, was favorite among the first. In her case the favoritism seemed outwardly caused by her very light color, and of course she was remarkably intelligent as well. In my case, my father seemed partial to me because of my "smartness" and forthrightness, but more obviously because of my hair, which was the longest and "best" in the family.

And yet, my father taught me two things that have been important   16
to me: he taught me not to bother telling lies, because the listener might be delighted with the truth, and he told me never to cut my hair. Though I have tried not to lie, the sister he rejected and I loved became a beautician, and one of the first things she did—partly in defiance of him— was to cut my shoulder-blade-length hair. I did not regret it so much while in high school and college (everyone kept their hair short, it seemed), but years later, after I married, I grew it long again, almost as long as it had been when I was growing up. I'd had it relaxed to feathers. When I walked up to my father, as he was talking to a neighbor, I stooped a little and placed his hand on my head. I thought he'd be pleased. "A woman's hair is her glory," he'd always said. He paid little attention. When the black power movement arrived, with its emphasis on cropped natural hair, I did the job myself, filling the face bowl and bathroom floor with hair and shocking my husband when he arrived home.

Only recently have I come to believe he was right in wanting me to   17
keep my hair. After years of short hair, of cutting my hair back each time it raised its head, so to speak, I have begun to feel each time as if I am mutilating my antennae (which is how Rastafarians, among others, think of hair) and attenuating my power. It seems imperative not to cut my hair anymore.

I didn't listen to my father because I assumed he meant that in the   18
eyes of a *man*, in his eyes, a woman's hair is her glory (unfortunately, he wore his own head absolutely cleanshaven all his life); and that is probably what he did mean. But now I begin to sense something else, that

there is power (would an ancient translation of glory *be* power?) in uncut hair itself. The power (and glory) perhaps of the untamed, the undomesticated; in short, the wild. A wildness about the head, as the Rastas have discovered, places us somehow in the loose and spacious freedom of Jah's universe. Hippies, of course, knew this, too.

As I write, my own hair reaches just below my ears. It is at the dangerous stage at which I usually butt my forehead against the mirror and in resignation over not knowing "what to do with it" cut it off. But this time I have thought ahead and have encased it in braids made of someone else's hair. I expect to wear them, braces for the hair, so to speak, until my own hair replaces them. Eventually I will be able, as I was when a child, to tie my hair under my chin. But mostly I would like to set it free. [19]

My father would have loved Jesse Jackson. On the night Jesse addressed the Democratic convention I stayed close to my radio. In my backwoods cabin, linked to the world only by radio, I felt something like my father must have, since he lived most of his life before television and far from towns. He would have appreciated Jesse's oratorical gift, and, unlike some newscasters who seemed to think of it primarily as technique, he would have felt, as I did, the transformation of the spirit of the man implicit in the words he chose to say. He would have felt, as I did, that in asking for forgiveness as well as votes and for patience as well as commitment to the Democratic party, Jackson lost nothing and won almost everything: a cleared conscience and peace of mind. [20]

My father was never able to vote for a black candidate for any national or local political office. By the time black people were running for office and occasionally winning elections, in the late sixties and early seventies, he was too sick to respond with the exhilaration he must have felt. On the night of Jackson's speech, I felt it for him; along with the grief that in neither of our lifetimes is the United States likely to choose the best leadership offered to it. This is the kind of leader, the kind of ever-growing, ever-expanding spirit *you* might have been, Daddy, I thought— and damn it, I love you for what you might have been. And thinking of you now, merging the two fathers that you were, remembering how tightly I hugged you as a small child returning home after two long months at a favorite aunt's, and with what apparent joy you lifted me beside your cheek; knowing now, at forty, what it takes out of body and spirit to go and how much more to stay, and having learned, too, by now, some of the pitiful confusions in behavior caused by ignorance and pain, I love you no less for what you were. [21]

RESPONDING TO "FATHER"

Freewrite about a parent, a grandparent, or a significant older relative whose ideas were different from yours but who, nevertheless, influenced you when you were growing up.

Responding through Interpretation

1. In your reading journal, briefly characterize Walker's "two fathers." What has she learned from the two men who make up her father?
2. How did Alice Walker's relationship with her father influence her choice of a husband and other decisions about relationships?
3. What does Walker's hair represent in the essay? How does her attitude toward her hair change over time?

Responding through Discussion

1. Discuss with your group a relative about whom you have strong feelings. Trace the process of your relationship with this relative and highlight some of the stages it has passed through. What is the status of your relationship with that person now?
2. Spend some time in the group brainstorming about important images from your childhood that stick in your mind—images that are connected with one of your relatives or caregivers. Allow time for each member to share his or her most vivid image and to explain why it is important.

Responding through Writing

1. Take one of the images you came up with in the group discussion and write a journal entry describing every detail of it that you can remember. Close your eyes and go back into the memory in order to recapture details and feelings you had when you were a child. After describing the event or image, write about what it has meant to you throughout your life.
2. Write an essay in which you describe your relationship with a parent or parent figure who has influenced your life. Show how this relationship has progressed over the years. What have you learned about yourself through this relationship?

My Dad and Walker's "Father"

Beverley Skinner

A native and current resident of Alameda, California, Beverley Skinner has raised four children and is now a grandmother. She is a returning student in evening school, currently majoring in business administration. The following essay, written for her English class, compares Skinner's own attempts to understand her father with those of Alice Walker.

I felt myself shiver as I read the essay "Father," by Alice Walker. While reading it, I realized that my relationship with my father had similarities to Walker's relationship with her father. I agree with Alice Walker's statement that "it is more difficult to write about my father than about my mother." Though my childhood was not particularly good, some of my best memories were of the good times I shared with my father, who was not often home because of his long tours in the Navy. For the first eleven years of my life, I did not realize that problems existed in our family. For the next five or six years I tried to understand my father, and what caused him to become an alcoholic. I idolized the man I thought my father to be, the one I needed. Like Alice Walker, I was not able to accept my father for what he was, understand his pain, and forgive him "until after his death."

Unlike Alice Walker, I was not the last child. Our relationship was not a "casualty of exhaustion and circumstances." There were seven children in our family, and I was my father's first. My first mistake in our relationship was that I was created female instead of male. Consequently, neither my father nor my mother would name me for fear of offending the other. As I grew up, I could never seem to do anything to suit either of my parents. I wanted to dance, but dancing was not acceptable. Dancing lessons cost money, and I would be the one wanting to spend hard-earned money frivolously.

Somehow though, I, again unlike Alice Walker, became "my father's favorite," and my mother's least favorite. Maybe one reason I became his favorite was that, like Walker did with her dad, I "share many of my father's characteristics, physical and otherwise." Sometimes I also think I was favored and disfavored because it gave my parents an outlet for their anger toward each other. My father would do something special for me to get even with my mother, and my mother would

dole out a punishment to me to get even with him. It was difficult trying to please both of them, while staying out of their way and their arguments.

My father, like Walker's, was "two fathers." I like to remember the   4
father who did not drink, who took me to the park to play, who took the
whole family to the drive-in Saturday nights, who cooked Sunday dinner for us, and who watched Gumby with me before he went to work.
I remember that on one hot July day he went out and bought water-
melons for all the kids on our block. We sat outside eating and laughing and challenging my dad to watermelon seed spitting contests. Another time he came home from work and loaded all seven of us kids in
the car and took us to the park to see the Giants play an exhibition game.
I also remember my first trip to the beach; he came home from work hot
and tired, and off we went.

When I was ten, my father fell from the second story of our apart-   5
ment building and sustained head injuries that developed into a brain
tumor. Because of the tumor, he had periods of time that he did not know
who anyone was, including himself. He was quite often violent during
these blackouts. It was about then that I realized he drank too much. This
is when I began to be at "odds with my father," which, like Walker, "in
my heart, I have never wanted to be."

After my father's accident, we spent most of our Saturdays driving   6
to the State Hospital to see him. When he was able to come home from
the hospital, he continued to drink, and his violent attacks became worse.
He never tried to physically hurt me, but he did hurt one of my sisters
and the twins. There were more times when he was drunk and did not
know what he was doing than there were good times. That was the
"other father," the one I had to learn to forgive and love with all his
faults.

Like Alice Walker, "what I regret most about my relationship with   7
my father is that it did not improve until after his death." I was thirteen
years old the last time I saw him; he died just after my twenty-second
birthday. At thirteen I did not understand many things he did, but at
twenty-two I could accept and understand him better. Without all the
complications that life hands out, in different circumstances my father
could have been the best. Behind the alcohol he was a sensitive and caring man. It might have been his sensitivity, in part, which caused the
drinking problem indirectly responsible for the tumor and ultimately for
his death. Daddy, I too "love you for what you might have been," for
what I know in my heart you wanted to be.

RESPONDING TO "MY DAD AND WALKER'S 'FATHER'"

Freewrite about your father's or mother's childhood. What do you know about how either of them grew up?

Responding through Interpretation

1. What similarities does Skinner find between her relationship with her father and Walker's relationship with *her* father?
2. Skinner develops two processes in her essay: the process through which her father gradually deteriorated and her own process of coming to accept him as he "might have been." What do these two processes reveal about her current feelings for her father?

Responding through Discussion

1. As a group, look over Skinner's essay and discuss whether or not you think it is an appropriate response to Walker's essay. What do you see as the strengths and the weaknesses of Skinner's essay?

Responding through Writing

1. Take a brief scene from either Walker's or Skinner's essay and imagine it in full detail. Close your eyes and let your imagination go. Then write a journal entry in which you expand the scene further by using your own imagination.
2. Write a fantasy about your ideal parent—either the kind of parent you would like to have or the kind of parent you would like to be.

Alice Walker's "Father": A Process of Understanding and Acceptance

Shu Fan Lee

A native of Hong Kong, Shu Fan Lee came to the United States as a teenager, settling in San Francisco. He went to several community colleges in the Bay Area before transferring to the University of California. In the following essay Shu Fan Lee analyzes the process of discovery in Alice Walker's "Father" and makes some comparisons with his own evolving relationship with his father, who lived away from his family for a number of years when Shu was growing up.

The essay "Father" by Alice Walker is an exploration of the evolution of 1 her relationship with her father. She felt at odds with him much of her life, but as an adult came to understand and accept him. She writes, "[F]or a long time I felt so shut off from him that we were unable to talk." However, as she frees herself from her negative memories, she begins to see the "other" father whom her older siblings had seen and told her about. Walker's memory of her father is actually a self-examining process that she uses to help release herself from her early, negative judgment of her father. After analyzing the process Walker went through, I was reminded of my own family life and the difficulties I had in accepting my own father, who lived far away from us in Taiwan as I was growing up in China.

Walker claims in the beginning of her essay that "writing about 2 people helps us to understand them." This shows her intention to recount the parent-child relationship she had with her father, even though reliving the relationship might be a bitter process. With the help of a description of her father from her older siblings that contrasted vividly with her own memories, Walker begins to question her initial impression of him. This is a common reevaluation process for adults who have become more mature as they grow older and gain more life experience. A person's own experience with his or her children might act as the catalyst to motivate a person to review the relationship with parents during his or her childhood.

Walker recalls some of the conflicts that she had with her father and 3 tries to put the positive and negative impressions together to make some sense out of her memories of the man. Although it was difficult to do this when she was away at college, in later years, after she has become a parent, the release of her stubbornness allows her to see a more accurate image of why he took certain positions, such as not letting her cut her hair. The negative image of her father gradually fades away as she tries to pull bits and pieces of positive accounts together, forming a more complete vision of her father, in contrast to her narrow and biased early images of him. At last she comes to gain "the father she didn't know."

As she continues to write about him, her search for the real picture of her father seems to become easier. She starts to understand her father's efforts on behalf of civil rights for blacks in America. This allows her to to appreciate her father within a historical perspective as she resolves her inner conflicts about him. Walker becomes more excited as she discovers herself starting to love her father for what he "might have been." The negative impact on her of her father's disillusion and exhaustion gradually washed away. Her effort to relate the "two fathers" she saw in him pays off as the process of reevaluation is completed.   4

It is particularly delightful for me to realize that Walker successfully completes her journey of searching for her "real" father because of a similar problem that I had in searching for an understanding of my own father. My father was estranged from me during most of my childhood since we only met for a few days each year. I remember waiting for him anxiously at the airport when he returned twice a year from Taiwan, where he managed a restaurant. He was such a stranger to me that I did not dare to utter a sound when he appeared at the gate. My father and I failed to communicate with each other through a lack of contact.   5

Just as Walker feels how ethically disoriented her father is after her unfair punishment, I also believed as a child that my father was unable to distinguish between right and wrong in relation to his family. I remember one time when my mother came home from a Mah Jong game and found that my little brother still had not finished his homework. Maybe she had lost in the game, so she punished my brother a little too harshly. My brother cried so loudly that my father went into the kitchen and threw all the dishes onto the floor, breaking them into pieces. He scolded my mother so hard that she ran out of the home crying. I did not know what my mother had done wrong to deserve this kind of scolding, for it was absolutely natural to me that my brother had to be punished for his negligence in not completing his homework. From that experience I came to regard my father as an ethically disoriented person.   6

After reading Walker's "self-therapy" process that came through 7
continuous reassessments of her relationship with her father, I have
come to believe that my father also must have some positive qualities
that have been obscured to me through our lack of contact. I now feel
that the time he scolded my mother so hard was due to the fact that he
loved my brother, and all of us, so much. He only stayed with us for a
brief period of time each year, so it was painful for him to see us quar-
rel. As my mother would say whenever she gave us pocket money from
him, "This is from your father. He supports the whole family without
complaints. You have to understand how lonely he is in Taiwan alone.
Separated from the family. Separated from those he loves."

To pursue more understanding about my father would probably be 8
a process as bitter as what Walker went through. However, to use
Walker's expression: Daddy, damn it—I think it's worth it.

RESPONDING TO "ALICE WALKER'S 'FATHER': A PROCESS OF UNDERSTANDING AND ACCEPTANCE"

Freewrite about a hardship you have seen one of your parents or guardians
go through.

Responding through Interpretation

1. How does Shu Fan Lee's approach to the Walker essay differ from that
   of Beverley Skinner? In what ways is his response similar to hers?
2. Lee devotes most of his essay to analyzing the process that Walker went
   through in coming to understand and accept her father. What stages of
   the process does he point out, and what transitions and topic sentences
   does Lee use to draw attention to these stages?

Responding through Discussion

1. Discuss both Lee's and Skinner's essays in your group. Compare their
   writing styles, their organization, and the material included or omitted,
   and study each essay's weaknesses and strengths. What have you learned
   about writing your own essays from studying these two student essays?

Responding through Writing

1. In your journal, speculate on the forces that might sometimes have kept
   you from communicating honestly with one or both of your parents.
2. Write a paper in which you say to your parents something you wished
   you had said to one or both of them when you were growing up. Don't

be afraid to use humor; even with very serious subjects, humor can be both appealing and informative.

_____

MAKING CONNECTIONS

As you might have realized after reading the pieces in this chapter, family relationships can be complicated and sometimes painful experiences for many people. Certainly our family is one of the most intensely emotional areas of our lives, a confusing puzzle that we may never completely solve. Think back over the selections in this unit and write down one or two ideas that you got from this chapter on family.

1. *The process of rebellion and separation.* Several of the pieces in this unit explore the inclination of children to separate themselves from their family through rebellion and to establish their own independence. Look back at Wright's "Reunion," Walker's "Father," Didion's "On Going Home," and the student essays by Charlie Wu, Beverley Skinner, and Shu Fan Lee. Study some of the parallels in these essays and note what strategies the authors have taken in order to separate themselves from their families. Then write an essay, using your own family as an example if you like, about the pattern of rebellion that is so often a part of the parent-child relationship.

2. *The influence of poverty on family life.* Much has been written by sociologists on the impact of poverty on families. When there is never quite enough to eat, when both parents come home exhausted and unhappy from long workdays, when new opportunities don't exist because the money's not there, then family life can become a rather grim struggle for economic survival. Olsen's short story "I Stand Here Ironing" and Walker's "Father" vividly present families who have suffered because of poverty. Write a paper that explores how these two works depict a family dramatically affected by poverty. You can use references from your own life, as well as references based on observations you've made about others' lives.

3. *Children of immigrant parents.* America is, in John F. Kennedy's words, "a nation of immigrants." Our literature increasingly reflects the experience of being an immigrant or a child of an immigrant to this country. Alberto Alvaro Rios in "Nani" writes about his Spanish grandmother; Amy Tan in "Snapshot" writes about her Chinese mother and grandmother; and Amy Marx in "My Grandfather's Memories" writes about her German-Jewish grandfather. If you grew up in an immigrant family—if either your parents or grandparents

came from another country—write an essay in which you explain the process of cultural change that children of immigrants go through growing up in America. Use your own observations and experiences or perhaps information from your relatives as specific examples.

4. *The positive aspects of family.* Look back through the eleven selections in this chapter and make a note of some of the experiences you find which show the good and inspirational side of living in a family. Write a paper in which you champion the positive aspects of growing up with strong family connections, despite problems, pressures, negative feelings, and so forth.

CHAPTER 5

Gender

Introduction

ELIZABETH CADY STANTON   You Should Have Been a Boy!

SCOTT RUSSELL SANDERS   The Men We Carry in Our Minds . . . and How They Differ from the Real Lives of Most Men

QUYNHCHAU TRAN   The Battle Between Men and Women

GREG MATTHEWS   Indiscriminate Discrimination

MARGE PIERCY   A Work of Artifice

WAKAKO YAMAUCHI   And the Soul Shall Dance

RICK CARY   Coming Out

JULIUS LESTER   Being a Boy

NINA WOODLE   On Being Female

MAGNOLIA TSE   What about Being a Girl?

Making Connections

INTRODUCTION

Journal Entry

Think about a problem you have which seems to be related to your being male or female. Spend some time analyzing whether or not this is a real or an imagined problem. If you were the opposite gender, would the problem change? Write a journal entry explaining this problem and how you might be able to overcome it.

Just as traditional family structures are being challenged and redefined, so also are the gender structures that have supported male and female roles for many centuries. Since the structures have begun to shake loose, we are no longer sure what is truly gender-related and what is habit, convenience, or social constriction. Today we are surrounded by a continuous stream of questions about gender roles—questions that not long ago would never have been even thought of, much less asked:

Who should be the breadwinner in the family?

Who should be the primary caregiver for children?

Which gender should take the lead in asking for dates?

Who should have the final say in making decisions?

Which jobs should be reserved for one gender or the other?

Who controls the money?

What rights do gays, lesbians, and bisexuals have?

In this chapter on gender, you will have an opportunity to examine many of the common dilemmas of gender that people growing up in our society encounter. Elizabeth Cady Stanton, one of the early leaders in the women's rights movement, lived much of her life feeling she had been born the wrong gender. In "You Should Have Been a Boy!" Stanton writes about the struggle she faced in trying to take the place of her deceased brother in her father's life. Scott Sanders in "The Men We Carry in Our Minds . . ." expresses his confusion over society's hostility toward men as being the privileged class and gender when his own life has proved quite the opposite. Rick Cary in "Coming Out" reveals the torments and dilemmas that homosexuals live with from an early age when they are struggling with sexual orientations that don't fit society's pictures. In "Being a Boy" Julius Lester powerfully presents the downside of being a boy and laments the early socialization that forces young girls and boys "into those narrow, constricting cubicles labeled female and male."

Two powerfully poetic pieces, Marge Piercy's poem "A Work of Artifice" and Wakako Yamauchi's "And the Soul Shall Dance," eloquently illuminate the anger and despair—and the twisted lives—that can result when human beings are thwarted by gender roles and societal stereotyping.

The selections in this chapter will give you an opportunity to question your own ingrained gender assumptions. As you read, begin to identify which of your views on gender roles come from within you and your own thinking and which of your views are at least partially derived from society's expectations.

You Should Have Been a Boy!

Elizabeth Cady Stanton

Born in 1815, Elizabeth Cady Stanton was an early leader in the abolitionist movement and the temperance movement; she was also a pioneer in the women's rights and suffrage movement in America. She was educated in Troy, New York, at the Emma Willard Seminary. Stanton is best remembered for her "Declaration of Sentiments" (1848), delivered at the Seneca Falls Convention as a statement of the rights and grievances of women. In the following essay, from her autobiography *Eighty Years and More: Reminiscences 1815–1897*, Stanton reflects on her troubled relationship with her father, a judge, with whom she studied law for some years.

When I was eleven years old, two events occurred which changed   1
considerably the current of my life. My only brother, who had just
graduated from Union College, came home to die. A young man of great
talent and promise, he was the pride of my father's heart. We early felt
that this son filled a larger place in our father's affections and future
plans than the five daughters together. Well do I remember how tenderly
he watched my brother in his last illness, the sighs and tears he gave vent
to as he slowly walked up and down the hall, and, when the last sad
moment came, and we were all assembled to say farewell in the silent
chamber of death, how broken were his utterances as he knelt and
prayed for comfort and support. I still recall, too, going into the large
darkened parlor to see my brother, and finding the casket, mirrors, and
pictures all draped in white, and my father seated by his side, pale and
immovable. As he took no notice of me, after standing a long while, I
climbed upon his knee, when he mechanically put his arm about me and,
with my head resting against his beating heart, we both sat in silence,
he thinking of the wreck of all his hopes in the loss of a dear son, and I
wondering what could be said or done to fill the void in his breast. At
length he heaved a deep sigh and said: "Oh, my daughter, I wish you
were a boy!" Throwing my arms about his neck, I replied: "I will try to
be all my brother was."

Then and there I resolved that I would not give so much time as   2
heretofore to play, but would study and strive to be at the head of all
my classes and thus delight my father's heart. All that day and far into
the night I pondered the problem of boyhood. I thought that the chief
thing to be done in order to equal boys was to be learned and coura-

geous. So I decided to study Greek and learn to manage a horse. Having formed this conclusion I fell asleep. My resolutions, unlike many such made at night, did not vanish with the coming light. I arose early and hastened to put them into execution. They were resolutions never to be forgotten—destined to mold my character anew. As soon as I was dressed I hastened to our good pastor, Rev. Simon Hosack, who was always early at work in his garden.

"Doctor," said I, "which do you like best, boys or girls?"   3

"Why, girls, to be sure; I would not give you for all the boys in   4
Christendom."

"My father," I replied, "prefers boys; he wishes I was one, and I intend to be as near like one as possible. I am going to ride on horseback and study Greek. Will you give me a Greek lesson now, doctor? I want to begin at once."   5

"Yes, child," said he, throwing down his hoe, "come into my library   6
and we will begin without delay."

He entered fully into the feeling of suffering and sorrow which took   7
possession of me when I discovered that a girl weighed less in the scale of being than a boy, and he praised my determination to prove the contrary. The old grammar which he had studied in the University of Glasgow was soon in my hands, and the Greek article was learned before breakfast.

Then came the sad pageantry of death, the weeping of friends, the   8
dark rooms, the ghostly stillness, the exhortation to the living to prepare for death, the solemn prayer, the mournful chant, the funeral cortège, the solemn, tolling bell, the burial. How I suffered during those sad days! What strange undefined fears of the unknown took possession of me! For months afterward, at the twilight hour, I went with my father to the new-made grave. Near it stood two tall poplar trees, against one of which I leaned, while my father threw himself on the grave, with outstretched arms, as if to embrace his child. At last the frosts and storms of November came and threw a chilling barrier between the living and the dead, and we went there no more.

During all this time I kept up my lessons at the parsonage and made   9
rapid progress. I surprised even my teacher, who thought me capable of doing anything. I learned to drive, and to leap a fence and ditch on horseback. I taxed every power, hoping some day to hear my father say: "Well, a girl is as good as a boy, after all." But he never said it. When the doctor came over to spend the evening with us, I would whisper in his ear: "Tell my father how fast I get on," and he would tell him, and was lavish in his praises. But my father only paced the room, sighed, and

showed that he wished I were a boy; and I, not knowing why he felt thus, would hide my tears of vexation on the doctor's shoulder.

Soon after this I began to study Latin, Greek, and mathematics with a class of boys in the Academy, many of whom were much older than I. For three years one boy kept his place at the head of the class, and I always stood next. Two prizes were offered in Greek. I strove for one and took the second. How well I remember my joy in receiving that prize. There was no sentiment of ambition, rivalry, or triumph over my companions, nor feeling of satisfaction in receiving this honor in the presence of those assembled on the day of the exhibition. One thought alone filled my mind. "Now," said I, "my father will be satisfied with me." So, as soon as we were dismissed, I ran down the hill, rushed breathless into his office, laid the new Greek Testament, which was my prize, on his table and exclaimed: "There, I got it!" He took up the book, asked me some questions about the class, the teachers, the spectators, and evidently pleased, handed it back to me. Then, while I stood looking and waiting for him to say something which would show that he recognized the equality of the daughter with the son, he kissed me on the forehead and exclaimed, with a sigh, "Ah, you should have been a boy!"

RESPONDING TO "YOU SHOULD HAVE BEEN A BOY!"

Freewrite about how you think being born male or female has been accepted in your family.

Responding through Interpretation

1. Notice how Stanton repeats and varies the idea of the title "You Should Have Been a Boy!" throughout the essay. Make a list of the different ways she states this idea. What does this repetition contribute to the effectiveness of the essay?
2. What evidence does the author use to show how devastated her father is at the loss of his son?
3. Imagine Stanton ten years later, at the age of twenty-one. In your reading journal, write a description of the kind of woman you think she became. Support your opinions with evidence from the essay.

Responding through Discussion

1. As a group, discuss whether or not you think that fathers today still consider daughters as less important than sons. Share your group's views with the class as a whole.

2. Carry the previous discussion further: Brainstorm together about when, where, and how the preference for male children began. Then do some reading about the topic. Discuss how the effects of this attitude are still seen in our country today.

Responding through Writing

1. Think back to your own early childhood and the kind of acceptance you feel you received from your parents and relatives. Then write a journal entry about how you were treated in comparison to your siblings or cousins of the opposite sex.

2. Sometimes young boys and girls find inspiration and encouragement from a friend of the family, as Stanton did with Reverend Hosack. Write an essay about an adult—such as a relative, family friend, teacher, coach—who made you feel special when you were a child.

The Men We Carry in Our Minds . . . and How They Differ from the Real Lives of Most Men

Scott Russell Sanders

Sanders grew up in poverty in rural Tennessee and Ohio. He is a social activist and writer who has written on peace, environmentalism, family, and male/female relationships. The following essay, which appeared originally in *Milkweek Chronicle* in 1984, was reprinted in Sanders's book of essays, *Paradise of Bombs* (1987). In "The Men We Carry in Our Minds . . .," Sanders examines some of the negative and damaging stereotypes of males which society holds.

This must be a hard time for women," I say to my friend Anneke. "They 1 have so many paths to choose from, and so many voices calling them."

"I think it's a lot harder for men," she replies. 2

"How do you figure that?" 3

"The women I know feel excited, innocent, like crusaders in a just 4 cause. The men I know are eaten up with guilt."

"Women feel such pressure to be everything, do everything," I say. 5 "Career, kids, art, politics. Have their babies and get back to the office a week later. It's as if they're trying to overcome a million years' worth of evolution in one lifetime."

"But we help one another. And we have this deep-down sense that 6 we're in the *right*—we've been held back, passed over, used—while men feel they're in the wrong. Men are the ones who've been discredited, who have to search their souls."

I search my soul. I discover guilty feelings aplenty—toward the 7 poor, the Vietnamese, Native Americans, the whales, an endless list of debts. But toward women I feel something more confused, a snarl of shame, envy, wary tenderness, and amazement. This muddle troubles me. To hide my unease I say, "You're right, it's tough being a man these days."

"Don't laugh," Anneke frowns at me. "I wouldn't be a man for any- 8 thing. It's much easier being the victim. All the victim has to do is break free. The persecutor has to live with his past."

How deep is that past? I find myself wondering. How much of an 9 inheritance do I have to throw off?

When I was a boy growing up on the back roads of Tennessee and   10
Ohio, the men I knew labored with their bodies. They were marginal
farmers, just scraping by, or welders, steelworkers, carpenters; they
swept floors, dug ditches, mined coal, or drove trucks, their forearms
ropy with muscle; they trained horses, stoked furnaces, made tires, stood
on assembly lines wrestling parts onto cars and refrigerators. They got
up before light, worked all day long whatever the weather, and when
they came home at night they looked as though somebody had been
whipping them. In the evenings and on weekends they worked on their
own places, tilling gardens that were lumpy with clay, fixing broken-
down cars, hammering on houses that were always too drafty, too leaky,
too small.

The bodies of the men I knew were twisted and maimed in ways vis-   11
ible and invisible. The nails of their hands were black and split, the
hands tattooed with scars. Some had lost fingers. Heavy lifting had
given many of them finicky backs and guts weak from hernias. Racing
against conveyor belts had given them ulcers. Their ankles and knees
ached from years of standing on concrete. Anyone who had worked for
long around machines was hard of hearing. They squinted, and the skin
of their faces was creased like the leather of old work gloves. There were
times, studying them, when I dreaded growing up. Most of them
coughed, from dust or cigarettes, and most of them drank cheap wine
or whiskey, so their eyes looked bloodshot and bruised. The fathers of
my friends always seemed older than the mothers. Men wore out sooner.
Only women lived into old age.

As a boy I also knew another sort of men, who did not sweat and   12
break down like mules. They were soldiers, and so far as I could tell they
scarcely worked at all. But when the shooting started, many of them
would die. This was what soldiers were *for,* just as a hammer was for
driving nails.

Warriors and toilers: these seemed, in my boyhood vision, to be the   13
chief destinies for men. They weren't the only destinies, as I learned from
having a few male teachers, from reading books, and from watching television. But the men on television—the politicians, the astronauts, the
generals, the savvy lawyers, the philosophical doctors, the bosses who
gave orders to both soldiers and laborers—seemed as remote and un-
real to me as the figures in Renaissance tapestries. I could no more imagine growing up to become one of these cool, potent creatures than I
could imagine becoming a prince.

A nearer and more hopeful example was that of my father, who had   14
escaped from a red-dirt farm to a tire factory, and from the assembly line

to the front office. Eventually he dressed in a white shirt and tie. He carried himself as if he had been born to work with his mind. But his body, remembering the earlier years of slogging work, began to give out on him in his fifties, and it quit on him entirely before he turned 65.

A scholarship enabled me not only to attend college, a rare enough feat in my circle, but even to study in a university meant for the children of the rich. Here I met for the first time young men who had assumed from birth that they would lead lives of comfort and power. And for the first time I met women who told me that men were guilty of having kept all the joys and privileges of the earth for themselves. I was baffled. What privileges? What joys? I thought about the maimed, dismal lives of most of the men back home. What had they stolen from their wives and daughters? The right to go five days a week, 12 months a year, for 30 or 40 years to a steel mill or a coal mine? The right to drop bombs and die in war? The right to feel every leak in the roof, every gap in the fence, every cough in the engine as a wound they must mend? The right to feel, when the layoff comes or the plant shuts down, not only afraid but ashamed? 15

I was slow to understand the deep grievances of women. This was because, as a boy, I had envied them. Before college, the only people I had ever known who were interested in art or music or literature, the only ones who read books, the only ones who ever seemed to enjoy a sense of ease and grace were the mothers and daughters. Like the menfolk, they fretted about money, they scrimped and made do. But, when the pay stopped coming in, they were not the ones who had failed. Nor did they have to go to war, and that seemed to me a blessed fact. By comparison with the narrow, ironclad days of fathers, there was an expansiveness, I thought, in the days of mothers. They went to see neighbors, to shop in town, to run errands at school, at the library, at church. No doubt, had I looked harder at their lives, I would have envied them less. It was not my fate to become a woman, so it was easier for me to see the graces. I didn't see, then, what a prison a house could be, since houses seemed to me brighter, handsomer places than any factory. I did not realize—because such things were never spoken of—how often women suffered from men's bullying. Even then I could see how exhausting it was for a mother to cater all day to the needs of young children. But if I had been asked, as a boy, to choose between tending a baby and tending a machine, I think I would have chosen the baby. (Having now tended both, I know I would choose the baby.) 16

So I was baffled when the women at college accused me and my sex of having cornered the world's pleasures. I think something like my bafflement has been felt by other boys (and by girls as well) who grew up 17 in dirt-poor farm country, in mining country, in black ghettos, in Hispanic barrios, in the shadows of factories, in Third World nations—any place where the fate of men is just as grim and bleak as the fate of women.

When the women I met at college thought about the joys and privileges of men, they did not carry in their minds the sort of men I had known in my childhood. They thought of their fathers, who were bankers, physicians, architects, stockbrokers, the big wheels of the big cities. They were never laid off, never short of cash at month's end, never lined up for welfare. These fathers made decisions that mattered. They ran the world.   18

The daughters of such men wanted to share in this power, this glory. So did I. They yearned for a say over their future, for jobs worthy of their abilities, for the right to live at peace, unmolested, whole. Yes, I thought, yes yes. The difference between me and these daughters was that they saw me, because of my sex, as destined from birth to become like their fathers, and therefore as an enemy to their desires. But I knew better. I wasn't an enemy, in fact or in feeling. I was an ally. If I had known, then, how to tell them so, would they have believed me? Would they now?   19

RESPONDING TO "THE MEN WE CARRY IN OUR MINDS . . ."

Freewrite about whether you think it is more difficult to be a man or a woman living in today's world.

Responding through Interpretation

1. What are the two types of men that influenced Sanders as he was growing up? Why didn't the images of men in books and on television influence him?
2. Why does Sanders feel that most poor, working-class men would be "baffled" by the accusations made by the women he met at college? Do you agree or disagree with him?
3. Look through the essay and make note of several images and comparisons that Sanders uses which you think are especially vivid and accurate.

Responding through Discussion

1. Discuss what it was like being a male or a female in your family. You can bring in your perceptions about how it was for your siblings and your parents if that seems relevant to your own experience.

2. Take a look at how you feel the media have influenced your own ideas about males and females. Allow time for all group members to contribute some of the images from media (television, movies, advertising, etc.) which they feel have had an impact on shaping the way they view males and females.

Responding through Writing

1. Sanders says: "The only ones who ever seemed to enjoy a sense of ease and grace were the mothers and daughters." Write a journal entry that responds to Sanders's statement—do you agree with him?
2. How do your ideas about men compare with those of Sanders? How would these ideas be different if you were the opposite gender or from a different social class? Write a paper in which you agree or disagree with Sanders's views of gender differences and expectations, using examples and observations from your own experience to support your position.

The Battle between Men and Women

Quynhchau Tran

Quynhchau Tran is the daughter of Vietnamese parents and feels she is very lucky to have grown up in America where there is more social equality for women. She attended DeAnza College and wrote the following essay for her freshman composition class in response to an assignment that asked her to report on what she has learned about women's roles in Vietnam.

There is a Vietnamese saying which goes like this: "If a girl stays at   1
home, she ought to respect her father; if she is married, she has to obey her husband; and if her husband dies, she is subject to listen to her son." To Americans and other people in developed societies, this saying may seem out of date. However, in Vietnam, it still reflects women's roles in society particularly—and in the world generally. From inside the house to outside in the world, from all walks of life to specific professional fields, women's positions in Vietnam are clearly defined as one step behind men. Vietnamese women have been limited by these stereotypes for years, and only recently have they begun to struggle to gain equal rights with men.

Several decades ago, women's status in Vietnam was considered   2
much lower than that of men. My grandmother's life is a good illustration of the status of women as compared with the status of men of her time. She was born in a small village in Vietnam in 1910. Her parents had four children, and she was the only girl in the family. When her brothers and she grew up, her father prepared a very good education for all his children—except her. He told her that because she was a girl, education was not important. She had to stay home and help her mother to take care of the house by cooking and sewing, he told her, and then when she matured, she would get married.

My grandmother acted like a servant both for her parents and then   3
later for her husband and her family. She had no right to argue with her husband over anything. My grandmother told me that the worst thing in her life was that she couldn't write or read, but she had to accept her life as it was. At that time, people recognized the inferior position of women in Vietnam, and this position was firmly established. During my grandmother's days, instead of revolting, women accepted the way things were without complaining. I think society strongly affected peo-

ple's attitudes. As modern values have influenced Vietnam in more recent years, people have opened their minds and women's roles have
been gradually changing.

For example, my mother's life was much better than my grand-   4
mother's. My mother was allowed to go to school like the boys, and she
had the opportunity to show her intelligence in her studies. She was always the top one in her classes. Moreover, my mother had a special ability in drawing, and she dreamed she would be an architect. She told my
grandfather about her dream, and my grandfather was very surprised.
He couldn't believe what my mother said. In his mind, women shouldn't
have a dream like that. According to him, women should dream about
a family with a good husband and children rather than dreaming of becoming an architect or an engineer. Jobs like these were not popular for
women in Vietnam.

As we see, stereotypes strongly affected my mother when she was   5
growing up in Vietnam. These stereotypes became a barrier for her and
stopped her from achieving her dream. But she didn't give up completely. My grandfather didn't allow her to attend college; however, my
mother refused to give up and struggled with my grandfather and with
the social stereotypes. She argued that women and men do not have any
different level of intelligence quotient. Therefore, why can't women obtain as equal an opportunity in their lives as men? Eventually, instead
of obeying my grandfather by staying home and getting married, my
mother decided to go to college without my grandfather's permission.
She had to leave her house to live on campus in order to attend college.
After four years, she got a BA degree and worked in one of the most famous companies in Vietnam. Because of my mother's courage, my
grandfather has changed his way of evaluating women. Nowadays,
Vietnamese women's roles have changed greatly. Women participate in
fields which were only for men before—such as science, engineering, and
politics. In order to gain this high position in society, they had to struggle against stereotypes that have been a part of the minds of the Vietnamese people for centuries.

I am a lucky woman to live in America where women and men   6
have equal rights. I can choose whatever major that I am interested in.
I have many freedoms and the opportunity to show my abilities without being afraid of stereotypes. I remember last year when I told my
mother that I had decided to major in civil engineering, she smiled and
smoothed my hair and said: "You can choose whatever you want if you
have enough ability to achieve it and the important thing is you have to
enjoy it." I was very happy when I heard my mother's advice. I thought

that if my grandfather heard about my dream, he would react differently from the way my mother did.

Today, in America, men and women can participate in any field   7
without having to distinguish between the ones for men and the ones for women. I think that when society becomes more developed, then the stereotype itself will disappear and men and women all over the world will have access to the same positions.

RESPONDING TO "THE BATTLE BETWEEN MEN AND WOMEN"

Freewrite about some of the changes you are aware of in women's roles from your mother's generation to your own.

Responding through Interpretation

1. What was the Vietnamese attitude about women's roles when Tran's grandmother grew up? How has it changed? Does Tran present a consistent view concerning this matter?
2. Tran develops her essay with illustrations from her own experiences. Which details do you find the most vivid?.

Responding through Discussion

1. With your group, jot down some of the details you know about how women are treated in different cultures. In your discussion, let each member contribute what he or she knows, either firsthand or through reading, about some of the practices and attitudes toward women in other countries. Bring your findings back to the class as a whole.

Responding through Writing

1. In your journal, write a response to Tran's essay. How do you imagine her grandmother's life to have been? Her mother's? Using evidence from Tran's essay, describe what you think Tran's life as a woman will be like in this country.
2. Women have traditionally been undereducated and underprepared for employment as compared with men. Write a paper in which you express your opinion about whether or not women should receive an education equal to men's. Do women need an education as much as men do? What if some women don't work outside the home—will their education be wasted? Support your ideas with information from outside sources when necessary.

Indiscriminate Discrimination

Greg Matthews

Born in Oakland, California, Greg Matthews has lived his entire life in the San Francisco Bay Area. Coaching swimming has been a positive experience that has led Greg to think of himself as a teacher; he plans to get teaching certification and to become a mathematics instructor. Greg's biggest problem with writing is getting started; although an excellent student in his other classes, he entered his college composition class with a strong case of "writing phobia," which he has worked hard to overcome through freewriting and journal keeping. Greg Matthews wrote the following essay in response to the question, "Do you believe that men are discriminated against in our society?"

When I hear people talk about sexual discrimination, I immediately think of a woman being oppressed by a man in some way. However, today some men are making their own claims of sexual discrimination. In the workplace some men argue that they are being denied promotions so that some women may be promoted to meet quotas for gender equality. In physically demanding jobs, such as those of police officers and firefighters, some men feel that less qualified women are given hiring preferences for reasons of gender-based quotas. Male athletes in high school and college also complain about the way that some men's sports have been cut back or discontinued, while new women's athletic programs have been added at many schools. Although the three examples mentioned above may appear to be cases of male gender discrimination, in practice, the examples are not as simple and clear-cut as they might appear.

In the first example the claim is that a less qualified woman gets promoted ahead of a more qualified man. Usually, when I hear a statement like this, it comes from the individual, or a close friend of his, who has been passed up for the promotion. This being true, I would have to consider the possibility that there is some bias to the claims. When you don't get something that you expect to get, it is normal to place the blame on somebody else. Although businesses are not going to promote totally unqualified people, they may, for their own reasons, hire someone who appears to be a less qualified person. However, what appears to be true and what is true are often two different things.

Imagine that a newspaper company is interviewing several writers for a new column. The final round of interviews contains several experienced, highly regarded male writers and a few talented but not so well-known female writers. The newspaper ends up selecting one of the female writers. One male writer feels discriminated against, so he inquires as to the basis for the final decision. The interviewers on the panel explain that they wanted the column written from a female perspective to reach more of their female readers. In this example, a particular well-known male writer may have been superior to his female competitors in some respects of his craft, but he was not the best choice given the specific circumstances of the available position.

Let's take another imaginary example. In this case, some men feel   4
they are unfairly discriminated against in the hiring of new police and firefighter cadets. In these two professions, individuals who try out for the available positions are subjected to rigorous physical tests and are given oral examinations as well. The men lodge a complaint because they are certain that they outperformed the female candidates on the physical tests because of superior strength and endurance. However, equality quotas may not have been the only reason some women were chosen over male applicants; the women may have done substantially better on the oral examinations, making them stand out despite somewhat lower performance on physical-based tests. In the life and death situations modern police and firefighters must face, intelligence, mastery of technology, resourcefulness, and empathy are sometimes more important than sheer muscle power.

In the third case involving male sports programs, most of the recent   5
cutbacks in male sports, particularly football, have been made due to budgetary restraints. These cutbacks have angered male athletes and coaches, who feel that it is unfair to cut their programs while leaving women's sports untouched or while even adding more female athletic competitions. However, the reality is that at almost all schools there are fewer female sports programs than there are male sports, and the average budget for individual female sports is considerably lower than the budget for their male equivalents. In a case when the athletic budget is severely limited, it seems only fair to make cuts which tend to provide more equity between male and female athletic programs. Cutting one very expensive sport such as the typically all-male football program, for example, might allow for the creation of two lower-cost female competitive sports and still result in a net savings for the institution.

In conclusion, I believe that the opportunity does exist today for men   6
to be discriminated against in hiring and in certain areas of education, but not at a significant enough level to raise alarm. Any sincerely believed and substantiated claim of male discrimination should be taken

seriously by affirmative action officials, just as any such claim should be taken seriously if filed by a member of any other group. However, the more common complaints by males today are more like those discussed in the body of this essay: matters of chance and necessary change, rather than systematic discrimination.

RESPONDING TO "INDISCRIMINATE DISCRIMINATION"

Freewrite about a case of male discrimination that you have read or heard about, witnessed, or personally experienced.

Responding through Interpretation

1. The essay begins with a brief listing of situations in which males have claimed sexual discrimination. How does Matthews use the situations he lists in his introduction to develop in the body of his paper his critique of male claims of discrimination?
2. Greg Matthews uses examples that are "hypothetical." He acknowledges these hypothetical examples by such transitions as "let's take another imaginary example." Do the hypothetical situations he provides seem logical? Do they create strong and relevant support for his main points? Why or why not?

Responding through Discussion

1. Working in groups that are equally balanced, if possible, with males and females, discuss the issue of discrimination against males. Make note of any actual cases of such discrimination, no matter how seemingly insignificant, that members have personally witnessed or experienced, either at school, at work, or elsewhere in society. Each group should report back to the entire class on its findings.

Responding through Writing

1. Write an essay in which you argue either for or against the position that Matthews takes in his essay on the prevalence of male discrimination, providing examples from your own experience, from reading, or from the stories shared in class discussion by other students.
2. Write a narrative essay about an instance in which you witnessed, participated in, or were a victim of male discrimination. Include major steps or stages in the discrimination involved, and describe your responses, both immediate and long term.

A Work of Artifice

Marge Piercy

Originally from Detroit, Michigan, Marge Piercy is the author of many novels, poems, and stories as well as an advocate of social and environmental change. Piercy often writes on gender-related issues. Her most recent novel is *The Longings of Women* (1994). The following poem, "A Work of Artifice" from *Circles in the Water* (1982), uses an image of a bonsai, a tree that is trimmed to deliberately keep it small, to make a comment on the way society limits women by imposing rigid images and standards on them.

The bonsai tree
in the attractive pot
could have grown eighty feet tall
on the side of a mountain
till split by lightning.   5
But a gardener
carefully pruned it.
It is nine inches high.
Every day as he
whittles back the branches   10
the gardener croons,
It is your nature
to be small and cozy,
domestic and weak;
how lucky, little tree,   15
to have a pot to grow in.
With living creatures
one must begin very early
to dwarf their growth:
the bound feet,   20
the crippled brain,
the hair in curlers,
the hands you
love to touch.

RESPONDING TO "A WORK OF ARTIFICE"

Freewrite about a "typical" physical or mental quality, ascribed to either men or women, that you believe is socially—rather than biologically—created.

Responding through Interpretation

1. The gardener carefully prunes the little tree, keeping it small. Why? What *could* have been the fate of the tree?
2. What is implied by the last two lines of the poem, "The hands you/love to touch"? Why do you think that the author uses words from an advertising slogan for dish soap ("Palmolive. For the hands you love to touch") as the basis for her poem's conclusion?
3. What does the title add to the poem? What relationship do you see between the title and the text of the poem?

Responding through Discussion

1. Get together with your group and leaf through a few current magazines. Point out product advertisements that seem to define or accentuate gender-role characteristics. Share your findings with the rest of the class.
2. Brainstorm within your group to come up with examples of ways that both men and women may be "stunted" or limited in their physical and mental potential by social roles and standards. Think of some of the "pots" that determine the way people grow.

Responding through Writing

1. In your journal, write your response to what is a "proper" appearance and/or behavior for males or females. What would it be like if society set no norms at all for how women and men should look and act as representative members of their gender group?
2. Write an essay in which you compare several kinds of limits placed on males and females. For which gender, if either, do the limits imposed seem most rigid and confining?

And the Soul Shall Dance

Wakako Yamauchi

Like the narrator in the following story, Wakako Yamauchi is a Japanese American who grew up on a farm in California's Imperial Valley. During the 1940s, her family was interned with many other Japanese Americans at a concentration camp. Yamauchi started writing late in life, and has seen success with stories such as "Surviving the Wasteland Years" (1988) and "Maybe" (1988). Her stories and plays are collected in *Songs My Mother Taught Me* (1994). "And the Soul Shall Dance" deals with the impact of an immigrant woman's alcoholism on her own health and on the well-being of her family.

It's all right to talk about it now. Most of the principals are dead, except, of course, me and my younger brother, and possibly Kiyoko Oka, who might be near forty-five now, because, yes, I'm sure of it, she was fourteen then. I was nine, and my brother about four, so he hardly counts at all. Kiyoko's mother is dead, my father is dead, my mother is dead, and her father could not have lasted all these years with his tremendous appetite for alcohol and pickled chilies—those little yellow ones, so hot they could make your mouth hurt; he'd eat them like peanuts and tears would surge from his bulging thyroid eyes in great waves and stream down the dark coarse terrain of his face.

My father farmed then in the desert basin resolutely named Imperial Valley, in the township called Westmoreland; twenty acres of tomatoes, ten of summer squash, or vice versa, and the Okas lived maybe a mile, mile and a half, across an alkaline road, a stretch of greasewood, tumbleweed and white sand, to the south of us. We didn't hobnob much with them, because you see, they were a childless couple and we were a family: father, mother, daughter, and son, and we went to the Buddhist church on Sundays where my mother taught Japanese, and the Okas kept pretty much to themselves. I don't mean they were unfriendly; Mr. Oka would sometimes walk over (he rarely drove) on rainy days, all dripping wet, short and squat under a soggy newspaper, pretending to need a plow-blade or a file, and he would spend the afternoon in our kitchen drinking sake and eating chilies with my father. As he got progressively drunker, his large mouth would draw down and with the stream of tears, he looked like a kindly weeping bullfrog.

Not only were they childless, impractical in an area where large fam- 3
ilies were looked upon as labor potentials, but there was a certain
strangeness about them. I became aware of it the summer our bathhouse burned down, and my father didn't get right down to building
another, and a Japanese without a bathhouse . . . well, Mr. Oka offered
us the use of his. So every night that summer we drove to the Okas for
our bath, and we came in frequent contact with Mrs. Oka, and this is
where I found the strangeness.

Mrs. Oka was small and spare. Her clothes hung on her like loose 4
skin and when she walked, the skirt about her legs gave her a sort of
webbed look. She was pretty in spite of the boniness and the dull calico
and the barren look; I know now that she couldn't have been over thirty.
Her eyes were large and a little vacant, although once I saw them fill with
tears; the time I insisted we take the old Victrola over and we played our
Japanese records for her. Some of the songs were sad, and I imagined
the nostalgia she felt, but my mother said the tears were probably from
yawning or from the smoke of her cigarettes. I thought my mother resented her for not being more hospitable; indeed, never a cup of tea appeared before us, and between them the conversation of women was totally absent: the rise and fall of gentle voices, the arched eyebrows, the
croon of polite surprise. But more than this, Mrs. Oka was *different*.

Obviously she was shy, but some nights she disappeared altogether. 5
She would see us drive into her yard and then lurch from sight. She was
gone all evening. Where could she have hidden in that two roomed
house—where in that silent desert? Some nights she would wait out our
visit with enormous forbearance, quietly pushing wisps of stray hair behind her ears and waving gnats away from her great moist eyes, and
some nights she moved about with nervous agitation, her khaki canvas
shoes slapping loudly as she walked. And sometimes there appeared to
be welts and bruises on her usually smooth brown face, and she would
sit solemnly, hands on lap, eyes large and intent on us. My mother hurried us home then: "Hurry, Masako, no need to wash well; hurry."

You see, being so poky, I was always last to bathe. I think the Okas
bathed after we left because my mother often reminded me to keep the
water clean. The routine was to lather outside the tub (there were buck-
ets and pans and a small wooden stool), rinse off the soil and soap, and
then soak in the tub of hot hot water and contemplate. Rivulets of per-
spiration would run down the scalp.

When my mother pushed me like this, I dispensed with ritual, 6
rushed a bar of soap around me and splashed about a pan of water. So
hastily toweled, my wet skin strapped the clothes to me, impeding my

already clumsy progress. Outside, my mother would be murmuring her many apologies and my father, I knew, would be carrying my brother whose feet were already sandy. We would hurry home.

I thought Mrs. Oka might be insane and I asked my mother about   7
it, but she shook her head and smiled with her mouth drawn down and said that Mrs. Oka loved her sake. This was unusual, yes, but there were other unusual women we knew. Mrs. Nagai was brought by her husband from a geisha house; Mrs. Tani was a militant Christian Scientist; Mrs. Abe, the midwife, was occult. My mother's statement explained much: sometimes Mrs. Oka was drunk and sometimes not. Her taste for liquor and cigarettes was a step in the realm of men; unusual for a Japanese wife, but at that time, in that place, and to me, Mrs. Oka loved her sake in the way my father loved his, in the way of Mr. Oka, and the way I loved my candy. That her psychology may have demanded this anesthetic, that she lived with something unendurable, did not occur to me. Nor did I perceive the violence of emotions that the purple welts indicated—or the masochism that permitted her to display these wounds to us.

In spite of her masculine habits, Mrs. Oka was never less than a   8
woman. She was no lady in the area of social amenities; but the feminine in her was innate and never left her. Even in her disgrace, she was a small broken sparrow, slightly floppy, too slowly enunciating her few words, too carefully rolling her Bull Durham, cocking her small head and moistening the ocher tissue. Her aberration was a protest of the life assigned her; it was obstinate, but unobserved, alas, unheeded. "Strange" was the only concession we granted her.

Toward the end of summer, my mother said we couldn't continue   9
bathing at the Okas'; when winter set in we'd all catch our death from the commuting and she'd always felt dreadful about our imposition on Mrs. Oka. So my father took the corrugated tin sheets he'd found on the highway and had been saving for some other use and built up our bathhouse again. Mr. Oka came to help.

While they raised the quivering tin walls, Mr. Oka began to talk. His   10
voice was sharp and clear above the low thunder of the metal sheets.

He told my father he had been married in Japan previously to the   11
present Mrs. Oka's older sister. He had a child by the marriage, Kiyoko, a girl. He had left the two to come to America intending to send for them soon, but shortly after his departure, his wife passed away from an obscure stomach ailment. At the time, the present Mrs. Oka was young and had foolishly become involved with a man of poor reputation. The family was anxious to part the lovers and conveniently arranged a marriage

by proxy and sent him his dead wife's sister. Well that was all right, after all, they were kin, and it would be good for the child when she came to join them. But things didn't work out that way, year after year he postponed calling for his daughter, couldn't get the price of fare together, and the wife—ahhh, the wife, Mr. Oka's groan was lost in the rumble of his hammering.

He cleared his throat. The girl was now fourteen, he said, and begged   12
to come to America to be with her own real family. Those relatives had forgotten the favor he'd done in accepting a slightly used bride, and now tormented his daughter for being forsaken. True, he'd not sent much money, but if they knew, if they only knew how it was here.

"Well," he sighed, "who could be blamed? It's only right she be with   13
me anyway."

"That's right," my father said.   14

"Well, I sold the horse and some other things and managed to buy   15
a third-class ticket on the Taiyo-Maru. Kiyoko will get here the first week of September." Mr. Oka glanced toward my father, but my father was peering into a bag of nails. "I'd be much obliged to you if your wife and little girl," he rolled his eyes toward me, "would take kindly to her. She'll be lonely."

Kiyoko-san came in September. I was surprised to see so very nearly   16
a woman; short, robust, buxom: the female counterpart of her father; thyroid eyes and protruding teeth, straight black hair banded impudently into two bristly shucks, Cuban heels and white socks. Mr. Oka brought her proudly to us.

"Little Masako here," for the first time to my recollection, he touched   17
me; he put his rough fat hand on the top of my head, "is very smart in school. She will help you with your school work, Kiyoko," he said.

I had so looked forward to Kiyoko-san's arrival. She would be my   18
soul mate; in my mind I had conjured a girl of my own proportion: thin and tall, but with the refinement and beauty I didn't yet possess that would surely someday come to the fore. My disappointment was keen and apparent. Kiyoko-san stepped forward shyly, then retreated with a short bow and small giggle, her fingers pressed to her mouth.

My mother took her away. They talked for a long time—about Japan,   19
about enrollment in American school, the clothes Kiyoko-san would need, and where to look for the best values. As I watched them, it occurred to me that I had been deceived: this was not a child, this was a woman. The smile pressed behind her fingers, the way of her nod, so brief, like my mother when father scolded her: the face was inscrutable, but something—maybe spirit—shrank visibly, like a piece of silk in

water. I was disappointed; Kiyoko-san's soul was barricaded in her un-enchanting appearance and the smile she fenced behind her fingers.

She started school from third grade, one below me, and as it turned   20
out, she quickly passed me by. There wasn't much I could help her with
except to drill her on pronunciation—the "L" and "R" sounds. Every
morning walking to our rural school: land, leg, library, loan, lot; every
afternoon returning home: ran, rabbit, rim, rinse, roll. That was the extent of our communication; friendly but uninteresting.

One particularly cold November night—the wind outside was icy;   21
I was sitting on my bed, my brother's and mine, oiling the cracks in my
chapped hands by lamplight—someone rapped urgently at our door. It
was Kiyoko-san; she was hysterical, she wore no wrap, her teeth were
chattering, and except for the thin straw zori, her feet were bare. My
mother led her to the kitchen, started a pot of tea, and gestured to my
brother and me to retire. I lay very still but because of my brother's restless tossing and my father's snoring, was unable to hear much. I was
aware, though, that drunken and savage brawling had brought Kiyoko-
san to us. Presently they came to the bedroom. I feigned sleep. My
mother gave Kiyoko-san a gown and pushed me over to make room for
her. My mother spoke firmly: "Tomorrow you will return to them; you
must not leave them again. They are your people." I could almost feel
Kiyoko-san's short nod.

All night long I lay cramped and still, afraid to intrude into her   22
hulking back. Two or three times her icy feet jabbed into mine and
quickly retreated. In the morning I found my mother's gown neatly
folded on the spare pillow. Kiyoko-san's place in bed was cold.

She never came to weep at our house again but I know she cried: 23
her eyes were often swollen and red. She stopped much of her giggling
and routinely pressed her fingers to her mouth. Our daily pronunciation drill petered off from lack of interest. She walked silently with her
shoulders hunched, grasping her books with both arms, and when I
spoke to her in my halting Japanese, she absently corrected my prepo-
sitions.

Spring comes early in the Valley; in February the skies are clear   24
though the air is still cold. By March, winds are vigorous and warm and
wild flowers dot the desert floor, cockleburs are green and not yet tenacious, the sand is crusty underfoot, everywhere there is a smell of things
growing and the first tomatoes are showing green and bald.

As the weather changed, Kiyoko-san became noticeably more cheer-   25
ful. Mr. Oka who hated so to drive could often be seen steering his dusty
old Ford over the road that passes our house, and Kiyoko-san sitting in

front would sometimes wave gaily to us. Mrs. Oka was never with them. I thought of these trips as the westernizing of Kiyoko-san: with a permanent wave, her straight black hair became tangles of tiny frantic curls; between her textbooks she carried copies of *Modern Screen* and *Photoplay*, her clothes were gay with print and piping, and she bought a pair of brown suede shoes with alligator trim. I can see her now picking her way gingerly over the deceptive white peaks of alkaline crust.

At first my mother watched their coming and going with vicarious 26
pleasure. "Probably off to a picture show; the stores are all closed at this hour," she might say. Later her eyes would get distant and she would muse, "They've left her home again; Mrs. Oka is alone again, the poor woman."

Now when Kiyoko-san passed by or came in with me on her way 27
home, my mother would ask about Mrs. Oka—how is she, how does she occupy herself these rainy days, or these windy or warm or cool days. Often the answers were polite: "Thank you, we are fine," but sometimes Kiyoko-san's upper lip would pull over her teeth, and her voice would become very soft and she would say, "Drink, always drinking and fighting." And those times my mother would invariably say, "Endure, soon you will be marrying and going away."

Once a young truck driver delivered crates at the Oka farm and he 28
dropped back to our place to tell my father that Mrs. Oka had lurched behind his truck while he was backing up, and very nearly let him kill her. Only the daughter pulling her away saved her, he said. Thoroughly unnerved, he stopped by to rest himself and talk about it. Never, never, he said in wide-eyed wonder, had he seen a drunken Japanese woman. My father nodded gravely, "Yes, it's unusual," he said and drummed his knee with his fingers.

Evenings were longer now, and when my mother's migraines drove 29
me from the house in unbearable self-pity, I would take walks in the desert. One night with the warm wind against me, the dune primrose and yellow poppies closed and fluttering, the greasewood swaying in languid orbit, I lay on the white sand beneath a shrub and tried to disappear.

A voice sweet and clear cut through the half-dark of the evening: 30

> Red lips press against a glass
> Drink the purple wine
> And the soul shall dance

Mrs. Oka appeared to be gathering flowers. Bending, plucking, 31
standing, searching, she added to a small bouquet she clasped. She held

them away; looked at them slyly, lids lowered, demure, then in a sudden and sinuous movement, she broke into a stately dance. She stopped, gathered more flowers, and breathed deeply into them. Tossing her head, she laughed—softly, beautifully, from her dark throat. The picture of her imagined grandeur was lost to me, but the delusion that transformed the bouquet of tattered petals and sandy leaves, and the aloneness of a desert twilight into a fantasy that brought such joy and abandon made me stir with discomfort. The sound broke Mrs. Oka's dance. Her eyes grew large and her neck tense—like a cat on the prowl. She spied me in the bushes. A peculiar chill ran through me. Then abruptly and with childlike delight, she scattered the flowers around her and walked away singing:

> Falling, falling, petals on a wind . . .

That was the last time I saw Mrs. Oka. She died before the spring   32
harvest. It was pneumonia. I didn't attend the funeral, but my mother said it was sad. Mrs. Oka looked peaceful, and the minister expressed the irony of the long separation of Mother and Child and the short-lived reunion; hardly a year together, she said. We went to help Kiyoko-san address and stamp those black-bordered acknowledgments.

When harvest was over, Mr. Oka and Kiyoko-san moved out of the   33
Valley. We never heard from them or saw them again and I suppose in a large city, Mr. Oka found some sort of work, perhaps as a janitor or a dishwasher and Kiyoko-san grew up and found someone to marry.

RESPONDING TO "AND THE SOUL SHALL DANCE"

Freewrite: Explore your feelings about the role that gender plays in alcoholism. What might lead a woman to abuse alcohol?

Responding through Interpretation

1. "And the Soul Shall Dance" is a complex story that raises many deep issues about families and the relationship between men and women—husbands and wives, daughters and fathers. In your reading journal, make a note of the gender issues you can identify in the story and interpret the story's perspective on each of them.
2. What does the narrator of the story discover about Mrs. Oka as the story progresses over time? In your notebook, make a chronological list of events that revealed new information to the young narrator.

3. What is the significance of the scene when the narrator catches Mrs. Oka dancing? How does this scene relate to the story's title?

Responding through Discussion

1. With your group, read some of the key passages aloud. Look at the story each passage portrays of men and women. Study sentences such as "Her taste for liquor and cigarettes was a step in the realm of men" and ". . . the feminine in her was innate and never left her." Look at what the men do and at what the women do. Discuss all the aspects of gender that you can identify in the story. Report to the rest of the class what the group discovers.
2. Do you think that Mr. Oka's daughter, Kiyoko-san, contributed to the final deterioration of Mrs. Oka? Allow group members to respond by giving their opinions pro or con about this question. Be sure to support opinions with evidence from the story.

Responding through Writing

1. In your journal, write an imaginary scene in which Mrs. Oka speaks aloud her thoughts and feelings. Use details and evidence from the story itself whenever possible.
2. "And the Soul Shall Dance" deals with drinking problems within a particular ethnic community. Write an essay in which you discuss the causes of drinking by men or women within a racial or cultural group to which you belong—or about which you have some special knowledge.

Coming Out

Rick Cary

The following essay was written by Rick Cary when he was twenty-four.
It appeared in a collection of writings by gay and lesbian youth, titled *One
Teenager in Ten* (1983) and edited by Ann Heron. Because of the intimate
nature of his essay, Rick has used a pseudonym.

Coming out means different things to different people. For me as a gay   1
man, it refers to a long process of self-discovery that led me to realize
and celebrate my sexuality. It also refers to my telling others that I'm gay.
My coming out process led me to say to myself and others, "I'm gay and
proud."

I was a "late bloomer." My sexual awareness dawned more slowly   2
than it did for many folks. During high school I thought certain boys
were good looking; I worried about having an erection in the locker
room. But I didn't think this was unusual. I figured all boys admired an
attractive male body.

I don't think I had heard the word "gay," only "fag." What I had   3
heard about them was negative, and I certainly didn't feel like a per-
vert. I knew no one who was gay, and no one questioned my assumed
heterosexuality. I dated girls and went steady a few times, but I never
loved any of them. Still, I didn't think I was different from other guys,
until. . . .

One day, while a senior, I was in a shopping mall bookstore and saw   4
a magazine that included a picture of a naked man modeling jewelry. I
liked what I saw. Thinking it to be a magazine for men, I bought a copy.
Later, to my surprise, I read on the cover that it was "a magazine for
women"! I then began to suspect that I was *not* like other boys. Something about me was different; my self-discovery had begun.

I entered college at a major state university as a naive eighteen-year-   5
old from a small southern town. I had yet to meet a homosexual, but that
was to change. I met Jerry, a member of a campus gay organization who
spoke to my psychology class. Although I cannot remember his words,
I do recall his presence. Blond and attractive, he sat on a table's edge,
his legs swinging freely as he spoke comfortably about being gay. Being
gay no longer seemed unimaginable. He was no stereotype, but flesh and
blood. Like me. And I began to wonder: am I gay?

The summer following my freshman year provided an emotional 6
turning point. I worked in a hamburger joint with Pete, a guy from high
school. His eyes and smile captivated me, and I recall that he'd occasionally touch my arm and pat my behind. I loved to be with him, and
when I returned to college in the fall I thought of him constantly. I was
nineteen and had never felt so warmly about anyone. But I never told
him I loved him. I couldn't; it was too scary. Yet my love for him added
fuel to a fire that was lighting a path toward my sexual awareness.

Throughout college I struggled to understand my sexuality. Was I 7
going through a "homosexual phase"? What did my feelings mean? I
struggled to understand the implications of being gay. Was being gay a
sign of psychological sickness or immaturity? Was homosexuality a sin?
My many questions boiled down to two: Am I gay? Is being gay OK?

I needed help to sort things out. So I read a lot of books on homo- 8
sexuality from psychological and Christian perspectives. I also talked
with a psychologist and several ministers who accepted me. They let me
explore my sexual feelings honestly. They supported me as I wrestled
to understand not only my sexuality, but myself as a human being.

When I started my senior year, I was still unclear about my sexual- 9
ity. I had dated women with increasing frequency, but never felt love
for any of them. I discovered that I could perform sexually with a
woman, but heterosexual experiences were not satisfying emotionally.
I felt neither love nor emotional oneness with women. Indeed, I had concluded that I was incapable of human love.

During that year I again experienced love like I had felt for Pete. 10
Stephen was a hall-mate, and I was drawn to him physically and emotionally. I longed to be with him. We teased each other, but I was afraid
to tell him of my love. My feelings for Stephen provided more fuel for
the fire.

At the age of twenty-one, I looked at the evidence in my life. I real- 11
ized that the only people I had loved were men, and now I loved
Stephen. During college my gay feelings had grown increasingly strong;
my sexual fantasies and dreams were about men. Although I had not had
sex with a man, I knew how I felt. Through counseling and reading I became able to say "Gay *is* good." I realized that being gay is neither a sickness nor a sin. During my final semester, after four years of conscious
struggle, I was able to say, "I am gay and proud."

I went to my first gay dance (was I scared!) and had a wonderful 12
time. Right after graduation I met Stuart. We fell in love, and for the first
time I shared love and sex with a man. I felt whole and at peace with

myself and with God. Finally I had come to see my sexuality with clarity. I could affirm and celebrate my gayness. I had come out.

My coming out includes telling others I'm gay. Some gays tell everybody, but that's not my style. I have chosen to be selective in telling others. The Bible says, "Do not throw your pearls before swine, lest they trample them under foot and turn to attack you." Well, my gayness is one of my treasured pearls, a pearl I own after paying a great price of personal struggle. I won't share that treasure with everybody. However, I have come out to many folks whom I care about and with whom I have significant relationships.   13

Most of the non-gay people who know I'm gay are friends. I began coming out to friends while a senior in college. Coming out was scary then . . . and still is! I never know how someone will react to my gayness. Some friends suspected all along; others were totally surprised. Some said "So what?"; others were upset. I've told several dozen friends and none have rejected me. Oh, many have struggled to understand my gayness, but they were willing to struggle. And my coming out has often led to deeper, more open relationships. I've been fortunate; other gays have experienced more rejection than I have.   14

Over the years, I've learned a few things about how to come out to someone. I need to tell my friend that I want to share something very personal, something that she or he may not understand at first. I want my friend to know that I desire a deeper friendship. I need to avoid coming out when I'm angry with someone. I want my coming out to be an act of love; the sharing of a treasured pearl with a friend. I also remind myself that an initial reaction of disbelief or anger is common. If my friend is upset, he or she may need time to wrestle with my gayness. I can offer to be there and answer questions (and often there are lots of questions!), but I cannot make my friend accept me. Every time I come out to someone I risk losing that friend. With each individual I decide if I want to take the risk.   15

Perhaps nothing is riskier than coming out to parents. I came out to my parents at the same time I came out to myself, but I wasn't prepared for their reaction. How I wish I could have read the Switzer's book *Parents of the Homosexual* before I came out to them. I could have had more realistic expectations, for the Switzers described my parents' reactions with amazing accuracy.   16

Mom and Dad first reacted with disbelief. "You can't be gay! You must be mistaken." They were so upset they sent me back to school and said, "Don't come back home until we say you can." Those were the most   17 painful words I've ever heard. For a brief moment I considered suicide, but I had friends and ministers to turn to for support. I was not alone.

After a few weeks they re-established contact with me. They real- 18 ized they could not run from the issue. After the initial shock, they felt a flood of emotions. *Anger.* They were angry with me for causing them so much pain and for refusing to see a psychiatrist. They were angry with everyone who might have "made" me gay—college friends, the minis- ters who counseled me, and finally, themselves. They felt guilty and wondered, "How did we fail?" *Fear.* They knew it's tough being gay in our society, and they feared I was throwing away my college education and promising future. *Sadness.* The "little Ricky" they knew was no longer the same. Their expectations for me, especially a wife and chil- dren, were suddenly taken away. Much had changed, and they grieved for the loss of their dreams for my life . . . and their lives too.

That's a lot of heavy emotion, and I felt emotional too. I was angry 19 with them for their reaction. I feared for my future and felt sad that our relationship was strained. The first year was incredibly tense, so tense that it was often terribly uncomfortable for us to be together. We have talked some about my gayness, but we most often avoid the topic. It's scary for all three of us. Yet we *need* to struggle with each other and our relationships. Happily, they have often demonstrated their love for me in recent years. I am still their son, and our lives go on.

Thus far in my life, I have come out selectively, but one day I may 20 decide to come out very publicly as some gays have done. A part of me wants to do that, but for now I choose otherwise. Each gay must make his or her choice. Coming out, to oneself and to others, is an in- tensely personal and individual experience. Each coming out story is unique. This has been mine, but the story has not ended because I am continually coming out. I will always need to reaffirm the goodness of my gayness and share that pearl with people I care about. I am com- ing out.

RESPONDING TO "COMING OUT"

Freewrite about your deepest feelings and attitudes about male and/or fe- male homosexuality.

Responding through Interpretation

1. What were the various steps that led Cary to determining that he was gay? Make a list of the sequence of events.

2. Which of the events described by Cary did you find most effective? Describe it in your own words in your reading journal and explain why it seems significant to you.
3. Look at Cary's paragraphing. Do you see any paragraphs that you think could be combined? Are there any you think should be expanded? Are there any you think should be deleted?

Responding through Discussion

1. Evaluate Cary's success in relating the story of his coming out. Did he succeed in eliciting your empathy and understanding? Why or why not?
2. Discuss prejudiced behavior that you have heard of or witnessed toward homosexuals. What are the most common prejudices? How do these prejudices affect others?

Responding through Writing

1. After the group discussion about prejudice against gays, write an entry in your journal responding to what was said. What did you learn? How did the discussions affect your preconceptions about "appropriate" sexual behavior and society's response to homosexuality?
2. Write a paper about a time when you experienced a "coming out"—that is, a time when you found out what was true for you and found the courage to tell the truth even though you knew there might be consequences. What motivated you to come forth with the truth? What was the outcome? Were there any consequences?

Being a Boy

Julius Lester

Julius Lester attended college at Fisk University and has taught since 1971 at the University of Massachusetts, where he has been a professor of African-American studies as well as Near Eastern and Judaic studies. Lester has written many books including *Do Lord Remember Me* (1984), *Lovesong: Becoming a Jew* (1988), and most recently, *And All Our Wounds Forgiven* (1994). In the following article, written originally for *Ms.* magazine in 1973, Lester reflects on his childhood experiences in order to explore the impact of stereotypes of "masculine" and "feminine" behavior on the consciousness of a young boy.

As boys go, I wasn't much. I mean, I tried to be a boy and spent many childhood hours pummeling my hardly formed ego with failure at cowboys and Indians, baseball, football, lying, and sneaking out of the house. When our neighborhood gang raided a neighbor's pear tree, I was the only one who got sick from the purloined fruit. I also failed at setting fire to our garage, an art at which any five-year-old boy should be adept. I was, however, the neighborhood champion at getting beat up. "That Julius can take it, man," the boys used to say, almost in admiration, after I emerged from another battle, tears brimming in my eyes but refusing to fall.   1

My efforts at being a boy earned me a pair of scarred knees that are a record of a childhood spent falling from bicycles, trees, the tops of fences, and porch steps; of tripping as I ran (generally from a fight), walked, or simply tried to remain upright on windy days.   2

I tried to believe my parents when they told me I was a boy, but I could find no objective proof for such an assertion. Each morning during the summer, as I cuddled up in the quiet of a corner with a book, my mother would push me out the back door and into the yard. And throughout the day as my blood was let as if I were a patient of 17th-century medicine, I thought of the girls sitting in the shade of porches, playing with their dolls, toy refrigerators and stoves.   3

There was the life, I thought! No constant pressure to prove oneself. No necessity always to be competing. While I humiliated myself on football and baseball fields, the girls stood on the sidelines laughing at me, because they didn't have to do anything except be girls. The rising   4 of each sun brought me to the starting line of yet another day's Olympic decathlon, with no hope of ever winning even a bronze medal.

Through no fault of my own I reached adolescence. While the pressure to prove myself on the athletic field lessened, the overall situation got worse—because now I had to prove myself with girls. Just how I was supposed to go about doing this was beyond me, especially because, at the age of 14, I was four foot nine and weighed 78 pounds. (I think there may have been one 10-year-old girl in the neighborhood smaller than I.) Nonetheless, duty called, and with my ninth-grade gym-class jockstrap flapping between my legs, off I went.

To get a girlfriend, though, a boy had to have some asset beyond the fact that he was alive. I wasn't handsome like Bill McCord, who had girls after him like a cop-killer has policemen. I wasn't ugly like Romeo Jones, but at least the girls noticed him: "That ol' ugly boy better stay 'way from me!" I was just there, like a vase your grandmother gives you at Christmas that you don't like or dislike, can't get rid of, and don't know what to do with. More than ever I wished I were a girl. Boys were the ones who had to take the initiative and all the responsibility. (I hate responsibility so much that if my heart didn't beat of itself, I would now be a dim memory.)

It was the boy who had to ask the girl for a date, a frightening enough prospect until it occurred to me that she might say no! That meant risking my ego, which was about as substantial as a toilet-paper raincoat in the African rainy season. But I had to thrust that ego forward to be judged, accepted, or rejected by some girl. It wasn't fair! Who was she to sit back like a queen with the power to create joy by her consent or destruction by her denial? It wasn't fair—but that's the way it was.

But if (God forbid!) she should say Yes, then my problem would begin in earnest, because I was the one who said where we would go (and waited in terror for her approval of my choice). I was the one who picked her up at her house where I was inspected by her parents as if I were a possible carrier of syphilis (which I didn't think one could get from masturbating, but then again, Jesus was born of a virgin, so what did I know?). Once we were on our way, it was I who had to pay the bus fare, the price of the movie tickets, and whatever she decided to stuff her stomach with afterward. (And the smallest girls are all stomach.) Finally, the girl was taken home where once again I was inspected (the father looking covertly at my fly and the mother examining the girl's hair). The evening was over and the girl had done nothing except honor me with her presence. All the work had been mine.

Imagining this procedure over and over was more than enough: I   9
was a sophomore in college before I had my first date.

I wasn't a total failure in high school, though, for occasionally I   10
would go to a party, determined to salvage my self-esteem. The parties
usually took place in somebody's darkened basement. There was generally a surreptitious wine bottle or two being passed furtively among
the boys, and a record player with an insatiable appetite for Johnny
Mathis records. Boys gathered on one side of the room and girls on the
other. There were always a few boys and girls who'd come to the party
for the sole purpose of grinding away their sexual frustrations to Johnny
Mathis's falsetto, and they would begin dancing to their own music before the record player was plugged in. It took a little longer for others
to get started, but no one matched my talent for standing by the punch
bowl. For hours, I would try to make my legs do what they had been
doing without effort since I was nine months old, but for some reason
they would show all the symptoms of paralysis on those evenings.

After several hours of wondering whether I was going to die ("Julius   11
Lester, a sixteen-year-old, died at a party last night, a half-eaten Ritz
cracker in one hand and a potato chip dipped in pimiento-cheese spread
in the other. Cause of death: failure to be a boy"), I would push my way
to the other side of the room where the girls sat like a hanging jury. I
would pass by the girl I wanted to dance with. If I was going to be refused, let it be by someone I didn't particularly like. Unfortunately, there
weren't many in that category. I had more crushes than I had pimples.

Finally, through what surely could only have been the direct inter-   12
vention of the Almighty, I would find myself on the dance floor with a
girl. And none of my prior agony could compare to the thought of actually dancing. But there I was and I had to dance with her. Social cus-
tom decreed that I was supposed to lead, because I was the boy. Why?
I'd wonder. Let her lead. Girls were better dancers anyway. It didn't matter. She stood there waiting for me to take charge. She wouldn't have
been worse off if she'd waited for me to turn white.

But, reciting "Invictus" to myself, I placed my arms around her,   13
being careful to keep my armpits closed because, somehow, I had managed to overwhelm a half jar of deodorant and a good-size bottle of
cologne. With sweaty armpits, "Invictus," and legs afflicted again with
polio, I took her in my arms, careful not to hold her so far away that she
would think I didn't like her, but equally careful not to hold her so close
that she could feel the catastrophe which had befallen me the instant I
touched her hand. My penis, totally disobeying the lecture I'd given it

before we left home, was as rigid as Governor Wallace's jaw would be if I asked for his daughter's hand in marriage.

God, how I envied girls at that moment. Wherever *it* was on them, it didn't dangle between their legs like an elephant's trunk. No wonder boys talked about nothing but sex. That thing was always there. Every time we went to the john, there *it* was, twitching around like a fat little worm on a fishing hook. When we took baths, it floated in the water like a lazy fish and God forbid we should touch it! It sprang to life like lightning leaping from a cloud. I wished I could cut it off, or at least keep it tucked between my legs, as if it were a tail that had been mistakenly attached to the wrong end. But I was helpless. It was there, with a life and mind of its own, having no other function than to embarrass me.   14

Fortunately, the girls I danced with were discreet and pretended that they felt nothing unusual rubbing against them as we danced. But I was always convinced that the next day they were all calling up their friends to exclaim: "Guess what, girl? Julius Lester got one! I ain't lyin'!"   15

Now, of course, I know that it was as difficult being a girl as it was a boy, if not more so. While I stood paralyzed at one end of a dance floor trying to find the courage to ask a girl for a dance, most of the girls waited in terror at the other, afraid that no one, not even I, would ask them. And while I resented having to ask a girl for a date, wasn't it also horrible to be the one who waited for the phone to ring? And how many of those girls who laughed at me making a fool of myself on the baseball diamond would have gladly given up their places on the sidelines for mine on the field?   16

No, it wasn't easy for any of us, girls and boys, as we forced our beautiful, free-flowing child-selves into those narrow, constricting cubicles labeled *female* and *male*. I tried, but I wasn't good at being a boy. Now, I'm glad, knowing that a man is nothing but the figment of a penis's imagination, and any man should want to be something more than that.   17

RESPONDING TO "BEING A BOY"

Freewrite exploring some of your feelings about what "being a boy" or "being a girl" means to you.

Responding through Interpretation

1. Do you think Lester's experiences are typical of adolescent expectations and pressures? Explain why or why not.

2. Interpret the meaning of Lester's concluding sentence. In what sense is he "glad"?

3. Lester creates a number of witty and unusual similes—nonliteral comparisons. Go through the essay and choose several that appeal to you and then create several similes of your own. Give some thought to how you, as a writer, can incorporate the use of more unusual comparisons into your own work.

Responding through Discussion

1. Discuss the practice of dating with your group, from both a male and a female perspective. Look over Lester's analysis of the drawbacks of dating and use those as a departure point for the discussion.

2. Consider, with your group, some of the cultural factors that might cause adolescence to be such a difficult period in the life of a young person. You might begin your discussion with thinking about how cultural stereotypes that come from the mass media, religious imagery, and family traditions contribute to the difficulty.

Responding through Writing

1. After thinking further about Lester's essay, write a journal entry in which you reminisce about some of your own adolescent experiences. How do they parallel or how are they different from Lester's?

2. Write a paper that explores some of the ways in which social expectations and dating patterns for both young males and females have changed since Lester's youth.

On Being Female

Nina Woodle

Nina Woodle works hard to balance the responsibilities of being a parent with working at a full-time job and attending college where she is study-ing business management. Woodle wrote the following essay, a response to Julius Lester's "On Being a Boy," for her class in English composition.

Julius Lester's idea of the simplicity of being a female as he presents it in his autobiographical essay, "Being a Boy," is in my opinion far from reality. At times when I was growing up as a Hispanic female, I felt the males were given power at birth while society unfairly assigned roles for the females. In comparing my own life experiences with Lester's, I feel it was and still is difficult to pass through life's growing phases as a woman.   1

Coming from a third-generation Mexican-American family, my sister and I were passed over when it came to academics. When we brought home the "A's" we would get our, "That's nice *mija* (daughter), but don't forget, boys don't like to be around girls that are too smart." In contrast, when our brothers brought home the "B's" it would be fiesta time since they, like Lester, had already earned their "A's" in machoism and cowboys.   2

It also wasn't fun being on the receiving end of the hair pulling and shoving that we encountered when little boys "liked" us. They didn't understand the emotions they were feeling and would often express those feelings in a painful act. Could this possibly be how Lester really got those scarred knees of his? A retaliation, maybe from a girl?   3

Lester's humiliation on the football and baseball fields is minor in comparison to the humiliation I went through when taking the manda-tory cooking classes we females were required to take in high school. It was a grueling experience and I hated it. At that time in my life, staying home and having babies was not my idea of an exciting future. I was too busy taking business classes and hanging out with the "Future Business Leaders of America" students. One day in cooking class, my FBLA lead-ership skills proved their worth when I, the leader of our kitchenette, for-got to add a main ingredient to our cake, the yolk! When my team noticed our cake wasn't rising and was never going to, I quickly assessed the op-tions and laid out a plot for the team. We were going to swap cakes with another kitchenette. I remember the precise timing and excellent execu-tion in which my co-conspirators carried out the scheme. By the time the   4 members of the other kitchenette knew they had a flat cake waiting for them, we were busily frosting ours. This was one time when I didn't allow humiliation to get the best of me like it did with Lester; I used my brain.

Lester's description of his experience of having to ask a girl to dance   5
brought me back to a time when I first felt the unfairness of the "given" power a male possessed. This enlightenment came to me at the tender age of thirteen. It happened in an era when square dancing was part of the physical education program. I had been ill for a week and upon my return to school my girlfriends anxiously warned me that all girls who didn't get picked to dance would get an "F" for the day. I froze—There we all were, the boys on one end of the auditorium and the girls on the other. I recall the boy's gym teachers in a corner attempting to adjust the volume on the record player with echoing words of DO-SE-DOS blasting out, while the girl's gym teachers stood with grading sheets in their hands smiling down at us, a look of pity in their eyes. Suddenly a hushed silence overcame the auditorium and a whistle was blown. It reminded me of the beginning of a horse race with the girls being the finish line.

At last the boys started coming our way; I looked at my classmates,   6
my sweaty hands clasped together, not knowing what I was going to do. Then I realized the truth: I didn't have a choice in the matter, but the boys did. Imagine that, a male having the power to decide who would get an "A." In the midst of this enlightenment, I was able to focus on two male shoes standing in front of me and a hand in front of my face. It then hit me; a boy was asking me to dance. I remember my body automatically stood up and allowed him to take it by the hand to join other couples in a square. It (my brain) eventually rejoined my body later telling me over and over, "You didn't get an 'F.' "

All in all, in comparing my own personal experiences with Lester's,   7
I can see, as Lester does at the end of his essay, that life isn't easy for either gender when it is looked at from both sides. This comparison has brought me to the conclusion that females and males alike go through varying degrees of uncertainty throughout life. We agonize through the physical development of our bodies because growth is inevitable; then as adults we mature mentally at our own pace, some faster than others, some slower. I believe it doesn't matter whether you end up being a male or a female. Being *human* is difficult.

RESPONDING TO "ON BEING FEMALE"

Freewrite about a time when you felt powerful about being your particular gender.

Responding through Interpretation

1. What were the expectations about girls in Woodle's family? How did she feel about these expectations?
2. Find what you consider to be Woodle's main statement. Then find all the other statements that support this main point.

Responding through Discussion

1. Commenting about the boys in her gym class having to ask the girls to dance, Woodle says: "I didn't have a choice in the matter, but the boys did." Focus the group discussion on this widely accepted practice of the males asking and the girls accepting. Make a list of the different areas in male/female interaction where this practice is still the norm and let group members discuss their feelings and ideas about each one.

Responding through Writing

1. Write a journal entry in which you discuss the division of labor within your own family. Compare and contrast the chores for which each member of the family is usually responsible. Are some chores done by the whole family? If so, how is this accomplished? Are some of the chores rotated among the family members? What suggestions could you make for improving the division of labor in your family?
2. Evaluate the extent to which Woodle understands and/or misunderstands Lester's points and analyses. Use textual evidence to support your claims.

What about Being a Girl?

Magnolia Tse

Born in Hong Kong, Magnolia Tse came to live in San Francisco when she was twelve years old. She enjoys fencing, singing in the church choir, and talking on the telephone. She is majoring in molecular cell biology, and eventually she would like to become a surgeon. Magnolia Tse wrote the following essay for her English class after reading Julius Lester's "Being a Boy." Notice how she draws on her own experiences of growing up in a traditional Chinese family to respond to several of Lester's points.

Boys face a lot of pressures as they grow up. These pressures, however, change as they reach adolescence. Some boys like Julius Lester, the author of the essay "Being A Boy," envy girls because they feel that girls have it easier; girls never have to do anything but sit around. Nevertheless, girls face a lot of pressures as they grow up, just as boys do. I disagree with Lester's position in his essay because I think that girls have just as hard a time as boys as they grow up.

Do boys such as Lester realize that we girls are usually forced to play dolls and help out at home, and that we often do not like it at all? Boys are free to play football and are allowed to come home smelly and dirty. Yet, since we are girls, we have to help out at home. "If you don't learn, you will grow up not knowing anything about housekeeping and cooking. Nobody would want a wife like that. . . ." Those are my mother's favorite threats. As a bunch of ten- to twelve-year-old boys roll around on the ground playing football after school, the girls at that same age are picked up by their mothers to go home. Even as the girls beg their mothers to allow them to stay or take the bus home with the guys, going home late would seem to be impossible. They are girls, and thus they should not hang around in the yard because it may not be safe; they should go home and finish their homework.

Lester believed that girls led the easy life: "Throughout the day as my blood was let . . . I thought of girls sitting in the shade of porches, playing with their dolls, toy refrigerators and stoves." However, in many cases, girls are forced to help set the table for dinner or to go grocery shopping with their mothers. When I was a child, I always wanted to walk around or to stay after school with my friends or even go to their houses to play video games. I hated to clean the house, let alone my room. Nevertheless, I always ended up having to go home to be trained by my mother to be a successful housewife. I only knew back then that if I didn't do well, nobody would want me. Compared to this, guys' efforts to prove themselves by setting fire to a garage seem far less stressful.

Lester remembers that "the girls stood on the sidelines laughing at   4
me . . . they didn't have to do anything except be girls." Girls may have seemed like they were just "being there" to Lester, but guys often underestimate the pressure that girls are under toward our appearance. What about the dress code? Guys can wear the same three or four pairs of jeans all year round and nobody is likely going to say anything. The situation is definitely different for girls. If they wear the same pair of pants and skirts all the time, other girls will notice. I admit that we girls like to gossip, and if someone is always wearing the same thing all the time, we would talk about her for sure. Guys do face this problem every once in a while, but their clothes don't change much, while girls, in contrast, have to live up to the latest styles. Many times I get the impression that my clothes and haircut are out of style and I need to do something about it. If I want to look good, I have to go shopping all the time. The pressure that we feel causes us to spend hundreds of dollars every few months. And what for? We feel the need to look our best so that guys will ask us out.

Lester states that "Boys were the ones who had to take the initiative   5
and all the responsibilities." However, girls are the ones who have to look good at all times to attract guys. Lester has a point that guys always have to make the first move, and it is very hard for them to do so. But what about us? Girls have to worry about the dances that are coming up as well as whether or not they will be asked to go. If we try too hard to ask a guy to be our dates, others will laugh at us and say that we are desperate. Can we afford such an insult? I remember that I had to wait almost for three weeks before the guy that I liked asked me to go to the winter ball. I'd even had my dress picked out and ready to go. I never had enough courage to ask him, and therefore I had to wait around for him to do so. "It was the boy who had to ask . . . until it occurred to me that she might say no!" In my opinion, Lester misunderstands the point that being rejected is far better than not being asked at all. Boys can always go to dances and parties alone and meet girls, but most of the girls that I know would rather die than go to a party dateless. Now who is more lucky?

Lester writes at the end of his essay, "No, it wasn't easy for any of   6
us, girls and boys. . . ." Thus he encourages us, the readers, not to be

blinded by little incidents and to understand that being either a boy or a girl can be a struggle. Lester comes to realize that he misjudged the opposite sex due to jealousy, and that it is obviously hard for girls as well as for boys to grow up in today's society. I totally agree.

RESPONDING TO "WHAT ABOUT BEING A GIRL?"

Freewrite about a time when you went out on a date with someone but felt uncomfortable because of "gender expectation"—the way you were "supposed to act" as either a boy or a girl.

Responding through Interpretation

1. What arguments does Magnolia Tse give to prove that girls have it as hard as boys do? Evaluate her reasons.
2. Which of Lester's statements does Tse respond to? How well did she interpret his points?

Responding through Discussion

1. Compare Tse's essay to Woodle's. How are the writers alike and different in their response to Lester and in the use of their own experiences as examples? Which essay did you like best, and why?

Responding through Writing

1. As a journal entry, write a memory of a school dance or party that was painful for you. Write in depth about only one event.
2. Take time to look through some current magazines. Then write a paper about what you think the new dress styles for your gender are trying to convey. What are some of the images being communicated through clothing? How do the images fit with the reality of the times?

MAKING CONNECTIONS

Some say that gender is destiny in that it predetermines what you can and can't do; others argue that it only seems that way because we have been brainwashed into believing that gender predetermines destiny. Either way, differences between the two genders is one of those topics that continues to be argued. It seems we are constantly redefining what is male and what is female. And while we have surely closed the wide gap between the genders and have become more "unisex," some differences will always remain.

Whether you see these differences as good or bad depends upon your own experiences and perceptions. It is hoped that the selections in this chapter have given you an opportunity to discover more about yourself as a female or a male. The following ideas for writing may take you even further along the path.

1. *Families and gender.* Julius Lester in "Being a Boy" and Elizabeth Cady Stanton in "You Should Have Been a Boy!" both describe the emotional hardships of growing up under strong expectations based on gender. Compare the ways these two authors describe male and female requirements and restrictions. What hardships did each of the authors undergo? Which author's perspective do you identify with most? Have you had any experiences that seem similar to either of these two authors' experiences?

2. *Gender roles that deform the individual.* Marge Piercy, Rick Cary, Wakako Yamauchi, and Scott Russell Sanders all illustrate the numerous problems that can occur for men and women when society will not accept the uniqueness of the individual and tries to "deform" him or her into rigid gender roles. Discuss the negative impact of gender roles on the individual, using examples from readings in the text as well as from your own experiences.

3. *Growing up male in America.* Scott Russell Sanders and Julius Lester share experiences of growing up male; both emphasize some of the struggles and pain experienced by males and attempt to dispel some stereotypes about male privilege. Compare the two views on male identity presented by these authors. Explain the struggles these two writers describe. Which viewpoint seems closest to your own—and why? From your perspective, what do you think growing up male in this country is like?

4. *Growing up female in America.* Nina Woodle, Magnolia Tse, Wakako Yamauchi, Elizabeth Cady Stanton, and Marge Piercy all paint memorable portraits of the damage that can occur when females are put into restricted roles. Sometimes, females fight big battles against these restrictions and ultimately benefit from the fight. Other women, such as those described by Piercy and Yamauchi, are never able to express themselves enough to fight and are ultimately crippled and irreparably damaged by these restrictions. Write a paper in which you use the information from Piercy's and Yamauchi's writings in order to explain how you think today's women might break out of such restrictions.

CHAPTER 6

Nature

Introduction

LEWIS THOMAS	On Embryology
LINDA HOGAN	Walking
DAVID KERR	Strawberry Creek: A Search for Origins
JEFF HUNZE	Lessons from the Earth
WILLIAM STAFFORD	Traveling through the Dark
PETER TAYLOR	A Walled Garden
JOHN T. NICHOLS	What Is a Naturalist, Anyway?
ANNIE DILLARD	Sojourner
ELIZABETH MARSHALL THOMAS	Do Dogs Have Thoughts and Feelings?
KIRSTEN SIMON	Dogs in Transition
LORI PASCERELLA	Dogs and Empathetic Observation

Making Connections

197

INTRODUCTION

Journal Entry

Freewrite about all the associations you have with the word *nature*. Begin with your earliest memories of this word and trace your ideas up to the present. Write long enough to surprise yourself, to uncover concepts and attitudes that lie deep below the surface.

The word *nature* is thrown around a good bit, especially by advertisers who want to emphasize the purity and superiority of their products. Slogans come at us from all sides, telling us that this product is "naturally grown" or that this one is "nature's own." We go around talking about "Mother Nature," "doing what comes naturally," and "our real nature." But what do these phrases really mean? Do we think of nature as something outside of the ordinary? Of something cleaner and better? Safer? Is it the great outdoors—animals, trees, and rocks? Where do we humans fit into the natural world? What about the dark and dangerous side of "nature"—the tornados, the predators, the decay and death?

You may have felt many positive responses about nature when you wrote your journal entry. Perhaps you've been fortunate enough to spend a lot of time in contact with nature and feel that you know the natural world firsthand. However, "getting away from it all" and "going back to nature" are not so easy for people who live in cities—even moderately sized ones. Think for awhile about the way you spend most of your time in an average week—in a classroom, in libraries, working after school, going home to watch TV and relax indoors, going out to movies or concerts. How much time do you have left over to really spend observing, studying, or experiencing the power of nature? How often do you create opportunities for yourself to get away and soak up the natural world? Even if you live in a rural area, you may see nature as something to use rather than to enjoy; you may become so accustomed to nature that you hardly see the splendor in it anymore.

We hope you will gain a new understanding of and a renewed inspiration from nature through reading the selections in this chapter. Most are written by "naturalists," people who really love nature and have a passion for the natural world of plants and animals. Many of these writers wish to do something through their lives and writing to restore humanity to a close, balanced relationship with nature. Lewis Thomas in "On Embryology" marvels about nature's greatest miracle—the union of sperm and egg to create human life. Linda Hogan in "Walking" and Annie Dillard in "Sojourner" take you on a nature ramble and point out simple but astonishing quirks of the natural world. Student writers David Kerr and Jeff Hunze offer their own close observations and responses to the world of nature. In "What Is a Naturalist, Anyway?" John T. Nichols defines and describes what this elusive term means to him. William Stafford in his poem "Traveling through the Dark" and Peter Taylor in his short story "A Walled Garden" look at the darker side of nature, deeply questioning our true relationship to the natural world. The chapter ends with the subject of dogs, a subject most people have strong feelings about. Elizabeth Thomas asks "Do Dogs Have Thoughts and Feelings?" and is answered in two essays from student writers Kirsten Simon and Lori Pascerella. You will probably have much to say in response to these three writers; we hope that the other readings in this chapter also will give you new ideas about your relationship to Mother Nature.

On Embryology

Lewis Thomas

Lewis Thomas was an outstanding physician and a highly respected
medical researcher who served as the president of the Memorial Sloan-
Kettering Cancer Center in New York City. His writing career was no
less illustrious than his career as a doctor. His first book, *Lives of a
Cell: Notes of a Biology-Watcher*, was published in 1974 and was
awarded the National Book Award for nonfiction. Thomas published
four other books that also reveal him to be an astute observer of both
nature and human nature. The following essay, "On Embryology," is
a chapter from his second book, *The Medusa and the Snail: More
Notes of a Biology Watcher*, published in 1979. In this selection, Lewis
Thomas raises some provocative ideas that are still relevant nearly
twenty years later.

A short while ago, in mid-1978, the newest astonishment in medicine,   1
covering all the front pages, was the birth of an English baby nine
months after conception in a dish. The older surprise, which should still
be fazing us all, is that a solitary sperm and a single egg can fuse and
become a human being under any circumstance, and that, however
implanted, a mere cluster of the progeny of this fused cell affixed to
the uterine wall will grow and differentiate into eight pounds of baby;
this has been going on under our eyes for so long a time that we've
gotten used to it; hence the outcries of amazement at this really minor
technical modification of the general procedure—nothing much, really,
beyond relocating the beginning of the process from the fallopian tube
to a plastic container and, perhaps worth mentioning, the exclusion of
the father from any role likely to add, with any justification, to his
vanity.

There is, of course, talk now about extending the technology beyond   2
the act of conception itself, and predictions are being made that the
whole process of embryonic development, all nine months of it, will ultimately be conducted in elaborate plastic flasks. When this happens, as
perhaps it will someday, it will be another surprise, with more headlines.
Everyone will say how marvelously terrifying is the new power of science, and arguments over whether science should be stopped in its
tracks will preoccupy senatorial subcommittees, with more headlines.
Meanwhile, the sheer incredibility of the process itself, whether it occurs

in the uterus or *in* some sort of *vitro*, will probably be overlooked as much as it is today.

For the real amazement, if you want to be amazed, is the process. 3 You start out as a single cell derived from the coupling of a sperm and an egg, this divides into two, then four, then eight, and so on, and at a certain stage there emerges a single cell which will have as all its progeny the human brain. The mere existence of that cell should be one of the great astonishments of the earth. People ought to be walking around all day, all through their waking hours, calling to each other in endless wonderment, talking of nothing except that cell. It is an unbelievable thing, and yet there it is, popping neatly into its place amid the jumbled cells of every one of the several billion human embryos around the planet, just as if it were the easiest thing in the world to do.

If you like being surprised, there's the source. One cell is switched 4 on to become the whole trillion-cell, massive apparatus for thinking and imagining and, for that matter, being surprised. All the information needed for learning to read and write, playing the piano, arguing before senatorial subcommittees, walking across a street through traffic, or the marvelous human act of putting out one hand and leaning against a tree, is contained in that first cell. All of grammar, all syntax, all arithmetic, all music.

It is not known how the switching on occurs. At the very beginning 5 of an embryo, when it is still nothing more than a cluster of cells, all of this information and much more is latent inside every cell in the cluster. When the stem cell for the brain emerges, it could be that the special quality of brainness is simply switched on. But it could as well be that everything else, every other potential property, is switched off, so that this most specialized of all cells no longer has its precursors' option of being a thyroid or a liver or whatever, only a brain.

No one has the ghost of an idea how this works, and nothing else in 6 life can ever be so puzzling. If anyone does succeed in explaining it, within my lifetime, I will charter a skywriting airplane, maybe a whole fleet of them, and send them aloft to write one great exclamation point after another, around the whole sky, until all my money runs out.

RESPONDING TO "ON EMBRYOLOGY"

Freewrite on some of the questions you had as a child about how babies are born. Try to recapture some of your early thoughts about how human life begins.

Responding through Interpretation

1. How does the essay define embryology?
2. Each of the essay's paragraphs contains intriguing information about new developments in birth and fertilization technology. How does Thomas attempt to explain scientific procedures and developments for the average reader? Is he successful?
3. Thomas's key tone or feeling in the essay is that of "amazement" at the miraculous advances in recent scientific developments. How does he communicate this sense of amazement through the language and examples he uses?

Responding through Discussion

1. Brainstorm with your group about the 1978 event Thomas describes. What do you know about it? Do some reading about the English baby who was conceived in a dish. Have Lewis Thomas's predictions come true? Bring your discoveries back to the entire class.
2. Discuss with the members of your group your beliefs and opinions about the ethics of using technology to influence conception, embryo development, and birth. Be sure each member has a chance to contribute. Have someone make a list of all the pros and cons, which you can later share with the class.

Responding through Writing

1. Write an imaginative piece in your journal in which you pretend that you are an infant being born into today's world.
2. Develop an essay in which you show how birth practices and attitudes have changed over the years. Support your statements with information from your reading as well as with illustrations from your own experiences. Include information about people who have used artificial birth conception—either people you know or people you have read about.

Walking

Linda Hogan

A Native American, Hogan has said that her writing "comes from and goes
back to the community, both the human and the global community." The
essay "Walking" first appeared in *Parabola* magazine in 1990 and was
reprinted in *Dwellings* (1995), a collection of Hogan's writings about nature and her own culture and heritage. In "Walking," Hogan describes her
observations of a natural scene on a series of walks, and by doing so defines the kind of cyclic change that takes place in nature.

It began in dark and underground weather, a slow hunger moving   1
toward light. It grew in a dry gully beside the road where I live, a place
where entire hillsides are sometimes yellow, windblown tides of
sunflower plants. But this one was different. It was alone, and larger than
the countless others who had established their lives further up the hill.
This one was a traveler, a settler, and like a dream beginning in conflict,
it grew where the land had been disturbed.

I saw it first in early summer. It was a green and sleeping bud, rais-   2
ing itself toward the sun. Ants worked around the unopened bloom,
gathering aphids and sap. A few days later, it was a tender young flower,
soft and new, with a pale green center and a troop of silver gray insects
climbing up and down the stalk.

Over the summer this sunflower grew into a plant of incredible   3
beauty, turning its face daily toward the sun in the most subtle of ways,
the black center of it dark and alive with a deep blue light, as if flint had
sparked an elemental fire there, in community with rain, mineral, mountain air, and sand.

As summer changed from green to yellow there were new visitors   4
daily: the lace-winged insects, the bees whose legs were fat with pollen,
and grasshoppers with their clattering wings and desperate hunger.
There were other lives I missed, lives too small or hidden to see. It was
as if this plant with its host of lives was a society, one in which moment
by moment, depending on light and moisture, there was great and diverse change.

There were changes in the next larger world around the plant as   5
well. One day I rounded a bend in the road to find the disturbing sight
of a dead horse, black and still against a hillside, eyes rolled back. Another day I was nearly lifted by a wind and sandstorm so fierce and hot

that I had to wait for it to pass before I could return home. On this day
the faded dry petals of the sunflower were swept across the land. That
was when the birds arrived to carry the new seeds to another future.

In this one plant, in one summer season, a drama of need and sur-   6
vival took place. Hungers were filled. Insects coupled. There was escape,
exhaustion, and death. Lives touched down a moment and were gone.

I was an outsider. I only watched. I never learned the sunflower's   7
golden language or the tongues of its citizens. I had a small understanding, nothing more than a shallow observation of the flower, insects,
and birds. But they knew what to do, how to live. An old voice from
somewhere, gene or cell, told the plant how to evade the pull of gravity
and find its way upward, how to open. It was instinct, intuition, necessity. A certain knowing directed the seedbearing birds on paths to an-
cestral homelands they had never seen. They believed it. They followed.

There are other summons and calls, some even more mysterious   8
than those commandments to birds or those survival journeys of insects.
In bamboo plants, for instance, with their thin green canopy of light and
golden stalks that creak in the wind. Once a century, all of a certain kind
of bamboo flower on the same day. Whether they are in Malaysia or in
a greenhouse in Minnesota makes no difference, nor does the age or size
of the plant. They flower. Some current of an inner language passes between them, through space and separation, in ways we cannot explain
in our language. They are all, somehow, one plant, each with a share of
communal knowledge.

John Hay, in *The Immortal Wilderness*, has written: "There are occa-   9
sions when you can hear the mysterious language of the Earth, in water,
or coming through the trees, emanating from the mosses, seeping
through the undercurrents of the soil, but you have to be willing to wait
and receive."

Sometimes I hear it talking. The light of the sunflower was one lan-   10
guage, but there are others, more audible. Once, in the redwood forest,
I heard a beat, something like a drum or heart coming from the ground
and trees and wind. That underground current stirred a kind of knowing inside me, a kinship and longing, a dream barely remembered that
disappeared back to the body.

Another time, there was the booming voice of an ocean storm thun-   11
dering from far out at sea, telling about what lived in the distance, about
the rough water that would arrive, wave after wave revealing the dis-
turbance at center.

Tonight I walk. I am watching the sky. I think of the people who   12
came before me and how they knew the placement of stars in the sky,
watched the moving sun long and hard enough to witness how a certain angle of light touched a stone only once a year. Without written
records, they knew the gods of every night, the small, fine details of the
world around them and of immensity above them.

Walking, I can almost hear the redwoods beating. And the oceans   13
are above me here, rolling clouds, heavy and dark, considering snow.
On the dry, red road, I pass the place of the sunflower, that dark and secret location where creation took place. I wonder if it will return this
summer, if it will multiply and move up to the other stand of flowers in
a territorial struggle.

It's winter and there is smoke from the fires. The square, lighted win-   14
dows of houses are fogging over. It is a world of elemental attention, of
all things working together, listening to what speaks in the blood.
Whichever road I follow, I walk in the land of many gods, and they love
and eat one another.

Walking, I am listening to a deeper way. Suddenly all my ancestors   15
are behind me. Be still, they say. Watch and listen. You are the result of
the love of thousands.

RESPONDING TO "WALKING"

Freewrite about an experience you've had with nature which still seems important to you.

Responding through Interpretation

1. Why is the essay entitled "Walking"? What are the different levels of
   meaning implied by this title in relationship to the essay?
2. Discuss Linda Hogan's way of seeing. Take note of the details she gives
   and explain why you found certain ones particularly meaningful.
3. In your reading notebook, briefly explain, from Hogan's point of view,
   why the sunflower, a "traveler," knows how to live.

Responding through Discussion

1. Go on a nature walk by yourself or with your group, if possible. Stop several times during the walk and write an observation of what you see, hear,

feel. Share what you have written with your group and later with the class as a whole.
2. With your group, discuss some of the changes you have observed in the natural world during your lifetime. Keep the discussion specific to members' own observations and experiences.

Responding through Writing

1. In your journal, make a list of images you remember seeing in nature and describe why these images have meaning for you.
2. Write an essay in which you present, define, and discuss several lessons that you have learned from being in and observing the natural world. Develop each major point with a concrete description from nature. Incorporate some of the ideas and images used in your journal entry.

Strawberry Creek: A Search for Origins

David Kerr

David Kerr, a longtime resident of Berkeley, California, wrote the following paper for his critical thinking class and published it in a class anthology on nature. In his paper, Kerr uses his own boyhood explorations in an attempt to understand and to define the history and secret pattern of a buried urban creek.

On warm summer days as if there were some great parental conspiracy, my friends and I would be sent out of our respective homes to "get some sun" and "go for a hike and explore nature." The irony of these requests would be that we would very often explore nature without ever getting any sun at all. 1

Once we decided to trace Strawberry Creek from the flatlands where I lived to its hidden beginnings. This had to be done underground. Our starting point was alongside a road in lower Berkeley (we often called lower Berkeley the flatlands or flats). Here the creek exited a tunnel on its way to the Bay. At an early period in the city's history, it was decided by those in charge of such things to bury all of the creeks in the flatlands, in order to build homes there as well as all over downtown. Even though the creeks had been covered over, they still flowed through these now ancient tunnels, perfect kid-size tunnels with perfect kid-size tunnel mouths. 2

Armed with flashlights, candles, lighters, and matches, we entered the tunnel for Strawberry Creek at this small, partially concealed outlet on the side of the road among the bushes. We would wind our way through the city underground. At least that is what we hoped. A big part of the adventure for us was finding out if this was truly the same Strawberry Creek that coursed through the university and Strawberry Canyon. There was no other way of knowing without tracing the creek backwards. 3

Entering the tunnel, we tried to balance ourselves on any flat rocks we could find, some of which were covered with a fine green moss from the occasional flow of water that passed over them. We tried our best to stay dry, something that was to be a losing battle. Inside the tunnel, we discovered that there was a small dry ledge upon which we could walk. Our strange mixture of lights created long and short dancing shadows 4

on the walls and rushing water. The rocks in the creek seemed almost
alive as our flashlight beams crossed over them. The whole scene was
straight out of some old horror movie—which made us all a little nervous.

In the tunnel, as we discovered after a short while, there were a num-   5
ber of side tunnels. In the hope of finding out what these side tunnels
were for, we entered one. There was no flowing water as in the main tunnel; it was dry. The ground was very smooth and silky with soft ripples
like an ancient ocean bed hidden for years. As our steps left the impressions of our tennis shoes, it was like being the first man on the moon.

As we continued on, we could see the roots of trees dangling down   6
above our heads. Leonard observed, "Don't you feel like you're in a car-
toon or something?" He grabbed a large root and started to swing
around from it. I asked, "What the hell do you think you're doing,
Leonard?" He came back with authority, "Trying to pull the tree into the
tunnel, of course." Well, there was no arguing with that, so we let him
swing. This little side tunnel somehow ended up back at the main tunnel; at least we hoped this was the main tunnel. Here it was not so easy
to walk as in the side tunnels, because there was flowing water and no
dry, silted mud to walk on.

More often than not, as we traversed the tunnel, we had to walk in   7
the creek water because the dry edges had become too small to walk on.
As we walked with the creek water rushing over our feet, soaking our
shoes, we started making jokes about coming across giant rats or some
great albino alligator who would gobble us up. We had heard stories of
children bringing back alligators from Florida that end up in the sewers
of New York. These alligators supposedly attacked sewer workers there;
so why not here? Never mind that we were on the other side of the country. Then of course there were the giant mutant rats that were lurking
around the next bend. It had to be true. My friend Leonard also pointed
out that in this great exploration of nature, "Strawberry Creek does run
through the university." He commented with his best all-knowing voice,
"Some careless student has dumped something radioactive into the
creek." This without question had given birth to giant mutant rats which
were certainly going to eat us for a tasty little snack. We never did get
eaten; we did, on the other hand, come to the end of the tunnel at the
entrance of the university. At least one mystery was solved: It is the same
creek.

Strawberry Creek enters the tunnel at the university at around Cen-   8
ter and Oxford Streets where we had just exited. The creek at this point
is surrounded by a small grove of redwoods through which the sun was

still shining as we emerged. It was a bit of a shock to see the sun again after having spent the last few hours underground. We were tired and a bit wet; nonetheless, we were only half done in our search for the creek's origins.

As we followed the creek through the university, we wound around buildings and under bridges rather than underground. The creek led us through different groves of trees, some bay laurel, some redwood, and some live oak. At a point near the Life Sciences building, there is a calm area that has created a pond. There is an abundance of water life here; it provided a momentary stop in our search. We cupped our hands and tried to scoop up water striders. They raced away the second our hands touched the water, yet always returned (as if to torture us) to where you have placed your hand in the water. Somehow we were never able to capture any at all. After giving up our efforts with the water striders, we followed the creek to the other side of the campus. Here, much to our dismay, we could no longer follow the creek; the tunnel under the stadium was too small for us. Crossing over to the other side of the stadium we tried to pick up Strawberry Creek where it starts before it enters the tunnel. I don't remember whether or not we ever did find that end of the tunnel. Somewhere we picked up our journey for the origins of the creek in Strawberry Canyon.

As we hiked up the canyon alongside the creek, the creek started to split into different tributaries. We followed one of them which led us to a fenced area, the botanical gardens for the university. Unable to continue here, we followed a fire trail that this part of the creek had led us to. As we hiked up the trail we could see another part of the creek continuing up the canyon. This again led us to another part of the botanical gardens fence through which we could pass.

At this point, we gave up our search for the mythical origins of Strawberry Creek, yet we continued on to a part of the canyon called Woodbridge Memorial Grove. When we arrived at this small grove of redwoods with its tilted bay tree from which we, as others have, once hung a rope to swing from, we found our rope had once again been cut away from the tree. The day was gone, so we headed home where dinner awaited.

RESPONDING TO "STRAWBERRY CREEK: A SEARCH FOR ORIGINS"

Freewrite about a memorable time in your childhood when you and your friends explored nature.

Responding through Interpretation

1. Describe the important events Kerr and his friends experienced in making their exploration of Strawberry Creek. What are some of the emotions that Kerr communicates through his descriptions?

2. In one sense, Kerr's essay has no conclusion; the friends simply go home for supper after walking to the redwood grove where they played as children. What is implied by the essay's lack of a formal conclusion? Do you consider this an effective ending, or would you rather have had a more formal conclusion?

Responding through Discussion

1. Before beginning your discussion, have the group write for 10 minutes and make a list of all the details they remember from Kerr's essay. Then discuss what each of you has learned about Strawberry Creek—its history, shape, origins, uses, etc. Give examples of closely observed, clear details from the essay which you feel define the creek through the use of description.

Responding through Writing

1. Write a journal entry about the value of children being allowed to explore nature alone or with a group of other children. What do you think young children learn from being in nature and observing it closely?

2. Using some of the information from both your freewrite and your journal entry above, write a paper that explains and defines several major lessons children learn from nature. Which of these lessons are most valuable to them as children? Which of the lessons can be carried over into adulthood? Use your own experiences and observations in deciding upon the lessons you will discuss.

Lessons from the Earth

Jeff Hunze

Born in a small town in central Alaska, Jeff Hunze attended high school in Alaska and moved to San Francisco where he attended community college, majoring in biology and anthropology. He wrote the following essay for his English class after reading some essays about the lessons people learn from the natural world.

Growing up in rural Alaska, I learned about nature early. Many of my first lessons were given to me simply through spending time in some of the wilder places on earth. I have seen amazing things, displays of power I can hardly comprehend, beauty so delicate it breaks your heart to look at it. I never tire of watching the daily miracle of life on our small planet. The lessons I have been taught by nature are by far the most important to me. They are what guides me through life, what binds everything together for me. Some teachers I have had in high school and in college have been very good, but none of them compare to what I have been shown painted so clearly by nature. Of these lessons, none are so striking as the fragile beauty, durability, and tenacity of life. I have learned respect, appreciation for beauty and strength, and I have come to realize how fleeting and precious every moment of life is. Above all, I have experienced peace in the great silence of nature, and I have learned the art of introspection.

Respect is something usually earned, but nature commands our respect, and it only takes one lesson learned poorly to finish us off. The first job I ever held was as a commercial fisherman at the age of fifteen. My co-workers and I thought it great fun to take the fishing skiffs out and water-ski among pods of dolphins feeding on the migrating salmon. As their huge, white-patched fins rose gleaming in the sun six or seven feet above the water, I came to see the incredible power and grace of these great creatures. It was the first time it had occurred to me that I might not be immortal, or even very important in the grand scheme of things. The sea is a great equalizer; it has no qualms about killing humans any more than it does about destroying any other being or thing. Fishing for salmon in a boat only eighteen feet long, I came to feel tiny, vulnerable, and insignificant. Respect for nature grows quickly at times like these, as you see the power and complete indifference of nature up close.

Yet nature is more than just raw power—it is also composed of the   3
millions of delicate living things that inhabit our planet. The contradic-
tion that much of the natural world is both fragile and at the same time
tenacious and resilient is found everywhere. It is a miracle to see how
tiny flowers adorn the cracks in the pavement of a freeway, how song-
birds nest in the harshest desert landscapes, and how the flawlessly
spun web of a spider exists through rain and wind. I learned about the
fragile resiliency of nature firsthand at age seventeen, when I worked as
a wrangler in interior Alaska in Denali State Park. On one of our range
rides, we were sitting by a river and we saw something in the water bobbing and trying to swim. On taking a closer look we found it was a moose
calf that had been washed away from its mother in the crossing somewhere upstream. The calf only weighed about twenty pounds when we
found him, soaking wet, terrified and exhausted. He was so tired that
he fell asleep on the way back to camp, wrapped in a blanket, his little
head bobbing in my lap. Yet he was a tough little guy, mean as a snake
at times, but resilient! I was amazed at his will to live and his ability to
adapt. He was one of my best lessons in that fragile tenacity found in so
many of nature's creatures.

Beauty can be found everywhere, if we are attentive and undis-   4
tracted by loud noises and the rapid pace of modern life. I have experienced beauty often in nature, and I have come to believe that what allows me to experience it there is the silence. I have hiked deep into the
back country and heard a silence there so profound that it literally made
my ears ring. In such fleeting moments, with no noise from outside to
clutter my thoughts, an easy peace comes over me. I feel guided inward,
given an ability and opportunity to understand the intricate connections
between myself and all that surrounds me, how everything is balanced
and how I am part of that balance.

Sitting still at midnight at 13,000 feet on a perfectly still night,   5
watching the moon cross the night sky, completing part of its great
circle, I have found peace. Just letting the crystalline mountain air
wash over me is enough somehow to dispel much of the fear and confusion that make life difficult sometimes. Most importantly, nature
puts things in perspective. How small we are indeed, small, but tenacious.

RESPONDING TO "LESSONS FROM THE EARTH"

Freewrite about a lesson you have learned from nature.

Responding through Interpretation

1. Briefly describe the main lessons Hunze says he has learned from nature. Does he define and explain each lesson clearly? What incidents does he use to clarify his ideas?

2. How does Hunze's long introductory paragraph set the stage for the rest of his essay and arouse your interest in his subject?

Responding through Discussion

1. Hunze uses many vivid details and a number of fairly long sentences. Together with your group, look over his essay and point out instances where you feel his language is especially effective and where you feel it is not. What are some of the techniques Hunze uses in his essay that you could adapt in your own essays? Review these techniques with the class as a whole.

Responding through Writing

1. In your journal, write a response to Jeff Hunze's concluding sentence: "Most importantly, nature puts things in perspective. How small we are indeed, small, but tenacious." Use examples from your own experiences with nature.

2. Think about your own relationship with nature. What are some of the varied experiences you have had with it? Do you feel nature has been your friend or your enemy? Write an essay in which you define your relationship with nature, using examples from your own life to illustrate your statements.

Traveling through the Dark

William Stafford

William Stafford was born and raised in Kansas. He taught English at Lewis and Clark College in Portland from 1948 until 1980. A recipient of the National Book Award for *Traveling through the Dark* (1963), he also was the author of many other books of poetry, including *Passwords* (1991). His essays are collected in *Writing the Australian Crawl: Views on the Writer's Vocation* (1978). Stafford, a conscientious objector during World War II, had faith in the power of nature to teach us about ourselves. The poem that follows, "Traveling through the Dark," explores the darker side of the human relationship with nature, the sacrifices of natural creatures that people feel they must make in order to survive.

Traveling through the dark I found a deer
dead on the edge of the Wilson River road.
It is usually best to roll them into the canyon:
that road is narrow; to swerve might make more dead.

By glow of the tail-light I stumbled back of the car   5
and stood by the heap, a doe, a recent killing;
she had stiffened already, almost cold.
I dragged her off; she was large in the belly.

My fingers touching her side brought me the reason—
her side was warm; her fawn lay there waiting,   10
alive, still, never to be born.
Beside that mountain road I hesitated.

The car aimed ahead its lowered parking lights;
under the hood purred the steady engine.
I stood in the glare of the warm exhaust turning red;   15
around our group I could hear the wilderness listen.

I thought hard for us all—my only swerving—,
then pushed her over the edge into the river.

RESPONDING TO "TRAVELING THROUGH THE DARK"

Freewrite about a time when you experienced the death or loss of an animal.

Responding through Interpretation

1. In your reading notebook, briefly summarize the story of the poem: Who is traveling? What happens?
2. What central conflict does the speaker in the poem experience that leads him to hesitate before pushing the dead deer over the edge of the canyon?
3. The title implies that this is a poem about darkness. Go through the poem and underline all the imagery of darkness that the poem suggests to you. What does the poem reveal to you about real—and symbolic—darkness?

Responding through Discussion

1. Discuss in your group the different responses to the poem that each member had. Then look at these key lines one by one and discuss each of them in relationship to the content of the poem:

    > It is usually best to roll them into the canyon:
    > that road is narrow; to swerve might make more dead.
    >   . . .
    > I stood in the glare of the warm exhaust turning red;
    > around our group I could hear the wilderness listen.

2. Discuss with your group some of the ways you feel that human beings treat animals without compassion.

Responding through Writing

1. Write an essay in which you explore your views about the ways we sacrifice animals to make our human lives easier.
2. Think about all the functions that animals serve and have served in the world. Write a paper describing several ways in which we human beings are dependent on animals.

A Walled Garden

Peter Taylor

Born in Tennessee in 1917, Peter Taylor has enjoyed a long, successful career as a writer and teacher. He is considered a master of the short story and has published eight books of stories as well as numerous plays and several novels. In 1987, Taylor won the Pulitzer Prize for his novel *A Summons to Memphis*. Most of his stories are about the Deep South—its unusual characters, its tragedies and romances, and its tensions. "A Walled Garden" originally appeared in *The New Republic* and is collected in *The Old Forest and Other Stories* (1986).

No, Memphis in autumn has not the moss-hung oaks of Natchez. Nor, my dear young man, have we the exotic, the really exotic orange and yellow and rust foliage of the maples at Rye or Saratoga. When our five-month summer season burns itself out, the foliage is left a cheerless brown. Observe that Catawba tree beyond the wall, and the leaves under your feet here on the terrace are mustard and khaki colored; and the air, the atmosphere (who would dare to breathe a deep breath!) is virtually a sea of dust. But we do what we can. We've walled ourselves in here with these evergreens and box and jasmine. You must know, yourself, young man, that no beauty is native to us but the verdure of early summer. And it's as though I've had to take my finger, just so, and point out to Frances the lack of sympathy that there is in the climate and in the eroded countryside of this region. I have had to build this garden and say, "See, my child, how nice and sympathetic everything can be." But now she does see it my way, you understand. You understand, my daughter has finally made her life with me in this little garden plot, and year by year she has come to realize how little else there is hereabouts to compare with it.

And you, you know nothing of flowers? A young man who doesn't know the zinnia from the aster! How curious that you and my daughter should have made friends. I don't know under what circumstances you two may have met. In her League work, no doubt. She *throws* herself so into whatever work she undertakes. Oh? Why, of course, I should have guessed. She simply *spent* herself on the Chest Drive this year. . . . But my daughter has most of her permanent friends among the flower-minded people. She makes so few friends nowadays outside of our little circle, sees so few people outside our own garden here, really, that I find it quite strange for there to be someone who doesn't know flowers.

No, nothing, we've come to feel, is ever very lovely, really lovely, I   3
mean, in this part of the nation, nothing *but* this garden; and you can well
imagine what even this little bandbox of a garden once was. I created it
out of a virtual chaos of a backyard—Franny's playground, I might say.
For three years I nursed that little magnolia there, for one whole summer did nothing but water the ivy on the east wall of the house; if only
you could have seen the scrubby hedge and the unsightly servants'
quarters of our neighbors that are beyond my serpentine wall (I suppose,
at least, they're still there). In those days it was all very different, you
understand, and Frances's father was about the house, and Frances was
a child. But now in the spring we have what is truly a sweet garden here,
modeled on my mother's at Rye; for three weeks in March our hyacinths
are an inspiration to Frances and to me and to all those who come to us
regularly; the larkspur and marigold are heavenly in May over there beside the roses.

But you do not know the zinnia from the aster, young man? How   4
curious that you two should have become friends. And now you are impatient with her, and you mustn't be; I don't mean to be too indulgent,
but she'll be along presently. Only recently she's become incredibly
painstaking in her toilet again. Whereas in the last few years she's not
cared so much for the popular fads of dress. Gardens and floral design
have occupied her—with what guidance I could give—have been pretty
much her life, really. Now in the old days, I confess, before her father
was taken from us—I lost Mr. Harris in the dreadfully hot summer of
'48 (people don't generally realize what a dreadful year that was—the
worst year for perennials and annuals, alike, since Terrible '30. Things
died that year that I didn't think would *ever* die. A dreadful summer)—
why, she used then to run here and there with people of every sort, it
seemed. I put no restraint upon her, understand. How many times I've
said to my Franny, "You must make your own life, my child, as you
would have it." Yes, in those days she used to run here and there with
people of every sort and variety, it seemed to me. Where was it you say
you met, for she goes so few places that are really *out* anymore? But Mr.
Harris would let me put no restraint upon her. I still remember the
strongheadedness of her teens that had to be overcome and the testiness
in her character when she was nearer to twenty than thirty. And you
should have seen her as a tot of twelve when she would be somersault-
ing and rolling about on this very spot. Honestly, I see that child now,
the mud on her middy blouse and her straight yellow hair in her eyes.

When I used to come back from visiting my people at Rye, she   5
would grit her teeth at me and give her confidence to the black cook. I
would find my own child become a mad little animal. It was through

this door here from the sun room that I came one September afternoon—just such an afternoon as this, young man—still wearing my traveling suit, and called to my child across the yard for her to come and greet me. I had been away for the two miserable summer months, caring for my sick mother, but at the sight of me the little Indian turned, and with a whoop she ran to hide in the scraggly privet hedge that was at the far end of the yard. I called her twice to come from out that filthiest of shrubs. "Frances Ann!" We used to call her by her full name when her father was alive. But she didn't stir. She crouched at the roots of the hedge and spied at her travel-worn mother between the leaves.

I pleaded with her at first quite indulgently and good-naturedly and described the new ruffled dress and the paper cutouts I had brought from her grandmother at Rye. (I wasn't to have Mother much longer, and I knew it, and it was hard to come home to this kind of scene.) At last I threatened to withhold my presents until Thanksgiving or Christmas. The cook in the kitchen may have heard some change in my tone, for she came to the kitchen door over beyond the latticework that we've since put up, and looked out first at me and then at the child. While I was threatening, my daughter crouched in the dirt and began to mumble things to herself that I could not hear, and the noises she made were like those of an angry little cat. It seems that it was a warmer afternoon than this one—but my garden does deceive—and I had been moving about in my heavy traveling suit. In my exasperation I stepped out into the rays of the sweltering sun, and into the yard which I so detested; and I uttered in a scream the child's full name, "Frances Ann Harris!" Just then the black cook stepped out onto the back porch, but I ordered her to return to the kitchen. I began to cross the yard toward Frances Ann—that scowling little creature who was *incredibly* the same Frances you've met—and simultaneously she began to crawl along the hedgerow toward the wire fence that divided my property from the neighbor's.

I believe it was the extreme heat that made me speak so very harshly and with such swiftness as to make my words incomprehensible. When I saw that the child had reached the fence and intended climbing it, I pulled off my hat, tearing my veil to pieces as I hurried my pace. I don't actually know what I was saying—I probably couldn't have told you even a moment later—and I didn't even feel any pain from the turn that I gave my ankle in the gully across the middle of the yard. But the child kept her nervous little eyes on me and her lips continued to move now and again. Each time her lips moved I believe I must have raised my voice in more intense rage and greater horror at her ugliness. And so, young man, striding straight through the hedge I reached her before she had climbed to the top of the wire fencing. I think I took her by the arm above the elbow, about here, and I said something like, "I shall have to punish you, Frances Ann." I did not jerk her. I didn't jerk her one bit, as she wished to make it appear, but rather, as soon as I touched her, she relaxed her hold on the wire and fell to the ground. But she lay there—in her canniness—only the briefest moment looking up and past me through the straight hair that hung over her face like an untrimmed mane. I had barely ordered her to rise when she sprang up and moved with such celerity that she soon was out of my reach again. I followed—running in those high heels—and this time I turned my other ankle in the gully, and I fell there on the ground in that yard, this garden. You won't believe it—pardon, I must sit down. . . . I hope you don't think it too odd, me telling you all this. . . . You won't believe it: I lay there in the ditch and she didn't come to aid me with childish apologies and such, but instead she deliberately climbed into her swing that hung from the dirty old poplar that was here formerly (I have had it cut down and the roots dug up) and she began to swing, not high and low, but only gently, and stared straight down at her mother through her long hair—which, you may be sure, young man, I had cut the very next day at my own beautician's and curled into a hundred ringlets.

RESPONDING TO "A WALLED GARDEN"

Freewrite about ways you used to escape from the grown-ups when you were a child. Did these escapes ever get you into trouble?

Responding through Interpretation

1. The opening paragraph makes it immediately clear that "The Walled Garden" is a story about something far more important than the garden itself. Study the first paragraph, especially the paragraph's last two sentences, and write down what you think Taylor intends to convey to the reader through these statements.
2. Trace Frances Ann's life with her mother, as given in the story. What were the major events disclosed by her mother? What impact did each of these have on Frances Ann as she grew up? What is the significance of the mother having her daughter's hair cut and "curled into a hundred ringlets"?
3. Think about the connection Taylor suggests between nature and children. In what ways are children like nature? How are children like gardens that need proper tending by parents? To further understand Taylor's story, write a comparison of young children to a garden.

Responding through Discussion

1. Together with your group, go back over the story and note Taylor's physical descriptions of the garden. See if you can describe it as it looked before and after the mother has "transformed" it. Discuss with the group what other meanings the various descriptions of the garden suggest.

2. On a deeper level, this story is about a mother's relationship with her young daughter and how the mother has forced her will on her daughter. Discuss this idea in your group, drawing upon your own experiences and observations. When does parental control protect children and enable them to grow in positive ways, and when does it thwart and damage them?

Responding through Writing

1. In your journal, write a detailed response to this story. How did it affect you? What are the different emotions it brought up in you? What do you think about the story in general? Is it believable? What do you think Taylor's point was in writing the story?

2. Study Taylor's story for tone and ideas and then try your hand at writing a brief story told by one person. Be sure to keep the story from the speaker's point of view only. Choose your own subject matter. Try setting your story in a "natural," outdoors environment.

What Is a Naturalist, Anyway?

John T. Nichols

John Nichols was raised in a family of naturalists. His grandfather, a curator at the American Museum of Natural History for a number of years, had a large collection of stuffed and live birds and other natural creatures which he kept at his 600-acre estate in Mastic, Long Island. John Nichols went on to become a novelist concerned with conservation issues; his *Milagro Beanfield War* has been made into a film, and he recently completed a photo-essay on the environment, *The Sky's the Limit*. The following definition of a naturalist is excerpted from a speech he made at the American Museum of Natural History.

One of the traits that marked my grandfather, and that he passed on to   1
my dad, who passed it on to me, was his curiosity about almost everything in the natural world. Grandpa was an eclectic man of science. To earn a living, he wound up specializing in fishes, but he was also an avid and respected ornithologist, a fan of weasels, a good man with a bat (the flying kind), a turtle junkie—and was intrigued by almost everything else. In a 1916 article entitled "Primarily Unadaptive Variants," he ran through a wide gamut of discussion, including observations on black-backed gulls and Spanish mackerels, tree squirrels and bay-breasted warblers, black bears and wild guinea pigs.

The man was also a philosopher and poet, and he had a sometimes   2
wacky sense of humor. The same mind that ranged so widely over the mysteries of natural history was also capable of conjuring up my favorite poem of childhood:

> I had a niece
> Who ate a piece
> Of candle grease.
>
> For goodness sake,
> How it did make
> Her stomach ache.
>
> Run, run, anyone
> Get a gun.

> Because we love her
> We can't let her suffer,
> We'll shoot her and stuff her.

All these reflections on my grandfather lead me to ask, "What is a nat-   3
uralist, anyway?" This same question was asked by my Grandpa in a short
autobiography he wrote in 1923. He answered his own query in this manner, and it is the way he defined himself:

> *A naturalist, it would seem, is one interested in natural phenomena. The term
> may be further limited, however. All persons working in the broad field of sci-
> ence deal with natural phenomena, but the modern tendency to specializa-
> tion has carried the majority of scientists into fields of thought far removed
> from those of the old-fashioned naturalist; and in the study of animals, for in-
> stance, there are anatomists, cytologists, physiologists, geneticists, etc., so nu-
> merous, that in its narrower sense it is convenient to reserve the term natu-
> ralist for those investigating life from an older, different viewpoint. A
> naturalist takes the most obvious first phenomenon, the individual animal,
> for the basic unit of his science, and instead of cataloguing its parts, investi-
> gates its place in nature, and that of the larger units, such as the species, of
> which it is an integral part.*

My grandfather's definition of a naturalist reminds me of a statement   4
by John Muir, which I feel best describes the situation of all life on earth.
Muir said, "Whenever we try to pick out anything by itself, we find it
hitched to everything else in the universe."

Of course, that's obvious, and it should be the first building block   5
of all knowledge. Yet in a world that has reached its current technological ascendancy largely through specialization, we have all but forgotten that nothing exists apart from everything else. And so we find ourselves in a major-league pickle that features a diminishing ozone layer,
the greenhouse effect, and perhaps ultimately, the premature end of
most evolution on earth.

The responsibility of scientists in this dilemma was emphatically dri-   6
ven home to me some years back when I was working with the European film director Costa-Gavras on a movie (never produced) about the
daily lives of some nuclear physicists. All of them were brilliant, dedicated, and compassionate people, but their dependency on government
money for the perpetuation of their scientific specialties ultimately led
them to create a technology of megadeath. During my research for this
film, I repeatedly came across warnings by various knowledgeable authors on the danger of the growing chasm between human values and
the scientific enterprise. Biologist Jacques Monod, for instance, pro-

claimed that "any mingling of knowledge with values is unlawful, forbidden." Sociologist Max Weber put it this way: "Whoever lacks the capacity to put on blinders, so to speak . . . may as well stay away from science." And science historian Steve J. Heims once wrote that "in the nineteenth century, any consideration of social responsibility in connection with scientific research became a direct violation of the standards and values of the profession. Thus, falling into a false innocence was the price paid for 'benefits' of scientific progress."

Two of the more interesting thinkers I met in my reading were the   7
astrophysicist Freeman Dyson and the physicist Max Born. In his book *Disturbing the Universe,* Dyson speaks of how some modern molecular biologists have adopted a narrow definition of scientific knowledge, "by reducing the complex behavior of living creatures to the simpler behavior of the molecules out of which the creatures are built . . . [results in a] reduction of the apparently purposeful movements of an organism to purely mechanical movements of its constituent parts." Elaborating on how this tendency has transformed the entire modern workplace, Max Born says that "most workmen know only their special tiny manipulation in a special section of the production process and hardly ever see the complete product." So, "naturally, they do not feel responsible for the product or its use." Born then states that this kind of technical specialization, which "separates action from effect," reached its zenith in Nazi Germany, where mass murderers "pleaded not guilty because they 'did their job' and had nothing to do with its ultimate purpose."

While Born felt that scientific research   8

> has led to an enormous widening of the horizon of knowledge . . . this gain is paid for by a bitter loss. The scientific attitude is apt to create doubt and skepticism toward traditional, unscientific knowledge and even toward natural, unsophisticated actions on which human society depends.

Born concludes:

> I am haunted by the idea that this break in human civilization caused by the discovery of the scientific method may be irreparable. The political and military horrors and complete breakdown of ethics which I have witnessed in my lifetime may be not a symptom of social weakness, but a necessary consequence of the rise of science—which in itself is among the highest intellectual achievements of man.

Now it may seem that I have strayed a bit far afield from my tall, lanky   9
grandfather, dressed in a rumpled blue suit and a tattered old fedora, with a pipe hanging out of his mouth, squinting as he notched yet another box tur-

tle and then leaned over slowly to set it free in the grass. Yet I have always felt that in that man, and in the legacy he passed on to my father and thus to me, there was an important lesson to be learned. It was evident in his strength of character, in his personality and his view of the world, in the disciplines he chose to follow, in the curiosity he had for many things, and in the humility that typified his way of doing science. But most importantly, my grandfather saw the natural world as an interconnected whole: he understood, and sympathized with, "the complete product."

Today, science is much more sophisticated than he ever could have   10 imagined. Yet in this world of vast complexity, instant communication, and technological sophistication, we seem to have completely lost track of the overall scheme of things. This has led to what many see as a building ecological catastrophe, perhaps of insurmountable proportions. And interestingly, it seems as if my grandfather's perception of the world, placing value on biodiversity, is increasingly one that the environmental movements of today are adopting as their own in order to save the globe. At a recent meeting of the American Society of Ichthyologists and Herpetologists, an organization that my grandfather helped to found, between a fourth and a third of the presentations dealt with conservation, endangered species, environmental damage, biodiversity, species protection, and the relationship of "anthropogenic perturbation of the extirpation of species." I find that both sad and hopeful. Sad because, obviously, each day there are many fewer snakes and fishes and salamanders out there to learn about. (Approximately 3,000 species became extinct in the United States alone last year.) But I also feel hopeful because obviously the conscience of science today is struggling to learn how to rectify the situation.

In a book called *The Tangled Wing*, the biological anthropologist   11 Melvin Konner writes, "We are losing the sense of wonder, the hallmark of our species and the central feature of the human spirit." And he believes that:

> at the conclusion of all our studies we must try once again to experience the human soul as soul, and not just as a buzz of bioelectricity, the human will as will, and not just a surge of hormones: the human heart not as a fibrous, sticky pump, but as the metaphoric organ of understanding.

I think my grandfather probably always operated on those presump-   12 tions. He was awed by the mystery of things. And he never could ignore his own emotional responses to a beautiful seascape or butterfly simply because he understood a great deal about the factual components that made it beautiful.

So, "What is a naturalist, anyway?" Well, I would propose that a   13
naturalist is a person whose curiosity is boundless. He or she is interested in kinkajous and sticklebacks, in astronomy, French wine, magpies,
baseball, prairie rattlesnakes, quantum mechanics, corn on the cob, great
sperm whales, and even Bolsheviks and hummingbirds. A naturalist is
a person who tries to delight in everything, is in love with the whole of
life, and hopes to walk in harmony across this earth. A naturalist might
also be a lunatic like myself who would like to overthrow an economic
system based on planned obsolescence and conspicuous consumption
because he believes that it is a formula for planetary suicide. Put another
way, a naturalist probably understands that human growth for the sake
of growth is the ideology of the cancer cell. So a naturalist most likely
gets a vasectomy or a tubal ligation after 1.8 children and sends lots of
money to Planned Parenthood. In a naturalist's life style, a lot less "stuff"
is consumed, so that all the other critters he or she loves can use that un-
exploited biological capital for their own benefit and survival.

In short, a naturalist chooses not to be anthropocentric, believing,   14
rather, that everything has an equal right to life on earth—whether it's
an elephant, a peasant from El Salvador, an African cichlid, or a tiny bac-
terium. A naturalist understands, and defends, the product as a whole.
I feel certain that the answer to our future lies in this world view. And
I am grateful I learned it as a child, because it has enriched my life im-
measurably.

RESPONDING TO "WHAT IS A NATURALIST ANYWAY?"

Freewrite about a person (it can be yourself, a member of your family, or a
person you know) whom you think of as a naturalist. What are the characteristics that make the person a naturalist?

Responding through Interpretation

1. Nichols gives a number of definitions of a naturalist throughout the
   essay. Find the statements he uses to define a naturalist and underline
   them. Then look through the essay and note the *examples* and ideas from
   others which he incorporates to further clarify his definitions. Write a
   brief summary in your reading notebook which covers all the important
   points of Nichols's definition.
2. The author provides many quotations from such authorities as Max
   Weber, Freeman Dyson, and Max Born. How do these quotations support Nichols's points? Which of the quotations do you find most interesting and relevant?

3. What did Nichols learn about the "chasm" in science while working on the film about nuclear physicists?

Responding through Discussion

1. Choose a professor on campus in one of the life sciences departments, such as ecology, biology, botany, or geology. Interview, in a group if at all possible, the professor and ask what he or she thinks about Nichols's accusations against scientists. Before going to the interview, get together as a group and extract key statements from Nichols's essay so you will be well-informed during the session.
2. Discuss some of the statements Nichols made about our "ecological catastrophe." As a group, come up with a short list of practical steps that might be taken to ward off this catastrophe. Report back to the class with your suggestions.

Responding through Writing

1. In your journal, write an extended definition of some term that interests you. Use some of Nichols's ideas for making your own definition lively and fun to read.
2. Write an essay in which you develop Nichols's definition of a naturalist by providing some specific examples from your own experience or reading. Use your freewrite, your journal entry, and your responses to Nichols's essay as sources of information for your paper.

Sojourner

Annie Dillard

Annie Dillard has delighted a wide audience of readers with her close observations and deep meditations on the natural world ever since she published her first book of nonfiction, *Pilgrim at Tinker Creek,* which won
the Pulitzer Prize in 1974. Born and raised in Pennsylvania, Dillard obtained both her B.A. and M.A. degrees from Hollins College in Virginia.
In addition to a book of poems and a novel, Annie Dillard has written several other nonfiction books. The following piece, "Sojourner," is excerpted
from *Teaching a Stone to Talk* (1982). Dillard has described herself as "a
poet . . . with a background in theology and a penchant for quirky facts."

If survival is an art, then mangroves are artists of the beautiful: not only   1
that they exist at all—smooth-barked, glossy-leaved, thickets of lapped
mystery—but that they can and do exist as floating islands, as trees
upright and loose, alive and homeless on the water.

I have seen mangroves, always on tropical ocean shores, in Florida   2
and in the Galápagos. There is the red mangrove, the yellow, the button, and the black. They are all short, messy trees, waxy-leaved, laced
all over with aerial roots, woody arching buttresses, and weird leathery
berry pods. All this tangles from a black muck soil, a black muck matted like a mud-sopped rag, a muck without any other plants, shaded,
cold to the touch, tracked at the water's edge by herons and nosed by
sharks.

It is these shoreline trees which, by a fairly common accident, can   3
become floating islands. A hurricane flood or a riptide can wrest a tree
from the shore, or from the mouth of a tidal river, and hurl it into the
ocean. It floats. It is a mangrove island, blown.

There are floating islands on the planet; it amazes me. Credulous   4
Pliny described some islands thought to be mangrove islands floating
on a river. The people called these river islands *the dancers,* "because in
any consort of musicians singing, they stir and move at the stroke of the
feet, keeping time and measure."

Trees floating on rivers are less amazing than trees floating on the   5
poisonous sea. A tree cannot live in salt. Mangrove trees exude salt from
their leaves; you can see it, even on shoreline black mangroves, as a thin
white crust. Lick a leaf and your tongue curls and coils; your mouth's a
heap of salt.

Nor can a tree live without soil. A hurricane-born mangrove island   6
may bring its own soil to the sea. But other mangrove trees make their
own soil—and their own islands—from scratch. These are the ones
which interest me. The seeds germinate in the fruit on the tree. The ger-
minated embryo can drop anywhere—say, onto a dab of floating muck.
The heavy root end sinks; a leafy plumule unfurls. The tiny seedling,
afloat, is on its way. Soon aerial roots shooting out in all directions trap
debris. The sapling's networks twine, the interstices narrow, and water
calms in the lee. Bacteria thrive on organic broth; amphipods swarm.
These creatures grow and die at the trees' wet feet. The soil thickens, ac-
cumulating rainwater, leaf rot, seashells, and guano; the island spreads.

More seeds and more muck yield more trees on the new island. A   7
society grows, interlocked in a tangle of dependencies. The island rocks
less in the swells. Fish throng to the backwaters stilled in snarled roots.
Soon, Asian mudskippers—little four-inch fish—clamber up the mangrove roots into the air and peer about from periscope eyes on stalks,
like snails. Oysters clamp to submersed roots, as do starfish, dog whelk,
and the creatures that live among tangled kelp. Shrimp seek shelter
there, limpets a holdfast, pelagic birds a rest.

And the mangrove island wanders on, afloat and adrift. It walks tee-   8
tering and wanton before the wind. Its fate and direction are random. It
may bob across an ocean and catch on another mainland's shores. It may
starve or dry while it is still a sapling. It may topple in a storm, or pitch-
pole. By the rarest of chances, it may stave into another mangrove island
in a crash of clacking roots, and mesh. What it is most likely to do is drift
anywhere in the alien ocean, feeding on death and growing, netting a
makeshift soil as it goes, shrimp in its toes and terns in its hair.

We could do worse.   9

I alternate between thinking of the planet as home—dear and fa-   10
miliar stone hearth and garden—and as a hard land of exile in which we
are all sojourners. Today I favor the latter view. The word "sojourner"
occurs often in the English Old Testament. It invokes a nomadic people's
sense of vagrancy, a praying people's knowledge of estrangement, a
thinking people's intuition of sharp loss: "For we are strangers before
thee, and sojourners, as were all our fathers: our days on the earth are
as a shadow, and there is none abiding."

We don't know where we belong, but in times of sorrow it doesn't   11
seem to be here, here with these silly pansies and witless mountains, here
with sponges and hard-eyed birds. In times of sorrow the innocence of
the other creatures—from whom and with whom we evolved—seems

a mockery. Their ways are not our ways. We seem set among them as among lifelike props for a tragedy—or a broad lampoon—on a thrust rock stage.

It doesn't seem to be here that we belong, here where space is curved, 12
the earth is round, we're all going to die, and it seems as wise to stay in bed as budge. It is strange here, not quite warm enough, or too warm, too leafy, or inedible, or windy, or dead. It is not, frankly, the sort of home for people one would have thought of—although I lack the fancy to imagine another.

The planet itself is a sojourner in airless space, a wet ball flung across 13
nowhere. The few objects in the universe scatter. The coherence of matter dwindles and crumbles toward stillness. I have read, and repeated, that our solar system as a whole is careering through space toward a point east of Hercules. Now I wonder: what could that possibly mean, east of Hercules? Isn't space curved? When we get "there," how will our course change, and why? Will we slide down the universe's inside arc like mud slung at a wall? Or what sort of welcoming shore is this east of Hercules? Surely we don't anchor there, and disembark, and sweep into dinner with our host. Does someone cry, "Last stop, last stop"? At any rate, east of Hercules, like east of Eden, isn't a place to call home. It is a course without direction; it is "out." And we are cast.

These are enervating thoughts, the thoughts of despair. They crowd 14
back, unbidden, when human life as it unrolls goes ill, when we lose control of our lives or the illusion of control, and it seems that we are not moving toward any end but merely blown. Our life seems cursed to be a wiggle merely, and a wandering without end. Even nature is hostile and poisonous, as though it were impossible for our vulnerability to survive on these acrid stones.

Whether these thoughts are true or not I find less interesting than 15
the possibilities for beauty they may hold. We are down here in time, where beauty grows. Even if things are as bad as they could possibly be, and as meaningless, then matters of truth are themselves indifferent; we may as well please our sensibilities and, with as much spirit as we can muster, go out with a buck and wing.

The planet is less like an enclosed spaceship—spaceship earth— 16
than it is like an exposed mangrove island beautiful and loose. We the people started small and have since accumulated a great and solacing muck of soil, of human culture. We are rooted in it; we are bearing it with us across nowhere. The word "nowhere" is our cue: the consort of musicians strikes up, and we in the chorus stir and move and start twirling

our hats. A mangrove island turns drift to dance. It creates its own soil as it goes, rocking over the salt sea at random, rocking day and night and round the sun, rocking round the sun and out toward east of Hercules.

RESPONDING TO "SOJOURNER"

Freewrite about a plant or tree that you have observed. Describe it and explain what you know about it.

Responding through Interpretation

1. What two elements is Dillard comparing? How does she say they are similar? Different?
2. What is the central meaning of Dillard's essay? What is she really talking about? What is a sojourner?
3. Dillard says: "Our life seems cursed to be . . . a wandering without end." In your reading notebook, write an extended explanation of this idea as you understand it through Dillard's eyes.

Responding through Discussion

1. From Dillard's descriptions, what do you imagine a mangrove to look like? Go through and study the spots where she gives the reader specific physical descriptions. Why does Dillard find them so fascinating? If possible, locate a picture of a mangrove and see how it compares with Dillard's descriptions.
2. Before beginning the discussion, take 10 minutes in the group to jot down plants or other natural wonders you would like to know more about. Share these in the group and take time for group members to give whatever information they know about them.

Responding through Writing

1. Study Dillard's essay further. What do you notice about her style? Her organization? In your journal, write an evaluation of what you like and don't like about her presentation.
2. Write an essay in which you describe one object of nature very fully, using some of the same kinds of techniques of description and evaluation which Dillard has used. After you have fully described the object, move into a philosophical discussion of how this natural object is similar to our lives on the planet earth. Include a photograph or a drawing of the object in your paper, if possible.

Do Dogs Have Thoughts and Feelings?

Elizabeth Marshall Thomas

Elizabeth Marshall Thomas is an anthropologist who spent a number of years observing a group of dogs that she owned and bred at her home in Cambridge, Massachusetts. She moved to a more rural environment in Virginia where she allowed her dogs to return to a "natural" life, free of human beings. The results of her observations and interactions with these dogs can be seen in her best-selling book, *The Hidden Life of Dogs*, from which the following excerpt is taken. "Do Dogs Have Thoughts and Feelings?" explores several terms that are important issues in trying to define and understand the inner worlds of animals: anthropomorphism, cynomorphism, and empathetic observation.

Do dogs have thoughts and feelings? Of course they do. If they didn't, there wouldn't be any dogs. That being said, however, a book on dogs must by definition be somewhat anthropomorphic, and reasonably so, since our aversion to the label is misplaced. Using the experience of one's species to evaluate the experience of another species has been a useful tool to many of the great wildlife biologists. The more experienced the investigator, the more useful the tool. Consider George Schaller's observation of a mother leopard and her son: "At times [the two leopards] had ardent reunions, rubbing their cheeks and bodies sinuously and licking each other's face, obviously excited and delighted with the meeting. Witnessing such tenderness, I realized that these leopards merely masked their warm temperament and emotional depth beneath a cold exterior."* 1

In contrast is the observation of a former neighbor of mine, now deceased—a psychiatrist, actually—who saw a bird fly into the glass of his picture window and fall to earth, stunned. In a moment, a second bird swooped down, picked up the first, and flew away with it. In a quite moving anthropomorphization, the psychiatrist assumed that the second bird was a male, the mate of the first, and had come to her rescue. However, since birds never carry their loved ones, and grab other birds only to kill them, the second bird was surely not a helper at all but a predator taking advantage of the first bird's plight. If the 2

---

*George Schaller, *Golden Shadows, Flying Hooves* (New York: Knopf, 1973), p. 196.

psychiatrist had been more familiar with the ways of the natural world, he probably wouldn't have made that particular assumption.

We are not the only species to apply our values and our experience 3 when interpreting other creatures. Dogs do it too, sometimes with no more luck than the psychiatrist. When a dog with a bone menaces a human observer, the dog actually assumes that the person wants the slimy, dirt-laden object, and is applying dog values, or cynomorphizing. Nevertheless, most animals, including dogs, constantly evaluate other species by means of empathetic observation. A dog of mine once assessed my mood, which was dark, over a distance of about one hundred yards, and changed his demeanor from cheery to bleak in response. He was in a pen that I was approaching, and as I rounded the corner he caught sight of me. I was sad at heart but not showing it in a way that any of the people around me had noticed, but the dog saw at once that something was wrong. Over the great distance he stared at me a moment, as if to be sure that he was really seeing what he thought he was seeing, and then, evidently deciding that his first impression had been accurate, he drooped visibly. I was so impressed with his acuity that I cheered up again, and so did he!

I was equally impressed by a female housecat, Lilac, whom I happened to be carrying home one evening, when on the way I decided to look in a nearby field to see if by chance any deer were grazing. I must have tensed a little as I got near the field, and perhaps walked a bit more quietly, but whatever it was, Lilac felt the change, instantly recognized it as a prelude to hunting, and leaned forward, ears up, eyes wide, claws sticking into my arm, ready to spring at whatever I might be stalking.

As a further note on anthropomorphism, the reader may notice references herein to a dog's smile. All dogs smile, which is to say their faces become pleasant and relaxed, with ears low, eyes half shut, lips soft and parted, and chin high. This is a dog smile. Yet a few dogs also emulate human smiles, and hence they themselves are anthropomorphizing. In the presence of human beings these dogs will draw back their lips grotesquely to bare their teeth, making the same face we make. At the same time, these dogs may also roll over to reveal their bellies submissively, showing that they understand exactly what our smiles mean.

And finally, anthropomorphism can help us interpret the act of 6 showing the belly—the act that symbolizes what puppies do when submitting to adult dogs. By the act, dogs say to us, *Do as you will with us, since we are helpless puppies in your presence.* To understand the act, we can look at the human parallel: the way many religious people—Christians, for example—behave toward God. We call God the parent and ourselves his children. When we kneel to pray, we diminish our height, so that we look more like young children. Our prayerful position with raised eyes suggests that we are clasping God around the knees and looking up, as if he were facing us and looking straight down, not as if he were, say, off on the horizon. What's more, just as many of us pray at specified hours—upon getting up in the morning or going to bed at night, for instance—many dogs do their ritual submission at certain times of day. My husband's dog, for example, elects to show his belly to my husband right after they both get up in the morning. Why? No one knows for sure, but by now they both expect it.

Do dogs think we're God? Probably not. But just as we think of   7
God's ways as mysterious, dogs find our ways capricious and mysterious, often with excellent reason. Every day the humane societies execute thousands of dogs who tried all their lives to do their very best by their owners. These dogs are killed not because they are bad but because they are inconvenient. So as we need God more than he needs us, dogs need us more than we need them, and they know it.

RESPONDING TO "DO DOGS HAVE THOUGHTS AND FEELINGS?"

Freewrite about an experience you had with a dog or a cat that led you to believe that animals have thoughts and feelings.

Responding through Interpretation

1. What is anthropomorphism? Why does Thomas believe it is acceptable in writing about dogs?
2. In your reading journal, make a list of all the examples that Thomas gives about animal behaviors. What purpose does each of these examples serve in supporting Thomas's points?
3. What does Thomas say are the parallels between the way religious people act toward God and the way dogs act toward their owners?

Responding through Discussion

1. With your group, discuss your experiences with household pets who seemed very much like human beings. Take time to write down a list of behaviors (only one pet at a time) which you considered to be parallel to the behavior of humans.
2. Discuss Thomas's essay. Allow the members of the group who agree with her to explain why they do; then allow the members of the group who

disagree with her to explain why they do. Report your most important points—both pros and cons—back to the class.

Responding through Writing

1. In your journal, write an extended definition of one of the key terms Thomas uses in her essay. Use examples from your own observations or experiences to illustrate your point.
2. Write an essay about one of your household pets that seemed to you to be very much like a human being—at least to you. Bring in some of Thomas's ideas, as well as some of the ideas gained from the group discussions.

Dogs in Transition

Kirsten Simon

Kirsten Simon grew up in Germany and came to live in northern California several years ago after spending years traveling in Europe, North Africa, Israel, and India, where she studied massage healing techniques. She is a professional masseuse who is returning to college to study somatic psychology. Kirsten Simon wrote the following essay for her English class in order to explore the complex ways that pets and their owners interact and often come to resemble one another, after reading Elizabeth Marshall Thomas's "Do Dogs Have Thoughts and Feelings?"

Elizabeth Marshall Thomas's reflections on proper and improper   1
anthropomorphism of pets in her essay "Do Dogs Have Thoughts and Feelings?" made me recall my own observations of the relationship between people and their dogs. Have you ever noticed how much owners and their dogs look alike? I have been entertained by this phenomenon for many years. In parks, on downtown sidewalks, and along hiking trails I have witnessed women in high heels strolling with their coiffed and perfumed poodles, plump housewives dragging their overfed Cocker Spaniels, and fit joggers running with their slender, energetic Retrievers. Are dogs really like their owners or are owners making their dogs into reflections of themselves? I believe that the latter is true. People often project human characteristics onto their dogs; however, unlike humans, dogs cannot advance to human levels of consciousness, reasoning and self-revelation.

Anthropomorphism is often a tool used by people attempting to cre-   2
ate closeness with their pets. For example, my friend Maryanne considers her Standard Poodle, Beau, to be well-mannered, often referring to him as a "gentleman" when he behaves. Dogs can act in a human manner, but their motivation for that behavior is related to their instinctive need to survive. Pleasing the owner assures the dog food, shelter and comfort. His behavior results from training and conditioning. He remembers that a certain activity is rewarded with a treat. My friend Isabelle's Retriever, Bessy, has learned that every time she brings the paper into the house she is rewarded with a Doggie Biscuit. After having repeated this many times, Bessy now brings in the paper habitually and the biscuit can be substituted by a petting gesture, or words of approval. Bessy has taken her lesson a step further, and she now brings Is-

abelle all kinds of things like socks and books in order to get rewards. Isabelle often says, "Bessy is bringing me gifts." By anthropomorphizing her dog she gets the love and validation she has lacked since her children left the house. In Isabelle's mind Bessy feels as lonely as she feels and shows Isabelle her love and need for company by bringing her gifts. However, Bessy is simply following her conditioned responses.

The closeness between dogs and humans has its origin in the similarities of dog pack structures and human family structures. Michael Leneham writes in his article "Four Ways to Walk a Dog" that the wild dog "travels in a pack that is roughly comparable to a slightly extended human family: a mating pair, a generation or two of their offspring, and a few related adults—aunts and uncles, if you will . . . and [the pack] hunts cooperatively." People also have to cooperate with each other to earn their livings. Even the fact that people and dogs share comparable basic instincts, and employ similar methods to survive, does not mean that dogs have become more human because dogs cannot reason. For example, man uses reasoning to consciously plan his family while the dog acts on instinct to create his family. Man can take steps to create the family of his choice employing the options of birth control and abortion, while the dog controlled by his instincts will have puppies every year. Therefore, dog owners also have to be responsible for the family planning of their dogs. Because dogs do not have reasoning available to them, they are dependent upon their owners throughout their lives. They may act human, but they can never become the equal to a human being.

It can be dangerous if people anthropomorphize their dogs and present them as human-like beings because there is always a chance that a dog's instincts will overrule their conditioned behavior. Our mailman told me that he has been bitten several times by dogs whose owners assured him that the dog never bites. I learned an equally painful similar lesson when, as a child, I became friendly with our neighbor's bulldog, Boris, who was introduced to me as friendly and safe. I used to play with him every day after school until one day he attacked me while I was helping my neighbor bring in some groceries. I thought that Boris must have been afraid that I would steal his food. Today I believe that Boris was actually challenging me because he thought that I was the lowest human pack member. Dog trainer Bill Koehler points out that "occasionally a pet dog will try its luck. It may challenge the owner's authority by simply disobeying, or in extreme cases it may mount an actual physical attack." Therefore a dog is always a wild animal first even if he is trained well.

It is common that people deceive themselves with the illusion that 5
their dogs have become human. I believe that one reason why people
do this is because it is easier for them to fulfill their needs by developing relationships with dogs rather than with other people. People have
more complex personalities and are less dependent than dogs. However,
if people meet the challenge of getting their needs met in relationships
with other people, their needs will be met more authentically than they
can be by their dogs.

RESPONDING TO "DOGS IN TRANSITION"

Freewrite about a memorable encounter—good or bad—that you've had
with your own or someone else's pet.

Responding through Interpretation

1. What particular concerns does Simon share with Thomas? Does Simon
   seem to agree or disagree with Thomas's ideas about dogs and their owners?
2. Simon develops her essay by using concrete examples and descriptive
   details. Go through the essay and note details you consider to be effective.

Responding through Discussion

1. With your group, look back over both Thomas's and Simon's essays. Discuss which point of view you agree with most and why. Bring your
   group's decision and ideas back to the class for further discussion.

Responding through Writing

1. In your journal, write a letter to Kirsten Simon expressing your opinion
   about her essay—both the content and the way she has written it.
2. Whether you agree or disagree with Thomas, write your own essay arguing against anthropomorphism of household pets. What are some of
   the drawbacks of this practice?

Dogs and Empathetic Observation

Lori Pascerella

Lori Pascerella is a returning student who works full-time as a telephone installer and repairer. She enjoys sports and the out-of-doors. She is also a cancer survivor whose close relationship with her animals helped get her through a difficult period in her treatment and recuperation. The following essay was written in her English class as a response to Elizabeth Marshall Thomas's "Do Dogs Have Thoughts and Feelings?" Lori Pascerella directed her essay to an audience of pet lovers. Notice how Pascerella explores definitions of key terms and issues in the Thomas essay, such as animal thoughts, feelings, language, and empathetic observation, drawing upon her own extensive contact with pets for examples.

We pet lovers all know our animals have thoughts and feelings; it seems   1
to be the rest of the world that is confused. Elizabeth Marshall Thomas
wrote convincingly in an excerpt from *The Hidden Life of Dogs*, "Do Dogs
Have Thoughts and Feelings?", that of course dogs have thoughts and
feelings and are aware of our needs. One of the ways dogs show emotion
is through empathetic observation, the power to understand another's
feelings and to pay close attention to them. This often is expressed by a
dog in its own language, which helps to communicate the special
relationship that exists between dog and owner.

Zephyr is my golden retriever who speaks to me daily with his eyes   2
and expressions. I have three dogs and three cats in my household, and
they all have their own personality and speak to me in their own language. Every morning Zephyr wakes me up by laying his soft golden
colored head and wet black nose near my face on my bed. When I wake
up, his big puppy-like face and eyes are staring at me, while his tail is
swishing back and forth in the air. "Wake up Mom, I am hungry, I have
to go out," he seems to say expressively. I reach down and scratch his
head, and he just melts and has no more cares in the world.

He always feels so happy when he's included in my daily adven-   3
tures. When I choose to leave him at home, he dramatically stands in the
corner with his head hanging down full of sadness. Just as you would
suspect, as soon as I pick up my car keys Zephyr runs over to me, wag-
ging his tail full of excitement. He looks at me with that irresistible face,
"Can I go, Mom?" Being the sucker that I am, I load him into my truck
with his head sticking out of the window and his ears flopping in the
wind as we drive down the road.

Zephyr's feelings of bewilderment, confusion and worry became 4
strongly relevant last year when I became very ill. I went through
surgery and follow-up treatments for six to eight months. Every time I
came home from a treatment Zephyr greeted me at the door faithfully
making sure I was all right. He would always lie beside me when I was
in bed not feeling well. He seemed to be aware of the fact that something
wasn't right with me, but he wasn't quite sure what. He would always
give me loads of unconditional love. As pet owners we are fortunate to
have such a special relationship in our life: the bond that you experience
with your animal is like no other.

Over the year that I was ill, Zephyr grayed considerably. His eye- 5
brows and face turned white, and he looks much older than he really is.
It is almost like he was the one that was ill and went through all the treatments. At first I thought it was my imagination, but a lot of people close
to me have noticed the change also. Our animals are very in tune to us
on an emotional level. They pay attention to our feelings and have the
power to understand us.

Most of the feelings expressed by animals in my experience are very 6
simple and straightforward: They are often sleepy, hungry, playful, anxious, and sometimes aggressive. As pet owners we all recognize these
expressions and actions easily. Animal behavior patterns and personalities differ extremely, but all seem to have that quality of giving unconditional love.

The strong feelings of love and compassion I receive from my pets 7
are irreplaceable. Their thoughts and feelings come through to me clearly
from their expressive actions and faces. I do feel they are very conscious
of the way you're feeling, as shown through my experience with my illness. As pet owners I'm sure you would have no arguments; we are a
special breed of people who receive a certain type of unconditional love
that could never be replaced.

RESPONDING TO "DOGS AND EMPATHETIC OBSERVATION"

Freewrite about the advantages (or disadvantages) of having a pet in the
family.

Responding through Interpretation

1. What particular aspects of the relationship between pet and master does
   Pascerella focus on? How does her point of view differ from Simon's?
2. How does Pascerella use her experiences with her dog, Zephyr, to develop her own definition of anthropomorphism?

Responding through Discussion

1. Look over all three essays again—Thomas's, Simon's, and Pascerella's. What similarities do you see? What differences? Discuss the strengths and weaknesses of each of the essays. If the group decided to put together an anthology of readings about pets, which of these three essays would you choose to publish? Why?

Responding through Writing

1. Close your eyes for a few moments and imagine that you are a kind of animal. Take time to really feel what it might be like to be this animal. Which animal did you become in your imagination? Write a journal entry about what you imagined and how you felt while doing so.
2. Expand your freewrite about the advantages (or disadvantages) of having a pet in the family into a full-length paper. Support your position with concrete facts and specific examples.

MAKING CONNECTIONS

The concept of "nature" is a broad one and covers many different facets of being a human being living in the natural world. The natural world is everything that we see, feel, touch, experience. We are part of the natural world; the elements in our bodies parallel the same elements we find around us in the natural world. Nearly all the selections in this chapter describe some aspect of the unity between Mother Nature and all living things.

1. *Solitude in nature.* Linda Hogan's "Walking," Annie Dillard's "Sojourner," and William Stafford's "Traveling through the Dark" all use personal, meditative experiences to make points about the connection between natural creatures and human feelings and ideas. Compare these readings and make notes about how they are alike and how they are different. Which parts of each piece did you like best? Using these three selections as inspiration, write your own meditative paper about being alone in nature and what you learned.
2. *Human beings and animals.* William Stafford's poem and Elizabeth Thomas's essay and the two student essays by Kirsten Simon and Lori Pascerella talk about the relationship between human beings and animals. Look at some of the ways humans use animals—even the household pets that we love. Write an essay that gives your opinion on this issue.

3. *Only too human.* Peter Taylor's short story "A Walled Garden," is about the use of one human being by another, and Lewis Thomas's essay "On Embryology" takes a look at human intervention in the most fundamental process of all—how an embryo is created. Look back at these two pieces and decide for yourself what each writer's attitude is about people. Then write an essay on the "downside" of being human. Are human beings basically good . . . or bad? What is behind our desires to control everything—other people, nature, animals, the human conception process?

4. *You and nature.* Refresh your memory about the concept of being a "naturalist" by looking back over the essays by Hogan, Nichols, and Dillard and the two student essays by Hunze and Kerr. All these selections provide different pieces of the picture of what it means to be a naturalist. Is a naturalist someone who simply enjoys nature? Someone who spends a great deal of time outside looking at nature and collecting and cataloging it? Is a naturalist someone who writes about nature? Teaches others about it? Do you consider yourself a naturalist? Using ideas from these five essays, write your own essay about you and nature—about nature as your teacher, your nurturer, your pleasure, your enemy, or whatever relationship you have with nature.

CHAPTER 7

Health

Introduction

DONALD M. MURRAY	Reflections from a Sick Bed
GEOFFREY KURLAND	A Doctor's Case
DICKON CHAN	The Health Care Plan I Favor
KIRSTEN SIMON	Massage-Message
ROBIN BECKER	Medical Science
WILLIAM CARLOS WILLIAMS	The Use of Force
PERRI KLASS	Learning the Language
ANNA QUINDLEN	The War on Drinks
BILL MOYERS	The Art of Healing
KATHERINE RAZUM	Doctor, Do You Care?
DEREK COLLINS	Responding to "The Art of Healing"

Making Connections

243

INTRODUCTION

Journal Entry

Write for a few minutes about your ideas about health. What does it mean to you to be healthy? Do you consider yourself to be in good health for your age? If not, what are some steps you could take to enjoy better health? Do you have any particular health problems or handicaps?

Health has become a national obsession for many Americans today. Although we spend billions each year on medical training and hospital construction and have the most advanced medical technology in the world, many American children are out of shape and overweight, thousands of people still die prematurely of preventable diseases, and, while the life span has increased, the quality of life and health care for most elderly people has deteriorated. Think for a few minutes about this elusive thing called "health." Is health primarily the absence of disease? What about feeling *healthy* most of the time instead of tired, plagued by minor symptoms, and overstressed? If we're unhealthy, what will it take to become healthy? And if we're already fairly healthy, what will it take to keep us that way and perhaps even improve our well-being?

In part because of the high cost and complexity of modern medicine, many people avoid going to the doctor if at all possible and take nonprescription medication to ease the symptoms if they feel ill. As Donald Murray reminds us in his essay "Reflections from a Sick Bed," family doctors once came to the home and prescribed bed rest and a few basic medications for a variety of illnesses. In contrast, few of us today have a close relationship with one particular physician for most of our lives. The trend now is toward specialists, and while we might get more "expert" help, we seldom feel connected to, much less even remember, the various doctors we go to. We now depend on exact "scientific" diagnoses rather than the general "bed rest" that Murray found so restorative in his boyhood.

Perri Klass in her essay on medical jargon and Robin Becker in her poem "Medical Science" both give us a hard look into the highly technological medical world which more and more of us feel bewildered by and excluded from. Geoffrey Kurland's nightmare battle with leukemia ("A Doctor's Case") reminds us that even doctors get sick and must adjust to cures that seem to have no human hand or face behind them. Anna Quindlen in "The War on Drinks" spotlights a health menace that people create for themselves:

alcohol. This calls to mind how many people today self-medicate their personal problems by using mood-altering and habit-forming substances such as prescription medicines, drugs, and alcohol and eventually cause themselves irreparable physical damage. Bill Moyers, however, offers us hope that perhaps the state of medicine is changing and that more doctors and hospitals are trying to pay more attention to their patients' emotional and psychological needs—a change that the student essays in this chapter, especially the one on massage by Kirsten Simon, argue in favor of.

Probably one of the most memorable selections in this chapter is the short story "The Use of Force" by William Carlos Williams, a poet and fiction writer who also happened to be a medical doctor. Williams brilliantly illuminates for us the very complex power relationship that often goes on beneath the surface with doctors and their patients. As you look at all the selections in this chapter, consider the issue of power: Who has ultimate control over your health—the medical profession; other "healers" who use an approach that emphasizes the link between body, mind, and spirit; or you?

Reflections from a Sick Bed

Donald M. Murray

Donald M. Murray has written for the *Boston Globe* and has taught jour-
nalism for many years at the University of New Hampshire. He is the author of many successful textbooks and several essay collections on the art
of writing. The following essay, from Murray's collection *Expecting the
Unexpected* (1989), evokes a time when doctors made house calls and
young patients were prescribed lengthy periods of "bed rest" as a cure for
many common childhood ailments.

At 62, I don't take miracle drugs for granted. At 62, I don't take 63 for   1
granted, but I know I've gotten this far because of pills that are still magic
to me and drugs that still make me wonder.

I can still remember the red quarantine cards of the houses with scar-   2
let fever inside. I still dream of the hearse that so carefully, so slowly
backed down a neighboring driveway, turned in the street, taking away
Butler Mitchell who had polio. We had an abundance of justified fears,
blood poisoning and food poisoning, rheumatic fever, diphtheria, ty-
phoid, the flu that had touched every family I knew, consumption,
whooping cough, measles (German and native), mumps, chicken pox,
small pox, pneumonia—I had double lobar.

Things were scary all right and they were treated with medicines   3
that tasted like medicine: no cherry syrup then. Children today
would take parents to court who poured acidy things into their
throats that tasted as if they were made of mashed tree roots,
squashed beetles, shaved toad—and probably were. I can still hear
the rip of a mustard plaster being removed, and sometimes, in a
strange social situation when people turn away and I am left alone
with a glass of tomato juice in my hand, I imagine the guests have
smelled the odor of ointments that were massaged into my flesh
when I was young.

In a time when I have rarely heard the word *poultice* and medicine   4
tastes so good that the great worry is that children will steal it and make
themselves sick on a cure, I grow nostalgic for my sickly childhood, in
which God punished me for my sins with sickness and my parents punished me with their treatments. The good part came afterward during a
period described by that wonderful, long, musical word so rarely heard
today: convalescence.

Now I am not romanticizing the experience of children today or yes-   5
terday who battle fatal disease, but I do remember—with a surprising
nostalgia—the prescription that followed the crisis of those old-
fashioned diseases: bed rest.

As a boy, I often heard Dr. Bartlett rumble, "Now, Donald, you'll   6
have to stay in bed for a week or two."

"A week?" I'd yell as my mother said, "Shush."   7

"At least a week. I'll come by and we'll see about that second one."   8

He smiled as he said that and I suspect that he knew, more than I   9
did then, how much I looked forward to long days in bed with no
school—and no after-school.

The gang would come by the house in the morning shouting, "Mur-   10
ray, Murray," on their way to school, and I'd appear at the window and
wave them on. They'd grin and yell and cavort—they knew I was fak-
ing it to get out of school, and I mimed a response that played to such
an idea. In the afternoon, I'd hear, "Murray, Murray," again and I'd signal how much I wished I could go out to play.

I was lying. They would leave, and I would return to the warm tan-   11
gle of quilts, blankets, and pillows in which I would spend those long,
lonely days without time. Sometimes I feel that I have lived my life on
the resources I developed when I was my only companion.

In that bed I was free of all the pressures to conform and belong. On   12
the street, I was a coward playing the role of a tough kid, and never quite
making it. Alone I didn't have to worry about what others thought of
me, how I was dressed, how I spoke, how I walked. Turning inward I
could travel further than I could biking the streets of North Quincy.

I read without plan or counsel. My teachers assigned books, such as   13
Lorna Doone. I had always been a more adventuresome reader than
school, in those days, would allow. I read sports stories and reread tales
of adventure and exploration, such as Admiral Byrd's *Alone.* As a
teenager I joined and paid for the packages that came from the Book-of-
the-Month. Membership, in my neighborhood, had to be kept a secret.
It was open season on intellectuals. Eyeglasses could get you beaten up.
Glasses and books took a form of manliness I had not yet achieved.

In bed I read Baptist sermons, sometimes the Bible, even mother's   14
magazines, the *Woman's Home Companion* and *McCall's, Ladies Home Journal,* and I believe something called the *Delineator.*

I was doing badly in school but I was a reader, an insatiable, promis-   15
cuous reader of stories about love and home-making, hockey and history; I read the *Boston Globe* and the *Boston Herald,* the *Record,* the *Post,*
Quincy Patriot Ledger. When I found an author, such as Sabatini or Ho-

ratio Alger or Kenneth Roberts, I would search for all the books by that author, gorging myself the way I did when I found a new ice cream flavor such as black raspberry.

I took advantage of every accident to expand my secret curriculum. My father, for some reason, was given a book I found in his desk drawer. I asked to read it and he blushed. He told me he had not read it. It had been a gift from a college man he worked with. It was a dirty book and a Commie book. Ceremonially we walked to another neighborhood to put the book in a stranger's trashcan. 16

The book was *Anna Karenina* by Tolstoy. The next day I went to the Wollaston Public Library and introduced myself to the world of Russian fiction. 17

These books were all, like the *National Geographic* maps on my ceiling, invitations to escape. I didn't read these books, I went into them. I joined the march to Quebec; I was in the Russian railroad station, my nostrils filled with coal smoke. I even entered into the alien worlds of my mother's fiction reading. I moved back and forth in time, crossed oceans, became lonely housewives, sad old men, and more than once a young lover. 18

I would also travel into my radio, becoming Jimmy Foxx or Tiny Thompson in the net for the Bruins. I played in the big bands with Dorsey and Miller and Goodman. Walter Damrosch introduced me to Tchaikovsky, Sibelius, and Debussy. I followed the convoluted plots of the soapies, surely good training for an intellectual, and got goosebumps hearing the convention hall boom "We want Willkie." 19

What I read, what I heard on the radio, what I dreamed in my daydreams and my night dreams, what I thought and what I imagined, all ran together. It was all part of a rich tapestry of memory and imagination, experience lived and relived. And the best part of it often was when the radio was off and the books and the magazines and the newspapers slid from the bed to the floor. And I was just there, in my bed, able to follow my mind wherever it went. 20

Those imaginings of mine were so vivid that sometimes, when I was in a real war, I was disappointed that it was, well, boring, and my life has to some degree always been like that, a wonderful blurring between what was, what might be, what might have been, with make believe often more real than real believe. I learned in those lonely days of a sickly childhood something that many Americans have never seemed to learn, that there are worse things than being in a room by yourself. 21

I can remember one afternoon looking out the window on Chester Street, where I watched the leaves on the maple tree slowly turn, palms 22

out toward the sun. That was a better lesson than most I learned in
school.

I want no sickly second childhood to provide matching bookends   23
to my life, but sometimes, in retirement, when the present is too present,
I will take to bed and practice the art of convalescence, tracing a map on
the ceiling with my imagination, reading a mystery and putting it aside
to continue the story, watching the leaves outside the window to see if
I can catch them turning toward the sun.

RESPONDING TO "REFLECTIONS FROM A SICK BED"

Freewrite about a time when being sick and in bed was a pleasurable experience for you. How did you occupy your time?

Responding through Interpretation

1. How were the kinds of illnesses Murray experienced over half a century
   ago different from those of today? What are some of today's illnesses
   that weren't diagnosed in those days?
2. What does Murray mean when he says "I didn't read these books, I went
   into them"? How did Murray's approach to reading compare with the
   way he listened to the radio?
3. Describe what Murray observed in nature while sick in bed. What were
   the deeper meanings behind what he saw? What did his sick-bed experience teach him about himself and his own life?

Responding through Discussion

1. Before beginning the group discussion on "sick-bed learning," take 10
   minutes for the group to make a list of interesting things they learned
   while in bed—such as information from reading or watching television,
   personal insights and realizations, etc.
2. Donald Murray is a fine writer, much respected by the general public.
   He's also an outstanding teacher and journalist. What could you learn
   from him as a writer? Go over his essay in the group and point out aspects of his writing style that seem particularly effective to you as a
   reader. Read some of the passages aloud in the group. Make a group list
   of all the strong points of Murray's writing.

Responding in Writing

1. Write a journal entry in response to Murray's statement, "Sometimes I
   feel that I have lived my life on the resources I developed when I was

my only companion." What do you think he means by this? What ideas does it give you about yourself? What in your own life has given you the resources you now use?

2. Using your freewrite, your journal entry, your reading notebook entries, as well as Murray's essay, write a paper in which you explore the idea of how positive emotions and experiences can contribute to healing. Use some of your own experiences as examples.

A Doctor's Case

Geoffrey Kurland

Geoffrey Kurland is a pediatric pulmonologist at Children's Hospital at the University of Pittsburgh in Pennsylvania. He wrote the following article, which appeared in *Newsweek* in April 1991, a year after he was successfully treated for hair-cell leukemia. Dr. Kurland is active in cancer survivor groups.

I was sitting, trying to write letters with the IV in my left arm. I was in   1
the back room of my hematologist's office: with its desk, examining table and worn back issues of magazines, where the "chemo" was blessed and administered. I waited as the initial fluids infused, feeling the room-temperature solution tingle up to my shoulder as it mixed with my body-temperature blood.

The day was gray, with snow forecast. The Pittsburgh view from the   2
11th-floor window had changed over the months of treatment only in the amount of afternoon light. They'd made special accommodations for me: the 4 P.M. chemotherapy allowed me to be a doctor as long as possible before relinquishing myself to the role of patient. The nurse came in to administer the medication designed to kill my leukemic cells, to change IV bags and then to leave me in solitude. I lay down on the examining table, insulated from its cold leather by the thin white paper; I turned away from the room with its fluorescent brightness and faced the wall. Sleep came easily, as the combination of leukemia, chemotherapy and my busy schedule had left me extremely drowsy. An hour later I awoke as the nurse took out my IV, saying it was time to go home, reminding me the next dose was in two weeks.

As best I could, I walk-ran to my car and drove home, cursing the slow   3
drivers, red lights, distance and my increasing nausea. I slogged up the dark stairs to the bathroom, talked myself out of vomiting as I undressed, and took what I called my "magic meds." The first was designed to prevent the rapidly rising nausea, but was of insufficient strength. The second was an amnestic, a memory-eradicating drug that rendered the former's insufficiency unimportant. I set my alarm for four hours later, the time for repeat doses. I called home; my mother answered with a voice that knew who was calling. The conversation was brief: yes, my blood counts had been reasonable; yes, I got my chemo; yes, I was home; yes, I was going to sleep; yes, don't call me; yes, I would be OK . . .

My next brush with reality would be 24 hours later when, still for- 4
getful, reeling and drained, I would try to drink or eat. Any vomiting in
the previous day was like a dream, a short wretchedness full of the
smell of cold porcelain and unwashed floors that might or might not
have actually happened. I hated being alone. I hated being sick alone.
Yet I didn't want to be seen as sick and out of control. As a physician, I
had always been the one in charge of the patient, of the illness. Now it
was upside down, backward, ultimately and inexplicably wrong: I was
the patient, controlled by my illness and its treatment.

I kept up a frenetic pace on clinical service, with regular months and 5
weekends on call, available to my patients and to the physicians and students I taught. I continued my research, despite the interruptions of
days missed. I still continued running several miles every day between
chemotherapy treatments. All this in a vain effort to appear whole and
unscathed by illness. In the days immediately following my diagnosis,
I found myself in the library reading about my illness, only to become
depressed when looking at the ominous survival curves and, inevitably,
reading case histories that sounded all too familiar.

When I was hospitalized for a month with fever, I looked forward 6
to having visitors. But when they arrived I didn't want them, preferring
solitary desolation to seeing the pain in their faces. My life was being attacked and destroyed, but I was used to battles that were private, not
public. I remember the face of the Mayo Clinic specialist when he told
me my diagnosis. I had seen him because a mass had been found on my
chest X-ray, which I had taken because I thought I'd cracked a rib from
a persistent cough. His look said everything even before he took a
slightly deeper breath: "Listen to this, I don't want to have to say this
twice." He explained my diagnosis as I, benumbed with disbelief, heard
almost none of his words after "hairy-cell leukemia." I felt as if I were a
spirit in the room, watching the two of us; I felt more sorry for him than
me because of the news he carried.

Division and Multiplication

The counsel of the hematologist on the day of diagnosis—the need for my 7
spleen to be removed and, later, a major chest operation to remove the
mass—had little impact on me. My mind was frozen, paralyzed and sub-
servient to my fate. I tried not to betray my panic while I fought back tears
and told myself to "be brave," although the idea of "being brave" was as remote as other feelings during the first days and weeks of facing the hidden
foe that was taking over my life. Like the vomiting that was to come, it all
seemed a dream.

And then over a year ago my bone marrow was declared "clean"; I   8
was delivered into the state of grace known as remission. I was finished
with chemotherapy, rid of the evil that was my own DNA, with my altered life before me. The leukemia had given no respite in its relentless
mission. It had no rules except division and multiplication, and took part
of me with it when it left, changing forever that part of me which remained. For those cells didn't just die, leaving no trace. Friends feel the
weight of my fight. When I'm asked how I am, the answer "fine" is no
longer enough. I have to add that my chest X-ray is unchanged and
"counts" are normal, without a sign of relapse. My chest X-ray will
never be normal: the wires holding my sternum together, the metal clips
on blood vessels will always be there.

My life may be another two months or 40 years. I'll always be able   9
to taste the "chemo," the metallic taste awakening my nausea. But those
days immediately following chemotherapy are distant memories. The
leukemia, through my genetic code, added its own helix to the turns of
my life. The twists of the days I cannot find and recall, the solitary nights,
the vomiting, the fear, all are a silent, gauzy part of me with which I still
struggle. They're another component of the price paid, one of the things
no one mentions except at the time of diagnosis, when they state the obvious: "This will change your life . . ." Even if you win.

RESPONDING TO "A DOCTOR'S CASE"

Freewrite about what you imagine it would be like for a physician to become seriously ill. Would it be easier for a doctor to cope with a possibly
fatal illness because of his or her training?

Responding through Interpretation

1. How does Kurland bring his experience of being a doctor to the writing
   of this essay?
2. What does Kurland mean when he says that disease "took part of me with
   it when it left, changing forever that part of me which remained"? How
   exactly was he changed, and what general conclusions can you draw from
   his experience about disease and survival?
3. Examine some of the specific details of his illness and response to treatment provided in the essay. What did you learn from these details about
   the physical and psychological effects of leukemia?

Responding through Discussion

1. In your group, discuss the effectiveness of Kurland's narrative of his illness. What impact did it have? Did his being a doctor make any difference in its impact? Together with your group, write a letter to Geoffrey Kurland telling him how his article affected you.
2. Think about doctors you've known or heard about who became seriously ill. Discuss with your group the stories of these doctors' lives. What happened to them? How did their own illness affect their lives as doctors? As people?

Responding through Writing

1. Write a journal entry about the distance that patients often feel from their doctors. Does the world of medicine and hospitals seem dehumanizing and impersonal to you? How did Kurland's article affect your attitude?
2. Write a paper about some successful medical treatment you have either experienced or witnessed. For example, has your life or the life of someone you know ever been saved by medical science? Highlight the positive aspects of the medical profession: Tell stories about the good people, the good treatment, the good hospital—in other words, show the "upside" of getting medical treatment.

The Health Care Plan I Favor

Dickon Chan

Dickon Chan arrived in San Francisco from Hong Kong when he was eighteen and attended community college to work toward an aircraft maintenance certificate; he eventually would like to transfer to a four-year college. Dickon Chan had been in this country only three years when he wrote the following essay for his English class on the subject of a national health plan. Notice how Chan uses disturbing experiences in his own family, as well as information gained though reading and conversations, to support his arguments about the need for a national health plan.

On a Saturday afternoon some 18 months ago, my mother opened her   1
mail and started to cry. Why? Kaiser had turned down her application
for medical insurance due to traces of blood found in her urine. My
mother was very worried, for we were then new immigrants and my
father faced a similar fate as he had hypertension. Angered, I began to
consider how ridiculous it was that a person in America, a developed
country, could be denied medical care. In developed countries such as
Canada, Australia and the United Kingdom, there are various types of
national health care plans for the citizens, and America seems to be the
only exception.

The various health care plans available in some of the developed   2
countries include both national and government-sponsored and/or coordinated approaches. In the United Kingdom, a national health care
plan not only is available to all citizens but is also extended to all visitors and overseas students. All enjoy free medical treatments and prescriptions. My brother, who went to study in Scotland some five years
ago, was twice admitted to the hospital for glaucoma operations. He did
not have to pay even a cent for both operations. In addition, he received
several pounds sterling for traveling allowances. The good points of
such national health care plans are that people do not have to worry
about their medical expenses. However, the bad points are that the system may be subject to abuse and is a heavy financial burden for the government.

Both Canada and Australia have implemented government-   3
sponsored and/or coordinated health care plans. All new immigrants are
required to pay for their medical insurance for the first year in Australia
and for the first six months in Canada. The plan also covers all preexist-

ing conditions. After the first year of residence for immigrants, the plan will be taken over by the government on payment of minimal charges. This would appear to be a practical solution as the government can have at least some income to add to its health care resources. Again, this type of plan might be subject to abuse. It is not uncommon to read news of unethical doctors, in conspiracy with their patients, who cheat the government on consultation fees or unnecessary laboratory tests. I know of a doctor in Australia who, in order to get more money, refers patients to his laboratory for unnecessary blood or other biochemical tests.

However, in view of the unhappy experience of my parents and   4
many others in America, I still feel the U.S. government should seriously consider introducing some sort of workable and efficient health care plans for her citizens. President Clinton in his election platform vowed to work out a national health care plan for the American people, and I support him on this issue.

Of the two plans I mentioned above, I would vote for the government-   5
sponsored and/or coordinated health care plan. The plan should be paid for partly by the employer, partly by the employee, and to some extent by the government. In this way, it would not be too great a financial burden. For the unemployed, the government could help finance their bills. In order to avoid abuse, I would suggest that the government set up trained nursing teams who are responsible for examining all patients in the first instance. They can prescribe simple medicines and patients can only be seen by a doctor upon referral by a member of the nursing teams.

Until recently, when they managed to get a medical insurance plan,   6
my parents had to worry every day and to pray not to have to go to a hospital which could easily have cost them a fortune. I think no one will disagree with me that health care is a basic need for every citizen. It is vital that some sort of comprehensive health care plan be introduced; to do otherwise would only reflect upon the irresponsibility of the government. As a developed country, America should take positive steps to implement a workable health care plan.

RESPONDING TO "THE HEALTH CARE PLAN I FAVOR"

Freewrite about the needs of your family (or other families that you know) for medical insurance. Do you have it? Have you ever needed or used it?

Responding through Interpretation

1. Dickon Chan contrasts the American medical system with the systems used in Britain, Canada, and Australia. What contrasts does he point out?

2. Examine the opening paragraph of the essay. How does Chan use the story of his parents' lack of a medical plan to introduce his criticism of American health care? When and where does he continue to refer to his parents as a way to unify his essay? How effective do you think Chan is in achieving unity?

Responding through Discussion

1. With your group, discuss Chan's argument and whether or not you agree with him. What do you think about his proposal? Draw on your family's and your own experiences with medical insurance as a basis for the discussion.

Responding through Writing

1. Write a journal entry in which you evaluate Chan's argument. How effective was it? What additional arguments would you have added?
2. Write an essay giving your own opinion about the health care system in America. Do you think America should have a national health plan? If so, what kind? What would be the benefits? The drawbacks?

Massage-Message

Kirsten Simon

Kirsten Simon is a professional masseuse who is returning to college to study somatic psychology, which emphasizes the mind-body connection in relationship to health. She wrote the following essay, which emphasizes the beneficial effects of massage, for her English class.

Relax! That's an order! But how? Our achievement-oriented society   1
provides us with plenty of clues on how to succeed in our competitive
world. If we want to keep up with the pace, there are loads of strong
coffee and fast food to help keep us going. On our way to the top,
however, don't be surprised if some of us are detoured to a hospital.
Many of us sacrifice our health in order to attain our goals, and our
health care system supports us in abusing our bodies by repairing
us instead of teaching us good preventive habits. Because obtaining
success in our society generally demands the most from our minds,
many of us have lost touch with our bodies. My experience is that
when my body is healthy and relaxed, it serves me in all that I
am doing. Being relaxed gives me a wealth of strength and energy, and
the most beneficial method of relaxation I have found is massage.
Massage is a technique that recognizes the body's integral role in our
lives. Massage nurtures, restores, energizes, and preserves the body,
and I believe it is one of the most effective tools of preventive health
care.

The benefits of massage have not yet been fully appreciated by med-   2
ical doctors. Doctors generally feel that massage practitioners do not possess sufficient training to engage in the recovery process. Doctors are
more likely to use physical therapists because physical therapists are required to complete a three-year-long training prior to licensing; massage
therapists are only required to take one hundred hours of training prior
to certification, and typically only eight hours are devoted to anatomy
study. Also, doctors are reluctant to be supportive of massage therapy
because massage techniques are not based on as much scientific research
as conventional medical practice. However, doctors cannot ignore the
evidence that massage heals. In her article "Working Out with Massage," Mirka Knaster quotes internationally respected track coach Bill
Dellinger as saying that "one runner who had a plantar fascia problem
and was absolutely unable to do anything" received massage therapy

for two weeks, "and he was running, when most orthopedic surgeons weren't doing much for him."

My friend Barbara's speedy recovery from tuberculosis with the help of regular massage provides further support for the healing bene- fits of massage therapy. Barbara used to work two jobs in addition to raising her son alone. She also ate poorly and did nothing to relieve her stress. During this time, she contracted tuberculosis from one of her house-cleaning clients. Barbara recovered by cutting back on her work, improving her diet and receiving at least one massage per week. She be- lieves that she was struck with tuberculosis because her immune system was weak due to poor circulation. Her weekly massages not only re- lieved her stress, but also gave her better circulation through different kneading techniques. In "Working Out with Massage," Mirka Knaster recounts the result of a French study which found that "massage was necessary for stimulating circulation and increasing the oxygen-carrying capacity of the blood." The effectiveness of massage in addition to the other steps she took amazed her medical doctor. He was surprised by how quickly she recuperated because, normally, recovery from tuber- culosis takes much longer when the treatment consists only of antibi- otics. Barbara still receives weekly massages, and she feels that they contribute greatly to her continued good health.

Another argument against massage therapy is that it is an invasion of privacy. Many people feel uncomfortable being touched by someone whom they are not familiar with. They feel that nurturing touch should only be between people who are close, and between lovers. However, many people do not receive nurturing touch from either their lovers or the people whom they are close to. Massage practitioners can offer a safe and respectful environment for their clients to satisfy the very human need to be touched. Lucinda Lindell, author of *The Book of Massage,* says that "touch is of vital importance. It gives reassurance, warmth, pleasure, and comfort." I find her assertion to be true not only as a recipient of mas- sage, but also as a provider of massage. In my massage practice I have witnessed clients who initially were uncomfortable being touched be- cause as children they received so little physical affection. These clients shared in common low levels of self-esteem because they did not feel worthy of attention. In the process of providing my clients with nur- turing, respectful massages, they began feeling better about themselves. For example, one of my female clients had been in an unhappy marriage when I first started working with her. She was constantly told by her hus- band that she was at fault for everything that went wrong in their rela- tionship. Feeling reassured by the attention she got during her mas-

3

4

sages, she started to feel better about herself, and then she not only ended her painful relationship, but also started to take art classes to further her creative talents which will enable her to work in a profession she truly enjoys. She is having her first art show next spring.

Medical doctors have many invaluable abilities to help heal the sick   5
which massage therapists do not have. For example, a massage therapist cannot perform surgery or adjust bones. However, massage therapy can be as important to the maintenance and well-being of our health as more sophisticated medical procedures can be. If our goal is to be healthy and stay healthy, I believe that relaxing therapeutic massage can help us to achieve that goal. We have to educate people in taking care of themselves by emphasizing a proper diet, sufficient relaxation, exercise, and a positive mental approach. Spending time, energy, and money on preventive health care which includes massage should take priority over having total reliance on medical doctors to help us after we become ill.

RESPONDING TO "MASSAGE-MESSAGE"

Freewrite about your opinion on whether or not massage is a true health benefit.

Responding through Interpretation

1. What does Simon believe to be the benefits of massage?
2. What are the arguments Simon finds against massage? How does she answer these arguments?

Responding through Discussion

1. In a general discussion, let all group members tell what they know about massage and if they've ever experienced it firsthand. At the end of the discussion, make a list of all the other information you would like to know about the therapeutic effects of massage.

Responding through Writing

1. In your journal, write a brief account of the many different ways you have learned to relax. Explain more fully the relaxation method you enjoy the most.
2. Do some further reading about massage and write a paper explaining some of the ways massage is already being used in the health field. What is the history of massage therapy? Are there any real measurable, "scientific" benefits? If so, what are they?

Medical Science

Robin Becker

Formerly a college professor of writing at Massachusetts Institute of Technology, Robin Becker is a poet and an editor. She is poetry editor for *The Women's Review of Books* and the author of a collection of poetry, *Backtalk* (1982). Her poem "Medical Science" comments on the emotional impact of hospitalization and medical technology.

My father's heart is on television
at the hospital. Lonely and a little embarrassed, it beats blindly on
the videotape, hoping for the best. Like family
members of a game-show contestant, my mother and I stand off
to the side, proud of the healthy culvert doing its chores.   5
The doctor explains that this is the artery of
a much younger man, and I think of the parts of my father's
body assembled in a shop from the odds and ends
of others. Now the doctor
is speaking very quickly, as if she could hide   10
the sad blocked door of the right
ventricle, unable to pass its burden of blood
from one room to another. When the lights go on, I
expect to see it, sore and swollen, counting
off the seconds with its bad arm. My mother   15
takes a few steps, respectfully, holding her
pocketbook, waiting to be addressed. We have seen
the unshaven face of the heart, the cataract
eyes of the heart, the liver-spotted hands
of the heart. Seated in the cafeteria, my mother whispers   20
that my father's heart is a miracle, that it has already been dead
and recalled twice.

RESPONDING TO "MEDICAL SCIENCE"

Freewrite about a time you visited a relative or a friend in the hospital.

Responding through Interpretation

1. What does the doctor explain about the father's heart? What does she try
   to conceal from the mother and daughter?

2. What meanings are suggested by the title of the poem, "Medical Science"?

3. Becker describes the heart in a series of complex comparisons:

> *... We have seen*
> *the unshaven face of the heart, the cataract*
> *eyes of the heart, the liver-spotted hands*
> *of the heart. ...*

Write your interpretation of these comparisons in your reading journal.

Responding through Discussion

1. Get together with your group and have two different members read the poem out loud very slowly. Make notes of any additional meanings or ideas you got from hearing the poem read aloud. Afterward, the group can discuss several aspects of the poem: the images, the language, the form, and the underlying meaning.

2. Discuss various experiences that group members have had in having medical tests—or being with someone who was having tests done. What kind of machinery was used? What was the impact of such testing on the human beings involved?

Responding through Writing

1. In your journal, rewrite Becker's poem into a scene for a story or play. What happens? Who are the people? What do they do and say? What do you think happens after this visit to the hospital?

2. Write a paper giving your experiences with one particular new medical technology. What impact has it had on people, both emotionally and physically? Do you think that this medical technology helps people to get well faster? Is the new technology worth what it costs?

The Use of Force

William Carlos Williams

William Carlos Williams spent most of his life in Paterson, New Jersey, where he wrote unceasingly throughout his long career as a practicing physician. Known primarily as one of America's most outstanding poets (his three volumes of collected poems run over 1000 pages), Williams has also published numerous other books of stories, essays, and literary criticisms. As a doctor and a poet, Williams was always fascinated by people, saying they "always absorbed me. I lost myself in the very properties of their mind." The following short story, "The Use of Force," was first published in 1938 in his second collection of stories, *Life along the Passaic River.*

They were new patients to me, all I had was the name, Olson. Please come down as soon as you can, my daughter is very sick.

When I arrived I was met by the mother, a big startled looking woman, very clean and apologetic who merely said, Is this the doctor? and let me in. In the back, she added, You must excuse us, doctor, we have her in the kitchen where it is warm. It is very damp here sometimes.

The child was fully dressed and sitting on her father's lap near the kitchen table. He tried to get up, but I motioned for him not to bother, took off my overcoat and started to look things over. I could see that they were all very nervous, eyeing me up and down distrustfully. As often, in such cases, they weren't telling me more than they had to, it was up to me to tell them; that's why they were spending three dollars on me.

The child was fairly eating me up with her cold, steady eyes, and no expression to her face whatever. She did not move and seemed, inwardly, quiet; an unusually attractive little thing, and as strong as a heifer in appearance. But her face was flushed, she was breathing rapidly, and I realized that she had a high fever. She had magnificent blonde hair, in profusion. One of those picture children often reproduced in advertising leaflets and the photogravure sections of the Sunday papers.

She's had a fever for three days, began the father and we don't know what it comes from. My wife has given her things, you know, like people do, but it don't do no good. And there's been a lot of sickness around. So we tho't you'd better look her over and tell us what is the matter.

As doctors often do I took a trial shot at it as a point of departure. Has she had a sore throat?

Both parents answered me together, No . . . No, she says her throat 7
don't hurt her.

Does your throat hurt you? added the mother to the child. But the 8
little girl's expression didn't change nor did she move her eyes from my
face.

Have you looked? 9

I tried to, said the mother, but I couldn't see. 10

As it happens we had been having a number of cases of diphtheria 11
in the school to which this child went during that month and we were
all, quite apparently, thinking of that, though no one had as yet spoken
of the thing.

Well, I said, suppose we take a look at the throat first. I smiled in 12
my best professional manner and asking for the child's first name I said,
come on, Mathilda, open your mouth and let's take a look at your throat.

Nothing doing. 13

Aw, come on, I coaxed, just open your mouth wide and let me take 14
a look. Look, I said opening both hands wide, I haven't anything in my
hands. Just open up and let me see.

Such a nice man, put in the mother. Look how kind he is to you. 15
Come on, do what he tells you to. He won't hurt you.

At that I ground my teeth in disgust. If only they wouldn't use the 16
word "hurt" I might be able to get somewhere. But I did not allow myself to be hurried or disturbed but speaking quietly and slowly I approached the child again.

As I moved my chair a little nearer suddenly with one cat-like move- 17
ment both her hands clawed instinctively for my eyes and she almost
reached them too. In fact she knocked my glasses flying and they fell,
though unbroken, several feet away from me on the kitchen floor.

Both the mother and father almost turned themselves inside out in 18
embarrassment and apology. You bad girl, said the mother, taking her
and shaking her by one arm. Look what you've done. The nice man. . . .

For heaven's sake, I broke in. Don't call me a nice man to her. I'm 19
here to look at her throat on the chance that she might have diphtheria
and possibly die of it. But that's nothing to her. Look here, I said to the
child, we're going to look at your throat. You're old enough to understand what I'm saying. Will you open it now by yourself or shall we have
to open it for you?

Not a move. Even her expression hadn't changed. Her breaths how- 20
ever were coming faster and faster. Then the battle began. I had to do it.
I had to have a throat culture for her own protection. But first I told the
parents that it was entirely up to them. I explained the danger but said

that I would not insist on a throat examination so long as they would take the responsibility.

If you don't do what the doctor says you'll have to go to the hospital, the mother admonished her severely.   21

Oh yeah? I had to smile to myself. After all, I had already fallen in love with the savage brat, the parents were contemptible to me. In the ensuing struggle they grew more and more abject, crushed, exhausted while she surely rose to magnificent heights of insane fury of effort bred of her terror of me.   22

The father tried his best, and he was a big man but the fact that she was his daughter, his shame at her behavior and his dread of hurting her made him release her just at the critical moment several times when I had almost achieved success, till I wanted to kill him. But his dread also that she might have diphtheria made him tell me to go on, go on though he himself was almost fainting, while the mother moved back and forth behind us raising and lowering her hands in an agony of apprehension.   23

Put her in front of you on your lap, I ordered, and hold both her wrists.   24

But as soon as he did the child let out a scream. Don't, you're hurting me. Let go of my hands. Let them go I tell you. Then she shrieked terrifyingly, hysterically. Stop it! Stop it! You're killing me!   25

Do you think she can stand it, doctor! said the mother.   26

You get out, said the husband to his wife. Do you want her to die of diphtheria?   27

Come on now, hold her, I said.   28

Then I grasped the child's head with my left hand and tried to get the wooden tongue depressor between her teeth. She fought, with clenched teeth, desperately! But now I also had grown furious—at a child. I tried to hold myself down but I couldn't. I know how to expose a throat for inspection. And I did my best. When finally I got the wooden spatula behind the last teeth and just the point of it into the mouth cavity, she opened up for an instant but before I could see anything she came down again and gripping the wooden blade between her molars she reduced it to splinters before I could get it out again.   29

Aren't you ashamed, the mother yelled at her. Aren't you ashamed to act like that in front of the doctor?   30

Get me a smooth-handled spoon of some sort, I told the mother. We're going through with this. The child's mouth was already bleeding. Her tongue was cut and she was screaming in wild hysterical shrieks. Perhaps I should have desisted and come back in an hour or more. No doubt it would have been better. But I have seen at least two children   31 lying dead in bed of neglect in such cases, and feeling that I must get a diagnosis now or never I went at it again. But the worst of it was that I too had got beyond reason. I could have torn the child apart in my own fury and enjoyed it. It was a pleasure to attack her. My face was burning with it.

The damned little brat must be protected against her own idiocy, one says to one's self at such times. Others must be protected against her. It is social necessity. And all these things are true. But a blind fury, a feeling of adult shame, bred of a longing for muscular release are the operatives. One goes on to the end. 32

In a final unreasoning assault I overpowered the child's neck and jaws. I forced the heavy silver spoon back of her teeth and down her throat till she gagged. And there it was—both tonsils covered with membrane. She had fought valiantly to keep me from knowing her secret. She had been hiding that sore throat for three days at least and lying to her parents in order to escape just such an outcome as this. 33

Now truly she *was* furious. She had been on the defensive before but now she attacked. Tried to get off her father's lap and fly at me while tears of defeat blinded her eyes. 34

RESPONDING TO "THE USE OF FORCE"

Freewrite about how you felt about doctors when you were a child. Did you ever have any experiences similar to Mathilda's?

Responding through Interpretation

1. This may appear to be a simple story of a doctor's house call to look at a little girl's throat, but the real conflict goes on beneath the action that takes place physically. In your reading notebook, draw a line down the center of a page. On the left side, list the external actions that take place; on the right, list the emotions that take place with each action.
2. Write a brief description of the kind of person Mathilda is and the kind of person the doctor is. How do the unique personalities of patient and doctor create conflict in the story?
3. How does the title contribute to the story's meaning?

Responding through Discussion

1. "The Use of Force" is a good story to read aloud because it has a great deal of dialogue. In your group, assign parts and read the story out loud like a play. In addition to the four characters, you might like to have a

narrator who reads the parts that are not dialogue. Then discuss what else you learned about the story by playing these roles.

2. Outwardly, this is the story of a doctor's struggle with his young patient. Discuss the details in the story which illustrate medical treatment during the time the story was written—1938. How have practices changed today?

Responding through Writing

1. Write a journal entry giving your opinion about the doctor in the story. What kind of person is he? Is he justified in using force against the little girl?

2. The tension in "The Use of Force" hinges on the fact that diphtheria used to be a common and contagious disease that killed many children. Write a paper about childhood diseases you either have experienced or know something about.

Learning the Language

Perri Klass

Perri Klass graduated from Harvard Medical School in 1986 and is in practice as a pediatrician in Boston. Her point of view about needed reforms
in medical practices became public when her nonfiction reports about
going to medical school were published first in the *New York Times*, and
then later as a book *A Not Entirely Benign Procedure* (1987), from which
the following excerpt is taken. Klass has also published *Baby Doctor: A
Pediatrician's Training* (1992). In the following essay, Klass reveals some
of the motives behind medical jargon.

"Mrs. Tolstoy is your basic LOL in NAD, admitted for a soft rule-out   1
MI," the intern announces. I scribble that on my patient list. In other
words, Mrs. Tolstoy is a Little Old Lady in No Apparent Distress who
is in the hospital to make sure she hasn't had a heart attack (rule out a
Myocardial Infarction). And we think it's unlikely that she has had a
heart attack (a *soft* rule-out).

If I learned nothing else during my first three months of working in   2
the hospital as a medical student, I learned endless jargon and abbreviations. I started out in a state of primeval innocence, in which I didn't
even know that "s̄ CP, SOB, N/V" meant "without chest pain, shortness
of breath, or nausea and vomiting." By the end I took the abbreviations
so much for granted that I would complain to my mother the English
professor, "And can you believe I had to put down *three* NG tubes last
night?"

"You'll have to tell me what an NG tube is if you want me to sym-   3
pathize properly," my mother said. NG, nasogastric—isn't it obvious?

I picked up not only the specific expressions but also the patterns of   4
speech and the grammatical conventions; for example, you never say
that a patient's blood pressure fell or that his cardiac enzymes rose. Instead, the patient is always the subject of the verb: "He dropped his pressure." "He bumped his enzymes." This sort of construction probably reflects the profound irritation of the intern when the nurses come in the
middle of the night to say that Mr. Dickinson has disturbingly low blood
pressure. "Oh, he's gonna hurt me bad tonight," the intern might say,
inevitably angry at Mr. Dickinson for dropping his pressure and creating a problem.

When chemotherapy fails to cure Mrs. Bacon's cancer, what we say   5
is, "Mrs. Bacon failed chemotherapy."

"Well, we've already had one hit today, and we're up next, but at   6
least we've got mostly stable players on our team." This means that our
team (group of doctors and medical students) has already gotten one
new admission today, and it is our turn again, so we'll get whoever is
admitted next in emergency, but at least most of the patients we already
have are fairly stable, that is, unlikely to drop their pressures or in any
other way get suddenly sicker and hurt us bad. Baseball metaphor is pervasive. A no-hitter is a night without any new admissions. A player is
always a patient—a nitrate player is a patient on nitrates, a unit player
is a patient in the intensive care unit, and so on, until you reach the terminal player.

It is interesting to consider what it means to be winning, or doing   7
well, in this perennial baseball game. When the intern hangs up the
phone and announces, "I got a hit," that is not cause for congratulations.
The team is not scoring points; rather, it is getting hit, being bombarded
with new patients. The object of the game from the point of view of the
doctors, considering the players for whom they are already responsible,
is to get as few new hits as possible.

This special language contributes to a sense of closeness and pro-   8
fessional spirit among people who are under a great deal of stress. As a
medical student, I found it exciting to discover that I'd finally cracked
the code, that I could understand what doctors said and wrote, and
could use the same formulations myself. Some people seem to become
enamored of the jargon for its own sake, perhaps because they are so
deeply thrilled with the idea of medicine, with the idea of themselves as
doctors.

I knew a medical student who was referred to by the interns on the   9
team as Mr. Eponym because he was so infatuated with eponymous terminology, the more obscure the better. He never said "capillary pulsa-
tions" if he could say "Quincke's pulses." He would lovingly tell over
the multinamed syndromes—Wolff-Parkinson-White, Lown-Ganong-
Levine, Schönlein-Henoch—until the temptation to suggest Schleswig-
Holstein or Stevenson-Kefauver or Baskin-Robbins became irresistible
to his less reverent colleagues.

And there is the jargon that you don't ever want to hear yourself   10
using. You know that your training is changing you, but there are certain changes you think would be going a little too far.

The resident was describing a man with devastating terminal pancreatic cancer. "Basically he's CTD," the resident concluded. I reminded myself that I had resolved not to be shy about asking when I didn't understand things. "CTD?" I asked timidly.   11

The resident smirked at me. "Circling The Drain."   12

The images are vivid and terrible. "What happened to Mrs. Melville?"   13

"Oh, she boxed last night." To box is to die, of course.   14

Then there are the more pompous locutions that can make the beginning medical student nervous about the effects of medical training. A friend of mine was told by his resident, "A pregnant woman with sickle-cell represents a failure of genetic counseling."   15

Mr. Eponym, who tried hard to talk like the doctors, once explained to me, "An infant is basically a brainstem preparation." The term "brainstem preparation," as used in neurological research, refers to an animal whose higher brain functions have been destroyed so that only the most primitive reflexes remain, like the sucking reflex, the startle reflex, and the rooting reflex.   16

And yet at other times the harshness dissipates into a strangely elusive euphemism. "As you know, this is not entirely benign procedure," some doctor will say, and that will be understood to imply agony, risk of complications, and maybe even a significant mortality rate.   17

The more extreme forms aside, one most important function of medical jargon is to help doctors maintain some distance from their patients. By reformulating a patient's pain and problems into a language that the patient doesn't even speak, I suppose we are in some sense taking those pains and problems under our jurisdiction and also reducing their emotional impact. This linguistic separation between doctors and patients allows conversations to go on at the bedside that are unintelligible to the patient. "Naturally, we're worried about adeno-CA," the intern can say to the medical student, and lung cancer need never be mentioned.   18

I learned a new language this past summer. At times it thrills me to hear myself using it. It enables me to understand my colleagues, to communicate effectively in the hospital. Yet I am uncomfortably aware that I will never again notice the peculiarities and even atrocities of medical language as keenly as I did this summer. There may be specific expressions I manage to avoid, but even as I remark them, promising myself I will never use them, I find that this language is becoming my professional speech. It no longer sounds strange in my ears—or coming from my mouth. And I am afraid that as with any new language, to use it   19 properly you must absorb not only the vocabulary but also the structure, the logic, the attitudes. At first you may notice these new and alien assumptions every time you put together a sentence, but with time and increased fluency you stop being aware of them at all. And as you lose that awareness, for better or for worse, you move closer and closer to being a doctor instead of just talking like one.

RESPONDING TO "LEARNING THE LANGUAGE"

Freewrite about the manner in which a particular doctor or medical practitioner spoke to you on one occasion. Why do you still remember it?

Responding through Interpretation

1. In your reading journal, make note of all the medical jargon given as examples by Perri Klass and explain in regular language what each of the terms actually means.
2. What does Klass say are the benefits of this jargon to the medical profession? What does she say are the real dangers of it?
3. How are comparisons to sport, especially baseball, used in medical jargon, and what are the implications of such sports-related terms as "hit," "team," and "player"?

Responding through Discussion

1. Discuss in your group what you think Klass's attitude is about the language she is learning. Do you agree or disagree with her? Does it make any difference to the group that she is a medical doctor writing this essay?
2. Brainstorm in the group and come up with as many examples of medical jargon that you can all think of. Make a master list. Then have some fun writing a group paragraph using some of the funniest ones. Share your paragraph with the class as a whole.

Responding through Writing

1. Klass's essay is from a book of her essays entitled *A Not Entirely Benign Procedure*. In paragraph 17, she quotes an imaginary doctor as saying: "As you know, this is a not entirely benign procedure." In your journal, write what you think are the deeper meanings behind this statement. How is the language influenced by the medical procedure and vice versa? (Be sure you understand the meaning of the word *benign* before beginning.)

2. Think of another professional field that uses a specific jargon; nearly all professions do. Gather as many examples of the jargon used by, say, engineers, scientists, lawyers, college English teachers, café waiters and cooks, sales personnel, or any profession you're familiar with. Write a humorous account of how people in this profession talk and what they hope to accomplish by using this jargon. Like Klass has done, give specific examples of words and their intentions.

The War on Drinks

Anna Quindlen

Anna Quindlen graduated from Barnard College in 1974 and worked at the *New York Times* as a reporter and editor from 1977 to 1985. Since 1986 she has written a syndicated column for the *Times*, giving her personal views on social issues. Her first book, *Living Outloud* (1988), was composed of pieces from her column "Life in the 30's." In 1992 she received the Pulitzer Prize for commentary. She is also the author of a novel, *Object Lessons* (1992). "The War on Drinks" (1991) first appeared in the *New York Times*.

When she was in fourth grade the girl wrote, "What do you think it does   1
to somebody to live with a lot of pressure?" Starting at age 8 she had been
cashing the public assistance check each month, buying money orders,
paying the bills and doing the grocery shopping. One little brother she
walked to school; the other she dressed and fed before leaving him at
home.

Their mother drank.   2

"The pressure she was talking about wasn't even the pressure of   3
running an entire household," said Virginia Connelly, who oversees
substance abuse services in schools in New York City. "She didn't know
there was anything strange about that. The pressure she was talking
about was the pressure of leaving her younger brother at home."

Surgeon General Antonia Novello has opened fire on the alcohol in-   4
dustry, complaining that too much beer and wine advertising is aimed
at young people. Her predecessor, C. Everett Koop, did the same in
1988, and you can see how radically things have changed: Spuds
MacKenzie is out and the Swedish bikini team is in. There's a move afoot
to have warning labels on ads for beer, wine and liquor, much like the
ones on cigarettes. Dr. Novello didn't mention that; she said she would
be taking a meeting with the big guys in the liquor industry. That's not
enough.

There's no doubt that beer ads, with their cool beaches, cool women   5
and cool parties, are designed to make you feel you're cool if you drink,
milking a concern that peaks in most human beings somewhat shy of
the legal drinking age. And those sneaky little wine coolers are designed
to look like something healthy and fruit-juicy; kids will tell you they're
sort of like alcohol, but not really. This has joined "it's only beer" as a
great kid drinking myth.

(I've got a press release here from an organization called the Beer 6
Drinkers of America that notes that "many of the Founding Fathers
were private brewers" and goes on to rail against "special interests" that
would interfere with the right to a cold one. Isn't it amazing how much
time people have on their hands?)

But Dr. Novello should take note of what many counselors dis- 7
cover: that the drinking problem that damages kids most is the one that
belongs to their parents. The father who gets drunk and violent, the
mother who drinks when she's depressed, the parents whose personality shifts with the movements of the sun and the bottle. The enormous
family secret.

"An Elephant in the Living Room" is the title of one book for kids 8
whose parents drink. "When I was about ten years old, I started to realize that my dad had a drinking problem," it begins. "Sometimes he
drank too much. Then he would talk loudly and make jokes that weren't
funny. He would say unkind things to my mom in front of the neighbors and my friends. I felt embarrassed."

That's the voice of an adult who has perspective on her past. This 9
is the voice of a 12-year-old at a school in the kind of neighborhood
where we talk, talk, talk about crack though the abuse of alcohol is
much more widespread. She is talking about her father, who drinks:
"I hate him. He should just stay in his room like a big dog." This would
make a good commercial—the moment when your own kid thinks of
you as an animal.

The folks who sell alcohol will say most people use it responsibly, 10
but the fact remains that many people die in car accidents because of it,
many wind up in the hospital because of it, and many families are destroyed because of it. Dr. Novello is right to excoriate the commercials;
it is not just that they make drinking seem cool, but that they make it
seem inevitable, as though parties would not take place, Christmas never
come, success be elusive without a bottle. It's got to be confusing to see
vodka as the stuff of which family gatherings are made and then watch
your mother pass out in the living room.

This is the drug that has been handed down from generation to 11
generation, that most kids learn to use and abuse at home. I'd love to
see warning labels, about fetal alcohol syndrome and liver damage and
addiction. But it's time for a change, not just in the ads, but in the atmosphere that assumes a substance is innocuous because it's not illegal. For most of our children, the most powerful advertisement for alcohol may be sitting at the kitchen table. Or sleeping it off in the
bedroom.

RESPONDING TO "THE WAR ON DRINKS"

Freewrite about what you think most influences children to drink.

Responding through Interpretation

1. Although Quindlen believes the surgeon generals have tried to lead a "war on drinks," they have not been successful. What else could they do, in her opinion?
2. Why does Quindlen believe that parents who drink have such a powerful effect on their children? Do you agree that parents who drink damage their kids? In what ways?
3. Quindlen, as a journalistic writer, presents her brief argument against drinking through specific contemporary facts and anecdotes (brief narratives). Which anecdotes did you find most convincing?

Responding through Discussion

1. Quindlen calls alcohol "the drug that has been handed down from generation to generation, that most kids learn to use and abuse at home." Discuss her point of view with your group. Do you agree or disagree with her? What have been some of the personal experiences that members of the group are willing to share?
2. Before your next group discussion, have each member of the group watch television commercials and look for magazine ads that promote alcohol consumption. Bring some examples back to class and discuss how persuasive these are. What hidden messages lie behind the ads? Do they seem aimed at young people rather than at adults? Share your findings with the class as a whole.

Responding through Writing

1. Write a journal entry about the different ways that you have observed alcohol creating health and family problems.
2. Collect several youth-oriented ads for alcoholic beverages from newspapers or popular magazines; use them to illustrate a paper in which you explain how these ads appeal to the needs and interests of young people. Do you believe such ads are effective in influencing underage drinking?

The Art of Healing

Bill Moyers

Bill Moyers grew up in Marshall, Texas. He was a press secretary for President Lyndon Johnson and has been a television news commentator as well
as the producer and moderator of a number of successful educational television series on subjects such as poetry, creativity, the ideas of Joseph
Campbell, and healing. The following selection, from Moyers's book,
Healing and the Mind (1993), explores the ways in which caring, involved
physicians can help the healing process.

"Remember to cure the patient as well as the disease"

—Dr. Alvan Barach

Sirens wail through the night as ambulance after ambulance pulls up to   1
the emergency room of Parkland Memorial Hospital, the public hospital in Dallas, Texas. The emergency area is so crowded that patients' beds
line the hallways. Anyone who does not need immediate medical attention is sent to a packed waiting area. Men, women, and children sit
silently, often in pain, waiting for hours to see a doctor. During the day
more than 350 people may cram the waiting area of the outpatient clinic,
until the line extends beyond the hospital door to the sidewalk. It is not
unusual for some of these people, most of them poor, to wait ten or
twelve hours to receive fifteen minutes of basic medical care. Like all
public hospitals, Parkland is underfunded, overcrowded, and overwhelmed. Yet unlike most, it has resolved to change the way it practices
medicine.

The man behind the change is Dr. Ron Anderson, Parkland's chief   2
executive officer, a practicing internist and a Southern Baptist who has
been influenced both by Native American wisdom about healing and by
clinical experience demonstrating that patients benefit measurably when
their medical treatment includes attention to their emotional needs.

Following Ron Anderson on his rounds with medical students, I lis-   3
ten as he stops at the bedside of an elderly woman suffering from chronic
asthma. He asks the usual questions: "How did you sleep last night?"
"Is the breathing getting any easier?" His next questions surprise the
medical students: "Is your son looking for work?" "Is he still drinking?"
"Tell us what happened right before the asthma attack." He explains to
his puzzled students, "We know that anxiety aggravates many illnesses,

especially chronic conditions like asthma. So we have to find out what may be causing her episodes of stress and help her find some way of coping with it. Otherwise, she will land in here again, and next time we might not be able to save her. We cannot just prescribe medication and walk away. That is medical neglect. We have to take the time to get to know her, how she lives, her values, what her social supports are. If we don't know that her son is her sole support and that he's out of work, we will be much less effective in dealing with her asthma."

Modern medicine, with all its extraordinary technology, has accomplished wonders, but Anderson believes that caring is also a powerful medicine. The most striking example of his emphasis can be seen in Parkland's neonatal intensive care unit. Like hospitals across the country, Parkland is dealing with a sharp increase in premature and low-birth-weight babies. The hospital employs the latest technology to keep those infants alive, but saving them, Anderson says, is not enough. Equally important is promoting the emotional connection between parent and child. Scientific research has shown that without human contact, a baby will wither and its normal development will be stunted. Babies need to be touched.   4

Cindy Wheeler is a neonatal nurse. I watch as she introduces Vanessa, a fifteen-year-old mother, to her premature son for the first time. In a room outside the intensive care unit, Vanessa scrubs her hands and arms. Cindy helps her put a sterilized gown over her clothing and then don a mask that covers her nose and mouth. They proceed through the double doors into a series of open rooms with row after row of high-tech medical machinery. In the middle of these islands of hardware is an incubator, a technological womb for Malcolm, Vanessa's tiny son. Protected by this space-age bubble, Malcolm looks more like a fetus than a baby. He is covered with tape and dotted with intravenous needles; tubes connect him to a series of monitors and machines. Cindy knows that Vanessa is frightened and wants to run away. She takes the mother's hand and in a gentle voice begins to tell her that it will be okay, that the baby needs her. She guides Vanessa's finger to Malcolm's miniature hand, whispering that all babies, no matter how old, will respond to the touch of a mother's hand by gripping her finger. The moment is crucial. Vanessa's tense ambivalence will either disappear or cause her to flee. The tiny hand closes around her middle finger. The mother smiles and closes her eyes. Her relief is palpable.   5

For many women like Vanessa, Cindy tells me, a baby is a status symbol, the first they can call their own. Their dream of a Gerber baby, a Barbie doll, is shattered when the child is born very small or critically ill. "Our   6 mission," she says, "is to share our understanding of the loss they feel, and to help the mothers feel something positive from what otherwise can be a major disappointment and leave a deep psychological scar."

Many of the young mothers are from dysfunctional families. The hospital staff is often the closest they have come to having a nurturing family, and their experience in the neonatal unit is for some the first time they feel supported. To Cindy Wheeler and her colleagues, these teenage mothers are forced to make a decisive choice: to continue being controlled by their problems, or to take charge of their circumstances and, through caring, to make a difference. "Sometimes," says Cindy, "we get very angry at the mothers. A while ago, we saw mothers on drugs as a danger to their babies, and we kept them away from here. Just recently I became angry with a woman for taking drugs during her pregnancy. She was turning her baby into an addict. Her own baby! I wanted to slap her, but I controlled my anger. I told her that she should hold the baby because it was experiencing stress. Maybe it was the touch of that helpless child: whatever, the mother entered a drug rehabilitation program. And she's doing okay."

Listening to Cindy, I recall an essay by the physician and philosopher Lewis Thomas. Its point is that the dismay of being sick comes in part from the loss of close human contact; touch is medicine's real professional secret.

Far from Parkland, at Beth Israel Hospital in Boston, I hear similar opinions from Dr. Thomas Delbanco, an internist who has taken a sabbatical from his practice to head the Picker/Commonwealth Program for Patient-Centered Care. The issue of illness as a life crisis for patient and family, Delbanco says, has been given too little attention in the medical community. New studies are suggesting that patients who receive information and emotional support fare better on the average than those who do not. According to these studies, closer contact between physicians and patients can improve the chances of a good recovery.

Delbanco comes from a family of artists and plays the violin, an instrument whose uniqueness he compares to each individual's experience of illness. "There are two important parts of me," he says. "There is the physician and there is the musician. Music connects me with the importance of being replenished spiritually. And that is something that as a physician I must never forget. The patient before me is a human being with the same joys, sorrows, and complexities as myself. Doctors have to listen to what makes one person different from the other and constantly evaluate that distinction in order to figure out what makes one treatment work better for one person and not the other."

He introduces our team to Audrey and Ed Taylor. Audrey, who is   11
fifty-eight, works in computer graphics. She is about to experience one
of the most traumatic events in medicine—open heart surgery. Dr. Delbanco will follow her through the experience and interpret it for her and
her family: her husband, Ed, a retired firefighter; their son, Ed, Jr., an MIT
graduate with a degree in engineering, who now runs his own small construction company; and their daughter, Ruthie, an elementary-school
teacher. Audrey's ordeal will test the family. How they manage their col-
lective trauma, Delbanco explains, can affect Audrey's recovery from the
surgery. "The hospitalization of a loved one is a crisis for the whole family. Families can interfere with medicine or they can be the medicine. I
would say that respecting and facilitating family bonds may be more crucial to a patient's survival than the latest diagnostic procedure or therapeutic innovation. All too often they are left out of the picture. As doctors, we don't get into the house anymore. And we don't get that larger
context in the examining room.

"If we physicians also thought of ourselves as medicine," he says,   12
"we would treat people differently. The more informed you are as a patient and the more your family understands what is happening, the
more you and they will be able to make wiser decisions. Information is
hope. The terrible doctor robs the patient of hope. As physicians, we have
to treat the body and appeal to the mind—the patient's and the family's."

This rings true to me. When I was growing up, our family doctor in   13
Marshall, Texas, instinctively knew a lot about healing and the mind.
When he asked, "How are you feeling?" he was interested in more than
our stomachaches or fevers. He lived down the street, went to the church
on the corner, knew where my parents worked, knew our relatives and
family history—and he knew how to listen. He treated the patient holistically before anyone there ever heard of the term.

That was years ago. Today the practice of medicine in an urban, tech-   14
nological society rarely provides either the time or the environment to
encourage a doctor-patient relationship that promotes healing. Many
modern doctors also lack the requisite training for this kind of healing.
As Eric J. Cassell writes in *The Nature of Suffering and the Goals of Medicine*, "Without system and training, being responsive in the face of suffering remains the attribute of individual physicians who have come to
this mastery alone or gained it from a few inspirational teachers." Healing powers, Cassell continues, "consist only in and no more than in al-
lowing, causing, or bringing to bear those things or forces for getting better (whatever they may be) that already exist in the patient." The
therapeutic instrument in this healing is "indisputably" the doctor,

whose power flows not from control over the patient but from his or her own self-mastery. Modern physicians have mastered admirably the power of the latest scientific medicine. To excel at the art of healing requires the same systematic discipline.

Talking with different doctors during this journey, I realize that we do need a new medical paradigm that goes beyond "body parts" medicine, and not only for the patient's sake. At a time when the cost of health care is skyrocketing, the potential economic impact of mind/body medicine is considerable. Thinking about our medical system as a "health care" system rather than a "disease treatment" system would mean looking closely at medical education and our public funding priorities.   15

On this first stage of my journey, I realize that the subject of healing and the mind stretches beyond medicine into issues about what we value in society and who we are as human beings. As patients, we are more than lonely, isolated flecks of matter; we are members of families, communities, and cultures. As this awareness finds its way into hospitals, operating rooms, clinics, and doctors' offices, perhaps it will spread further, as well. Healing begins with caring. So does civilization.   16

RESPONDING TO "THE ART OF HEALING"

Freewrite about a good experience you've had with a caring medical professional.

Responding through Interpretation

1. Moyers provides several examples of caring doctors and nurses to make his ideas concrete. Briefly describe each of the examples and how effective you thought each was.
2. What does Moyers believe doctors need to master in order to excel in the art of healing and why? What new "medical paradigm" does he say is needed?
3. Moyers, along with the physician Lewis Thomas, believes that "touch is medicine's real professional secret." In your reading journal, interpret this statement and give your response to it.

Responding through Discussion

1. If possible, have group members informally interview a health care professional or read some current periodicals to see whether the new "caring" approaches discussed in Moyers's essay are being incorporated

more deliberately into medical care. Report back to the group and then to the class as a whole.

2. Discuss in the group the different experiences group members have had with doctors. Have you found doctors like the ones Bill Moyers mentions? What impact have different doctors had on you?

Responding through Writing

1. Write a journal entry about how medical care has changed since you were a child. How did you used to see doctors and nurses? How do you see them now? What vivid memories do you have of hospitals when you were little?
2. Moyers ends his essay by saying, "Healing begins with caring. So does civilization." Write a paper in which you argue for or against Moyers's position. Do you think society should put its resources into training medical specialists or into training family doctors?

Doctor, Do You Care?

Katherine Razum

Katherine Razum grew up in Arizona and currently lives in Oakland, California. She is taking courses in order to transfer to a four-year college where she hopes to be an English major and write plays and screenplays. Katherine Razum wrote the following essay for her critical thinking class in response to Bill Moyers's "The Art of Healing." As you read her essay, notice how Razum, using her own experiences with "holistic" treatments to support her position, thoughtfully examines some of the possible effects of training doctors to be holistically oriented generalists rather than specialists.

It is important for society to concentrate its resources on training medical   1
specialists to be proficient in implementing revolutionary, high-level medical technologies instead of on programs to train more general practitioners to use a holistic approach to healing. Scientists are literally on the verge of discovering the causes and cures of some of the most painful and deadly diseases of our time. As those technologies become realities, the medical community is duty-bound to master them.

Holism, as defined by Webster's dictionary, means, "The theory   2
that whole entities, and fundamental components of reality, have an existence other than as a mere sum of their parts." Holistic healing is not just healing physical ailments, but dealing with emotional and spiritual problems as well. Bill Moyers, author of *Healing and the Mind,* is a proponent of this approach. In an excerpt from his book he says, "Healing begins with caring." Anyone who dedicates his or her life to preserving health and saving lives obviously does care. So, in a sense, healing does begin with caring. However, it would be impossible for just anyone who is caring to be a healer without the benefit of medical training. In his statement, Moyers has overlooked the necessity of possessing the ability to diagnose and treat the patient's illness to begin the healing process.

When I was diagnosed with my third ulcer, the doctor tried a logi-   3
cal and caring approach rather than a clinical one. He asked me what was going on in my life that might cause stress. After we talked for awhile, he made some recommendations for cutting tension out of my life. He also recommended several books. Instead of writing a prescription for some heavy-duty drug (like the doctors before had done), he handed me a book called *When Bad Things Happen to Good People.* I de-

spise taking medication, so this was fine with me. It was reassuring to feel like he cared about me and my health. But he took a relatively serious medical condition and risked exacerbating it by assuming that I would read the book, that the book would work, and that I would be able to change my lifestyle. I didn't follow through on his recommendations and ended up needing a low-dosage ulcer medication. Moyers refers to modern-day medicine as "disease treatment," indicating that doctors are only prescribing medications to effect healing. While our country's doctors may be facing an overreliance on prescription drugs and medical technology, there is no refuting the conclusive results—such drugs are very often necessary to heal and save lives.

Moyers describes the philosophy of Dr. Thomas Delbanco, a physi-   4 cian in Boston. He believes that it is important for doctors to realize each patient's individuality and recommend treatment accordingly. This is an acceptable expectation of medical professionals. Delbanco also thinks that "information is hope." If a patient and his or her family are well-informed about what is happening in treatment, they will make better decisions. I think that information also relieves the anxiety that accompanies medical procedures. For instance, a recent trend with OB/GYN doctors is to talk the patient through every step of the examination or procedure. It has a calming effect as well as diminishing the threat of sexual misconduct that so many women fear. This caring approach should be taught as a medical courtesy or obligation.

We cannot expect general practitioners to be everything to everyone;   5 this would cause severe emotional distress to doctors, and possibly to patients as well. As an alternative to training doctors in holistic practices, we should equip them with reliable references to psychologists and ministers to complete the holistic system. To validate this concept, we would need to make this type of treatment available under most insurance plans. For instance, if prescribed, a patient would visit a professional trio (M.D., psychologist, and spiritual leader), and it would be covered by insurance as one charge.

Another alternative to training G.P.'s as holistic healers is teaching   6 nurses to be the primary caregivers. Nurses are responsible for most of the preparation and health maintenance of patients. Therefore, they are with patients more than the doctors are. Bill Moyers cites an example of a neonatal nurse, Cindy Wheeler, who shares stories about premature births, babies born with drug addictions, and babies that don't survive. She believes that it is her and her nursing staff's mission "to share [their] understanding of the loss [the mothers] feel, and to help the mothers feel something positive from what otherwise can be a major disappointment. . . ." I think it is very natural to expect your attending nurses to be kind, caring, and sympathetic. If they aren't, and there are some that aren't, they were misguided by their career counselor.

There are several drawbacks to Bill Moyers's plan to redirect focus   7 from specialists and high-level technology to general practitioners and holistic healing. For one, Health Maintenance Organizations (HMOs) would undermine any attempt at holistic healing because members are not allowed the freedom to choose their physicians. This would limit the potential for doctors to get to know their patients well and establish trust which are rudimentary elements of this approach to healing. Another disadvantage is that imposing such demands on physicians is unrealistic and unsympathetic. Finally, if doctors develop close relationships with all of their patients, they would suffer immeasurable grief when they lost them to death. In fact, doctors may lose more patients this way if we eliminate specialists and their ability to provide revolutionary, high-tech medicine. Society would pay the ultimate price when our medical professionals start burning out, becoming mentally and emotionally unstable, or even committing suicide because of excessive stress and excessive emotional involvement with each patient.

Moyers argues that "thinking about our medical system as a 'health   8 care' system rather than a 'disease treatment' system would mean looking closely at medical education and our public funding priorities." Yes, caring is an integral part of healing, but if the funding was taken away from medical programs that train specialists in the latest technologies, we may end up with a group of physicians who know how to care, but not how to heal.

RESPONDING TO "DOCTOR, DO YOU CARE?"

Freewrite about a time when you received or gave caring attention during your own or someone else's illness.

Responding through Interpretation

1. In response to Bill Moyers's essay, Razum notes several of Moyers's points about the lack of caring in our medical care and our overreliance on technology. List the major arguments she mentions from Moyers. Which ones did she leave out? On what points does she disagree with him?

2. Razum ends her essay with this statement:

> Yes, caring is an integral part of healing, but if the funding was taken away
> from medical programs that train specialists in the latest technologies, we

*may end up with a group of physicians who know how to care, but not how
to heal.*

In your reading notebook, write what you think Razum means and then
give your own opinion about this statement.

Responding through Discussion

1. As a group, look over Katherine Razum's essay and note the reasons she
   gives for disagreeing with Moyers. Do the effects described by her seem
   believable? Does she provide evidence to support them? Discuss whether
   or not the group found Razum's essay effective. What suggestions would
   you have for improving the essay?

Responding through Writing

1. In your journal write a narrative account about a time you went to a physician who had an influence on your feelings and attitudes about doctors.
2. Write a paper, using your own experiences with doctors and treatment,
   about how you think medical practices have changed during your lifetime. Incorporate material from your journal entry above if appropriate.

Responding to "The Art of Healing"

Derek Collins

Originally from Alberta, Canada, Derek Collins was working two jobs and attending community college full-time when he wrote the following essay in response to "The Art of Healing." Derek would like eventually to obtain an M.B.A. and possibly a law degree. In writing his essay, he wanted to present a balanced look at both family medicine and medical specialists. Notice how Collins draws upon his own experiences with doctors to support his arguments.

I was nineteen years old, waiting for my name to be called to see a   1
doctor. I had been sick for four weeks and put off seeing a physician.
When I finally got called, I was asked to wait some more. I waited what
seemed like an hour. When the doctor came, he asked me what was
wrong; I told him I was vomiting and couldn't control it. He looked at
me and said, "I will be back. The nurse will be in in a moment." That
was the last I saw of him.

This single experience was the worst moment in my life. I remem-   2
ber feeling like the visit would never end. I had a helpless feeling that
was accelerated to a panic state when I didn't receive the emotional support I needed and was regarded like a "body-part." I believe, in retro-
spect, the whole ordeal could have been lessened if my emotional needs
had been filled. During the visit I felt as if I were one of many, that I was
insignificant, yet I had a need for special attention, a need to be made to
feel really important, as many people do when they are sick.

I have heard stories about the days when most people saw family   3
doctors who knew all their patients personally and medically, who lived
within the community. Bill Moyers describes in the essay the variety of
community activities the general practitioners were involved in, such as
church work. I believe the relationships that come from an in-house
doctor create an ease and sense of security for the sick. The special
warmth generated from the ongoing relationships appeals to emotional
needs of patients. Patients get a boost in strength when sympathized
with. They get a "second wind" in their battle. I find that medical remedies to the body are only half of the treatment; a doctor that sympathizes
with and relates to patients will help them on the road to recovery.

Moyers's essay raises the important question of whether it is more   4
important to put resources into training medical specialists or general
practitioners. I feel that it is more important for medical resources to go

to the training of general practitioners. Most cases of sickness take just fundamental, rather than specialized, medical knowledge; therefore, more money for training doctors should be put into general medicine.

I also feel that some cases of major sickness can be abbreviated or even stopped by preventative medicine and personal attentiveness. For example, an anti-drinking advertisement says, "Stop teenage drinking before it happens." This ad shows that to stop teenage drinking and driving accidents we need to stop teenagers from drinking. I feel that if general practitioners got involved with prevention of drug and alcohol problems, using personal approaches, they could cure some sicknesses before they happen. By lending a more sympathetic ear, a trained doctor could also discover problems earlier, therefore starting treatment earlier. It could save many dollars in medical treatments to catch problems earlier, and it could mean life or death in some situations. For example, a doctor who has established relationships within the community could tell women to come in for a mammogram. A patient who is comfortable with her physician will do as she is advised. What is happening now is that some women feel uncomfortable or even scared to see physicians they do not know. This fear can lead to undiagnosed cancers that may develop into an irreversible problem.

I believe that significant medical resources should go to family practitioners; however, I do not see in the near future a shift in resources back from medical specialists. We have built many hospitals and have created a field of specialists within the medical profession. Many new life-saving technologies have been discovered because of the amount of resources put into specialists' education and training. Medicine is a very rewarding career financially, and job satisfaction does come from knowing that you came up with a technological advance that might save millions of lives. These factors motivate many doctors to specialize. A society where we build hospitals makes it seem that we do not need family practitioners. We have centralized medicine, which makes the doctor's work more productive. We can therefore spend the freed money to go to specialists. Some within the medical profession believe many doctors waste their talents as general practitioners. They feel nurses can be trained to do the bulk of the work that general practitioners used to do. The convenience of centralized medicine makes it so you can see a diagnosing physician, and see another doctor if necessary, and fill prescriptions all in the same place. This convenience is very beneficial to a patient who is not feeling well enough to run around.

Although there are some arguments for staying with centralized medicine, it is also a way for the medical profession to create job security and get more money. Centralized medicine like Kaiser gets rid of

competition by making a huge facility-hospital. It makes a general practitioner's job obsolete while creating job security for doctors at the
"super-clinic." In contrast, when we had decentralized medicine we had
general practitioners competing for patients. Doctors would come to
your house. They often lived within the community, like the doctors Bill
Moyers remembers from his childhood in Marshall, Texas. Decentralized medicine made doctors compete financially. It forced doctors to
keep rates reasonable. It would also make doctors more sympathetic and
caring to patients' needs. If you did not have these qualifications, as prescribed above, you would find yourself without work. As it is, we now
have centralized medicine that only benefits the medical profession. The
system as it is has cut back on the need for general practitioners, freeing
doctors to become specialists. This allows the medical profession to
charge higher rates for tests and technology that are not always necessary. On top of all that, we now have doctors at hospitals who do not
sympathize with patients and often treat patients in a condescending,
uncaring way. When I was sick with mononucleosis, I had to make three
separate visits to find the cause of my illness, yet I still had to pay for all
of these visits.

In conclusion, I believe specialized medicine allows people who   8
might not be able to get treatments for their problems to receive the benefit of new breakthroughs in medical technology, while centralized medicine makes it more convenient for ill patients to receive treatment faster
and with more ease. However, I feel we have lost touch with the basic
concept of medicine. Physical needs are not the only ones that have to
be addressed. The medical industry has forgotten, because of greed,
that emotional needs also must be addressed to complete the healing
process. If the medical profession could remember the emotional needs
of the patient that need to be fulfilled to complete the healing process,
we would have a happier, healthier, and a more financially equal nation.

RESPONDING TO "RESPONDING TO THE ART OF HEALING"

Freewrite on your attitudes about the rise of medical specialists.

Responding through Interpretation

1. What main point in Moyers's essay does Collins agree with and why?
   Which points does he disagree with?
2. Unlike Katherine Razum, who began her essay with a summary and definitions before bringing in her personal experience, Derek Collins be-

gins his argument with a direct personal narrative before introducing his main ideas. Which approach did you find more effective? Why?

Responding through Discussion

1. Discuss with your group whether or not you think Collins's experience with a doctor is a common one and, if so, can such experiences become serious problems?

Responding through Writing

1. In your journal, respond to the following sentence from Collins's conclusion:

   The medical industry has forgotten, because of greed, that emotional needs also must be addressed to complete the healing process.

   Do you agree? Why?
2. Write a paper that gives an account of an illness you once had in which you were sent from doctor to doctor for consultations and treatments. What was the outcome of this illness? What impact did the experience have on you? If you've had no direct experience, use the experiences of someone close to you or someone you know about.

MAKING CONNECTIONS

A great part of our lives is given over to maintaining our health. Without good health, nothing else matters that much. You know how it feels to be sick: All you can think about is getting better. Everything else you might want to do or usually do takes a back seat when you're ill. The readings in this chapter bring into focus all the physical and emotional levels that come into play when we need medical care. A number of the readings also point out the inadequacies of the medical system in responding to patients in a holistic way.

1. *Doctors and healing.* Several of the readings in this chapter focus on how doctors' concern for their patients can play a vital role in patients' recovery. Re-read some of the ideas set forth by Bill Moyers in "The Art of Healing," Perri Klass in "Learning the Language," and Katherine Razum in "Doctor, Do You Care?" Then write a paper in which you give your own suggestions for how doctors today could create closer and more trusting relationships with their patients.
2. *The deep effects of illness.* Donald Murray ("Reflections from a Sick Bed") and Geoffrey Kurland ("A Doctor's Case") both give personal

accounts of the emotional and physical effects of being ill. Write an essay about an illness you have had, whether serious or relatively benign, and illustrate how it changed the way you perceived things from that point on.

3. *Taking a look at medical practices.* Look through all the selections once again and take note of the different medical procedures that have been described in Williams's short story "The Use of Force," Becker's poem, "Medical Science," and the essays by Kurland, Klass, and Razum. What did you learn that you didn't already know? Write a paper in which you discuss some of the medical terminology and procedures that interested you most.

4. *Health hazards by our own hand.* Anna Quindlen's "The War on Drinks" is the only selection in this chapter that discusses a specific practice (drinking alcohol) that causes health problems. There are, of course, numerous others: smoking, doing drugs, overeating, eating the wrong foods, and so on. Choose another destructive practice that you feel should be brought to the public's attention, and write a paper similar to Quindlen's in which you argue for the elimination of that practice.

CHAPTER 8

Work

Introduction

RICHARD RODRIGUEZ	Labor
NANCY K. AUSTIN	Workable Ethics
JENNIFER HOLMES	The Work Ethic and Me
KEVIN (WING KUEN) HIP	Why I Hate Work
LAUREEN MAR	My Mother, Who Came from China, Where She Never Saw Snow
HEINRICH BÖLL	The Laugher
MAYA ANGELOU	Cotton Pickers
MICKEY KAUS	Yes, Something Will Work: Work
BARBARA EHRENREICH	A Step Back to the Workhouse?
NIKKI CORBIN	Why Workfare?
DEIRDRE MENA	Welfare versus Workfare

Making Connections

INTRODUCTION

Journal Entry

Freewrite for 10 minutes on your feelings about work. What do you associate with work? What part has work played in your life? What are the different kinds of work that you do? Would you be content not to have to do any kind of work at all? How would you occupy your time?

A great part of our lives is spent working. Although it is usually associated with wage labor, work also has other meanings. Some people work for the fun of it, as a hobby—fixing up their homes or cars, gardening, making clothes, or pursuing artistic interests such as painting, singing, or writing. Work done on one's own is usually thought of as more fulfilling than work done for hire.

However, salaried labor can also sometimes have great personal benefits as well as financial rewards. On the most basic level, a person who earns money and supports himself or herself can take pride in being independent and strong. Often, salaried work also brings us in contact with other workers, giving us an opportunity to be with people from different backgrounds from our own. Most of us have mixed feelings about work: We'd like to work, not because we have to, but because we want to—and we might yearn for the day when we don't have to work at all. Sometimes, however, without work to structure our days, we can grow despondent and wonder what to do with ourselves.

A country singer once changed his name to "Johnny Paycheck" to emphasize his identification with wage-earning people and the way wage labor wears us down. Some work taxes the brain; some taxes the body. Nearly every town, city, and country has been built on the backs of others, and it is this kind of hard physical labor that is explored in several of the readings in this chapter: Richard Rodriguez in "Labor," Maya Angelou in "Cotton Pickers," and Laureen Mar in her poem "My Mother Who Came from China" all paint graphic pictures of tough and monotonous physical labor that is numbing to the mind and destructive to the body.

Despite the negative aspects of labor, Mickey Kaus in "Something Will Work: Work" argues in favor of the work ethic as a way to solve social problems and increase individual self-esteem. Kaus and Barbara Ehrenreich ("A Step Back to the Workhouse?") both tackle the increasing problems of the welfare system—each from a different angle. Kaus thinks people should be made to work (or given job training) in exchange for government assistance, while Ehrenreich argues against it, saying that it's just another form of the ancient workhouse to force poor people to work for welfare checks.

Certain views about work are given in student Kevin Hip's essay, "Why I Hate Work," when he argues that work is stressful and painful for most people and we should stop trying to brainwash people into believing that work is good for you. Contrasting views are given in Jennifer Holmes's "The Work Ethic and Me," in which a department store worker traces the maturation that can come to young people from mastering the social world of the work place. Nancy Austin in her essay, "Workable Ethics," considers some of the difficult ethical choices that people must often make on the job; and Heinrich Böll's unusual short story, "The Laugher," might make you stop and think about what you would consider an ideal profession. If laughing for a living is not fun, what is?

Labor

Richard Rodriguez

The son of Mexican-American immigrants, Richard Rodriguez could not
speak English when he entered elementary school. Rodriguez went on to
graduate from Stanford and to continue his study of English Renaissance
literature at the University of California, Berkeley. Turning down university positions, Rodriguez decided to become a full-time writer. In the autobiographical work *Hunger of Memory* (1982) he uses his own successful educational experience to develop a critique of both bilingual education
and affirmative action. His most recent work is *Days of Obligation* (1992).

It was at Stanford, one day near the end of my senior year, that a friend   1
told me about a summer construction job he knew was available. I was
quickly alert. Desire uncoiled within me. My friend said that he knew I
had been looking for summer employment. He knew I needed some
money. Almost apologetically he explained: It was something I probably
wouldn't be interested in, but a friend of his, a contractor, needed
someone for summer to do menial jobs. There would be lots of shoveling
and raking and sweeping. Nothing too hard. But nothing more
interesting either. Still, the pay would be good. Did I want it? Or did I
know someone who did?

I did. Yes, I said, surprised to hear myself say it.   2

In the weeks following, friends cautioned that I had no idea how   3
hard physical labor really is. ("You only *think* you know what it is like
to shovel for eight hours straight.") Their objections seemed to me challenges. They resolved the issue. I became happy with my plan. I decided,
however, not to tell my parents. I wouldn't tell my mother because I
could guess her worried reaction. I would tell my father only after the
summer was over, when I could announce that, after all, I did know what
"real work" is like.

The day I met the contractor (a Princeton graduate, it turned out),   4
he asked me whether I had done any physical labor before. "In high
school, during the summer," I lied. And although he seemed to regard
me with skepticism, he decided to give me a try. Several days later, ex-
pectant, I arrived at my first construction site. I would take off my shirt
to the sun. And at last grasp desired sensation. No longer afraid. At last
become like a *bracero*. "We need those tree stumps out of here by tomorrow," the contractor said. I started to work.

I labored with excitement that first morning—and all the days after.   5
The work was harder than I could have expected. But it was never as tedious as my friends had warned me it would be. There was too much
physical pleasure in the labor. Especially early in the day, I would be
most alert to the sensations of movement and straining. Beginning
around seven each morning (when the air was still damp but the scent
of weeds and dry earth anticipated the heat of the sun), I would feel my
body resist the first thrusts of the shovel. My arm, tightened by sleep,
would gradually loosen; after only several minutes, sweat would gather
in beads on my forehead and then—a short while later—I would feel my
chest silky with sweat in the breeze. I would return to my work. A nervous spark of pain would fly up my arm and settle to burn like an ember
in the thick of my shoulder. An hour, two passed. Three. My whole body
would assume regular movements; my shoveling would be described
by identical, even movements. Even later in the day, my enthusiasm for
primitive sensation would survive the heat and the dust and the insects
pricking my back. I would strain wildly for sensation as the day came
to a close. At three-thirty, quitting time, I would stand upright and
slowly let my head fall back, luxuriating in the feeling of tightness re-
lieved.

   Some of the men working nearby would watch me and laugh. Two   6
or three of the older men took the trouble to teach me the right way to
use a pick, the correct way to shovel. "You're doing it wrong, too fuck-
ing hard," one man scolded. Then proceeded to show me—what persons
who work with their bodies all their lives quickly learn—the most eco-
nomical way to use one's body in labor.

   "Don't make your back do so much work," he instructed. I stood im-   7
patiently listening, half listening, vaguely watching, then noticed his
work-thickened fingers clutching the shovel. I was annoyed. I wanted
to tell him that I enjoyed shoveling the wrong way. And I didn't want
to learn the right way. I wasn't afraid of back pain. I liked the way my
body felt sore at the end of the day.

   I was about to, but, as it turned out, I didn't say a thing. Rather it   8
was at that moment I realized that I was fooling myself if I expected a
few weeks of labor to gain me admission to the world of the laborer. I
would not learn in three months what my father had meant by "real
work." I was not bound to this job; I could imagine its rapid conclusion.
For me the sensations were to be feared. Fatigue took a different toll on
their bodies—and minds.

   It was, I know, a simple insight. But it was with this realization that   9
I took my first step that summer toward realizing something even more

important about the "worker." In the company of carpenters, electricians, plumbers, and painters at lunch, I would often sit quietly, observant. I was not shy in such company. I felt easy, pleased by the knowledge that I was casually accepted, my presence taken for granted by men (exotics) who worked with their hands. Some days the younger men would talk and talk about sex, and they would howl at women who drove by in cars. Other days the talk at lunchtime was subdued; men gathered in separate groups. It depended on who was around. There were rough, good-natured workers. Others were quiet. The more I remember that summer, the more I realize that there was no single *type* of worker. I am embarrassed to say I had not expected such diversity. I certainly had not expected to meet, for example, a plumber who was an abstract painter in his off hours and admired the work of Mark Rothko. Nor did I expect to meet so many workers with college diplomas. (They were the ones who were not surprised that I intended to enter graduate school in the fall.) I suppose what I really want to say here is painfully obvious, but I must say it nevertheless: the men of that summer were middle-class Americans. They certainly didn't constitute an oppressed society. Carefully completing their work sheets; talking about the fortunes of local football teams; planning Las Vegas vacations; comparing the gas mileage of various makes of campers—they were not *los pobres* my mother had spoken about.

On two occasions, the contractor hired a group of Mexican aliens. They were employed to cut down some trees and haul off debris. In all, there were six men of varying age. The youngest in his late twenties; the oldest (his father?) perhaps sixty years old. They came and they left in a single old truck. Anonymous men. They were never introduced to the other men at the site. Immediately upon their arrival, they would follow the contractor's directions, start working—rarely resting—seemingly driven by a fatalistic sense that work which had to be done was best done as quickly as possible.

I watched them sometimes. Perhaps they watched me. The only time I saw them pay me much notice was one day at lunchtime when I was laughing with the other men. The Mexicans sat apart when they ate, just as they worked by themselves. Quiet. I rarely heard them say much to each other. All I could hear were their voices calling out sharply to one another, giving directions. Otherwise, when they stood briefly resting, they talked among themselves in voices too hard to overhear.

The contractor knew enough Spanish, and the Mexicans—or at least the oldest of them, their spokesman—seemed to know enough English to communicate. But because I was around, the contractor decided one day to make me his translator. (He assumed I could speak Spanish.) I

10

11

12

did what I was told. Shyly I went over to tell the Mexicans that the *patrón* wanted them to do something else before they left for the day. As I started to speak, I was afraid with my old fear that I would be unable to pronounce the Spanish words. But it was a simple instruction I had to convey. I could say it in phrases.

The dark sweating faces turned toward me as I spoke. They stopped 13
their work to hear me. Each nodded in response. I stood there. I wanted to say something more. But what could I say in Spanish, even if I could have pronounced the words right? Perhaps I just wanted to engage them in small talk, to be assured of their confidence, our familiarity. I thought for a moment to ask them where in Mexico they were from. Something like that. And maybe I wanted to tell them (a lie, if need be) that my parents were from the same part of Mexico.

I stood there.   14

Their faces watched me. The eyes of the man directly in front of me 15
moved slowly over my shoulder, and I turned to follow his glance toward *el patrón* some distance away. For a moment I felt swept up by that glance into the Mexicans' company. But then I heard one of them returning to work. And then the others went back to work. I left them without saying anything more.

When they had finished, the contractor went over to pay them in 16
cash. (He later told me that he paid them collectively—"for the job," though he wouldn't tell me their wages. He said something quickly about the good rate of exchange "in their own country.") I can still hear the loudly confident voice he used with the Mexicans. It was the sound of the *gringo* I had heard as a very young boy. And I can still hear the quiet, indistinct sounds of the Mexican, the oldest, who replied. At hearing that voice I was sad for the Mexicans. Depressed by their vulnerability. Angry at myself. The adventure of the summer seemed suddenly ludicrous. I would not shorten the distance I felt from *los pobres* with a few weeks of physical labor. I would not become like them. They were different from me.

RESPONDING TO "LABOR"

Freewrite about a temporary job you once had and how you related to your co-workers.

Responding through Interpretation

1. Why does Rodriguez realize that the words "real work" will never hold the same meaning for him as they do for his father?

2. What does the author realize about his distance from *los pobres?* Why does he feel "depressed by their vulnerability" and "angry at [him]self"?
3. Which specific descriptions and sensations does Rodriguez use to get across to his reader the feeling of hard physical labor? Write the ones you think are most vivid in your reading journal.

Responding through Discussion

1. Look over the essay with your group and exchange any information you have about the working world the author describes in "Labor." How is it different from or similar to the work world you know?
2. With your group, share a work experience that has helped you to rethink your values and lifestyle. After everyone has shared an experience, discuss what you learned that might parallel Rodriguez's summer experience in some ways.

Responding through Writing

1. Rodriguez learns much about his own bias and preconception about workers, both Anglo and Mexican, through his summer job. Write a journal entry about a work or a volunteer experience you had in which you learned about your own preconceptions and about how the people you worked with were different from what you had imagined them to be.
2. Write a paper in which you explore several aspects of physical labor as a way to earn a living—such as the construction work Rodriguez did. What do people learn or gain from such work, other than a paycheck? In addition to your own experiences and observations, do some outside reading to gain further information on the topic.

Workable Ethics

Nancy K. Austin

A management consultant in Capitola, California, Nancy Austin wrote the following essay for *Working Woman Magazine* (1992) after a disturbing experience with a demonstration at a medical association before which she was to give a speech. Austin felt caught in the middle between the demonstrators, with whom she identified, and her responsibilities to carry through with her speaking commitment. "Workable Ethics" presents some of her ideas on coping with ethical dilemmas that often arise in the workplace.

Knowing where to draw the line between private feelings and professional duties seems easy—until the moment they collide. When corporate conduct conflicts with your own sense of right and wrong, do you blow the whistle or keep quiet to protect your job? I faced just this sort of quandary a few months ago when I delivered the keynote address at the annual conference of one of the oldest and most respected professional medical associations in America. On the big day, exactly two minutes before my hosts and I stepped onto the stage, an association executive in a dark gray suit took us aside. He had just gotten word that a certain activist group intended to burst into the meeting and break up my presentation. If the protesters got past the guards posted at each door, I was to stay calm and move toward the back of the stage. The association president would then come forward to read a statement she had prepared, just in case.

I didn't feel very reassured. I was about to be thrust under bright lights before 3,000 people in a cavernous hall; I wanted to know what the protest was about. The answer still rings in my head: "The Dalkon Shield," one of my hosts said. The demonstrators would be protesting an award to be given later in the week at the conference to E. Claiborne Robins Sr. I felt dizzy, and my heart began to race. He was chair of A.H. Robins when it sold the disastrous contraceptive device. Another executive standing with us added, with a dismissive wave, "Oh, it all happened a long time ago, 20 years at least."

Twenty years precisely, I almost blurted out. I am a Dalkon Shield claimant. I have a six-digit claim number and a 41-page claim form, facts I was sure the protesters had latched on to. *They must know about me. Why else turn my session into their platform?*

1

2

3

Robins was to be recognized for a "lifetime of distinguished and   4
dedicated public service and contributions to his profession," and the
association hadn't told me. It wanted to grant the award quietly, but
word had leaked out.

The claimants are women and members of their families, number-   5
ing some 179,000, who say they've been damaged by the shield, a plastic intrauterine contraceptive device. They describe physical impair-
ments that include pelvic inflammatory disease, ectopic pregnancies
and permanent infertility. At least 20 deaths have been linked to the
shield. A.H. Robins has since declared bankruptcy and been acquired
by New York-based American Home Products. The Kansas Supreme
Court found that the company "deliberately, intentionally and actively
concealed the dangers of the Shield for year after year." In the eyes of
the claimants, E. Claiborne Robins Sr. heads the short list of responsible
parties.

All of this careened through my head as I took the stage. I felt I had   6
to go ahead with the speech. I kept telling myself I wouldn't be en-
dorsing their award by speaking at the meeting, though I couldn't shake
the sense that by living up to my professional contract, I would somehow be letting down all the claimants, myself included. What would
the others have me do? Come clean or keep my secret? Change my presentation right there and speak extemporaneously on corporate conscience? Stomp off the stage in disgust? No uninvited guests showed
up, but during each minute of my speech, I kept wondering what I
would do if they did.

When the body of moral principles that govern your day-to-day life   7
conflicts with the ethical practices of your company, clearing a path
through the tangle can be slow, arduous work. Suppose you had been
an Exxon employee when the *Valdez* spilled nearly 11 million gallons of
oil into Prince William Sound. Would it have been better to work for corporate reform from inside the company, or would quitting in protest
have had more impact—and would you have been willing to give up
your job over this? What if you had been a strongly pro-choice employee of the public-relations firm Hill and Knowlton when it took the
Roman Catholic Church on as a client to help defend and publicize its
anti-abortion position? Suppose you worked for Dow Corning and were
concerned about how it is handling responsibility for the effects of its
silicone breast implants. What should you do?

These are the kinds of questions that everybody faces in the course   8
of a normal career. The way you answer depends on where you mark
the boundary between your responsibility to your company and your

duty to yourself. Below, a few guideposts to help you through the shadowy terrain.

When the Pressure Is On

Even though all ethical decisions deserve in-depth consideration, often 9 there's no time for it. "Sometimes you have 30 seconds, sometimes an hour, but the impact is the same," says Kirk Hanson, a Stanford University management professor and president of the Business Enterprise Trust, a national ethics-research organization. "When you can't sleep on it, making these decisions is much tougher." The result is sometimes regret.

It's important to recognize, though, that rendering your decision 10 doesn't mean the case is closed—unless you want it to be. In my situation, the decision to give the speech, though I think it was the right one under the circumstances, was not the end of the story. I later called a trusted acquaintance at the host association and told her of the position her organization had put me in. I also let her know that I was writing this column. Both made me feel better about the quick decision I had made.

Sweat the Small Stuff

There is a way to prepare yourself for making complex ethical judgments 11 on the spot. It sounds corny, but the best way to meet these big challenges is to practice on the small ones you face every day. If you've been at a job for more than a week, you know the sorts of routine compromises that go with your professional territory. With just this information, you are well equipped to begin to establish where you feel comfortable drawing the line between personal standards and professional duty. How did you handle it when the boss pressed you to charge a client for more hours than you actually put in? Did you accept the Waterford vase from that customer? How about the tickets to the ballet and the World Series? Where ethical behavior is concerned, definitely sweat the small stuff—it's what will help you deal with tougher, more ambiguous situations later in your career.

Making my decision was easier because I had made similar, if less 12 dramatic, ones before. I know that if I had been a dues-paying member of the association I spoke before, I would likely have said straight out that the board had made a decision that I could not support. In fact, in the past I've threatened my standing as a panel member with one group by doing just that. But ethical behavior need not always be noisy. Here, I was not a member but a guest, invited to speak about good management, period.

Examine the Top Execs

Some things are out of the individual's control, however. Fundamentally, it's the chair, the chief executive and the senior officers who set the underlying ethical tone for the company. They show what counts through hundreds of small actions that are highly visible to everyone else. 13

If the everyday compromises you are asked to make in a company seem to consistently clash with your own sense of propriety, look hard at your bosses. If they aren't the sort of people whose ethics you respect, then you're bound for a head-on collision. Gary Edwards, president of the Ethics Resource Center, a nonprofit educational corporation in Washington, D.C., believes that "the moral responsibility of management is not to create an environment that encourages cheating. Certain systemic features—some incentive systems and meaningless performance evaluations—combine to break the backs of good people. The way they see it, they just did what was required of them. They're morally schizophrenic." If you find yourself in that position, the best move is usually to try to find a new job. 14

Working within the System

The alternative, if your company or department has systemic problems, is to stick around and try to make some changes for the better. It takes courage to be a public whistle-blower or even just to challenge everyday practices that send the wrong message throughout the company. But once top executives feel such pressure from an employee or a group of employees, or see negative headlines looming, the good news is that they can change. They might call in a group such as the Ethics Resource Center for help. The center's staff specializes in getting its clients to understand what has gone wrong and how to keep it from happening again. General Dynamics, which became a center client after it was caught overcharging on defense contracts, is now an ethical model. The Navy's ranking contracting officer even sends others to the rehabilitated firm to see how to do things right. 15

Edwards explains that a typical ethics overhaul begins with one-on-one discussions and extensive written surveys. But the real work is 16 aimed at the top dogs, who are the first to participate in programs designed to communicate values and ethical standards. The whole process takes six to eight months.

Whatever your choice when marking the boundary between what   17
you think is right and what your company does—whether you speak out or hold your peace—there will be people who think you've done the wrong thing. I'm sure many of you are disappointed that I gave my speech. You think I should have said something, given some sign that I was right and they were wrong. Of course all those sirens went off inside me when I heard about the award. In the end, what helped me draw that fine line was advice from a wise friend. "Follow your heart," she said. That I did.

RESPONDING TO "WORKABLE ETHICS"

Freewrite about a time when your personal sense of right and wrong was in conflict with what an employer or someone else "higher up" expected of you.

Responding through Interpretation

1. Why have the protesters decided to stage their demonstration during the award ceremony for E. Claiborne Robins Sr.? What is the speaker's inner conflict as she begins her speech? How do these events create an effective introduction to the arguments of the essay on workplace ethics?
2. What advice does Austin offer for those who are in positions where they have to make complex ethical decisions on a regular basis?
3. Why does Austin distinguish between having to make a snap judgment on an ethical issue and having the time "to sleep," or reflect, on the choice? What is the distinction?

Responding through Discussion

1. Take time in your group discussion for each member to contribute what he or she knows about the Dalkon Shield, the *Valdez* spill, and the Hill and Knowlton suit—all mentioned in Austin's essay. If necessary, do some preparatory reading. Then come up with your opinions about these cases, giving solutions you think might have been used.
2. Have group members interview one or two people in teaching or management positions on the issue of "workable ethics." Come together to compile your information and then present your findings to the class as a whole.

Responding through Writing

1. In your journal, describe a situation in which you had to make an ethical decision at work. What decision did you make and why? How did that decision affect your job and your subsequent attitude?
2. Write a paper in which you define what you consider to be good ethics in the workplace, giving examples from your own experience, observations, or reading. You might consider when it is ethical for an employee to "blow the whistle" on an employer or co-worker whose behavior seems dishonest or in some way unethical.

The Work Ethic and Me

Jennifer Holmes

Jennifer Holmes lived for several years in Alameda, California, where she attended college in the morning and worked in the afternoon as a clerk at Mervyn's, a large department store. She wrote "The Work Ethic and Me" in response to a question that asked whether she agreed that work helps build character.

Work is not just a way to earn money, but is also a way to build and strengthen our character and social interactions. Even though we initially go to work for money (and that is mostly everyone's first priority), interacting with people and working hard will, if not consciously, subconsciously help us to build character, enhance our social abilities, and provide us with insights that will help us to handle the problems that arise in our lives.

Most of us go to work to earn money, but while engaging in our everyday working experiences, we often come across experiences that strengthen our ability to interact well with others and to be responsible. My own work situation is a good example. Currently, I work at Mervyn's in Alameda. This is the first time that I have worked for a large company. I have only worked for them about five months, yet in this short period of time, I have learned that the better I can get along with my co-workers and superiors, the more pleasant my working environment can be. Being able to get along with others is building my character and also making me a more energetic and productive worker. For instance, I was recently given the boring task of cleaning our main stockroom. Because the person I worked with was someone whose company I enjoy, we got our work done more quickly. We were able to make light of the situation by talking and joking as we worked, and we found that the time seemed to pass more quickly as well.

Working also helps my social interactions by introducing me to a wide range of people who are rapidly becoming a part of my circle of friends. My work at Mervyn's has introduced me to people of all races, genders, and cultures. I have met a lot of new friends through my employment. In fact, one of my best friends works with me in the same department. We often spend time together shopping or just hanging out together in the breakfast room. Some of my co-workers have organized parties outside of work that I enjoyed very much; there are even couples who have met at Mervyn's and have formed strong relationships, including two people who just got married. I have also been able to form friendships with people who are a bit older than myself. Being a college student and having to support myself, I find it easier to interact with people I have met at work, and I try to combine my social life with work time whenever I get the opportunity.

My job also has strengthened my social interactions by putting me 4
in a position of having to get along with people whom I do not particularly like. There is a particular manager that I and many other workers do not care much for. I would rather not have to work with this person, who is rude and sarcastic, and often makes associates feel inadequate when they ask her questions. However, I have found that by smiling and acting friendly to her, she simply can't remain cold to me—although I must admit that I tend to avoid her as much as possible. However, I'm grateful to have had the opportunity to cope with people like my sarcastic manager at my current job. Without the ability to get along with unpleasant people, we can be really limited in our efforts to succeed within any social institution or environment.

Building character in the workplace happens everyday, even in the 5
most unpleasant encounters. For instance, two people in my department once told our area manager some nasty and untrue things about me. They told him that I did not do my job when my manager was not around and that I spent my time just wandering around the store. For a couple of weeks I felt very bad about these rumors and feared that I might be fired; finally, I got up the courage to speak to my manager. He sat me down and told me that I was doing my job fine, and that he and other managers were aware of my competence. Because I had started to believe these awful rumors, I felt like I was letting my department and myself down. I learned that I should not let other people put me on the defensive or make me anxious. This negative experience made my character stronger because I had to learn how to deal with people and their effect on me. It should not matter to me what people say about me as long as I know I am doing the best I can.

Working, character, and social interaction go hand in hand. Young 6
people build these abilities in the workplace not through a conscious training process, but through real-life, on-the-job events that they have to deal with. Rather than simply a way of providing extra income for eating out and entertainment, early job experiences are important guides in forming a person's character and social skills.

RESPONDING TO "THE WORK ETHIC AND ME"

Freewrite on whether you agree or disagree that working builds character.

Responding through Interpretation

1. Do you think Holmes's positive approach to on-the-job tensions is a typical one? How does it compare with your own or with that of others you have worked with?
2. Holmes sets forth her point of view that work helps to build character. Look through the essay and list the points and evidence she provides in order to support her belief.

Responding through Discussion

1. Discuss Holmes's essay in your group, both the strong points and the weak points. Did she persuade you of her point of view? If not, why not? If so, why? What advice would the group as a whole give her if she were to revise her essay?

Responding through Writing

1. Write a journal entry in which you take issue with Holmes's position on work. Even if you agree with her, pretend you don't and tell her why.
2. Write an essay in which you give your own views about the value of work. What do you personally find that it does for you? Use your own experiences as examples.

Why I Hate Work

Kevin (Wing Kuen) Hip

Originally from Hong Kong, Kevin Hip lived and worked in San Francisco
for a number of years as a cashier, as a waiter, and as a computer opera-
tor. He has studied business administration and hopes some day to own
his own business, so he can be the boss. He wrote the following essay for
his English composition class in response to a question that asked him to
give his views on whether work is good for one's character and values.

Although some people claim that they love their jobs and that working   1
builds character, in my opinion work is merely a way to earn money to
pay for basic needs such as food and shelter. Work itself is something
that most people hate to do, because work is a tedious way to spend time
and often produces tension and conflict, particularly when employers
take advantage of their workers.

Work is tedious because it is so boring to perform the same tasks day   2
after day, year after year. I have a relative who is an accountant. He told
me that he is tired of his job, for everyday he does the same thing: meeting with the managers in the morning, doing accounting work around
noon, and reporting to the boss before he gets off. I think that is why he
goes on frequent vacations and takes time off so often, since working is
so boring to him.

Furthermore, although workers receive money in exchange for their   3
labor, most jobs benefit the employers far more than they do the employee. Often a salesperson works hard each day and makes thousands
of dollars a week for the company; however, they only pay the employee about fifty dollars per day. Recently, I read an article about an
inventor who worked at a medical factory all his life and invented several popular cold medicine formulas. However, the company got all the
big profits from the patents while paying him only a regular wage.

Working is a stressful and painful experience for most people. Em-   4
ployees always have to be obedient to their bosses. We have to do everything the boss tells us, whether it is right or wrong. "You are right, sir!"
That is the only thing we can say when the managers scold us. We also
have to bear the unjust humiliation and bad temper of the bosses. Recently, I was having lunch at a restaurant and I saw how terribly the
owner treated the employees there. He yelled at them and threw the
order slips in the waiter's face, so that the waiter had to bow down and

pick them up off the floor. Yet all the employees kept quiet and seemed to ignore the boss's outbursts, since they needed to keep their jobs. Working in such an environment can degrade one's character and lead to bitterness and inner tension.

In fact, constantly working under the supervision of bosses can lead to bad judgment and even to an inferiority complex. My uncle works as an assistant manager at a company. "Yes sir!" is his favorite saying since this is what he says to his boss all the time. Most jobs don't allow employees to make important decisions for the company; all we can do is listen to the bosses and do whatever they say. Thus employees seldom develop the ability to think on their own or solve problems that come up on the job; when in doubt, they just wait for the boss to tell them what to do.   5

Finally, working tends to intensify and aggravate interpersonal conflicts. In order to be seen as competitive and to get promotions, employees often libel one another in front of the boss. I heard an ironic story about two best friends who were both working for a large company. In order to get a pending promotion, they made up stories about each other and created a great deal of struggle and bad feeling among the other workers at the company. They became enemies for life, and both were fired for their contribution to the negative work environment—yet they felt that they were simply doing what was expected of them: to be aggressive competitors struggling to get ahead.   6

Working, then, is simply a way of making money, and shouldn't be glorified as a valuable learning experience or a noble pursuit. If you want to learn something, read a good book or take a course at your local college. Don't expect too much from your boss; the only question he's likely to ask you is "Are you working hard?" and the only answer he wants to hear from you is "Yes sir!"   7

RESPONDING TO "WHY I HATE WORK"

Freewrite about why you work. What does the money you earn from working provide you? Would you work if you didn't need the money?

Responding through Interpretation

1. What position does Kevin Hip take on the question of whether work builds character? Explain why you either agree or disagree with him.
2. Re-read Hip's introductory and concluding paragraphs. Do you feel that he was consistent in his position from start to finish? How effective was

his introduction? His conclusion? What else would you advise him to add?

Responding through Discussion

1. In your group, let all the members explain why they currently work or don't work. Bring in past work experiences if appropriate. Then compare and contrast the different reasons for working or not working which were brought out in the discussion. Look for further reasons that might have been left out and add them; then report your findings to the class as a whole.

Responding through Writing

1. Imagine that you are a boss reading Hip's essay. What response would you have to his criticisms of employers? In your journal, give the boss's point of view.
2. Write a paper setting forth all the reasons you think high school and college students work. Provide examples of what you've observed firsthand or know about from your friends' experiences. Incorporate information from group discussion.

My Mother, Who Came from China, Where She Never Saw Snow

Laureen Mar

Laureen Mar, who comes from a Chinese-American immigrant family, is a poet and novelist who currently resides in Seattle, Washington. The following poem explores memories of her mother's labor in a garment factory. The garment industry is a major employer of recent immigrants; the work is hard and sometimes dangerous, and the pay is usually low.

In the huge, rectangular room, the ceiling
a machinery of pipes and fluorescent lights,
ten rows of women hunch over machines,
their knees pressing against pedals
and hands pushing the shiny fabric thick as tongues   5
through metal and thread.
My mother bends her head to one of these machines.
Her hair is coarse and wiry, black as burnt scrub.
She wears glasses to shield her intense eyes.
A cone of orange thread spins. Around her,   10
talk flutters harshly in Toisan wah.*
Chemical stings. She pushes cloth
through a pounding needle, under, around, and out,
breaks thread with a snap against fingerbone, tooth.
Sleeve after sleeve, sleeve.   15
It is easy. The same piece.
For eight or nine hours, sixteen bundles maybe,
250 sleeves to ski coats, all the same.
It is easy, only once she's run the needle
through her hand. She earns money   20
by each piece, on a good day,
thirty dollars. Twenty-four years.
It is frightening how fast she works.
She and the women who were taught sewing
terms in English as Second Language.   25
Dull thunder passes through their fingers.

*A Chinese dialect.

RESPONDING TO "MY MOTHER, WHO CAME FROM CHINA . . ."

Freewrite about a workplace where you or a family member has spent many hours. (The workplace might be home.)

Responding through Interpretation

1. What is the contrast between the kinds of coats the mother sews and the life she lives? What images in the poem connect the mother to the factory and the clothes that she sews?
2. Mar presents a controlled scene of the work in the factory, yet ends with the statement: "Dull thunder passes through their fingers." What do you think Mar means by this sentence?
3. Who is the speaker of the poem? Although she keeps repeating that the mother's job is "easy," what do you make of the fact that "only once she's run the needle through her hand"? Do you think the speaker is intentionally saying the opposite of what she really believes to be true? Explain.

Responding through Discussion

1. Read the poem aloud in your group at least twice and then discuss all the ideas the poem suggests to each of you. Have you or any family members worked in factories or in jobs in which you did the same things on the job day after day, year after year? What impact do you think jobs like this have on people?
2. Have group members do some reading about the "sweatshops" in this country. What kind of work is usually done in these places? Who are most of the workers? What are working conditions like now, and what were they like many years ago? Report back to your group and then to the class as a whole.

Responding through Writing

1. Close your eyes and briefly imagine the mother in the poem. Imagine her sitting at the sewing machine in the factory. What deeper qualities do you see in her, behind the mechanical work she is doing? Write a journal entry in which you describe all you can imagine about this woman from China.
2. Do some reading about the exploitation of immigrants in the workplaces of America. Historically, where have they been able to find work? Write an essay in which you argue for ways that immigrants could be better protected and valued as workers, despite their language limitations.

The Laugher

Heinrich Böll

Heinrich Böll was one of postwar Germany's most important writers and was honored with the Nobel Prize for literature in 1972. Though Böll was drafted and served in the German army, he consistently spoke out against the senselessness of war. Throughout his life, Böll was a strong defender of the intellectual freedom of writers. He is the author of many books, among them a novel *The Train Was on Time* (1949) about his devastating experiences as a soldier, *The Clown* (1963), and *The Safety Net* (1979). In the following short story, "The Laugher," Böll gives us a penetrating view of the artificial, unfulfilling nature of modern work.

When someone asks me what business I am in, I am seized with embarrassment: I blush and stammer, I who am otherwise known as a man of poise. I envy people who can say: I am a bricklayer. I envy barbers, bookkeepers and writers the simplicity of their avowal, for all these professions speak for themselves and need no lengthy explanation, while I am constrained to reply to such questions: I am a laugher. An admission of this kind demands another, since I have to answer the second question: "Is that how you make your living?" truthfully with "Yes." I actually do make a living at my laughing, and a good one too, for my laughing is—commercially speaking—much in demand. I am a good laugher, experienced, no one else laughs as well as I do, no one else has such command of the fine points of my art. For a long time, in order to avoid tiresome explanations, I called myself an actor, but my talents in the field of mime and elocution are so meager that I felt this designation to be too far from the truth: I love the truth, and the truth is: I am a laugher. I am neither a clown nor a comedian. I do not make people gay, I portray gaiety: I laugh like a Roman emperor, or like a sensitive schoolboy, I am as much at home in the laughter of the seventeenth century as in that of the nineteenth, and when occasion demands I laugh my way through all the centuries, all classes of society, all categories of age: it is simply a skill which I have acquired, like the skill of being able to repair shoes. In my breast I harbor the laughter of America, the laughter of Africa, white, red, yellow laughter—and for the right fee I let it peal out in accordance with the director's requirements.

I have become indispensable; I laugh on records, I laugh on tape, and television directors treat me with respect. I laugh mournfully, moderately, hysterically; I laugh like a streetcar conductor or like a helper in the grocery business; laughter in the morning, laughter in the evening, nocturnal laughter and the laughter of twilight. In short: wherever and however laughter is required—I do it.

It need hardly be pointed out that a profession of this kind is tiring, especially as I have also—this is my specialty—mastered the art of infectious laughter; this has also made me indispensable to third- and fourth-rate comedians, who are scared—and with good reason—that their audiences will miss their punch lines, so I spend most evenings in night clubs as a kind of discreet claque, my job being to laugh infectiously during the weaker parts of the program. It has to be carefully timed: my hearty, boisterous laughter must not come too soon, but neither must it come too late, it must come just at the right spot: at the pre-arranged moment I burst out laughing, the whole audience roars with me, and the joke is saved. 3

But as for me, I drag myself exhausted to the checkroom, put on my overcoat, happy that I can go off duty at last. At home I usually find telegrams waiting for me: "Urgently require your laughter. Recording Tuesday," and a few hours later I am sitting in an overheated express train bemoaning my fate. 4

I need scarcely say that when I am off duty or on vacation I have little inclination to laugh: the cowhand is glad when he can forget the cow, the bricklayer when he can forget the mortar, and carpenters usually have doors at home which don't work or drawers which are hard to open. Confectioners like sour pickles, butchers like marzipan, and the baker prefers sausage to bread; bullfighters raise pigeons for a hobby, boxers turn pale when their children have nose-bleeds: I find all this quite natural, for I never laugh off duty. I am a very solemn person, and people consider me—perhaps rightly so—a pessimist. 5

During the first years of our married life, my wife would often say to me: "Do laugh!" but since then she has come to realize that I cannot grant her this wish. I am happy when I am free to relax my tense face muscles, my frayed spirit, in profound solemnity. Indeed, even other people's laughter gets on my nerves, since it reminds me too much of my profession. So our marriage is a quiet, peaceful one, because my wife has also forgotten how to laugh: now and again I catch her smiling, and I smile too. We converse in low tones, for I detest the noise of the night clubs, the noise that sometimes fills the recording studios. People who do not know me think I am taciturn. Perhaps I am, because I have to open my mouth so often to laugh. 6

I go through life with an impassive expression, from time to time   7
permitting myself a gentle smile, and I often wonder whether I have ever
laughed. I think not. My brothers and sisters have always known me for
a serious boy.

So I laugh in many different ways, but my own laughter I have   8
never heard.

Translated by Leila Vennewitz

RESPONDING TO "THE LAUGHER"

Freewrite about your fantasy of the ideal profession.

Responding through Interpretation

1. Describe the narrator's profession. Where does he practice this profession? What is his specialty? Does he like his work?
2. What kind of person do you think the narrator actually is? Go through the story and find the statements he makes about himself that reveal his character and values. Write these in your reading notebook.
3. Go through the story and make note of the other people that the narrator mentions. What are his relationships like, and how are they influenced by the nature of his work?

Responding through Discussion

1. Have someone in the group read the story aloud slowly and see what else you understand from hearing it read aloud. Then discuss your insights about this story in the group. What criticism of work do you think lies below the surface of this story?
2. As a group, examine paragraph 5, in which the narrator justifies his behavior by giving examples of how people in other professions behave. Have each group member contribute examples that prove some of the old clichés—such as the shoemaker's children have no shoes, the dentist's family has rotten teeth, and so on. Give examples and have some fun. Laugh!

Responding through Writing

1. In your journal write a portrait of the narrator as you imagine him, based on Böll's descriptions in the story. Be sure you have some evidence from the story to back up each of the details you include in your portrait.

2. The narrator in this story seems, on the surface, to have the ideal profession: He earns a very good living by laughing, but he lets us know that he doesn't love his profession. Think of a profession that intrigues you. Do some reading about it. Imagine yourself being in that profession full-time. Then write a paper in which you first glamorize the profession and halfway through you switch gears and show the dark, dreary side of it.

Cotton Pickers

Maya Angelou

Maya Angelou was born in California but spent her early years with her grandmother, Annie Hutchinson, who ran a general store in Stamps, Arkansas. Angelou has worked as a dancer and an actress, and has written screenplays, poems, essays, and a continuing autobiography that began with the best-selling *I Know Why the Caged Bird Sings* (1969), from which the following selection is drawn. Angelou was invited by fellow Arkansan Bill Clinton to read one of her poems at his inauguration in 1993.

We lived with our grandmother and uncle in the rear of the Store (it was always spoken of with a capital *s*), which she had owned some twenty-five years.   1

Early in the century, Momma (we soon stopped calling her Grand-mother) sold lunches to the sawmen in the lumberyard (east Stamps) and the seedmen at the cotton gin (west Stamps). Her crisp meat pies and cool lemonade, when joined to her miraculous ability to be in two places at the same time, assured her business success. From being a mobile lunch counter, she set up a stand between the two points of fiscal interest and supplied the workers' needs for a few years. Then she had the Store built in the heart of the Negro area. Over the years it became the lay center of activities in town. On Saturdays, barbers sat their customers in the shade on the porch of the Store, and troubadours on their ceaseless crawlings through the South leaned across its benches and sang their sad songs of The Brazos while they played juice harps and cigar-box guitars.   2

The formal name of the Store was the Wm. Johnson General Merchandise Store. Customers could find food staples, a good variety of colored thread, mash for hogs, corn for chickens, coal oil for lamps, light bulbs for the wealthy, shoestrings, hair dressing, balloons, and flower seeds. Anything not visible had only to be ordered.   3

Until we became familiar enough to belong to the Store and it to us, we were locked up in a Fun House of Things where the attendant had gone home for life.   4

Each year I watched the field across from the Store turn caterpillar green, then gradually frosty white. I knew exactly how long it would be before the big wagons would pull into the front yard and load on the   5 cotton pickers at daybreak to carry them to the remains of slavery's plantations.

During the picking season my grandmother would get out of bed   6
at four o'clock (she never used an alarm clock) and creak down to her knees and chant in a sleep-filled voice, "Our Father, thank you for letting me see this New Day. Thank you that you didn't allow the bed I lay on last night to be my cooling board, nor my blanket my winding sheet. Guide my feet this day along the straight and narrow, and help me to put a bridle on my tongue. Bless this house, and everybody in it. Thank you, in the name of your Son, Jesus Christ, Amen."

Before she had quite arisen, she called our names and issued orders,   7
and pushed her large feet into homemade slippers and across the bare lye-washed wooden floor to light the coal-oil lamp.

The lamplight in the Store gave a soft make-believe feeling to our   8
world which made me want to whisper and walk about on tiptoe. The odors of onions and oranges and kerosene had been mixing all night and wouldn't be disturbed until the wooded slat was removed from the door and the early morning air forced its way in with the bodies of people who had walked miles to reach the pickup place.

"Sister, I'll have two cans of sardines."   9

"I'm gonna work so fast today I'm gonna make you look like you   10
standing still."

"Lemme have a hunk uh cheese and some sody crackers."   11

"Just gimme a coupla them fat peanut paddies." That would be   12
from a picker who was taking his lunch. The greasy brown paper sack was stuck behind the bib of his overalls. He'd use the candy as a snack before the noon sun called the workers to rest.

In those tender mornings the Store was full of laughing, joking,   13
boasting and bragging. One man was going to pick two hundred pounds of cotton, and another three hundred. Even the children were promising to bring home fo' bits and six bits.

The champion picker of the day before was the hero of the dawn. If   14
he prophesied that the cotton in today's field was going to be sparse and stick to the bolls like glue, every listener would grunt a hearty agreement.

The sound of the empty cotton sacks dragging over the floor and the   15
murmurs of waking people were sliced by the cash register as we rang up the five-cent sales.

If the morning sounds and smells were touched with the supernatural, the late afternoon had all the features of the normal Arkansas life.   16
In the dying sunlight the people dragged, rather than their empty cotton sacks.

Brought back to the Store, the pickers would step out of the backs   17
of trucks and fold down, dirt-disappointed, to the ground. No matter
how much they had picked, it wasn't enough. Their wages wouldn't
even get them out of debt to my grandmother, not to mention the stag-
gering bill that waited on them at the white commissary downtown.

The sounds of the new morning had been replaced with grumbles   18
about cheating houses, weighted scales, snakes, skimpy cotton and dusty
rows. In later years I was to confront the stereotyped picture of gay
song-singing cotton pickers with such inordinate rage that I was told
even by fellow Blacks that my paranoia was embarrassing. But I had seen
the fingers cut by the mean little cotton bolls, and I had witnessed the
backs and shoulders and arms and legs resisting any further demands.

Some of the workers would leave their sacks at the Store to be picked   19
up the following morning, but a few had to take them home for repairs.
I winced to picture them sewing the coarse material under a coal-oil lamp
with fingers stiffening from the day's work. In too few hours they would
have to walk back to Sister Henderson's Store, get vittles and load, again,
onto the trucks. Then they would face another day of trying to earn
enough for the whole year with the heavy knowledge that they were
going to end the season as they started it. Without the money or credit
necessary to sustain a family for three months. In cotton-picking time
the late afternoons revealed the harshness of Black Southern life, which
in the early morning had been softened by nature's blessing of groggi-
ness, forgetfulness and the soft lamplight.

RESPONDING TO "COTTON PICKERS"

Freewrite about a time when you performed or observed others perform hard
physical labor.

Responding through Interpretation

1. What does Angelou mean by "the remains of slavery's plantations"?
2. What does the grandmother's early morning prayer suggest about her values and lifestyle?
3. What stereotype caused Angelou to experience "inordinate rage"? Was
   her rage justified?

Responding through Discussion

1. Group members should share experiences of doing manual labor, such
   as agricultural or construction work, or observing manual laborers. Have

4

group members develop a position to present to the class as a whole on what a person can learn from manual labor and whether such work has any real benefits.

2. The way of life described in the essay still exists in some parts of the country—in the fields of California and Texas where migrant agricultural workers toil for low wages, as well as in some parts of the South. Group members should share their experiences and reading about exploited agricultural workers and their role in contemporary American society; report back to the class on group findings.

Responding through Writing

1. Write an essay in which you discuss the use of contrasting description in Angelou's essay to emphasize the feeling of disappointment and defeat experienced by the pickers in the evening in contrast to the optimism they felt in the morning. Use specific examples from the text.
2. Using your own experiences, write an essay about what can be learned or gained from doing manual labor.

Yes, Something Will Work: Work

Mickey Kaus

Mickey Kaus is the author of *The End of Equality* (1992), an analysis of social welfare in America. He is also an editor of and contributor to *The New Republic* and contributor to *Newsweek* and other national periodicals. The following article, which originally appeared in *Newsweek* in May of 1992, argues for government-created jobs as a solution not only to the "welfare problem" but to the social unrest that can result in urban crime and rioting.

Call it the "solutions gap." What distinguishes the L.A. riots of 1992 from   1
the L.A. riots of 1965 seems to be that in 1992 few Americans retain much confidence that the problems of the "ghetto poor" underclass can be overcome. Jack Kemp gets great press touting urban "enterprise zones," but does anybody but Kemp really think tax breaks will make businessmen flock to bombed-out South-Central Los Angeles?

What *would* solve the underclass problem? Start with the consensus   2
explanation for how the mainly black underclass was formed in the first place. As told by University of Chicago sociologist William Julius Wilson, the story goes like this: When Southern blacks migrated North, they settled, thanks to segregation, in urban ghettos. Then, beginning in the 1960s, two things happened. First, well-paying, unskilled jobs started to leave the cities for the suburbs. Second, middle-class blacks, aided by civil-rights laws, began to leave as well. This out-migration left the poorest elements of black society behind—now isolated and freed from the restraints the black middle class had imposed. Without jobs and role models, those left in the ghettos drifted out of the labor market.

But this story leaves a crucial question hanging—a question asked   3
by John Kasarda of the University of North Carolina: How were "economically displaced inner-city residents able to survive?" Kasarda's answer: "welfare programs." He notes that by 1982, in the central cities, there were more black single mothers who weren't working than who were. And 80 percent of these nonworking single mothers were getting some form of welfare, mainly Aid to Families with Dependent Children. AFDC not only provided an "economic substitute" for jobs, it provided that substitute in a form available, by and large, *only* to mothers in broken homes.

Bush spokesman Marlin Fitzwater had a point, then, when he   4
blamed ghetto poverty on welfare programs. Welfare may not have
been the main cause of the underclass, but it *enabled* the underclass
to form. Without welfare, those left behind in the ghetto would have
had to move to where the jobs were. Without welfare, it would have
been hard for single mothers to survive without forming working
families. Instead, between 1965 and 1974, the welfare rolls exploded—
from 4.3 million recipients to 10.8 million. Simultaneously, the proportion of black children in single-mother homes jumped from 33 to
over 50 percent.

So if welfare is what enabled the underclass to form, might not al-   5
tering welfare somehow "de-enable" the underclass? Certainly, if we're
looking for a handle on the culture of poverty, there is none bigger than
the cash welfare programs that constitute 65 percent of the legal income
of single mothers in the bottom fifth of the income distribution. Changing welfare to break the culture of poverty will take something much
more radical, however, than the mild welfare reform Congress enacted
in 1988. The 1988 law—which basically requires 10 percent of the welfare caseload to attend training classes or work part-time—is expected,
at best, to reduce welfare rolls by a few percentage points.

But what if cash welfare (mainly AFDC and food stamps) were re-   6
placed with the offer of a useful government job paying just below the
minimum wage? Single mothers (and anyone else) who needed money
would not be given a check. They would be given free day care for their
children. And they would be given the location of a government job site.
If they showed up and worked, they'd be paid for their work. To make
working worthwhile, the incomes of all low-wage workers would be
boosted to the poverty line by expanding the Earned Income Tax Credit.

FDR's Idea

In this regime, young women contemplating single motherhood would   7
think twice about putting themselves in a position where they would
have to juggle mothering with working. Life as it is too often lived in the
ghetto—in broken homes with no workers—would simply become impossible. The natural incentives to form two-parent families would re-
assert themselves. But even children of single mothers would grow up
in homes structured by the rhythms and discipline of work.

This is not a new idea. It's an obvious idea, even. It's basically the   8
approach Franklin D. Roosevelt took in 1935 when he replaced cash
welfare with government jobs in the Works Progress Administration

(WPA). Recently, a group of congressmen, led by Sen. David Boren of Oklahoma, proposed reviving the WPA, with about 75 percent of the jobs reserved for welfare mothers.

The objections to this idea are obvious, too. Replacing welfare with 9 a neo-WPA would be very expensive—a reasonable estimate is around $50 billion a year. There would be ample potential for boondoggles. And the transition from the current welfare system would be harsh. Many who now support themselves on AFDC would simply fail to work. For those who wind up destitute, there would have to be a beefed-up system of in-kind support (soup kitchens, shelters, and the like).

Nevertheless, for all these pitfalls, the WPA approach has a virtue 10 not shared by any of the other remedies offered up in the wake of the L.A. riots: it would work. Not within one generation, necessarily, or even two. But it would work eventually. Welfare is how the underclass (un-happily, unintentionally) survives. Change welfare, and the underclass will have to change as well.

RESPONDING TO "YES, SOMETHING WILL WORK: WORK"

Freewrite about which of Kaus's ideas you agree with and which you dis-agree with.

Responding through Interpretation

1. What proposal does Kaus give to change the "culture of poverty"?
2. What was the WPA? How does Kaus recommend we reinstate it?
3. How does Kaus lead the reader through his argument? Go through and underline key sentences in each paragraph. Does he develop his argu-ment logically? Is he convincing? Explain why or why not.

Responding through Discussion

1. Kaus brings in many names: Jack Kemp, William Julius Wilson, John Kasarda, Marlin Fitzwater, Franklin D. Roosevelt, and David Boren. Who are these people? In your group, discuss the authorities that Kaus cites in his essay, and let members contribute any information they have about these names. Decide whether or not they added impact to Kaus's piece.
2. With your group, consider Kaus's proposal for reinstating the WPA. Think about what would be involved in such a program. Argue for and

against it, and then vote on whether you think it could work and, if so, how? If not, why not? Present your decision to the class as a whole.

Responding through Writing

1. Write a journal entry in which you agree or disagree with Kaus's idea for providing jobs as a replacement for welfare. Do you think that having jobs would or would not create a respect for work? How realistic do you think Kaus's ideas are?
2. Write a paper responding to Kaus's final statement: "Change welfare, and the underclass will have to change as well." Explore the attitudes behind this statement. What exactly is Kaus saying? Do you agree?

A Step Back to the Workhouse?

Barbara Ehrenreich

Barbara Ehrenreich holds a Ph.D. from Rockefeller University and is a fellow at the Institute for Policy Studies in Washington, D.C. She writes regularly for *The New Republic, Mother Jones,* and *Time* magazine. She is the author of several books on social contemporary issues, including *Fear of Falling: The Inner Life of the Middle Class* (1989) and *The Worst Years of Our Lives: Irreverent Notes from a Decade of Greed* (1990). "A Step Back to the Workhouse" first appeared in *Ms.* magazine in 1987.

The commentators are calling it a "remarkable consensus." Workfare, as programs to force welfare recipients to work are known, was once abhorred by liberals as a step back toward the 17th-century workhouse or—worse—slavery. But today no political candidate dares step outdoors without some plan for curing "welfare dependency" by putting its hapless victims to work—if necessary, at the nearest Burger King. It is as if the men who run things, or who aspire to run things (and we are, unfortunately, talking mostly about men when we talk about candidates), had gone off and caucused for a while and decided on the one constituency that could be safely sacrificed in the name of political expediency and "new ideas," and that constituency is poor women.

Most of the arguments for workfare are simply the same indestructible stereotypes that have been around, in one form or another, since the first public relief program in England 400 years ago: that the poor are poor because they are lazy and dissolute, and that they are lazy and dissolute because they are suffering from "welfare dependency." Add a touch of modern race and gender stereotypes and you have the image that haunts the workfare advocates: a slovenly, over-weight, black woman who produces a baby a year in order to augment her welfare checks.

But there is a new twist to this season's spurt of welfare-bashing: welfare is being presented as a kind of *feminist* alternative to welfare. As Senator Daniel Patrick Moynihan (D.-N.Y.) has put it, "A program that was designed to pay mothers to stay at home with their children [i.e., welfare, or Aid to Families with Dependent Children] cannot succeed when we now observe most mothers going out to work." Never mind the startling illogic of this argument, which is on a par with saying that no woman should stay home with her children because other women do not, or that a laid-off male worker should not receive unemployment compensation because most men have been observed holding jobs. We are being asked to believe that pushing destitute mothers into the work force (in some versions of workfare, for no other compensation than the welfare payments they would have received anyway) is consistent with women's strivings toward self-determination.

Now I will acknowledge that most women on welfare—like most unemployed women in general—would rather have jobs. And I will further acknowledge that many of the proponents of workfare, possibly including Senator Moynihan and the Democratic Presidential candidates, have mounted the bandwagon with the best of intentions. Welfare surely needs reform. But workfare is not the solution, because "dependency"—with all its implications of laziness and depravity—is not the problem. The problem is poverty, which most women enter in a uniquely devastating way—with their children in tow.

Let me introduce a real person, if only because real people, as opposed to imaginative stereotypes, never seem to make an appearance in the current rhetoric on welfare. "Lynn," as I will call her, is a friend and onetime neighbor who has been on welfare for two years. She is also about as unlike the stereotypical "welfare mother" as one can get— which is to say that she is a fairly typical welfare recipient. She has only one child, which puts her among the 74 percent of welfare recipients who have only one or two children. She is white (not that that should matter), as are almost half of welfare recipients. Like most welfare recipients, she is not herself the daughter of a welfare recipient, and hence not part of anything that could be called an "intergenerational cycle of dependency." And like every woman on welfare I have ever talked to, she resents the bureaucratic hassles that are the psychic price of welfare. But, for now, there are no alternatives.

When I first met Lynn, she seemed withdrawn and disoriented. She had just taken the biggest step of her 25 years; she had left an abusive husband and she was scared: scared about whether she could survive on her own and scared of her estranged husband. He owned a small restaurant; she was a high school dropout who had been a waitress when she met him. During their three years of marriage he had beaten her repeatedly. Only after he threw her down a flight of stairs had she realized that her life was in danger and moved out. I don't think I fully grasped the terror she had lived in until one summer day when he chased Lynn to the door of my house with a drawn gun.

Gradually Lynn began to put her life together. She got a divorce and went on welfare; she found a pediatrician who would accept Medicaid and a supermarket that would take food stamps. She fixed up her apartment with second-hand furniture and flea market curtains. She was, by my admittedly low standards, a compulsive housekeeper and an overprotective mother; and when she wasn't waxing her floors or ironing her two-year-old's playsuits, she was studying the help-wanted ads. She spent a lot of her time struggling with details that most of us barely notice—the price of cigarettes, mittens, or of a bus ticket to the welfare office—yet, somehow, she regained her sense of humor. In fact, most of the time we spent together was probably spent laughing—over the foibles of the neighbors, the conceits of men, and the snares of welfare and the rest of "the system."

Yet for all its inadequacies, Lynn was grateful for welfare. Maybe if   8
she had been more intellectually inclined she would have found out that she was suffering from "welfare dependency," a condition that is supposed to sap the will and demolish the work ethic. But "dependency" is not an issue when it is a choice between an abusive husband and an impersonal government. Welfare had given Lynn a brief shelter in a hostile world, and as far as she was concerned, it was her ticket to *independence.*

Suppose there had been no welfare at the time when Lynn finally   9
summoned the courage to leave her husband. Suppose she had gone for help and been told she would have to "work off" her benefits in some menial government job (restocking the toilet paper in rest rooms is one such "job" assigned to New York women in a current workfare program). Or suppose, as in some versions of workfare, she had been told she would have to take the first available private sector job, which (for a non-high school graduate like Lynn) would have paid near the minimum wage, or $3.35 an hour. How would she have been able to afford child care? What would she have done for health insurance (as a welfare recipient she had Medicaid, but most low-paying jobs offer little or no coverage)? Would she have ever made the decision to leave her husband in the first place?

As Ruth Sidel points out in *Women and Children Last* (Viking), most   10
women who are or have been on welfare have stories like Lynn's. They go onto welfare in response to a crisis—divorce, illness, loss of a job, the birth of an additional child to feed—and they remain on welfare for two years or less. They are not victims of any "welfare culture," but of a society that increasingly expects women to both raise and support children—and often on wages that would barely support a woman alone. In fact, even some of the most vociferous advocates of replacing welfare with workfare admit that, in their own estimation, only about 15 percent

of welfare recipients fit the stereotype associated with "welfare dependency": demoralization, long-term welfare use, lack of drive, and so on.

But workfare will not help anyone, not even the presumed 15 percent of "bad apples" for whose sake the majority will be penalized. First, it will not help because it does not solve the problem that drives most women into poverty in the first place: how to hold a job *and* care for children. Child care in a licensed, professionally run center can easily cost as much as $100 a week per child—more than most states now pay in welfare benefits and (for two children) more than most welfare recipients could expect to earn in the work force. Any serious effort to get welfare recipients into the work force would require childcare provisions at a price that would probably end up higher than the current budget for AFDC. But none of the workfare advocates are proposing that sort of massive public commitment to child care.

Then there is the problem of jobs. So far, studies show that existing state workfare programs have had virtually no success in improving their participants' incomes or employment rates. Small wonder: nearly half the new jobs generated in recent years pay poverty-level wages; and most welfare recipients will enter jobs that pay near the minimum wage, which is $6,900 a year—26 percent less than the poverty level for a family of three. A menial, low-wage job may be character-building (from a middle-class vantage point), but it will not lift anyone out of poverty.

Some of my feminist activist friends argue that it is too late to stop the workfare juggernaut. The best we can do, they say, is to try to defeat the more pernicious proposals: those that are overcoercive, that do not offer funds for child care, or that would relegate workfare clients to a "subemployee" status unprotected by federal labor and civil rights legislation. Our goal, the pragmatists argue, should be to harness the current enthusiasm for workfare to push for services welfare recipients genuinely need, such as child care and job training and counseling.

I wish the pragmatists well, but for me, it would be a betrayal of women like Lynn to encourage the workfare bandwagon in any way. Most women, like Lynn, do not take up welfare as a career, but as an emergency measure in a time of personal trauma and dire need. At such times, the last thing they need is to be hustled into a low-wage job, and left to piece together child care, health insurance, transportation, and all the other ingredients of survival. In fact, the main effect of workfare may be to discourage needy women from seeking any help at all—a disastrous result in a nation already suffering from a child poverty rate of nearly 25 percent. Public policy should be aimed at giving impoverished mothers (and, I would add, fathers) the help they so urgently need—not only in the form of job opportunities, but sufficient income support to live on until a job worth taking comes along.

Besides, there is an ancient feminist principle at stake. The premise of all the workfare proposals—the more humane as well as the nasty—is that single mothers on welfare are *not working*. But, to quote the old feminist bumper sticker, EVERY MOTHER IS A WORKING MOTHER. And those who labor to raise their children in poverty—to feed and clothe them on meager budgets and to nurture them in an uncaring world—are working the hardest. The feminist position has never been that all women must pack off their children and enter the work force, but that all women's work—in the home or on the job—should be valued and respected.

15

RESPONDING TO "A STEP BACK TO THE WORKHOUSE?"

Freewrite about the two words *welfare* and *workfare*. What different images and ideas do these two words suggest to you?

Responding through Interpretation

1. How does Ehrenreich describe the welfare stereotypes that have been around for 400 years? In what ways does her essay attempt to refute these stereotypes? How successful do you think she is in doing so?
2. What is the "ancient feminist principle at stake" in the workfare argument, according to Ehrenreich? Do you agree that this is a feminist issue?
3. How does Ehrenreich use the story of her neighbor Lynn to prove her points? Do you think that she succeeds in proving her points through this narrative about her friend?

Responding through Discussion

1. Ehrenreich states that the biggest failure of workfare is that it makes no provision for child care. Look over the facts she brings in about child care and discuss in your group whether this is a valid argument against workfare. What could be done to better answer the need for child care for working mothers? Come up with some recommendations that you bring back to the whole class.
2. In your group, discuss the two different views about welfare and workfare presented by Kaus and Ehrenreich. How do these two authors' points of view differ? How are they alike? Which of them do you agree with most—and why?

Responding through Writing

1. In your journal, write a response to Ehrenreich's statement that "every mother is a working mother."
2. In her argument against workfare, Ehrenreich states: "A menial, low-wage job may be character-building . . . but it will not lift anyone out of poverty." Do some reading about both workfare and welfare and then write a paper in which you give your own argument for or against forcing poor people to work for poverty-level wages in order to receive public assistance.

Why Workfare?

Nikki Corbin

Born and brought up in rural Washington State, Nikki Vaughn Corbin moved to the San Francisco Bay Area when her husband was accepted at law school there. At the time she wrote the following essay on workfare proposals, she was working on a B.A. degree in history at San Francisco State College.

Many taxpayers today are angry about the welfare system. Most agree on the need for some type of reform; however, beyond that, the opinions differ tremendously. "Yes, Something Will Work: Work" by Mickey Kaus and "A Step Back to the Workhouse?" by Barbara Ehrenreich are two articles that reflect these differences. Kaus seems to stand behind the American ideal that to get ahead, one must work hard and persevere, while Ehrenreich is sympathetic to the welfare recipient's plight. Both these views seem understandable, yet Ehrenreich's position seems to me to be both more logical and more just than that of Kaus.

In his article on workfare, Mickey Kaus sets out to "solve the underclass problem." He begins by explaining how "the mainly black underclass" was formed, as if those on welfare are only of this ethnicity. The focus of his article on poverty centers around black people and single mothers. There is no mention of men who don't work and receive welfare. He blames the welfare system for supporting ghetto poverty rather than curing it: "Welfare may not have been the main cause of the underclass, but it *enabled* the underclass to form." Kaus says that without welfare, people would have been forced to move out of the inner cities to where the jobs had moved. Because the welfare system enabled poverty to form, he concludes that changes within the system might " 'de-enable' the underclass."

Kaus's solution is to change the system by giving welfare mothers a government job paying just below minimum wage, rather than a welfare check. Free child care is included in his plan; however, he neglects to mention the issue of medical benefits, which most minimum wage jobs do not include. Also, Kaus would like to see additional incentives to work through "expanding the Earned Income Tax Credit." Because women would have to work to get their check, they would "think twice about putting themselves in a position where they would have to juggle motherhood and working." Finally, because work nurtures family values, these mothers would be more likely to find marriage partners, or, if they chose to remain single, their children "would grow up in homes structured by the rhythms and discipline of work." Kaus also makes reference to Franklin Roosevelt, the American hero of the 30's and 40's, comparing his WPA, a program getting people back to work during the Depression, to welfare reform. This reference helps make Kaus's point that work ethics can create a solution for poverty.

In "A Step Back to the Workhouse?" Barbara Ehrenreich writes 4 about workfare, a program that forces welfare recipients to work. While she agrees that "Welfare surely needs reform," she contends that poverty, rather than laziness, is the problem that should be addressed. Ehrenreich describes her friend "Lynn" as a typical mother on welfare, who took her child and left an abusive relationship and who has only been on welfare for two years. Ehrenreich contends that welfare was Lynn's "ticket to independence" and asks what would have happened if she had "been told that she would have to 'work off' her benefits in some menial government 'job?' " (like restocking the toilet paper in rest rooms).

Ehrenreich also brings up the question of child care and health care 5 for these mothers forced to take low-paying jobs. If these benefits aren't continued after the mother begins to work, then the system makes it more beneficial for the mother to stay at home. Most women, she says, "go onto welfare in response to a crisis—divorce, illness, loss of job, the birth of an additional child to feed—and they remain on welfare for two years or less." Only 15 percent of all welfare recipients fit the stereotype of "welfare dependency," and even these few would not be helped by the new workfare program because it ignores the issue of what "drives most women into poverty in the first place: how to hold a job *and* care for children." Ehrenreich's solution is to teach women how to train themselves for a worthwhile job so that they are able to support themselves and their children, rather than forcing them to work at menial jobs that won't help them to improve their situation and will only keep them dependent on the system.

Although working for a welfare check doesn't seem unreasonable, 6 I think that Kaus's theory on the solution to get every American off welfare is misguided. His assumption that forcing women to work will recreate the "natural incentives to form two-parent families" ignores the fact that there are many happy, successful single-parent families in America today and that living with both a mother and a father is not necessarily the formula for a functional family environment. Also, homes are structured on much more than the "rhythms of discipline and work."

I agree with Ehrenreich that there needs to be a more structured plan to rehabilitate welfare recipients so that they can get away from being dependent on the system, but it seems reasonable that they should be able to make some contribution to the community while they are receiving welfare benefits. What if Lynn had been forced to restock toilet paper a few days a week in order to continue receiving her checks? Why can't people give back to a system that supports them and their children? Until the government is willing, however, to invest more in this program in ways to restructure it and provide money for health care and child care, the system will be one of dependency, rather than rehabilitation.

RESPONDING TO "WHY WORKFARE?"

Freewrite about the stereotypes commonly held about people on welfare.

Responding through Interpretation

1. Although Corbin begins by saying that Ehrenreich is more humane than Kaus, she actually ends up criticizing both of them. What flaws does she find in their arguments? Do her objections seem well-founded?
2. Corbin backs her summary of the two essays with quotations drawn from both essays. How well does she use these quotations and integrate them into her essay? Does she quote too much or not enough? Are any of the quotations too long or inadequately explained?

Responding through Discussion

1. Discuss Corbin's paper in your group. What effect did it have on different members of the group? What advice could the group give Corbin for improving her paper?

Responding through Writing

1. Corbin makes the statement: "What if Lynn had been forced to restock toilet paper a few days a week in order to continue receiving her checks? Why can't people give back to a system that supports them and their children?" Write a journal entry in which you react to Corbin's statement. How would you answer her questions?
2. If you have ever experienced poverty in your own family or have ever known someone well who lived in poverty, you are probably in a good position to write a paper explaining some of the effects of poverty on people. If you don't know much about poverty firsthand, do some reading to find out how poverty affects people's lives. Then write a paper that describes a life lived in poverty.

Welfare versus Workfare

Deirdre Mena

Deirdre Mena is a laboratory worker in the health services area who is going back to school in the evening to get a degree in biology. She wrote the following essay in response to the essays by Barbara Ehrenreich and Mickey Kaus on the subject of required work training and jobs for welfare mothers.

Workfare poses an interesting concept to today's financially over-   1
burdened, overly taxed citizens. Could it be the panacea we've all been hoping for? Conservative columnist Mickey Kaus thinks it could, but liberal writer Barbara Ehrenreich disagrees. I believe both of their essays have some strong arguments as well as some faults, but it is my view that workfare deserves a chance.

    In his "Yes, Something Will Work: Work" essay, Kaus briefs the   2
reader on why the "underclass" have remained the "underclass." He believes the reason why despair and hopelessness permeate ghetto life is because the inhabitants have no role models or available jobs. Moreover, Kaus argues that society enables people to remain in this mind frame and position by supporting welfare. He feels that we can rectify this misfortune by "disenabling" the "underclass" through workfare programs. Kaus's main premise is that welfare has encouraged mothers to break up the family unit because they know they will have welfare checks and food stamps to live on. He feels that by cutting the present benefits, these women would be forced to reevaluate their positions. Through the workfare program, the wheel would begin to turn in the other direction and slowly these people would be pulled out of their present morass.

    Kaus has a somewhat simplistic approach to curing poverty and de-   3
pendency, the chronic diseases of the "underclass." However, he is not blind to the downside of the workfare programs. He acknowledges that the transition would be difficult, but that we have no alternative. One of the major problems is that the program would be extremely expensive. Kaus also feels that it would encourage some boondoggling. He stresses that the transition would be difficult, and a strong support system would be essential for its success. Nevertheless, he is convinced that the program would work. Not overnight, but slowly, it would peel away the layers of despair and hopelessness enmeshed in the underclass culture of welfare.

In contrast, Barbara Ehrenreich believes the workfare proposition is   4
a way for many politicians to stereotype women who are living in crisis situations. In her essay "A Step Back to the Workhouse?," she refers
to society's portrayal of the stereotypical welfare mother as "a slovenly,
over-weight, black woman who produces a baby a year in order to augment her welfare checks." Ms. Ehrenreich refutes this image with an
anecdote of a neighbor surviving on welfare. Her friend is a young white
female struggling to better her lot in life. Ms. Ehrenreich states that 50%
of welfare recipients are white, with 74% of the population having one
to two children. She believes welfare is the only thing going for these
women in a "hostile world."

Furthermore, Ms. Ehrenreich feels that the politicians, mainly men,   5
who conceived this idea are totally out of line. According to the author,
their argument that the present welfare program pays "mothers to stay
at home . . . cannot succeed when we now observe most mothers going
out to work" is out of touch with reality. She shares the feminists' belief
that "every mother is a working mother" and single mothers who support themselves on welfare are "working the hardest." She believes
women on welfare would prefer to be working and contributing to society in a more productive manner. Ms. Ehrenreich thinks that "public
policy should be aimed at giving impoverished mothers . . . sufficient income support . . . until a job worth taking comes along." In addition, she
fears that women who participate in a workfare program would drown
in expenses such as child care and medical costs.

Ms. Ehrenreich takes the feminist viewpoint and believes mothers   6
are on welfare, not by choice but by necessity. I question the source of
her welfare demographics. I believe a lot of mothers are on welfare by
"choice" and some do have more children so they can supplement their
income. I work in East and West Oakland and have seen the anger and
resentment of the underclass, yet I also feel that some welfare recipients
choose to remain on public aid because they have no desire or motivation to improve themselves. Kaus suggests that welfare recipients have
no role models to lure them out of their environment; however, I believe
that there are many successful people of all ethnic backgrounds in this
country, and if the "underclass" so desired (or if they had to), they could
hold on to their dreams and work hard to achieve them.

Furthermore, I totally disagree with Ms. Ehrenreich's argument that   7
these women in "dire need" could not handle child care problems, health
insurance and "all the other ingredients of survival." Does she think that
these problems are exclusive to people in the ghetto? Every working

mother struggles with juggling child care, transportation and "all the other ingredients of survival."

I do agree with Ms. Ehrenreich that some women, like her friend Lynn, are striving to better themselves and get off the social system. But Kaus's idea of workfare would work for these people also. If the State offered free child care, the mother could work and earn a little money. She would learn new skills which she could hopefully apply to a position in the real work force. She may not get her dream job initially, but it would be a start. Ms. Ehrenreich refers to the menial jobs offered in New York's workfare program as an example of how unsuccessful and degrading these programs can be. Yet many recent immigrants to this country would be happy to have a job, even as "degrading" a one as stocking toilet rolls in public bathrooms. They have a dream, a dream for the next generation! People in the "underclass" society need to follow their example and have a dream of their own. I think there may be hope for them through programs such as workfare; at least it is a positive start!

8

RESPONDING TO "WELFARE VERSUS WORKFARE"

Freewrite by writing a letter to Deirdre Mena in which you respond to her essay.

Responding through Interpretation

1. In the early paragraphs of her essay, Mena paraphrases both Kaus's argument and Ehrenreich's argument. How thoroughly does she paraphrase each essay? Does she leave out or distort any key arguments either of them has made?
2. Mena brings in some of her own experiences and opinions toward the end of the essay. Are her examples effective? Why or why not?

Responding through Discussion

1. With your group, compare Corbin's critique of the authors and her final position with Mena's critique. Which student seems more objective and fair in her critique? Which supports her position more effectively? Why? Give specific examples in your discussion. Afterward, discuss what you have each learned that will help you in writing future papers.

Responding through Writing

1. Write a journal entry in which you imagine a day in the life of a young woman on welfare who has an eighteen-month-old baby and lives alone.

What would her normal day be like? What would be her biggest concerns? What would she do all day?

2. When you were growing up, did you attend a day care center while your mother worked? If not, did you have friends who did? Write a paper giving your opinions of parents who put young children into day care centers. What solutions could you offer for child care?

MAKING CONNECTIONS

If you look closely at the selections in this chapter, you will notice that many different professions were mentioned. Which struck you as the most interesting or the most unusual? Many forms of work were described, and were argued about by the different authors. Which of these forms of work would you like to do or like to avoid? Keep in mind your own work history and your current attitudes about work as you look over these writing ideas for a paper you might like to write about work.

1. *The future of workfare.* Mickey Kaus and Barbara Ehrenreich take totally opposite positions on workfare. Look over the two essays again and the notes you made for each. Write a paper in which you argue in favor of one of the author's positions. Take it point by point and show why you agree with one author and why you think the other author is wrong. You might end your paper by giving suggestions about how you think this issue might be resolved and how some of the differences might be reconciled. If you have the time and opportunity, interview a social worker and a welfare recipient to gain further information.

2. *The original work: hard physical labor.* Richard Rodriguez, Maya Angelou, and Laureen Mar explore some of the degrading effects of hard physical labor. Compare the views of hard labor presented by these three writers and then present your own opinion on the subject, using your own experiences and observations to support your opinion. What is the impact of hard labor on the worker? Does physical labor have any rewards other than a paycheck?

3. *The work ethic.* A number of essays promote the idea of "work for work's sake"—another phrase for "the work ethic" which holds that work of any sort is in itself good for the individual and promotes positive values. Do some reading on the work ethic. How did such an idea become a widespread ideal? What are the values of having a strong work ethic in a society? Refer also to the selections in this chapter for additional information and/or interview a professor on campus who might be knowledgeable about the work ethic in this country. Write up your

findings in an informative paper that also includes some of your own opinions.

4. *The work in your own future.* Think about all the kinds of jobs available to you at this stage in your life. What kind of work do you presently do? What kind of work do you hope to do in the near future? What do you consider your ideal profession? What are your career goals—where do you expect to be professionally in twenty years and how do you expect to get there? Write a paper in which you relate your own work history, how you feel about it, and where you expect to go in the future. Use information from any of the readings in this chapter which you feel you want to include; especially include any of the ideas in the pieces which directly affected your point of view.

CHAPTER 9

Community

Introduction

P. W. ALEXANDER   Christmas at Home

ARTHUR ASHE   Can a New "Army" Save Our Cities?

JULIAN CASTRO   Politics . . . *Maybe*

JEREMY TAYLOR   A Call to Service

TESS GALLAGHER   The Hug

TONI CADE BAMBARA   My Man Bovanne

DAVID MORRIS   Rootlessness

KATHRYN MCCAMANT   Cohousing and the American Dream
AND CHARLES DURRETT

EVAN MCKENZIE   Trouble in Privatopia

CECILIA FAIRLEY   Whatever Happened to the Neighborhood?

KIMBERLY CURTIS   Modern America: Metropolis or Necropolis?

Making Connections

INTRODUCTION

Journal Entry

Think about your own relationship to community and the associations you have with the word. Write about your experiences in being part of a community—either in the past or at present—and what value you have derived from being part of it. End your journal entry by describing the kind of ideal community you would like to be part of in the future.

The word *community* suggests a quiet way of life that once was common and still remains so in many parts of the world—including some small towns in America which still enjoy a feeling of community that has existed from one generation to the next. We think of a community as a place where people know one another well and have much in common culturally and socially, a place where residents spend most of their time, both at work and at play. The word *community* brings up many warm feelings for many people, perhaps even stirring a longing or nostalgia for a way of life that used to be.

The ideal community described in response to such a question is usually one with many shared facilities, for example, a marketplace where local people shop for food and other goods, community schools, and community recreation facilities such as parks and playing fields. In such a community people know one another by sight or by name, and the average person seems approachable because many activities and values are shared by most of the residents. In a tight-knit community people often gossip together, exchange news about neighbors and friends, and debate local issues. People in such a community would be likely to share a common language, although they may have some cultural differences, which are celebrated rather than criticized.

If you feel the above description bears little resemblance to the neighborhood or city you live in, you're not alone—the kind of community we have just described probably seems for most Americans today a vanishing world they may associate with the values of their grandparents, part of a less-populous, slower-moving, more stable society than the one to which most of us are accustomed. These "old-fashioned" ways of life offer much from which we can learn as we try to redesign the decayed, crime-ridden cities and neighborhoods of today to promote a greater sense of belonging and well-being for the citizens of tomorrow.

Read back over your journal entry to remind yourself of what kind of community you feel you would like to be part of. As you read through the selections in this chapter, compare your vision of a good community with some of the pictures described by others. P. W. Alexander in "Christmas at Home," Toni Cade Bambara in "My Man Bovanne," and Tess Gallagher in "The Hug" all paint graphic pictures of the ways communities both fail and succeed. These pieces poignantly show the separation of people by class, race, age, etc., and portray how this separation ultimately creates less community for all of us. Arthur Ashe, Julian Castro, and Jeremy Taylor promote the concept that organized service to others can build a better community and point out some ways in which this service might be structured.

Cities, of course, have robbed society of the small communities in which people were dependent upon each other. And yet cities are here to stay, and people continue to flock to them for all they offer. But is it possible to have a sense of community while living in a city? Some urban planners have changed their view of the city from one that is highly centralized and massive and is built straight up to one that is closer to the design of the smaller villages of the past, with many parks and green belts, with less reliance on cars and more on foot traffic, and with small businesses located in the heart of the community to eliminate the need for commuting. David Morris in his essay "Rootlessness" proposes such village-like communities, as do Kathryn McCamant and Charles Durrett in their essay on innovative, community-oriented housing, "Cohousing and the American Dream." On the other hand, sociologist Evan McKenzie, in "Trouble in Privatopia," presents a disturbing vision of a privatized community that rigidly excludes the world outside it and enforces strict rules to create uniformity of behavior and appearance.

Still, it is unlikely that architecture alone can build community. What is needed for a sense of belonging, a feeling of being part of a group of like-minded people, can't be built with bricks and mortar. It has to be built with hearts and caring. And as so many of the writers in this chapter show, it must all start with the individual: One person who cares and reaches out can begin to build "community."

Christmas at Home

P. W. Alexander

P. W. Alexander, a teacher and writer, was born in South Florida in 1951, one of ten children in a Mexican-American family. She was educated at San Francisco State University, received Montessori training at the University of California at San Diego, and is an advanced graduate student in education at Stanford University. Alexander has had a lifelong commitment to public service and has twice received humanities and arts fellowships to develop her own projects for children in her community. In the following essay, Alexander explores her feelings for her family and for the ideal of service in the community.

"It must have been fun growing up in a big family. I bet the holidays were great."

I look into the face of the woman standing before me. Her expression is some combination of curiosity, affirmation, and hope. It is a question I hear from time to time and not one as easily answered as asked. I can say, "Oh it was wonderful. We had a house full of people. We laughed, we cried, we fought and we made up. I had lots of sisters to love and to tease and to tell my darkest secrets." It is the second question, I bet the holidays were great, that causes me to hesitate, to look at the asker and wonder how much she really wants to hear.

As a child I did not look forward to the holidays. We have an expectation for holidays here in America. It is family time. We have a Norman Rockwell picture of the clan gathered around a long table, in the center of a comfortably furnished dining room, draped in freshly pressed linen and festooned with candles and flowers. At the center of attention is the huge bird, glistening, beckoning us to overeat. People are smiling. Children are neat, Sunday-best-dressed. It is a hopeful image, and I admit, I too am taken by it. It is a holiday scene that would have fit our family well. We had the well-furnished dining room. We had a long cherrywood table that could seat fourteen, three more chairs than our family needed. We had the yards of lace and linen and the wreaths, candles, centerpieces and china. My parents, however, had some other vision of how the holidays should be spent.

As a young child I simply accepted our family observance of holidays; I knew nothing else. It began with Halloween. In the morning we went to church and in the evening we collected for UNICEF. At first I thought little of the cup of money I brought home that was poured into a large glass jar and eventually spirited away somewhere. As I got older and greedier I began to dislike those nameless, faceless children in countries with odd names pointed out to me on the globe in the library. I wanted to take just one of those dimes and buy a full-size Snickers bar. I was glad when I became "too big" to go out trick or treating.

Thanksgiving and Christmas were equally painful. My mother would sign us all up to work at the soup kitchen. While other families watched televised parades, chased cousins under the piano and yelled at grandma because she had left her hearing aid home, we stood in line and served people from the fringe. We chopped and washed and sliced in the church kitchen. We wore old clothes because the work was messy and we didn't want to "show off." My brother and I were fascinated with the size of the ovens and the number of turkeys that they contained. We carried stacks of plates and bowls and dragged crates of vegetables across the concrete floors. My older brother had the most annoying habit of whistling or humming as he went about his kitchen chores. He was never a part of our kitchen shenanigans. We had games we played between ourselves—who could wash the most forks in one minute, how many cups of coffee could we carry on one tray without spilling. We stuck our fingers in pumpkin pies and covered the damage with whipped cream from a can.

One particularly cold Thanksgiving we were in West Virginia for the school holidays. My father found a place for us to serve. It was snowing hard. People came in long before the meal was ready. I remember them warming their hands on hot cups of coffee. I shivered in the warm church basement. They brought the icy wind inside with them. It was in their thin coats and wet shoes. The image of that red, cracked skin on their hands and faces stayed with me for a long time. I remember how much people would eat, and how quickly. I was scandalized at their table manners. Napkins were often left untouched at the side of their plates. My younger brother, Steven, relished these meals. He delighted in the piles of food and lack of rules. He announced once on the way home, "I ate mashed potatoes—with my fingers!" I had seen people surreptitiously stuffing unwrapped food into their pockets. They never left anything on the plate, not even a polite pea or a genteel stalk of asparagus.

As I got older, I began to ask more questions. Why don't they have homes? Why don't they have food? Why don't they work? And I always asked, WHY do WE have to do this? My mother's response was always the same. The same five words in the same calm, even voice. It was as if she had some perverse tape running inside her head that spewed out the same tired message time after time: "Because we have so much."

The year I was thirteen I thought we would all be saved the embar- 7 rassment, the humiliation, the torture of the slave galley. Grandmother was coming from Boston. Grandmother was a lady who always wore gloves. White gloves with little pearl buttons and lacy fingers. Grandmother would never ladle murky soup into plastic bowls or slice great slabs of turkey into scratched beige plates with little compartments. But Grandmother did. She did it with grace and humility. She hugged unwashed people with matted hair and open sores. She shook hands with their red, raw claws and she blessed them. She asked them to pray for her. She wrapped turkey legs in newspaper and openly invited people to take them home. She sat down next to a scruffy little girl and introduced herself as grandma. People smiled at her and showed her all the teeth they didn't have.

That night, my sister Katalina and I snuggled close together in my 8 top bunk and talked long into the night. She often crept up from her bed so we could whisper together after "lights out." We had never spoken much about our service. It was a dreaded event, something to complain about, one more reason to stand by our resolve never to sell our children into indentured servitude. But that night, that Thanksgiving that Grandmother came and took off her white lacy gloves and served gravy to poor people, that night we talked of other things.

We talked about how hard it was not to stare. We knew staring was 9 impolite. These people were so dirty, so poor, and so ugly. If they caught you looking at them they turned away quickly. There was something haunting in their eyes, something of pain and of shame and of sadness. They looked at the floor, at the plate of food heaped before them, at the crucifix on the wall over the table. "They have no dad." My sister Susana cried out in the darkness from her bed on the other side of the room. "Grandmother washed those two boys' hands in the kitchen sink and she sat by them and they told her they had no dad." I squeezed Katalina's hand. *No Dad.* Who took them to the beach, who gave them quarters for the movie, who told them stories at bedtime so they wouldn't have bad dreams?

A month later, at Christmas, Katalina and I gave away our two fa- 10 vorite books to the gift drive our church held. My older brother donated his bicycle and his skates. We didn't put up a tree that year but we did buy one and give it to some people we had read about in the newspaper. Their house and all their presents burned up in a fire.

I work at the homeless shelter and I stand in the serving line and ladle soup and gravy. I shake hands with people who don't bathe and I have on occasion hugged people with dried vomit on their clothing. Three years ago I came home on Thanksgiving with head lice. It is a small part of the job. It is a very small part of the experience. I am in service to my fellow human beings. I do this not out of any sense of duty or obligation, I do it because it is my family tradition. It would not be Thanksgiving or Christmas if I did not stand for a brief moment in front of my closet, gaze at my favorite party frock and feel a slight twinge of regret. It passes very quickly and then I put on my work clothes and I go to the church kitchen to do my service. I see the same hard, lined faces, the same out-of-fashion ragged clothes. I smell the same street dirt and sour alcohol. I hear the same stories of injustice and pain. The people whose eyes I avoided as a child I now seek. I search their faces for some harbinger of hope, some sign of change. If you ask me why I do it, I can only say, because I have so much.

⸻

RESPONDING TO "CHRISTMAS AT HOME"

Freewrite about your feelings on spending holidays serving others.

Responding through Interpretation

1. How does Alexander's essay serve as a response to the initial comment, "I bet the holidays were great." Were the holidays "great" for her and her family? If so, in what sense?
2. What does Alexander learn from her grandmother?
3. In your reading notebook, write down several of Alexander's images that seem particularly memorable for you. How do they contribute to her points about community service and family life?

Responding through Discussion

1. Go over the essay in your group and discuss your feelings about it and your opinions of it. Was doing service as a family on a holiday something you had thought of or experienced before? Do you think Alexander's portrayal is realistic? Why doesn't she offer hope, criticisms, solutions? What did the group learn from this essay?
2. Allow group members to share memories of childhood holidays where they interacted with the community beyond their immediate family—either through attending community celebrations and activities or through doing or receiving some form of service. What was there to learn from these experiences?

Responding through Writing

1. Alexander's mother and later Alexander herself state that they give service on holidays to others "because we have so much." In your journal, respond to this idea. What do you consider "so much"? If a person has "so much," why give it away?

2. Serving the community should ideally take place year-round. Do some research on opportunities for service in your community and write a paper that focuses on at least three of these opportunities, explaining what is needed and what college students might be able to contribute.

Can a New "Army" Save Our Cities?

Arthur Ashe

Arthur Ashe was a tennis champion, a graduate of UCLA, a sportswriter and commentator, and author of an autobiography, *Off the Court* (1981). He also wrote a book about the struggle of African-American athletes, *A Hard Road to Glory* (1988). Ashe spent his final years struggling with and writing about AIDS, from which he died in 1993. Ashe wrote the following editorial for the *Washington Post* (1992), shortly after the Los Angeles riots. In the editorial he proposes a path toward community revitalization through an ambitious national service program focusing on inner-city youth.

Once again, seething, residual anger has burst forth in an American city.   1
And the riots that overtook Los Angeles 10 days ago were a reminder of what knowledgeable observers have been saying for a quarter-century: America will continue paying a high price in civil and ethnic unrest unless the nation commits itself to programs that help the urban poor lead productive and respectable lives.

Once again, a proven program is worth pondering: national service.   2

Somewhat akin to the military training that generations of Ameri-   3
can males received in the armed forces, a 1990s version would prepare thousands of unemployable and undereducated young adults for quality lives in our increasingly global and technology-driven economy. National service opportunities would be available to any who needed it and, make no mistake, the problems are now so structural, so intractable, that any solution will require massive federal intervention.

In his much-quoted book, "The Truly Disadvantaged," sociologist   4
William Julius Wilson wrote that "only a major program of economic reform" will prevent the riot-prone urban underclass from being permanently locked out of American economic life. Today, we simply have no choice. The enemy within and among our separate ethnic selves is as daunting as any foreign foe.

Families rent apart by welfare dependency, job discrimination and   5
intense feelings of alienation have produced minority teenagers with very little self-discipline and little faith that good grades and the American work ethic will pay off. A military-like environment for them with practical domestic objectives could produce startling results.

348

Readings

Military service has been the most successful career training pro- 6
gram we've ever known, and American children born in the years since
the all-volunteer Army was instituted make up a large proportion of this
targeted group. But this opportunity may disappear forever if too many
of our military bases are summarily closed and converted or sold to the
private sector. The facilities, manpower, traditions, and capacity are already in place.

Don't dismantle it; rechannel it. 7

Discipline is a cornerstone of any responsible citizen's life. I was 8
taught it by my father, who was a policeman. Many of the rioters have
never had any at all. As an athlete and former Army officer, I know that
discipline can be learned. More importantly, it *must* be learned or it
doesn't take hold.

A precedent for this approach was the Civilian Conservation Corps 9
that worked so well during the Great Depression. My father enlisted in
the CCC as a young man with an elementary school education and he
learned invaluable skills that served him well throughout his life. The
key was that a job was waiting for him when he finished. The certainty
of that first entry-level position is essential if severely alienated young
minority men and women are to keep the faith.

We all know these are difficult times for the public sector, but here's 10
a chance to add energetic and able manpower to America's workforce.
They could be prepared for the world of work or college—an offer similar to that made to returning GIs after World War II. It would be a
chance for 16- to 21-year-olds to live among other cultures, religions,
races and in different geographical areas. And these young people could
be taught to rally around common goals and friendships that evolve out
of pride in one's squad, platoon, company, battalion—or commander.

We saw such images during the Persian Gulf War and during the 11
NCAA Final Four basketball games. In military life and competitive
sports, this camaraderie doesn't just happen; it is taught and learned in
an atmosphere of discipline and earned mutual respect for each other's
capabilities.

Ethnic hatred, like that portrayed in Los Angeles, is also taught and 12
learned.

A national service program would also help overcome two damag- 13
ing perceptions held by America's disaffected youth: that society just
doesn't care about minority youngsters and that one's personal best efforts will not be rewarded in our discriminatory job market. Harvard
professor Robert Reich has opined that urban social ills are so pervasive
that the upper 20 percent of Americans—that "fortunate fifth" as he

calls them—have decided quietly to "secede" from the bottom four-fifths, and the lowest fifth in particular. We cannot countenance such estrangement on a permanent basis. And what better way to answer skeptics from any group than by certifying the technical skills of graduates from a national service training program?

Now, we must act decisively to forestall future urban unrest. Republicans must put aside their aversion to funding programs aimed at certain cultural groups. Democrats must forget labels and nomenclature and recognize that a geographically isolated subgroup of Americans—their children in particular—need systematic and substantive assistance for at least another 20 years.   14

The ethnic taproots of minority Americans are deeply buried in a soil of faith and fealty to traditional values. With its accent on discipline, teamwork, conflict resolution, personal responsibility and marketable skills development, national service can provide both the training and that vital first job that will reconnect these Americans to the rest of us. Let's do it now before the fire next time.   15

RESPONDING TO "CAN A NEW 'ARMY' SAVE OUR CITIES?"

Freewrite about your response to Ashe's idea of having a national service. Do you think it would be a good idea for young people to be required to serve their communities?

Responding through Interpretation

1. What event triggered Ashe's editorial? Why does he believe the time has come to consider a national service program?
2. How does national service as Ashe depicts it replace military service as a training outlet for the poor? Why is military service no longer a viable option?
3. National service has many meanings—how does Ashe explain his program? What group will it serve? What particular ends will the program achieve? Who will pay for it?

Responding through Discussion

1. In a group discussion, brainstorm together about group members' views about the idea of a national service. Ashe refers to it as "a proven program." What does he mean? Did your group feel it is "proven"?
2. Share in your group any personal contact or experience each of you has had with government-sponsored service—whether on the national, state,

or city level. For example, have any of you served in the military, or in state fund-raising or cleanup campaigns, or in local summer programs for the youths of your city? Let group members who have had such experience discuss what they feel were the advantages and disadvantages of such programs for service.

Responding through Writing

1. In your journal, write a letter to Arthur Ashe telling him what you think about his ideas for a national service.
2. Ashe's program is expressed in general terms; he doesn't give any details of what such a program would be like. Read further about national service programs. Then, using some of Ashe's ideas, write up a program for a national service youth corps that would be very specific: Who would qualify? What kind of training would they receive? What would be their various duties to the community? What kind of pay would they receive? Who would fund the program? (You can come up with additional questions and concerns to add to the paper.)

Politics . . . Maybe

Julian Castro

Julian Castro was born and raised in San Antonio, Texas, in a family that was very involved in grass-roots politics for the Hispanic community. Recently he completed a project in community service, working with the Upward Bound Program. He wrote the following essay for his English class after reading the story "My Man Bovanne" and the essay by P. W. Alexander (both included in this chapter). Castro draws upon his memories of his mother and her commitment to activism as well as upon more recent experiences to create a reflective personal essay on the importance of service to others.

How many of these "functions" have I been to in my lifetime? They all seem the same to me now—the same speeches and speakers, the same cheese and ham sandwiches, the same people, ones whom I see only at these political gatherings, "functions" my mother calls them, and, of course, the same expectations of me. "So, what are you going to do after you finish school?" my mother's friend asks me. "Uhh . . ." Can he see my eyes float along the carpet?

I am told that when I was three years old I was involved in my first political campaign: I handed out flyers. Not of my own volition, but because my mother took part in the hustle and bustle of politics. Today, the very idea of politics makes many people's stomachs turn. Conventional wisdom (if we may call it that) is cynical about the motives of politicians and skeptical about the power of the political process to effect change. However, it was never like that for my mother. She sees political activism as an opportunity to change people's lives for the better. Perhaps that is because of her outspoken nature or because Chicanos in the early 1970s (and, of course, for many years before) had no other option. To make themselves heard, Chicanos needed the opportunity that the political system provided. In any event, my mother's fervor for activism affected the first years of my life, even as it touches it today.

I remember buttons and pens, posters, stickers, and pictures: "Viva La Raza!" "Black and Brown United!" "Accept me for who I am—Chicano." These and many other powerful slogans rang in my ears like war cries. And I remember my mother during that time. She worked for what seemed like an infinite number of nonprofit organizations. She sat on this committee and that board. There was the YWCA, Leadership 2000, and others that drift in and out of my memory. She got involved in the PTA at my school because she was the first to show up at a first-of-the-year meeting. Her list of things to do was miles long I thought. At seven or eight years old, I did not understand why my mother worked so diligently for these nonprofit organizations and political causes. I did not see what profit she gained from her work, and I wondered why she would give so much of herself. The slogans and discussions of this and that "-ism" meant nothing to me either.

As a twelve-year-old I liked to disagree with her about her politics. I questioned this stance and that remark. And I asked what in the world she was getting out of speaking up. Even as I continued to visit head-quarters and polls, I didn't think of it all as worthwhile. I have seen others of her generation go on to become successful, and I asked her why we did not have the nice house or good car that I saw others with. "Where are the benefits of what you have done?" I demanded.   3

Patiently, over several years, my mother explained to me why she and many others, she said, were trying to better the lives of all Chicanos—the typical, hardworking adult who is relegated by society to a low-income status, the impoverished mothers who, with numerous children to feed and not a single voice, wear badges of tribulation that are their faces. There weren't always Chicanos at this college or attending that major university, she explained. We used to be only farm workers, cooks or, if we were lucky, teachers. My grandmother was a maid, she reminded me.   4

These words my mother spoke again and again. She insisted that things were changing because of political activism, participation in the system. Maria del Rosario Castro has never held a political office. Her name is seldom mentioned in a San Antonio newspaper. However, today, years later, I read the newspapers, and I see that more Valdezes are sitting on school boards, that a greater number of Garcias are now doctors, lawyers, engineers and, of course, teachers. And I look around me and see a few other brown faces in the crowd at this university. I also see in me a product of my mother's diligence and of her friends' hard work. Twenty years ago I would not have been here.   5

Community service isn't always done in a soup kitchen or library, tutoring an adult to read. My opportunities are not a gift of the major-ity; they are the result of a lifetime of struggle and commitment endured by a *determined* minority. My mother is one of those persons. And each year I realize more and more how much easier my life has been made by the toil of past generations. I wonder what form *my* service will take, since I am expected by those who know my mother to continue the fam-   6 ily tradition. As far back as I can remember, I vowed never to become involved in politics. My young dreams of a fancy car and a nice house would fade as I contemplated a life of grass-roots organizing and committee meetings until all hours of the night. "I don't want to be poor!" I would tell my mom.

But profits don't have to be measured in bills. In fact, if we're lucky,   7
they are measured in happiness.

> *My eyes wander back onto his face and rest as they catch his. "Maybe politics," I answer with a straight smile. His eyes reflect damp brown fields turning into callused hands. The hands have in them pencils, the pencils, power. He laughs back at me.*

RESPONDING TO "POLITICS ... MAYBE"

Freewrite on the subject of children and politics: Can children understand political issues and learn from participating in campaigns?

Responding through Interpretation

1. What impact did his early involvement with political activism and community service have on Julian Castro's relationship with his mother and his values?
2. Julian Castro's mother never got elected to office or became a powerful political figure. What comment does the essay make on the relationship between political activism and the advancement of Chicanos and other minorities?

Responding through Discussion

1. Discuss in your group Castro's belief that people today generally are cynical about politics and think of it as a waste of time. What contact has each group member had with the political process, in this country or abroad? Do group members feel cynical about politics, or more optimistic, as Castro is?

Responding through Writing

1. Based on the information provided in the essay and your own imaginative response to it, write a narrative of a typical day in the life of Castro's mother, Maria del Rosario Castro.
2. Write an essay in which you discuss the major steps that minorities and other people outside of mainstream American life can take to gain success and power in this country. To what extent do you consider political involvement a part of that process?

A Call to Service

Jeremy Taylor

Jeremy Taylor grew up in a rural community in northern California. In his English composition class, Jeremy Taylor took part in a project in community service, after which he decided to write his final paper on the topic of service learning. In the following essay, he combines his own experiences with his research to present an argument for the integration of service learning into the college experience.

We need in education a transformation as far reaching as the one which has seized Eastern Europe and what was once the Soviet Union, as radical as the abrupt ending of the Cold War, as profound as the metamorphosis of America's vanquished enemies in World War II into its most dependable allies.

(Barber 10)

The test scores of American high school students are dropping rapidly, while our high school dropout rate, teenage drug abuse, and teenage pregnancy continue to increase. Today's educators are exploring learning approaches that will put our nation's young adults back on track. The introduction of community service into the classroom is a potential solution that is gaining momentum across the country. Through participation in community service learning projects, students can begin to better understand their role in a community and their responsibility to others. The introduction of community service into the classroom can be a vital part of the restructuring of our nation's educational goals as well as a valuable tool in teaching social responsibility.

By combining classroom work with community projects, students are able to see the applications of their knowledge. They learn well through this method because they are involved personally with the outcome; they do not have to feel like passive bystanders. This approach brings a sense of purpose back to education. Presently, classrooms are filled with students asking questions such as "Why do I need to learn this?" and "When am I ever going to use that?" Participating in service learning experiences in the "real world" helps students to begin to find some answers to these challenging questions. As students realize that knowledge gained through regular coursework and classroom learning can be applied outside the classroom, they gain a sense of motivation and purpose for learning.

355

Application of community service as a way to enhance and invigo-   3
rate the learning process is supported at many levels. After the passage
of the landmark Community Service Act of 1990, Senator Edward
Kennedy explained why he supports service learning:

> Service learning should be a central component of current efforts to re-
> form education. There are few better ways to inspire a child's interest
> in science than by allowing him or her to analyze and clean a polluted
> stream. There are few better ways to help a student's grammar than by
> having him or her tutor a recent immigrant learning to speak and write
> English. (772)

Along with Senator Kennedy, students, administrators, and teachers   4
all over the country are realizing the value of service learning. When students see their knowledge promoting the growth of the community, their
degree of knowledge retention is increased. As a sixteen-year-old member of an ambulance crew said, "In school you learn chemistry and biology and stuff and then forget it as soon as the test is over. Here you've got
to remember it because somebody's life depends on it (qtd. in Conrad 745).

In addition to increasing learning retention, studies also show that
students who participate in community service learning experiences de-   5
velop a more positive attitude toward others as well as a higher sense
of self-esteem; they also have fewer disciplinary problems (Conrad 747).
Most importantly, working with others on community service projects
can increase students' motivation to learn. Teacher Don Zwach of
Waseca, Minnesota, who incorporates community service into his curriculum, points to the significant impact that community service projects
have had on his students' motivation:

> This is the most enthusiastic class I've had in thirty years. You hear a
> lot about the problems of motivating students in the 1990s. But there's
> absolutely no problem motivating these young people. (qtd. in
> Kielsmeier 741)

Other teachers report that their academic goals are much more eas-   6
ily accomplished when students apply their knowledge to situations outside of the classroom. For example, after tutoring third and fourth
graders, seventeen-year-old Quinn Hammond said, "This taught me to
have a lot more patience and gave me a real good feeling. Volunteering
gave me a lot of respect for teachers" (qtd. in Kielsmeier 741).

Opponents of civic learning hold to the belief that the purpose of an   7
educational system is to educate, not to teach civic responsibility. They
claim that an academic institution has no right to coerce students into a
service behavior. Benjamin Barber captures the limitation of such "aca-

demic purism" in his book *An Aristocracy for Everyone* when he says that these educators believe in learning "not for career, not for life, not for democracy, not for money; for neither power nor happiness, neither career nor quality of life, but for its own pure sake" (203).

While the debate on whether to include community service in the academic curriculum grows more intense, this method of education through service is not new. When America's first colleges were established in the seventeenth and eighteenth centuries, service was one of their fundamental values and goals; they structured curriculums to support their belief in service to the church, service to the local community, and service to the emerging nation. In fact, Rutgers University was chartered in 1766 to promote "learning for the benefit of the community" (Barber 246).

From 1766 to the present many approaches and opinions have been offered on the subject of education through community service. Today's proponents work with ideas that are similar to those of John Dewey. In *Experience and Education,* published in 1913, Dewey developed the idea of stimulating academic achievement through actions directed toward others. Dewey spent much of his life trying to bring education and experience together in order to promote democracy as a "way of life and not just a political system" (qtd. in Barber 247). When Woodrow Wilson assumed the office of President, he encouraged a renewed interest in civic responsibility and service learning: "[A]s a nation we are becoming civically illiterate. Unless we find better ways to educate ourselves as citizens, we run the risk of drifting into a new kind of Dark Age" (qtd. in Barber 247).

In the 1950s, a new approach to civic education, the Citizenship Education Project, was developed by teachers from Columbia University. This program urged community involvement and participation and also contained the famous "Brown Box" with hundreds of ideas for community interaction (Conrad 744). The 1970s brought another new wave of reports condemning the passivity of our school systems. The National Committee on Secondary Education, the Panel on Youth of the President's Science Advisory Committee, and the National Panel on High School and Adolescent Education all supported the integration of education into the community (Conrad 744). By the mid-1980s, several pilot programs had been initiated, and community service programs began to appear in classrooms throughout the nation.

These historical facts provide a background for the educational innovations of the 1990s. Perhaps the most important step in the integration of public service into the classroom, the National and Community

Service Act of 1990, passed by the Congress of the United States, will provide funding for community service programs from kindergarten through college. This is the most thorough community service bill ever passed. The legislation provided federal appropriations of $62 million in 1991, $95.5 million in 1992, and $105 million in 1993 for community service programs. A major goal of this program is to inspire the interest in community service at a young age. Senator Edward Kennedy hopes that "by teaching young children to help others, we will also be encouraging the values that will help keep America strong for the next generation" (772).

Academic communities all over the country are beginning to realize the value of community service, and more programs are being introduced at the high school and college level. For example, service programs have been developed in Washington and Vermont. One program in particular, PennSERVE, developed in Pennsylvania, is achieving incredible success. PennSERVE emphasizes the link between the classroom and community service. Because of PennSERVE, the number of schools offering academic credit for service has doubled in two years and community service has become a common topic of debate (Briscoe 760). PennSERVE is just one of the many programs which has grown and flourished since the passage of the Community Service Act of 1990.

I was introduced to service learning through another type of program, a Community Service Writing Project; my experiences were memorable and beneficial. I chose to be placed in a Community Service English class because I had become bored with "regular" English, which I characterize as writing solely to please my teacher and receive a good grade. I looked forward to an English class that would expose me to community service in my first year of college. Through my English class, I decided to work at a public service organization that helped disadvantaged youth from nearby high schools prepare for college. Along with the four other students, I met with the organization's leader and discovered how our skills were to be utilized. Our group was to be responsible for developing a newsletter for prospective students and their parents. The newsletter was to include articles highlighting various aspects of the organization, so each person in our group wrote on a different topic. I chose to interview a new staff member, a classmate interviewed students who were involved with the program, and another group member researched the organization's incentive program to learn about how it rewarded students for their academic achievement.

While my finished product for the project was brief, the "behind the scenes" work was immeasurable and invaluable. I learned "real-life" skills while completing this project. First, I had to research the organization to prepare for my interview. It was then necessary to formulate questions for the interview and decide what my focus was going to be. During the interview I discovered how interviewing is an art and realized the difficulty of "staying on track" and directing the conversation toward key points. After the interview, it was necessary to review my notes, determine the focus of my article, and decide what information to include and what to leave out. Finishing this process, I wrote a draft and turned it into the organization. In an English class, after one turns in a paper the process is ended; this was not the case with my interview. The leader of the organization requested that I write another draft with a slightly different focus. While this was a new situation for me, I approached it as a challenge. Complying with the leader's suggestions, I wrote a revised article which addressed the issues she saw as important. This draft received approval to be placed in the newsletter and brought my writing project to a conclusion.

Although this project was lengthy and, at times, frustrating, it was   15
an invaluable experience. I was refreshed by writing with a purpose other than to receive an "A" and by knowing that my writing would be read by someone other than a professor. I felt a strong sense of responsibility to my organization, and I wanted to produce something of which I would be proud. But the writing was just a minimal part of the overall experience; this project introduced me to people, to ideas, and to situations that I would not have experienced in the classroom. It gave me a sense of pride, and illustrated that I am able to reach out to people in different ways and through different mediums. I would not trade my "real-life" experiences while working on this project for any other kind of essay assignment. Through my interaction with the organization and its members, I feel that in a subtle way this project has prepared me to participate more effectively in society.

In the early eighties, Ernest Boyer and Fred Hechinger asked that "a   16
new generation of Americans . . . be educated for life in an increasingly complex world . . . through civic education [that] prepares students of all ages to participate more effectively in our social institutions" (qtd. in Barber 248). Just as the world is changing around us, our educational system must change to meet the needs of today's students. The integration of civic education is an important part of that change. Community service, by showing us that we all have the means to contribute, can be the critical step in producing citizen graduates who realize their social responsibility and who will participate more effectively in our social institutions. Times have changed, yet our academic institutions have re-

mained the same. The call for change has been sounded. It won't fade; it will only grow louder.

Works Cited

Barber, Benjamin R. *An Aristocracy for Everyone: The Politics of Education and the Future of America.* New York: Ballantine Books, 1992.

Briscoe, John. "PennSERVE: The Governor's Office of Citizen Service." *Phi Delta Kappan* June 1991: 758–760.

Conrad, Dan and Diane Hedin. "School Based Community Service: What We Know from Research and Theory." *Phi Delta Kappan* June 1991: 743–749.

Kennedy, Edward M. "National Service and Education for Citizenship." *Phi Delta Kappan* June 1991: 771–773.

Kielsmeier, Jim and Joeseph Nathan. "The Sleeping Giant of School Reform." *Phi Delta Kappan* June 1991: 739–742.

RESPONDING TO "A CALL TO SERVICE"

Freewrite about your views on colleges incorporating community service learning into the curriculum. In which courses (if any) would community service work best?

Responding through Interpretation

1. The concept of using community service as a means of education dates back as far as 1766, according to Taylor. What are some of the early programs that preceded the current community service programs?
2. What kind of community service did Taylor do? What are some of the benefits and learning he gained from this service?

Responding through Discussion

1. How successful is Taylor in bringing in outside sources to back up his points? Which did you think were the most persuasive? Which others do you think he might have included? As a group, look over how Taylor has documented his paper and make notes on the form he used.

Responding through Writing

1. Taylor says toward the end of his essay: "I was refreshed by writing with a purpose other than to receive an A and by knowing that my writing

would be read by someone other than a professor." In your journal, respond to Taylor's statement. Do you need a "purpose" beyond a grade to motivate you in your writing?

2. Using Taylor's essay as a guide, write your own documented paper, arguing in favor of or against community service as a course assignment or as a way of earning money toward college tuition. Make reference to at least three outside sources of fact and opinion; use page numbers and author's last name for references to ideas and facts from your sources that you use to back up your own opinions. At the end of your paper, list your sources alphabetically as Taylor does in his essay on his "Works Cited" page.

The Hug

Tess Gallagher

Tess Gallagher grew up in Port Angeles, Washington. She attended the University of Washington and the University of Iowa and has taught creative writing at numerous colleges. She published her first collection of poems *Stepping Outside* in 1974 and has also written essays and short stories. One of her recent books, *Moon Crossing Bridge* (1992), is a collection of poems written after the sudden death of her husband, the writer Raymond Carver.

A woman is reading a poem on the street
and another woman stops to listen. We stop too,
with our arms around each other. The poem
is being read and listened to out here
in the open. Behind us   5
no one is entering or leaving the houses.
Suddenly a hug comes over me and I'm
giving it to you, like a variable star shooting light
off to make itself comfortable, then
subsiding. I finish but keep on holding   10
you. A man walks up to us and we know he hasn't
come out of nowhere, but if he could, he
would have. He looks homeless because of how
he needs. "Can I have one of those?" he asks you,
and I feel you nod. I'm surprised,   15
surprised you don't tell him how
it is—that I'm yours, only
yours, etc., exclusive as a nose to
its face. Love—that's what we're talking about, love
that nabs you with "for me   20
only" and holds on.
So I walk over to him and put my
arms around him and try to
hug him like I mean it. He's got an overcoat on
so thick I can't feel   25
him past it. I'm starting the hug
and thinking, "How big a hug is this supposed to be?
How long shall I hold this hug?" Already

we could be eternal, his arms falling over my
shoulders, my hands not   30
meeting behind his back, he is so big!

I put my head into his chest and snuggle
in. I lean into him. I lean my blood and my wishes
into him. He stands for it. This is his
and he's starting to give it back so well I know he's   35
getting it. This hug. So truly, so tenderly
we stop having arms and I don't know if
my lover has walked away or what, or
if the woman is still reading the poem, or the houses—
what about them?—the houses.   40

Clearly, a little permission is a dangerous thing.
But when you hug someone you want it
to be a masterpiece of connection, the way the button
on his coat will leave the imprint of
a planet in my cheek   45
when I walk away. When I try to find some place
to go back to.

RESPONDING TO "THE HUG"

Freewrite about the man in the poem whom the narrator hugs. Have you ever
talked to someone on the street who was a stranger to you?

Responding through Interpretation

1. "The Hug" revolves around a single incident, a quick moment in time.
   In your reading notebook, write a brief analysis that explains the events
   of the poem and the motivation of the narrator to hug the homeless man.
2. Who are the couple? Are they young or old? Married or not? Describe
   them. What kind of relationship do they have?
3. What does the image of "the imprint/of a planet in my cheek" suggest as
   a final meaning for the poem?

Responding through Discussion

1. Have a member of the group read the poem aloud very slowly. Then go
   back through and have each member contribute the image that he or she

found most meaningful. Discuss all the levels of meaning you see in the poem.

2. Go through the poem together and look at how the concept of home runs throughout the poem. Discuss all the aspects of home that you see reflected in the poem. Bring your ideas back to the class as a whole for further discussion.

Responding through Writing

1. Take a look at your ideas about love. Re-read Gallagher's lines at the end of the first stanza about love. Then write a journal entry about the different kinds of love you experience in your life. What experience have you had with the "for me only" love that Gallagher mentions?

2. Write an essay in which you take a position on whether or not it is possible to feel an intense love and caring for people you don't know personally. What inspires community work? Church giving? Programs for the poor and homeless? Use your own experiences and observations; include outside resources, such as Gallagher's poem, if appropriate to your essay.

My Man Bovanne

Toni Cade Bambara

Born in New York City, Toni Cade Bambara writes fiction, has taught writing and literature, has worked as a community organizer, and has developed documentaries detailing the African-American experience. Her writing includes the short story collection *Gorilla, My Love* (1972) and the novels *The Salt Eaters* (1980) and *If Blessing Comes* (1987). In the story "My Man Bovanne" Bambara presents an African-American family involved with community and political activities at the "grass-roots" level.

Blind people got a hummin jones if you notice. Which is understandable   1
completely once you been around one and notice what no eyes will force you into to see people, and you get past the first time, which seems to come out of nowhere, and it's like you in church again with fat-chest ladies and old gents gruntin a hum low in the throat to whatever the preacher be saying. Shakey Bee bottom lip all swole up with Sweet Peach and me explainin how come the sweetpotato bread was a dollar-quarter this time stead of dollar regular and he say uh hunh he understand, then he break into this *thizzin* kind of hum which is quiet, but fiercesome just the same if you ain't ready for it. Which I wasn't. But I got used to it and the onliest time I had to say somethin bout it was when he was playin checkers on the stoop one time and he commenst to hummin quite churchy seem to me. So I says. "Look here Shakey Bee, I can't beat you and Jesus too." He stop.

So that's how come I asked My Man Bovanne to dance. He ain't my   2
man mind you, just a nice ole gent from the block that we all know cause he fixes things and the kids like him. Or used to fore Black Power got hold their minds and mess em around till they can't be civil to ole folks. So we at this benefit for my niece's cousin who's runnin for somethin with this Black party somethin or other behind her. And I press up close to dance with Bovanne who blind and I'm hummin and he hummin, chest to chest like talkin. Not jammin my breasts into the man. Wasn't bout tits. Was bout vibrations. And he dug it and asked me what color dress I had on and how my hair was fixed and how I was doin without a man, not nosy but nice-like, and who was at this affair and was the canapes dainty-stingy or healthy enough to get hold of proper. Comfy and cheery is what I'm trying to get across. Touch talkin like the heel of the hand on the tambourine or on a drum.

But right away Joe Lee come up on us and frown for dancin so close to the man. My own son who knows what kind of warm I am about; and don't grown men call me long distance and in the middle of the night for a little Mama comfort? But he frown. Which ain't right since Bovanne can't see and defend himself. Just a nice old man who fixes toasters and busted irons and bicycles and things and changes the lock on my door when my men friends get messy. Nice man. Which is not why they invited him. Grassroots you see. Me and Sister Taylor and the woman who does heads at Mamies and the man from the barber shop, we all there on account of we grassroots. And I ain't never been souther than Brooklyn Battery and no more country than the window box on my fire escape. And just yesterday my kids tellin me to take them countrified rags off my head and be cool. And now can't get Black enough to suit em. So everybody passin sayin My Man Bovanne. Big deal, keep stepping and don't even stop a minute to get the man a drink or one of them cute sandwiches or tell him what's goin on. And him standin there with a smile ready case someone do speak he want to be ready. So that's how come I pull him on the dance floor and we dance squeezin past the tables and chairs and all them coats and people standin round up in each other face talkin bout this and that but got no use for this blind man who mostly fixed skates and skooters for all these folks when they was just kids. So I'm pressed up close and we touch talkin with the hum. And here come my daughter cuttin her eye at me like she do when she tell me about my "apolitical" self like I got hoof and mouf disease and there ain't no hope at all. And I don't pay her no mind and just look up in Bovanne shadow face and tell him his stomach like a drum and he laugh. Laugh real loud. And here come my youngest, Task, with a tap on my elbow like he the third-grade monitor and I'm cuttin up on the line to assembly.

"I was just talkin on the drums," I explained when they hauled me into the kitchen. I figured drums was my best defense. They can get ready for drums what with all this heritage business. And Bovanne stomach just like that drum Task give me when he come back from Africa. You just touch it and it hum thizzim, thizzim. So I stuck to the drum story. "Just drummin that's all."

"Mama, what are you talkin about?"

"She had too much to drink," say Elo to Task cause she don't hardly say nuthin to me direct no more since that ugly argument about my wigs.

"Look here, Mama," say Task, the gentle one. "We just trying to pull your coat. You were makin a spectacle of yourself out there dancing like that."

"Dancin like what?"

Task run a hand over his left ear like his father for the world and his 9
father before that.

"Like a bitch in heat," say Elo. 10

"Well uhh, I was goin to say like one of them sex-starved ladies get- 11
tin on in years and not too discriminating. Know what I mean?"

I don't answer cause I'll cry. Terrible thing when your own chil- 12
dren talk to you like that. Pullin me out the party and hustlin me into
some stranger's kitchen in the back of a bar just like the damn police.
And ain't like I'm old old. I can still wear me some sleeveless dresses
without the meat hanging off my arm. And I keep up with some thangs
through my kids. Who ain't kids no more. To hear them tell it. So I don't
say nuthin.

"Dancin with that tom," say Elo to Joe Lee, who leanin on the folks' 12
freezer. "His feet can smell a cracker a mile away and go into their shuf-
fle number post haste. And them eyes. He could be a little considerate
and put on some shades. Who wants to look into them blown-out fuses
that—"

"Is this what they call the generation gap?" I say. 13

"Generation gap," spits Elo, like I suggested castor oil and fricassee 14
possum in the milk shakes or somethin. "That's a white concept for a
white phenomenon. There's no generation gap among Black people. We
are a col—"

"Yeh, well never mind," says Joe Lee. "The point is Mama . . . well, 15
it's pride. You embarrass yourself and us too dancin like that."

"I wasn't shame." Then nobody say nuthin. Them standin there in 16
they pretty clothes with drinks in they hands and gangin up on me, and
me in the third-degree chair and nary a olive to my name. Felt just like
the police got hold to me.

"First of all," Task say, holding up his hand and tickin off the of- 17
fenses, "the dress. Now that dress is too short, Mama, and too low cut
for a woman your age. And Tamu's going to make a speech tonight to
kick off the campaign and will be introducin you and expecting you to
organize the Council of Elders—"

"Me? Didn't nobody ask me nuthin. You mean Nisi? She change her 18
name?"

"Well, Norton was supposed to tell you about it. Nisi wants to in- 19
troduce you and then encourage the older folks to form a Council of the
Elders to act as an advisory—"

"And you going to be standing there with your boobs out and that 20
wig on your head and that hem up to your ass. And people'll say, 'Ain't
that the horny bitch that was grindin with the blind dude?' "

"Elo, be cool a minute," say Task, getting to the next finger. "And   21
then there's the drinkin. Mama, you know you can't drink cause next
thing you know you be laughin loud and carryin on," and he grab another finger for the loudness. "And then there's the dancin. You been
tattooed on the man for four records straight and slow draggin even on
the fast numbers. How you think that look for a woman your age?"

"What's my age?"   22

"What?"   23

"I'm axin you all a simple question. You keep talkin bout what's   24
proper for a woman my age. How old am I anyhow?" And Joe Lee slams
his eyes shut and squinches up his face to figure. And Task run a hand
over his ear and stare into his glass like the ice cubes goin calculate for
him. And Elo just starin at the top of my head like she goin rip the wig
off any minute now.

"Is your hair braided up under that thing? If so, why don't you take   25
it off? You always did do a neat cornroll."

"Uh huh," cause I'm think how she couldn't undo her hair fast   26
enough talking bout cornroll so countrified. None of which was the subject. "How old, I say?"

"Sixtee-one or—"   27

"You a damn lie Joe Lee Peoples."   28

"And that's another thing," say Task on the fingers.   29

"You know what you all can kiss," I say, getting up and brushin the   30
wrinkles out my lap.

"Oh, Mama," Elo say, puttin a hand on my shoulder like she hasn't   31
done since she left home and the hand landin light and not sure it supposed to be there. Which hurt me to my heart. Cause this was the child
in our happiness fore Mr. Peoples die. And I carried that child strapped
to my chest till she was nearly two. We was close is what I'm tryin to tell
you. Cause it was more me in the child than the others. And even after
Task it was the girl-child I covered in the night and wept over for no reason at all less it was she was a chub-chub like me and not very pretty,
but a warm child. And how did things get to this, that she can't put a
sure hand on me and say Mama we love you and care about you and
you entitled to enjoy yourself cause you a good woman?

"And then there's Reverend Trent," say Task, glancin from left to   32
right like they hatchin a plot and just now lettin me in on it. "You were
suppose to be talking with him tonight, Mama, about giving us his basement for campaign headquarters and—"

"Didn nobody tell me nuthin. If grassroots mean you kept in the   33
dark I can't use it. I really can't. And Reven Trent a fool anyway the way

he tore into the widow man up there on Edgecombe cause he wouldn't take in three of them foster children and the woman not even comfy in the ground yet and the man's mind messed up and—"

"Look here," say Task. "What we need is a family conference so we can get all this stuff cleared up and laid out on the table. In the meantime I think we better get back into the other room and tend to business. And in the meantime, Mama, see if you can't get to Reverend Trent and—"   34

"You want me to belly rub with the Reven, that it?"   35

"Oh damn," Elo say and go through the swingin door.   36

"We'll talk about all this at dinner. How's tomorrow night, Joe Lee?"   37

While Joe Lee being self-important I'm wonderin who's doing the cookin and how come nobody ax me if I'm free and do I get a corsage and things like that. Then Joe nod that it's O.K. and he go through the swingin door and just a little hubbub come through from the other room. Then Task smile his smile, lookin just like his daddy, and he leave. And it just me in this stranger's kitchen, which was a mess I wouldn't never let my kitchen look like. Poison you just to look at the pots. Then the door swing the other way and it's My Man Bovanne standin there saying Miss Hazel but lookin at the deep fry and then at the steam table, and most surprised when I come up on him from the other direction and take him on out of there. Pass the folks pushing up toward the stage where Nisi and some other people settin and ready to talk, and folks gettin to the last of the sandwiches and the booze fore they settle down in one spot and listen serious. And I'm thinkin bout tellin Bovanne what a lovely long dress Nisi got on and the earrings and her hair piled up in a cone and the people bout to hear how we all gettin screwed and gotta form our own party and everybody there listenin and lookin. But instead I just haul the man on out of there, and Joe Lee and his wife look at me like I'm terrible, but they ain't said boo to the man yet. Cause he blind and old and don't nobody there need him since they grown up and don't need they skates fixed no more.   38

"Where we goin, Miss Hazel?" Him knowin all the time.   39

"First we gonna buy you some dark sunglasses. Then you comin with me to the supermarket so I can pick up tomorrow's dinner, which is goin to be a grand thing proper and you invited. Then we going to my house."   40

"That be fine. I surely would like to rest my feet." Bein cute, but you got to let men play out they little show, blind or not. So he chat on bout how tired he is and how he appreciate me taking him in hand this way. And I'm thinkin I'll have him change the lock on my door first thing. Then I'll give the man a nice warm bath with jasmine leaves in the water   41 and a little Epsom salt on the sponge to do his back. And then a good rubdown with rosewater and olive oil. Then a cup of lemon tea with a taste in it. And a little talcum, some of that fancy stuff Nisi mother sent over last Christmas. And then a massage, a good face massage round the forehead which is the worryin part. Cause you gots to take care of the older folks. And let them know they still needed to run the mimeo machine and keep the spark plugs clean and fix the mailboxes for folks who might help us get the breakfast program goin, and the school for the little kids and the campaign and all. Cause old folks is the nation. That what Nisi was sayin and I mean to do my part.

"I imagine you are a very pretty woman, Miss Hazel."   41

"I surely am," I say just like the hussy my daughter always say I was.   42

RESPONDING TO "MY MAN BOVANNE"

Freewrite on your feelings about older people: How are they served by your community? How do they serve the community?

Responding through Interpretation

1. How would you characterize the narrator in the story? What is her attitude toward her children, toward Bovanne, and toward the other people in her community? Write a brief description of her in your reading notebook.

2. Discuss Bovanne's role in the community, both when he was young and now that he is older. In what ways have he and the community changed over the years?

3. Why don't the children want their mother "dancing so close" to Bovanne? In what ways do the children's and the narrator's responses suggest that both children and mother are going through a big transition in their lives?

Responding through Discussion

1. Discuss the generation gap portrayed in "My Man Bovanne." What does the story show about the relationships between parents and children, between young people and old? What are the main conflicts? Find specific references in the story that illustrate these conflicts. Which of these conflicts, reactions, attitudes, etc., are ones that group members have experienced?

2. With your group, reminisce about older relatives or family friends who influenced your thinking and values. What did you learn from each of them?

Responding through Writing

1. Bambara's story is rich in unusual similes and images, such as when she says her son Task gives "a tap on my elbow like he the third-grade monitor and I'm cuttin up on the line to assembly." Go through the story and write down several of the ones that you like the best. Then write a few of your own in a paragraph about a dance or social event.

2. The narrator says toward the end of the story: "Cause you gots to take care of the older folks. . . . Cause old folks is the nation." Write a paper in which you agree or disagree with such a statement. Back up your opinion with some facts that you can gather from outside reading. Do "old folks" contribute anything of value to others? If so, what?

Rootlessness

David Morris

David Morris has written two books, *Neighborhood Power: The New Lo-calism* (1975) and *The New City States* (1983). He helps direct the Insti-tute for Local Self-Reliance in Washington, D.C., writes editorials, and contributes to social issue-oriented periodicals. The following article, first published in the *Utne Review* in 1990, examines the deterioration of our sense of community and what can be done to restore a sense of "rooted-ness" in America's towns and cities.

Americans are a rootless people. Each year one in six of us changes   1
residences; one in four changes jobs. We see nothing troubling in these statistics. For most of us, they merely reflect the restless energy that made America great. A nation of immigrants, unsurprisingly, celebrates those willing to pick up stakes and move on: the frontiersman, the cowboy, the entrepreneur, the corporate raider.

Rootedness has never been a goal of public policy in the United   2
States. In the 1950s and 1960s local governments bulldozed hundreds of inner city neighborhoods, all in the name of urban renewal. In the 1960s and 1970s court-ordered busing forced tens of thousands of children to abandon their neighborhood schools, all in the interest of racial harmony. In the 1980s a wave of hostile takeovers shuffled hundreds of billions of dollars of corporate assets, all in the pursuit of economic efficiency.

Hundreds of thousands of informal gathering spots that once nur-   3
tured community across the country have disappeared. The soda foun-tain and lunch counter are gone. The branch library is an endangered species. Even the number of neighborhood taverns is declining. In the 1940s, 90 percent of beer and spirits was consumed in public places. Today only 30 percent is.

This privatization of American public life is most apparent to over-   4
seas visitors. "After four years here, I still feel more of a foreigner than in any other place in the world I have been," one well-traveled woman told Ray Oldenburg, the author of the marvelous new book about pub-lic gathering spots, *The Great Good Place* (1990, Paragon House). "There is no contact between the various households, we rarely see the neigh-bors and certainly do not know any of them."

The woman contrasts this with her life in Europe. "In Luxembourg,   5
however, we would frequently stroll down to one of the local cafés in the evening and there pass a very congenial few hours in the company

of the local fireman, dentist, bank employee, or whoever happened to be there at the time."

In most American cities, zoning laws prohibit mixing commerce 6
and residence. The result is an overreliance on the car. Oldenburg cites the experience of a couple who had lived in a small house in Vienna and a large one in Los Angeles: "In Los Angeles we are hesitant to leave our sheltered home in order to visit friends or to participate in cultural or entertainment events because every such outing involves a major investment of time and nervous strain in driving long distances. In Vienna everything, opera, theaters, shops, cafés, are within easy walking distance."

Shallow roots weaken our ties in the neighborhood and workplace. 7
The average blue-collar worker receives only seven days' notice before losing his or her job, only two days when not backed by a union. The *Whole Earth Review* unthinkingly echoes this lack of connectedness when it advises its readers to "first visit an electronics store near you and get familiar with the features—then compare price and shop mail order via [an] 800 number."

This lack of connectedness breeds a costly instability in American 8
life. In business, when owners have no loyalty to workers, workers have no loyalty to owners. Quality of work suffers. Visiting Japanese management specialists point to our labor turnover rate as a key factor in our relative economic decline. In the pivotal electronics industry, for example, our turnover rate is four times that of Japan's.

American employers respond to declining sales and profit margins 9
by cutting what they regard as their most expendable resource: employees. In Japan, corporate accounting systems consider labor a fixed asset. Japanese companies spend enormous amounts of money training workers. "They view that training as an investment, and they don't want to let the investment slip away," Martin K. Starr of Columbia University recently told *Business Week.* Twenty percent of the work force, the core workers in major industrial companies, have lifetime job security in Japan.

Rootlessness in the neighborhood also costs us dearly. Neighborli- 10
ness saves money, a fact we often overlook because the transactions of strong, rooted neighborhoods take place outside of the money economy.

- Neighborliness reduces crime. People watch the streets where children play and know who the strangers are.
- Neighborliness saves energy. In the late 1970s Portland, Oregon, discovered it could save 5 percent of its energy consumption simply by

reviving the corner grocery store. No longer would residents in need of a carton of milk or a loaf of bread have to drive to a shopping mall.

- Neighborliness lowers the cost of health care. "It is cruel and unusual punishment to send someone to a nursing home when they are not sick," says Dick Ladd, head of Oregon's Senior Services. But when we don't know our neighbors we can't rely on them. Society picks up the tab. In 1987 home-based care cost $230 a month in Oregon compared to $962 per month for nursing home care.

Psychoanalyst and author Erich Fromm saw a direct correlation between the decline in the number of neighborhood bartenders and the rise in the number of psychiatrists. "Sometimes you want to go where everybody knows your name," goes the apt refrain of the popular TV show *Cheers*. Once you poured out your troubles over a nickel beer to someone who knew you and your family. And if you got drunk, well, you could walk home. Now you drive cross town and pay $100 an hour to a stranger for emotional relief.   11

The breakdown of community life may explain, in part, why the three best-selling drugs in America treat stress: ulcer medication (Tagamet), hypertension (Inderal), tranquilizer (Valium).   12

American society has evolved into a cultural environment where it is ever harder for deep roots to take hold. What can we do to change this?   13

- *Rebuild walking communities.* Teach urban planners that overdependence on transportation is a sign of failure in a social system. Impose the true costs of the car on its owners. Recent studies indicate that to do so would raise the cost of gasoline by as much as $2 a gallon. Recently Stockholm declared war on cars by imposing a $50 a month fee for car owners, promising to increase the fee until the city was given back to pedestrians and mass transit.
- *Equip every neighborhood with a library, a coffeehouse, a diversified shopping district, and a park.*
- *Make rootedness a goal of public policy.* In the 1970s a Vermont land use law, for example, required an economic component to environmental impact statements. In at least one case, a suburban shopping mall was denied approval because it would undermine existing city businesses. In Berkeley, citizens voted two to one to permit commercial rent control in neighborhoods whose independently owned businesses were threatened by gentrification.
- *Reward stability and continuity.* Today, if a government seizes property it pays the owner the market price. Identical homes have iden-

tical value, even if one is home to a third-generation family, while the other is occupied by a new tenant. Why not pay a premium, say 50 percent above the current market price, for every 10 years the occupant has lived there? Forty years of residence would be rewarded with compensation four times greater than the market price. The increment above the market price should go not to the owner but to the occupant, if the two are not the same. By favoring occupants over owners, this policy not only rewards neighborliness, but promotes social justice. By raising the overall costs of dislocation, it also discourages development that undermines rootedness.

- *Prohibit hostile takeovers.* Japanese, German, and Swedish corporations are among the most competitive and innovative in the world. But in these countries hostile takeovers are considered unethical business practices or are outlawed entirely.
- *Encourage local and employee ownership.* Protecting existing management is not the answer if that management is not locally rooted. Very few cities have an ongoing economic campaign to promote local ownership despite the obvious advantages to the community. Employee ownership exists in some form in more than 5,000 U.S. companies, but in only a handful is that ownership significant.
- *And above all, correct our history books.* America did not become a wealthy nation because of rootlessness, but in spite of it. A multitude of natural resources across an expansive continent and the arrival of tens of millions of skilled immigrants furnished us enormous advantages. We could overlook the high social costs of rootlessness. This is no longer true.

Instability is not the price we must pay for progress. Loyalty, in the plant   14
and the neighborhood, does not stifle innovation. These are lessons we've ignored too long. More rooted cultures such as Japan and Germany are now outcompeting us in the marketplace, and in the neighborhood. We would do well to learn the value of community.

RESPONDING TO "ROOTLESSNESS"

Freewrite about how well you know your neighbors.

Responding through Interpretation

1. According to Morris, what are the negative results of being "a nation of immigrants"?
2. What historical choices has the United States made that have destroyed neighborhoods and created rootlessness?

3. Look at Morris's opening sentence and his closing sentence. The first presents a problem; the last gives a solution to the problem. Now look at how Morris has developed his essay between those two ideas. Is he clear and convincing in his presentation? Why or why not?

Responding through Discussion

1. Discuss the respective neighborhoods of each group member and compare notes on how it used to be and how it is now. What has disappeared? What has been added? Are there any signs of revitalization, or what Morris calls "new rootedness"?
2. As a group project, go out into the community surrounding the college campus and make notes on what you see. Then take a look at the campus itself and make notes. Come back to the classroom and share the information you got from your observations. Did you find any signs of rootlessness? Any signs of rootedness?

Responding through Writing

1. Write a critique in your journal of Morris's suggestions for improving communities. Indicate which suggestions you feel are workable and which ones are unrealistic or even counterproductive. Include some suggestions of your own.
2. Study your own neighborhood and interview some inhabitants for signs of rootlessness or rootedness. Write an essay about your neighborhood—how it used to be; how it is now. Give specific changes you've observed and interpret what you think these changes mean.

Cohousing and the American Dream

Kathryn McCamant and Charles Durrett

McCamant and Durrett are architects who have worked in the area of community development. After observing in Europe small, community-
oriented cohousing projects that feature a shared common area, they participated in and currently live in a similar project in northern California.
They are the founders of the Cohousing Company, which designs and con-
sults in the development of cohousing projects. The following selection is
taken from their book, *Cohousing* (1988).

Traditional housing no longer addresses the needs of many people.   1
Dramatic demographic and economic changes are taking place in our
society, and most of us feel the effects of these trends in our lives. Things
that people once took for granted—family, community, a sense of
belonging—must now be actively sought out. Many people are mis-
housed, ill-housed, or unhoused because of the lack of appropriate
options. This article introduces a new housing model that addresses
such changes. Pioneered primarily in Denmark and now being adapted
in other countries, the cohousing concept reestablishes many of the
advantages of traditional villages within the context of late twentieth-
century life.

Several years ago, as a young married couple, we began to think   2
about where we were going to raise our children. What kind of setting
would allow us to best combine our professional careers with child rear-
ing? Already our lives were hectic. Often we would come home from
work exhausted and hungry, only to find the refrigerator empty. Between our jobs and housekeeping, when would we find the time to
spend with our kids? Relatives lived in distant cities, and even our
friends lived across town. Just to get together for coffee we had to make
arrangements two weeks in advance. Most young parents we knew
seemed to spend most of their time shuttling their children to and from
day care and playmates' homes, leaving little opportunity for anything
else.

So many people we knew seemed to be living in places that did not   3
accommodate their most basic needs; they always had to drive somewhere to do anything sociable. We dreamed of a better solution: an affordable neighborhood where children would have playmates and we
would have friends nearby; a place with people of all ages, young and
old, where neighbors knew and helped each other.

As architects, we had both designed different types of housing. We had been amazed at the conservatism of most architects and housing professionals, and at the lack of consideration given to people's changing personal needs. Single-family houses, apartments, and condominiums might change in price and occasionally in style, but otherwise they were designed to function pretty much as they had for the last 40 years. Perhaps our own frustrations were indicative of a larger problem: a diverse population attempting to fit into housing that is simply no longer appropriate for them.

Contemporary post-industrial societies such as the United States and Western Europe are undergoing a multitude of changes that affect our housing needs. The modern single-family detached home, which makes up 67 percent of American housing, was designed for a nuclear family consisting of a breadwinning father, a homemaking mother, and two to four children. Today, less than one-quarter of the United States population lives in such households. Rather, the family with two working parents predominates, while the single-parent household is the fastest growing family type. Almost one-quarter of the population lives alone, and this proportion is predicted to grow as the number of Americans over the age of 60 increases. At the same time, the surge in housing costs and the increasing mobility of the population combine to break down traditional community ties and place more demands on individual households. These factors call for a thorough reexamination of household and community needs, and the way we house ourselves.

As we searched for more desirable living situations, we kept thinking about the housing developments we had visited while studying architecture in Denmark several years earlier.

In Denmark, people frustrated by the available housing options developed a new kind of housing that redefine the concept of neighborhood to fit contemporary life-styles. Tired of the isolation and impracticalities of single-family houses and apartment units, they built or developed out of existing neighborhoods new housing that combines the autonomy of private dwellings with the advantages of community living. Each household has a private residence, but also shares extensive common facilities with the larger group, such as a kitchen and dining hall, children's playrooms, workshops, guest rooms, and a laundry. Although individual dwellings are designed to function independently and each has its own kitchen, the common facilities, and particularly common dinners, are an important aspect of community life.

As of last year, 67 of these communities had been built in Denmark, and another 38 were planned. They range in size from six to 80 households, with the majority between 15 and 33 residences. These communities are called *bofoellesskaber* in Danish ("living communities"), for which we have coined the term "cohousing." First built in the early 1970s, cohousing developments have quadrupled in number in the last five years. The Netherlands now features 30 cohousing communities and similar projects are being built in Sweden, France, Norway, and Germany.

Imagine . . . It's five o'clock in the evening, and Anne is glad the 9 workday is over. As she pulls into her driveway, she begins to unwind at last. Some neighborhood kids dart through the trees, playing a mysterious game at the edge of the gravel parking lot. Her daughter yells, "Hi Mom!" as she runs by with three other children.

Instead of frantically trying to put together a nutritious dinner, Anne 10 can relax now, spend some time with her children, and then eat with her family in the common house. Walking through the common house on her way home, she stops to chat with the evening's cooks, two of her neighbors, who are busy preparing dinner—broiled chicken with mushroom sauce—in the kitchen. Several children are setting the tables. Outside on the patio, some neighbors share a pot of tea in the late afternoon sun. Anne waves hello and continues down the lane to her own house.

After dropping off her things at home, Anne walks through the 11 birch trees behind the houses to the child-care center where she picks up her four-year-old son, Peter. She will have some time to read Peter a story before dinner, she thinks to herself.

Anne and her husband, Eric, live with their two children in a hous- 12 ing development they helped design. Not that either of them is an architect or builder: Anne works at the county administration office, and Eric is an engineer. Six years ago they joined a group of families who were looking for a realistic housing alternative. At that time, they owned their own home, had a three-year-old daughter, and were contemplating having another child—partly so that their daughter would have a playmate in their predominantly adult neighborhood.

Responding to a newspaper ad, Anne and Eric discovered a group 13 of people who expressed similar frustrations about their existing housing situations. The group's goal was to build a housing development with a lively and positive social environment.

In the months that followed, the group further defined its goals and 14 began the long, difficult process of turning its dream into reality. Some people dropped out, and others joined. Two and a half years later, Anne and Eric moved into their new home—a community of clustered houses that share a large common house. By working together, these people had created the kind of neighborhood they wanted to live in—a cohousing community.

Today Tina, Anne and Eric's eight-year-old daughter, never lacks   15
for playmates. She walks home from school with the other kids in the
community. Her mother is usually at work, so Tina goes up to the common house, where one of the adults makes tea and toast for the kids and
any adults who are around. Tina liked her family's old house, but this
place is much more interesting. There's so much to do; she can play outside all day, and, as long as she doesn't leave the community, her mother
doesn't worry about her.

John and Karen moved into the same community a few years after   16
it was built. Their kids were grown and had left home. Now they enjoy
the peacefulness of having a house to themselves; they have time to take
classes in the evenings, visit art museums, and attend an occasional play
in town. John teaches children with learning disabilities and plans to retire in a few years. Karen administers a senior citizens' housing complex
and nursing home. They lead full and active lives, but worry about getting older. How long will their health hold out? Will one die, leaving the
other alone? Such considerations, combined with the desire to be part
of an active community while maintaining their independence, led John
and Karen to buy a one-bedroom home in this community. Here they
feel secure knowing their neighbors care about them. If John gets sick,
people will be there to help Karen with the groceries or join her at the
theater. Common dinners relieve them of preparing a meal every night,
and their children and grandchildren can stay in the community's guest
rooms when they visit. John and Karen enjoy a house with no children,
but it's still refreshing to see kids playing outside.

Cohousing is a grass-roots movement that grew directly out of peo-   17
ple's dissatisfaction with existing housing choices. Its initiators draw inspiration from the increasing popularity of shared households, in which
several unrelated people share a house, and from the cooperative movement in general. Yet cohousing is distinctive in that each family or household has a separate dwelling and chooses how much they want to participate in community activities.

Cohousing also differs from most of the communes and intentional   18
communities we know in the United States, which are often organized
around strong ideological beliefs and may depend on a charismatic
leader to establish the direction of the community and hold the group
together. Based on democratic principles, cohousing developments es-
pouse no ideology other than the desire for a more practical and social
home environment. Cohousing communities are organized, planned,
and managed by their residents. The great variety in community size,
ownership structure, and design illustrates the many diverse applications of the concept.

In many respects, cohousing is not a new idea. In the past, most people lived in villages or tightly knit urban neighborhoods. Even today, people in less industrialized regions typically live in small communities. Members of such communities know one another for many years; they are familiar with one another's families and histories, talents and weaknesses. This kind of relationship demands accountability, but in return provides security and a sense of belonging. 19

In previous centuries, households were made up of at least six people. In addition to having many children, families often shared their homes with farmhands, servants, boarders, and relatives. A typical household might include a family with four children, a grandmother or an uncle, and one or more boarders who might also work in the family business. Relatives usually lived nearby. These large households provided both children and adults with a diverse intergenerational network of relationships in the home environment. The idea that the nuclear family should live on its own without the support and assistance of the extended family or surrounding community is relatively new, even in the United States. 20

To expect that today's small households, as likely to be single parents or single adults as nuclear families, should be self-sufficient and without community support is not only unrealistic but absurd. Each household is expected to prepare its own meals, do its own shopping, and so far as finances permit, own a vacuum cleaner, washing machine, clothes dryer, and other household implements, regardless of whether the household consists of two people or six, and whether there is a full-time homemaker or not. 21

People need community at least as much as they need privacy. We must reestablish ways compatible with contemporary American lifestyles to accommodate this need. Cohousing offers a new model for recreating a sense of place and neighborhood, while responding to today's needs for a less constraining environment. 22

RESPONDING TO "COHOUSING AND THE AMERICAN DREAM"

Freewrite about the kind of housing you grew up in. Did you enjoy a sense of community in your neighborhood?

Responding through Interpretation

1. What changes have taken place in society that make traditional housing inadequate for people today?

2. According to the authors, how is cohousing similar to village life or other kinds of earlier, closely knit communities? How do the authors describe the typical, larger households of the past?
3. What kinds of evidence and examples do the authors use based on their own personal experiences with cohousing? Did their examples seem convincing to you? Explain why or why not.

Responding through Discussion

1. Discuss the ideas in cohousing among your group. What do different members know about cohousing? Does it sound attractive to you as a way of life? Does it sound boring? Too idyllic? How convinced were you of the authors' point of view?
2. Have group members go out individually and investigate alternative types of housing that exist in their community—including shared housing, communal housing, religious communities, etc. Interview residents, if possible. How successful do these alternative homes seem to be? Share your findings with the group at first and later with the class as a whole.

Responding through Writing

1. The authors begin their closing paragraph with the statement: "People need community at least as much as they need privacy." Write a journal entry in which you respond to this statement.
2. Write a paper that evaluates the typical kinds of housing in your community—either the one you grew up in or the one you live in now. Which aspects of the housing in your community seem to work to build a sense of neighborhood and friendly sharing? Which aspects seem to work against a sense of neighborhood?

Trouble in Privatopia

Evan McKenzie

A professor of political science at Albright College in Pennsylvania, Evan McKenzie has written a book, *Privatopia: Homeowner Associations and the Rise of Residential Private Government* (1994), about the ways that private associations are beginning to replace the more public and diverse forms of government and community found in towns and cities. The following article, which appeared in the *Progressive* in October 1993, deals with the subject of his book.

A fifty-one-year-old grandmother in Santa Ana, California, received a   1
citation from her condominium association for allegedly violating one of the association's rules. The charged offense? "Kissing and doing bad things" while parked one night in the circular driveway. She acknowledged kissing a friend good night, but retained an attorney and threatened legal action. "Somebody, or a group, has decided to invade my privacy," an Associated Press story quoted her as saying. "And it just doesn't feel right to say, 'Let them get away with it.' "

Near Philadelphia, a homeowner paid a landscape architect to de-   2
sign and build a black fabric fence in his backyard to prevent his infant son from falling down a 400-foot slope at the rear edge of his lot. His homeowner association took him to court for violating a rule against fences. The owner fought back and won, saying, according to the *Philadelphia Inquirer*, "By God, when you have a 400-foot cliff, you need a fence."

These stories and many more like them are not just isolated neigh-   3
borhood conflicts: they are examples of life at the cutting edge of a new civic culture. They represent business as usual in walled, private, urban and suburban enclaves called common-interest housing developments (CIDs). For some, CID living means having to fight to defend a semblance of privacy and personal freedom, while the few residents who enforce the rules enjoy a degree of personal power over their neighbors that the Constitution denies to public officials.

Over the last thirty years, an alternative to the city has risen to   4
prominence in most rapidly growing areas. Since the early 1960s, large-scale "community builders" have constructed 150,000 common-interest housing developments, designed for hundreds or even hundreds of thousands of inhabitants.

CID housing is profitable because it allows builders to squeeze more   5
people onto less land and makes housing a mass-produced commodity.
Buyers and public officials are more likely to accept small individual lots,
narrow streets, and higher density if the development contains open
spaces and other facilities owned in common by all residents and maintained by a homeowner association.

Today, these developments house an estimated thirty million peo-   6
ple, or almost one-eighth of the U.S. population. In many parts of the
country, including much of the Sun Belt, nearly all new housing units
are some form of CID.

The rapid spread of CID housing is the largest and most dramatic   7
privatization of local government functions in American history. CID
residents pay monthly assessments to a homeowner association that
provides exclusive services. Within their gates and walls, CID dwellers
are protected by their own private security guards. They drive on streets
that are privately lit, cleaned, and maintained. Their swimming pools,
gyms, parks, and golf courses are private. Many CIDs also have exclusive access to shopping centers and even their own schools.

City officials who grant building permits are tempted by this private   8
infrastructure because it adds taxpayers at minimal public cost. However, this perspective may be shortsighted. With little notice or debate,
CID housing has begun to undermine the basic assumptions of urban
culture and establish a competing regime.

Millions of affluent homeowners are encouraged to secede from   9
urban America, with its endless flux and ferment, its spontaneity and
diversity and its unpredictable rewards and hazards. They are beckoned
to a privatized, artificial, utopian environment I call "Privatopia," where
master-planning, homogeneous populations, and private governments
offer the affluent a chance to escape from urban reality.

But those who opt for the good life in Privatopia pay for their ameni-   10
ties in more ways than their monthly assessments. The price of a ticket
to this Fantasyland includes a substantial loss of freedom and privacy.
CID residents live under the rule of their corporate board of directors,
an elected group of neighbors enforcing a set of restrictions created by
the developer to ensure that his master plan will never be altered.

These private governments operate outside the constitutional lim-   11
its that bind local authorities because CID activities are not "state action."
Moreover, courts often accept the legal fiction that CID restrictions are
private, voluntary arrangements among individuals. In truth, they are
non-negotiable boilerplate, drafted by the developer's lawyers and imposed on all residents.

In Rancho Bernardo, a large California development, there was a   12
restriction stating that "no truck, camper, trailer, boat, or any kind or
other form of recreational vehicle shall be parked" on the project. One
of the residents bought a new pickup truck with a camper shell, which
he used for personal transportation. The association took him to court
to prevent him from parking it under his own carport and to recover
$2,060 in fines it had assessed against him for this "violation." After
losing in the trial court, the management company appealed, only to
see the appellate court side with the resident and hold the company's
action unreasonable.

Yet this sort of action does not seem unreasonable to many CID res-   13
idents, particularly those who serve on boards of directors. They believe
the restrictions are good for property values, and feel that losing some
of your own freedom is a small price to pay for protection from the potential misdeeds of your neighbors. Richard Louv, in *America II,* quotes
one Rancho Barnardo resident as saying, "Sure, they have some rules,
like the one that regulates campers. But the community associations are
here to protect our interests, not let the community deteriorate. That's
not regulation; it's common sense. I don't know why anyone would
look at it differently than I do, do you?"

To answer that question, consider these examples of CID activities,   14
all reported in the press:

- Some community associations have banned display of the Ameri-   15
  can flag and political signs, prohibited distribution of newspapers,
  and barred political gatherings in the common areas.
- In Ashland, Massachusetts, a Vietnam veteran was told that he could   16
  not fly the American flag on Flag Day. The board backed down only
  after he called the press and the story appeared on the front page of
  a local newspaper.
- In Monroe, New Jersey, a homeowners association took a married   17
  couple to court because the wife, at age forty-five, was three years
  younger than the association's age-forty-eight minimum for resi-
  dency. The association won in the trial court. The judge ordered the
  sixty-year-old husband to sell, rent the unit, or live without his wife.
- In Fairbanks Ranch, an affluent CID in Southern California, behind   18
  six locked gates, there are forty-five private streets patrolled by private security officers who enforce a private speed limit. First-time
  speeders get a warning; the second offense brings a hearing before
  the board and a reprimand; a third offense means a $500 fine, and
  the car and driver are banned from the private streets for a month.

- In Vista, California, a homeowner whose income dropped because 19
  of a lost job and a divorce temporarily fell behind in paying her
  monthly association dues. The association obtained a lien on her
  property for the $192.04 in dues, plus attorneys' fees and costs. She
  resumed paying the dues on time, but when she disputed the
  amount of fees, late charges, and costs (which eventually brought
  the lien to $857.13), the association served her with a foreclosure
  summons. In desperation, the homeowner got an advance on a
  credit card and paid the full amount, but said, "To think that for a
  few dollars, they can come in and take your house out from under
  you—I can't believe it."
- In Fort Lauderdale, Florida, condominium managers ordered a cou- 20
  ple to stop entering and leaving their unit through their back door,
  claiming that they were wearing an unsightly path in the lawn by
  taking a short cut to the parking lot. The couple retained an attorney, who filed a lawsuit seeking a court's permission for the couple
  to use their own back door.
- In Boca Raton, Florida, an association took a homeowner to court for 21
  having a dog weighing more than thirty pounds, in violation of association rules. A court-ordered weighing ceremony was inconclu-
  sive, with the scales hovering around the thirty-pound mark. The
  association persisted with the suit nonetheless—willing to pay an
  attorney and use the courts to exclude a dog from the development
  for being even an ounce over the limit.
- In Bucks County, Pennsylvania, a woman bought a twenty-two- 22
  room stone farmhouse in 1980. Six years later, a CID was completed
  next to her property and a homeowner association was formed. In
  1988, a CID resident reviewed the plans for the development and
  discovered that the farmhouse was within the borders of the CID.
  The association began assessing the woman for membership dues
  and contended that she had to live by the association's rules. She refused, and the association sued her. A judge ordered her to pay
  $2,000 in fees and late charges. When she still refused to pay, the as-
  sociation obtained a lien on her house and scheduled a sheriff's sale
  at which it attempted to sell two of her cars and a lawn mower. When
  there were no takers, the association had to pay towing fees for the
  cars.
- Near Philadelphia is a development of $225,000 homes begun in the 23
  late 1980s. A family bought one in 1989, and brought their sons'
  metal swing set with them. One year later, the association told them
  to take it down, even though there were as yet no written rules re-

garding swing sets. When the rules finally appeared, they prescribed that all swing sets must be made of wood. Why? "It has to
do with what the overall community should look like," said an attorney for the association. The family then submitted a petition
from three-fourths of the homeowners supporting their swing set,
along with data from the Environmental Protection Agency warning against the danger to children (theirs were aged two and four)
from the poisonous chemicals used in pressure-treated wood, such
as that needed for outdoor swing sets. The association's response
was to impose a daily fine of ten dollars until the set was removed,
and to refuse offers to compromise, such as by painting the swing
set in earth tones.

For those who live outside CIDs in America's beleaguered cities, the   24
rapid spread of CIDs threatens to transform urban culture in ways some
find deeply disturbing. This "secession of the successful," as Robert
Reich calls it, deprives urban America of a vast amount of human and
economic resources. It promotes a two-class society of haves and have-
nots, the former enjoying a privatized set of what were formerly public
services, and the latter struggling to survive in cities faced with increasing responsibilities and shriveling revenues.

The city, Lewis Mumford tells us, is "a structure specially equipped   25
to store and transmit the goods of civilization." Cities are dense con-
centrations of a society's population, wealth and power—assets which,
for 6,000 years, have enabled cities to create, reflect, amplify, and communicate whatever a society has to offer the world.

Conservative scholar Charles Murray views CIDs as symbols of an   26
emerging caste society in which the affluent, freed from dependency on
public institutions, may come to regard cities as "an urban analog of the
Indian reservation"—places of deprivation and dysfunction for which
they feel no responsibility.

Urban theorist Mike Davis, in *City of Quartz*, paints the picture of a   27
privatized Los Angeles, architecturally redesigned to physically separate the two classes and protect the rich from the rest. He saw in this separation the potential for "approaching Helter-Skelter," even before 1992
brought the most intense urban riot in American history.

CIDs are, in a sense, a privatized, master-planned version of the   28
village-centered life that our species led for millennia, and that many romanticize today. For the rest of us, CIDs may speed the decline of cities
as centers of cultural, political, and economic power. Cities may come
to resemble the future Los Angeles of *Blade Runner*—desperate holding

pens, struggling to provide mere physical security and unable to afford other social services to all.

Ebenezer Howard, the Nineteenth Century English utopian whose vision of a master-planned "Garden City" launched the CID idea, was explicit about his intentions: "London must die," he wrote, "and a new city rise on the ashes of the old." 29

It is time to ask whether corporate builders should be allowed to continue spreading CIDs across the country, guided only by the calculus of private profit, or whether we should have an open, public discussion of the consequences—before the metropolis becomes a necropolis. 30

RESPONDING TO "TROUBLE IN PRIVATOPIA"

Freewrite: What is your opinion of common-interest housing developments (CIDs)? Do you feel they should be stopped or encouraged?

Responding through Interpretation

1. According to McKenzie, how do CIDs operate outside "constitutional limits" of ordinary governments?
2. What are some of the ways, as reported by McKenzie, that homeowners associations infringe on the liberties of individuals? McKenzie also provides a number of cases of suits and fines levied by homeowners associations. Which cases were most impressive to you?
3. In your reading journal, write down your interpretation of what McKenzie and others see as the biggest threats that CIDs pose to the rest of society. Do you agree or disagree with them?

Responding through Discussion

1. Discuss McKenzie's article with your group. What did you already know about "privatopias"? What did you learn about them? What are the pros and cons of privatopias? How effective was McKenzie in persuading you of his opinions?
2. McKenzie cites one critic as calling CIDS a "secession of the successful" and goes on to say that this "promotes a two-class society of haves and have-nots." Discuss this idea in your group. Then have the group brainstorm about some of the ways that CIDs could be less harmful to the cities they are close to.

Responding through Writing

1. Write a journal entry explaining what you think might be some of the positive benefits of living in a planned community based on the idea of

the old village. Or you can compare living in a city with living in a small town.

2. Do some further reading on privatopias. Consider such ideas as: Should the local and/or federal governments be involved in any way? Should there be more control over when, where, and how they are built? What impact do privatopias have on the rest of the population? Write a paper giving your opinion about privatopias and take a position on whether or not you think they should continue to be built. Use specific details and examples to support your point of view.

Whatever Happened to the Neighborhood?

Cecilia Fairley

Cecilia Fairley was born in northern California and grew up traveling extensively with her family. At the time she wrote the following essay for her English composition class, she was living in San Francisco, working as a nanny and doing part-time work at a research lab while majoring in neurobiology. In the following paper, Cecilia Fairley compares three different options for change in the community presented in this chapter, and presents her own suggestions for solutions.

Whatever happened to the villages of yesteryear? Where have all the public meetingplaces gone: the soda fountains, the local branch of public libraries, the neighborhood pub? Where has the sense of community gone or the extended family with neighbors and friends as honorary members? Whatever happened to knowing the business of the guy next door and the family next door to him? So much has changed from what is considered traditional American society that the existence of these things today is more rare than common. In the essays "Rootlessness," "Privatopia," and "Cohousing and the American Dream," the authors present three different views of America's current lack of a sense of community and what can be done to improve it.

According to David Morris in "Rootlessness," one in four Americans change jobs and one in six change homes every year. There is no sense of establishing yourself or making any type of connection to people around you. People move on without leaving traces of themselves behind, while new occupants find it difficult to meet anyone in the neighborhood when moving in. With no public meetingplaces such as the local bar, the family diner, or even a little supermarket on the corner, there's no indirect way to meet neighbors. Going door to door to announce your presence seems too forward for most people, so usually you may smile and greet your next-door neighbors without ever getting to know them.

A strong sense of community is necessary for many reasons. First, there's a basic level of surety in neighbors checking up on and looking out for each other, because without this, there's no sense of safety, no sense of common good. For example, would your neighbor call the police if an unscheduled moving van came to your apartment and started loading up the contents? How would they know your plans if you never really spoke to them? This lack of security becomes more obvious when considering the elderly living alone without a support system. If senior citizen neighbors hadn't been seen for a couple of days, would you think to look in on them to see that they were okay? In times past, society tended to look out more for the elderly and lend them a helping hand. Nowadays, however, old folks are simply ignored in most neighborhoods. Finally, with the fading out of public meetingplaces, no longer is there anything to do within walking distance of most residences. Friends, entertainment, or perhaps even your child's school can be located across town via a long car trip. This contrasts directly with European countries that have extensive local socializing at cafes and pubs. This distancing in America creates a sense of the neighborhood as a place of seclusion from the world, not as a place to take comfort in the people living around you.   4

In a small community, everyone knows everyone else's business, and this too is mainly how a village functions. In contrast, this occurs less often in today's more complicated world, in spite of a much greater population density. Yet many Americans are now nostalgic for the village life of the past and have made moves to recapture it. One large and fast-growing housing movement that would seem to be designed to wall out a disintegrating public community and to create a village-like private living environment is the CID (common-interest housing development). According to Evan McKenzie in "Trouble in Privatopia," CIDs are "walled, private, urban and suburban enclaves" where residents pay monthly assessment fees to a homeowner association for specific services: security guards, privately lit, cleaned and unkept streets, and often access to private swimming pools, gyms, and private parks. Although many residents are annoyed about the tendency of CID owner associations to overregulate and snoop into residents' private lives, most residents seem to feel that the rules are good for property values by protecting you from your neighbors. The subsequent loss of privacy and trust among residents seems not to greatly concern most people who live in CIDs.

Another not so obvious problem with CIDs is that there is a segregation of social classes since only the relatively wealthy can afford such exclusiveness. CIDs separate and insulate the upper class from problems outside and thus reduce any sense of civic responsibility. Furthermore, these communities aren't necessarily located near jobs, friends, and schools, so a good deal of time still wouldn't be spent at home. CID's would seem to offer little to create a renewed sense of community in our larger towns and cities.

Another alternative to the insufficiency of modern-day neighborhoods is a concept explored in "Cohousing and the American Dream"   6 by Kathryn McCamant and Charles Durrett. It is based upon a housing movement originating in Denmark called cohousing. Here a neighborhood is specifically designed by the residents. Each family has a private dwelling but shares extensive common facilities with the other residents such as kitchens and dining halls (including the chore of cooking for the entire group), playrooms for kids, guest rooms for visiting family and friends, a laundry, and various workshops. Each separate household has its own kitchen and appliances and therefore can function independently. This allows community sharing to not be a strict requirement. Yet due to the common space and chores, ultimately there is constant social interaction. These communities contain on average 14 to 33 separate households and individuals of a wide range of ages, from infants to senior citizens.

Cohousing offers many advantages for residents. Often it would be unnecessary to cook dinner when coming home from work because there would be shared meals made by assigned cooks. Children would probably have many playmates, and any adults who weren't working could keep an eye on them. Elderly people who require no medical care also could live here and would have company and people around to help out on days when they need it, thus providing an inexpensive alternative to a nursing home. In addition, with the inclusion of guest rooms in a common building, residents can provide sleeping arrangements for guests and family visits. With people constantly around, there would always be someone to interact with if you choose or you could retreat to the serenity of your own private domicile. 7

The disadvantages to such a lifestyle weren't discussed in the article, but the main problem would obviously be one of cooperation. With such a large group, things need to be organized and managed or chaos would ensue and all of the advantages of this lifestyle would be lost. To run more than one household would be similar to running a business, both in ensuring a completion of tasks and in a financial aspect. A committee would have to be formed in order to maintain such extensive common areas and the large number of households mentioned in the article. It would be in charge of apportioning tasks and in making sure of their completion, thus being very powerful in this community. To live in a society like this would be similar to having another job, unless the community paid someone to take care of these things. 8

Another disadvantage of this type of society is the lack of privacy. You would be offered companionship, and could retreat to your own home any time you needed to get away, but inevitably you are going to have to take part and do your duty in this type of a society. No doubt personality conflicts would occur. Also, living under the scrutiny of a 9

housing committee would be similar to living by the restrictions of the
homeowner's association's rules that MacKenzie describes in "Privatopia."

It is obvious after reading all three of these essays that the manner   10
in which most Americans live and the housing options that are available
to them today are inadequate for anyone's needs. On a large scale, people have lost all sense of a neighborhood or community fellowship in-
spite of being surrounded on all sides with other people. At closer perspective, most of the housing we have now was built originally for the
needs of the nuclear family which is now in the minority. Living isolated,
families experience a loss of security, of feeling safe and connected to the
place they live. Few people actually know their neighbors at all, and most
people remain only temporarily in any one area.

As for the solutions presented, to hide behind a walled, strictly ruled   11
community and to separate yourself from the real world hardly seems
a viable solution, although such separation occurs in CIDs and, to a
lesser extent, in cohousing. In the end, none of the needs mentioned
above would be met. Yet neither of these ideas should be discarded out
of hand in that they solve some problems and more importantly, they
bring attention to the fact that there is a real problem with housing and
a lack of neighborhoods. The best decision would be to then go a step
beyond and take into account problems they blatantly dismiss.

First and foremost, the solution is not to separate yourself from so-   12
ciety's problems, but rather to look for and implement feasible alternatives. A good way to start would be to create "walking communities" as
defined by David Morris in "Rootlessness." The idea is to plan neighborhoods to be self-sufficient and independent of auto transportation,
to make public services accessible to the public, and to build local cafes,
libraries, shopping districts, and parks that would be at furthest a short
trip on public transit away. Further, it is important to implement government policy to stop the destruction of neighborhoods by taking into
account the possible negative effects of mass commercialization and rebuilding. In addition, the government should give tax breaks and other
incentives to local businesses, especially those owned by residents of the
area.

All of this seems very practical and straightforward, but the prob-   13
lem with this or any other possible solution is a lack of funds. Where
would local government get this kind of money, especially if the neighborhood is poor to start with? There would have to be a substantial increase in taxes, and this might very well drive away people from a neighborhood that was in trouble already. And to lower taxes as a business

incentive wouldn't really solve the problem because this would draw investors from outside the neighborhood, allowing no local connection. In the end, the answer seems to be implementing as many neighborhood-strengthening policies as is financially feasible, trying to take into account the advantages offered by CIDs and cohousing: safety, public meetingplaces, a sense of community, and a place to belong.

In the end, it is obvious that with the space of America, and even the world, getting smaller every day, people need to interact and cooperate more with each other. Otherwise, all of the problems mentioned by the writers discussed above will become intensified, and we may lose our sense of community altogether. ₁₄

RESPONDING TO "WHATEVER HAPPENED TO THE NEIGHBORHOOD?"

Freewrite about the qualities you think make for a strong and enjoyable neighborhood or community.

Responding through Interpretation

1. What solutions does Fairley offer to regain a sense of neighborhood? What does she see as the biggest barrier to rebuilding our neighborhoods?
2. Study Fairley's introduction and conclusion. How strong do you find these two paragraphs? Do they serve to unify her essay? What advice could you give Fairley on improving her introduction and conclusion?

Responding through Discussion

1. With your group, reminisce about places that used to be part of your neighborhood but have now either disappeared or been replaced with something else. What did these places provide for you and your family and friends? Make a list of all the places you discuss and share them with the class as a whole.

Responding through Writing

1. In your journal, write a scene that you remember which took place in one of your neighborhood hangouts when you were young. Close your eyes and remember as many physical details about the place as you can and include some descriptions of it.
2. If you could design your ideal neighborhood, what would it be like? Write a paper in which you describe it in detail (include a drawing if you like); then explain how you think this neighborhood could actually be achieved. What would it take to build such a neighborhood?

Modern America: Metropolis or Necropolis?

Kimberly Curtis

A resident of Alameda, California, Kimberly Curtis is interested in the environmental movement, the natural sciences, and theology. Currently working toward a degree in education, she would like to teach children. In the following essay, Curtis compares and evaluates three essays on community, "Cohousing," "Privatopia," and "Rootlessness." Notice how Curtis tries to define *community*, paraphrases the articles, compares them, discovers both strong and weak points in each writer's perspective, and presents her own views on the subject.

American society is facing unprecedented challenges. The industrial   1
revolution has changed forever the meanings of *home* and *community*,
words that once conjured up images of family, food, fire, and fellowship.
"Trouble in Privatopia" by Evan McKenzie, "Rootlessness" by David
Morris, and "Cohousing and the American Dream" by Kathryn
McCamant and Charles Durrett all present different ideas about home
and community, examining the loss of community in our modern era
and exploring various models of alternative housing designed to
promote community restoration.

    To evaluate the problems and solutions put forth in these essays it   2
is necessary to establish a good definition of "community" and to evaluate the importance of community to society. "Community" is really a
social state or condition. So in a sense whether we live together in cities
or suburbs, a small town or a giant metropolis, we share community because we are creating a social or interactive experience with our fellow
human beings. We are sharing the same laws, paying the same taxes that
build and maintain our common living space. However, when we consider "community" and its meaning in our lives, we hardly consider it
in such a formal, rigid context. We are more likely to think of the corner
grocery store and its decline in the face of giant supermarket chains or
the neighborhood before it was bulldozed for the cause of progress. The
important things that stand out in our minds are not the actual buildings in the community, but the sense of belonging and the personal satisfaction that we feel from knowing others, being known by others, and
sharing life together as a "community." Human beings are by nature social creatures. Society was developed and evolved for centuries as a re-

sult of our innate social nature. The force of the industrial revolution, which all three writings allude to, has chaotically thrown the reasons that we live together as well as the places we live in into a radically new direction.

The common theme of loss of community is presented by all the authors in different ways. In "Cohousing" we are told that "Things that people once took for granted—family, community, a sense of belonging—must now be actively sought out." In "Rootlessness" author David Morris laments that "Hundreds of thousands of informal gathering spots that once nurtured community across the country have disappeared." McKenzie in "Privatopia" limits his writing to attacking the principles underlying CIDs, or "common-interest housing developments," more widely known as condominium-type developments. McKenzie implies a loss of community through CIDs by his analysis of "millions of affluent homeowners . . . encouraged to secede from urban America, with its endless flux and ferment, its spontaneity and diversity and its unpredictable rewards and hazards," to the more "predictable, controlled environments" that CIDs provide. While "Privatopia"'s examination of community is confined to urban communities, "Rootlessness" and "Cohousing" are inclusive of suburban as well as urban communities. The assumption is made by all the authors that homogeneous societal living is the preferred mode of human lifestyles.   3

The essence of "community" is the acknowledged interdependence   4
of each member. In "Privatopia" Evan McKenzie makes the bold statement that "CID housing has begun to undermine the basic assumptions of urban culture and establish a competing regime." An understanding of McKenzie's views is enhanced when one considers what is meant by "the basic assumptions of urban culture." In "Privatopia" McKenzie concentrates on "the competing regime" in terms of the establishment of CIDs and how they operate. The primary "basic assumption of urban culture" that he infers in his writing is that *we are all in it together.* This is inferred from his vehement opposition to the class separation and the exodus out of urban areas that he believes CIDs promote. He quotes several authorities in societal structure to substantiate his point. In "Cohousing" a similar idea is reflected in the authors' observation that "To expect that today's small households, as likely to be single parents or single adults as nuclear families, should be self-sufficient without community support is not only unrealistic but absurd." Again, we hear the idea reflected that *we are all in it together,* and also developed into a more expansive view that *we need each other.* Morris in "Rootlessness" also emphasizes the need of community: "Shallow roots [in a community]

weaken our ties in the neighborhood and workplace. . . . This lack of connectedness breeds a costly instability in American life."

All three essays contain the common call to return to a feeling of   5
community. In "Privatopia" McKenzie says that CIDs are a "privatized,
master-planned version of the village-centered life that our species led
for millennia, and that many romanticize today." The suggestions that
Morris makes in "Rootless" for rebuilding walking communities, equip-
ping every neighborhood with a library, coffeehouse, shopping area
and a park, are reflective of a "village" type of community concept. "Cohousing" gives a brief but insightful background into humanity's past
living situations:

> In the past, most people lived in villages or tightly knit urban neighborhoods.
> . . . Members of such communities know one another for many years; they are
> familiar with one another's families and histories, talents and weaknesses. This
> kind of relationship demands accountability, but in return provides security
> and a sense of belonging.

This stands in direct contrast to the future that McKenzie portrays in his quotation of scholar Charles Murray who predicts that class separation will cause
cities to become "places of deprivation and dysfunction for which they [the
inhabitants] will feel no responsibility."

While "Rootlessness" and "Cohousing" explore the unsatisfactory   6
living situations that we are in, "Privatopia" concentrates on an alternative, CIDs, where an estimated one-eighth of the US population is currently housed, and the problems that this alternative poses. "Privatopia"
views the main problems of the CIDs as the creation of a society of
"haves and have-nots," with the more affluent members exiting the
urban areas and establishing private communities that have their own
governments and common areas, such as parks and streets. McKenzie
perceives these communities as undermining social culture. While he
does not make an argument for a solution, he calls for us to examine the
situation and make our own evaluations. One of the best underlying
themes in his essay is that the creation and expansion of these CIDs
moves society in a certain direction by its very nature. He offers no personal criticism of the individuals who buy into these developments,
with their private roads, lights and security; after all, one would be hard-
pressed to argue against individuals who want to live in a safe and well-
maintained neighborhood. McKenzie makes a valuable point in directing our attention to the fact that this goal of living in a safe and
well-maintained neighborhood should be one that all of society is working toward achieving for all of its members. If one group of affluent people take it into their own hands to create their own "safe haven" to live

in and disregard everyone else, then what kind of social statement is that making? On the other hand, for many families today the CID offers the only affordable housing option, a point that McKenzie overlooks.

"Rootlessness" sees the rapid movement of the American family as   7
the cause of community loss. Morris believes that this has negative economic and emotional consequences. The solutions that he proposes are concrete ideas such as rebuilding walking communities, rewarding stability, prohibiting hostile takeovers and encouraging local ownership of business. These solutions are thought-provoking but not very realistic. To illustrate the lack of reasonability of one of Morris's suggestions, consider this: Morris suggests that if the government seizes private property, as in the case of urban development, that the government should pay a premium to the occupant if the occupant has resided there for at least ten years. Morris argues that this would reward stability and discourage thoughtless urban development. Although this is a nice idea, in the real world we live in it seems discriminatory, hardly a legally feasible proposal.

"Cohousing" sets forth the problem that traditional housing no   8
longer addresses the needs of many people and that housing options are limited. The main emphasis of the essay is the selling of the idea of "cohousing," a term coined by the authors to describe housing models that were developed in Denmark as "living communities." These cohousing communities are either newly built or built from existing structures. They comprise varying sizes of housing units designed to accommodate different types and sizes of families, each unit having its own kitchen and bathroom facilities. These developments also contain common kitchen and dining areas, shared guest accommodations, playrooms, laundry and the like.

"Cohousing" does not give any concrete operating details such as   9
dinner preparation rotation or the cost contribution required by each family. While I tend to favor the concepts in "Cohousing," the vagueness of the authors' explanation of the actual workings of this new type of community could be its demise. The idea that it is "a grass-roots movement that grew directly out of people's dissatisfaction with existing housing choices" was very appealing to me. However, the social concerns brought to light by McKenzie in "Privatopia" may not be satisfactorily answered by cohousing. Cohousing still has the potential to create a separate, class-bound society without real social and political involvement.

The best aspect of all three articles is their shared encouragement for us to take a look at where our modern society is heading and to partake   10
in the creation of its direction. Essentially society comprises people, not corporations or developers whose major directive is profit. People make

up community, people knowing people, people being known. While housing structures and alternatives are an important consideration, as well as one of our basic human needs, buildings are not what creates "community." Thus the decline of community in our society must be looked at from a broad, human perspective. The economic and technological factors that have preceded the decline of community must also be addressed if any real and lasting solution to community restoration is to be found. While technology has personally benefited many individuals in society, the costs that have been paid for technological advancement have been great, including loss of jobs, reliance on polluting vehicles that make commuter lifestyles possible, and the alienating, false sense of community created by television and radio. An honest evaluation of technology's value and failings needs to be made in the light of its impact upon our lives, not merely on our existence as private individuals, but on our lives as social creatures *who are all in it together and who need each other.*

RESPONDING TO "MODERN AMERICA: METROPOLIS OR NECROPOLIS?"

Freewrite about whether the group (or community) is more important than the individual.

Responding through Interpretation

1. Go back and read the section of the essay where Curtis gives her definition of *community*. Do you think she is accurate in her definition and explanation? Do you agree or disagree with her?
2. What is the common theme Curtis is responding to in the three essays? How effectively does she compare and evaluate them?

Responding through Discussion

1. When is the individual more important than the community—and vice versa? With your group, discuss how the rise of the individual might have affected community and neighborhoods. Is this necessarily bad or good? What are the drawbacks of being too involved in groups and communities, and what are the drawbacks of being too removed from others? What are the benefits?

Responding through Writing

1. What does Curtis mean when she says at the end of her essay that we are social creatures "who are all in it together and who need each other"? Write a journal entry in which you expand and explore her statement.

2. Write a paper in which you discuss the decline of "community" in today's world. Based on your own observations and experiences, what are some of the problems caused by a sense of not really belonging to the communities we live in?

MAKING CONNECTIONS

Now that you've read some of the selections in this chapter and have some information about the idea of community, you are better able to make your own decisions about the subject. Instead of taking for granted that strengthening community is a positive goal, think about the opposite viewpoint: Do strong communities weaken individual achievement and expression? If strong communities are such a desirable goal, why do cities continue to increase in population and small towns continue to decline? The following questions and writing suggestions might help to give you further ideas for developing your own opinions about communities.

1. *Cultural differences and tensions.* Several works in this chapter comment on tensions and misunderstandings that arise in community and society because of cultural differences. Take another look at the selections by Tess Gallagher, Toni Cade Bambara, Cecilia Fairley, Arthur Ashe, and P. W. Alexander. Write an essay in which you suggest possible changes in our educational system or community activities that would help to overcome cultural tensions and differences. Do you think that this goal is possible to achieve?

2. *Service to others.* Again, many of the selections in this chapter urge service to others as a way to improve life for all of us. See especially P. W. Alexander's "Christmas at Home," Tess Gallagher's poem "The Hug," and essays by students Julian Castro and Jeremy Taylor. Write a paper giving your opinion about community service as a way to improve relationships and establish a stronger sense of community.

3. *Loyalty in the neighborhood.* The decline of real neighborhoods is seen by several writers as the biggest issue in the lack of community. Compare such essays as "Cohousing and the American Dream," "Rootlessness," and "Trouble in Privatopia," as well as the papers by student writers Fairley and Curtis. What is your opinion about how housing affects a neighborhood (think about your own neighborhood at present)? Again, what are the advantages or disadvantages, from your point of view, of creating strong neighborhoods? Write a paper giving your opinions on the subject of how housing creates neighborhoods, which in turn create community.

4. *Politics and the community.* In what ways do you think politics either helps or destroys communities? Read again Arthur Ashe, Julian Castro, David Morris, and Kathryn McCamant and Charles Durrett. Drawing on your own observations and experiences, how do you think the government does or does not address the concerns of communities? Look at it from the city, the state, and the national levels. What kinds of legislation do you think might bring back a balance among neighborhoods, small towns, and large cities? Do additional reading if you need to and, if possible, conduct interviews with local politicians.

**BRINGING IDEAS TOGETHER:
MAKING FURTHER CONNECTIONS**

Even though you might not have read selections from each of the seven chapters of readings—and might not have read them in the order they were presented—we have placed here at the end of the book a few suggestions for writing which will highlight some of the connections between readings throughout the book. While we have organized readings under seven different categories—education, family, gender, nature, health, work, and community (each the title of a different chapter)—many of the readings bring up ideas that cross over into several of these categories. These additional writing suggestions will give you an opportunity to go back and read selections you might have missed and then to bring some of the ideas together in your own papers.

1. *Our multicultural society: Curse or blessing?* We have deliberately included in this book a number of pieces that give information and raise questions about the many cultures now so prevalent in this country. America has attracted an astounding number of immigrants over the past 100 years and has been called "a melting pot" of many different cultures. Go back through the book and make a note of all the selections that give perspectives on cultures different from what you might consider the normal white middle-class society which is so prominent in advertising. See, for example, Le, Kozol, and Rose in "Education"; Marx, Wu, Rios, Tan, and Walker in "Family"; Yamauchi in "Gender"; Rodriguez, Hip, Mar, and Angelou in "Work"; and Alexander, Gallagher, Bambara, and Castro in "Community."

   Bring together all you have learned about other cultures through these readings; then do some further reading about multicultural America and write a paper in which you present both the benefits and the problems created by so many cultures in one country.

2. *Poverty and our society.* The level of poverty in this country continues to spiral upward, outdistanced only by our national debt. Yet the United States clearly enjoys one of the highest standards of living of any country in the world. Many readings in *Responding Voices* show the effects of poverty on people's lives, especially these pieces: Kozol and Rose in "Education"; Olsen and Walker in "Family"; Sanders and Yamauchi in "Gender"; Rodriguez, Mar, Angelou, and Ehrenreich in "Work"; and Alexander, Gallagher, and Bambara in "Community."

Write a paper that pulls together some of the information about the effects of poverty on people's lives as shown in these readings. What did you learn about poverty through these readings? How do the things you learned compare with your own life? Do some further reading, and find out some of the reasons for the growing poverty and homelessness in America. Is it lack of jobs? Is it the welfare program? Is it because we no longer care about each other? Whatever happened to the War on Poverty? Give some reasons you've discovered for the continued poverty in this country.

3. *Family conflicts.* You are probably already aware of how many conflicts are caused by families themselves. The family, which is often portrayed as being a happy refuge in a hostile world, is frequently the very agent for causing unhappiness for a large number of individuals. This does not mean that there aren't many positive aspects of family life. Most of us want families, need them, love them. However, looking at some of the issues that cause the conflicts can be very enlightening. At least half of the readings in this book touch on family concerns: Jackson and Rose in "Education"; all the readings in "Family"; Stanton, Sanders, Yamauchi, Cary, Lester, Woodle, and Tse in "Gender"; Taylor in "Nature"; Murray, Becker, Williams, and Quindlen in "Health"; Rodriquez, Mar, Angelou, and Ehrenreich in "Work"; and Alexander, Castro, Taylor, and Bambara in "Community."

Read through these essays and identify some of the family conflicts that arise from gender, alcoholism, poverty, power struggles, work, etc. Choose one idea and write a paper giving your opinion about why this conflict causes so many problems; give some ideas for solving the conflict within families. You might do some further reading and perhaps conduct an interview with a family therapist. Then write a paper on family dynamics and communication. What are some of the ways a family can communicate more effectively and thereby become a more positive influence on the individual members?

4. *Separation from others: the need to become an individual.* Life is a constant process of connecting with others and then pulling apart to expe-

rience ourselves as individuals. Even in childhood, we seek out solitude, a chance to be alone with ourselves; we begin early in life to discover who we really are and to seek out opportunities to express ourselves. The uniqueness of the individual as an idea runs throughout many of the selections in *Responding Voices*. Look back through these selections and identify some of the ideas, particularly in Asimov, Holt, Woo, and Rose in "Education"; Goodman, Wright, Olsen, Tan, Didion, and Walker in "Family"; Stanton, Sanders, Piercy, Yamauchi, Cary, and Lester in "Gender"; Thomas, Hogan, Stafford, Taylor, and Dillard in "Nature"; Murray, Williams, and Moyers in "Health"; Rodriguez and Angelou in "Work"; and Gallagher and Bambara in "Community."

Write a paper in which you trace some of the ideas about individual expression in these readings. What do we learn from being alone? Consider the solitude that is essential in order for you to observe the world, to think, and to read and to write.

Acknowledgments

Alexander, P.W. "Christmas at Home" by P.W. Alexander. Reprinted by permission of the author.

Angelou, Maya. "Cotton Pickers" by Maya Angelou. From *I Know Why the Caged Bird Sings* by Maya Angelou. Copyright © 1969 by Maya Angelou. Reprinted by permission of Random House, Inc.

Ashe, Arthur. "Can a New 'Army' Save Our Cities" by Arthur Ashe, *Washington Post,* Sunday May 10, 1992. Reprinted with permission from The Washington Post and Jeanne Moutoussamy-Ashe.

Asimov, Isaac. "What Is Intelligence, Anyway?" by Isaac Asimov. Published by permission of The Estate of Isaac Asimov, c/o Ralph M. Vicinanza, Ltd.

Austin, Nancy K. "Ethics: Personal vs. Professional" by Nancy K. Austin, originally appeared in *Working Woman* Magazine, September 1992. Reprinted by permission of the author.

Bambara, Toni Cade. "My Man Bovanne" by Toni Cade Bambara. From *Gorilla, My Love* by Toni Cade Bambara. Copyright © 1971 by Toni Cade Bambara. Reprinted by permission of Random House, Inc.

Becker, Robin. "Medical Science" by Robin Becker reprinted from *Backtalk* with permission from Alicejames Books.

Böll, Heinrich. "The Laugher" by Heinrich Böll from *Heinrich Böll: Eighteen Stories.* Reprinted by arrangement with Verlag Kiepenheuer & Witsch, c/o Joan Daves Agency as agent for the proprietor. Copyright 1966 by Heinrich Böll.

Cary, Rick. "Coming Out" by Rick Cary, first appeared in *One Teenager in Ten.* © 1983, edited by Ann Heron. Reprinted by permission of Alyson Publications Inc., Los Angeles.

Didion, Joan. "On Going Home" from *Slouching Towards Bethlehem* by Joan Didion. Copyright © 1968 by Joan Didion. Reprinted by permission of Farrar, Straus & Giroux, Inc.

Dillard, Annie. "Soujourner" from *Teaching a Stone to Talk* by Annie Dillard. Copyright © 1982 by Annie Dillard. Reprinted by permission of HarperCollins Publishers, Inc.

Ehrenreich, Barbara. "A Step Back to the Workhouse?" by Barbara Ehrenreich as appeared in *Ms.* Magazine, November 1987. Reprinted by permission of the author.

Gallagher, Tess. "The Hug" copyright 1987 by Tess Gallagher. Reprinted from *Amplitude* with the permission of Graywolf Press, Saint Paul, Minnesota.

Goodman, Ellen. "Our Kids Are Not Just Copies of Us" by Ellen Goodman as appeared in *The Boston Globe,* August 30, 1993. © 1993, The Boston Globe Newspaper Co./Washington Post Writers Group. Reprinted with permission.

Rukeyser, Muriel. From "This Place in the Ways," by Muriel Rukeyser, from *A Muriel Rukeyser Reader*, 1994, W. W. Norton, New York, © William L. Rukeyser. Reprinted by permission.

Sanders, Scott Russell. "The Men We Carry in Our Minds . . . and How They Differ from the Real Lives of Most Men" by Scott Russell Sanders. Copyright © 1984 by Scott Russell Sanders; first appeared in *Milkweed Chronicle;* reprinted by permission of the author and Virginia Kidd, Literary Agent.

Stafford, William. "Traveling Through the Dark," copyright © 1977 William Stafford from *Stories That Could Be True* (Harper & Row). Reprinted by permission of The Estate of William Stafford.

Tan, Amy. "Snapshot: Lost Lives of Women" by Amy Tan. Copyright © 1991 by Amy Tan. First published in *Life* Magazine. Reprinted by permission of the author and the Sandra Dijkstra Literacy Agency.

Tan, Amy. Photo from "Snapshot: Lost Lives of Women" by Amy Tan. Copyright © 1991 by Amy Tan. First published in *Life* Magazine. Reprinted by permission of the author and the Sandra Dijkstra Literacy Agency.

Tannen, Deborah, "How Male and Female Students Use Language Differently," *The Chronicle of Higher Education,* June 19, 1991. Reprinted by permission of International Creative Management, Inc. Copyright © 1991 by Deborah Tannen.

Taylor, Peter. "A Walled Garden," from *The Old Forest and Other Stories* by Peter Taylor. Copyright 1941, 1945, 1947, 1949, 1951, 1958, 1959, 1979, 1981, 1985 by Peter Taylor. Used by permission of Doubleday, a division of Bantam Doubleday Dell Publishing Group, Inc.

Thomas, Elizabeth Marshall. Excerpt from *The Hidden Life of Dogs* by Elizabeth Marshall Thomas. Copyright © 1993 by Elizabeth Marshall Thomas. Reprinted by permission of Houghton Mifflin Company. All rights reserved.

Thomas, Lewis. "On Embryology, pp. 155–7," copyright © 1979 by Lewis Thomas, from *The Medusa and the Snail* by Lewis Thomas. Used by permission of Viking Penguin, a division of Penguin Books USA Inc.

Walker, Alice. "Father" from *Living by the Word: Selected Writings 1973–1987,* copyright © 1985 by Alice Walker, reprinted by permission of Harcourt Brace & Company.

Williams, William Carlos. "The Use of Force" by William Carlos Williams, from *Doctor Stories.* Copyright © 1938 by William Carlos Williams. Reprinted by permission of New Directions Publishing Corp.

Woo, Merle. "Poem for the Creative Writing Class, Spring 1982" by Merle Woo. Reprinted by permission of the author.

Wright, Lawrence. "Reunion" by Lawrence Wright. Reprinted with permission from Texas Monthly.

Yamauchi, Wakako. Reprinted, by permission, from Wakako Yamauchi, "And the Soul Shall Dance," in *Songs My Mother Taught Me: Stories, Plays and Memoir,* ed., Garrett Hongo (New York: The Feminist Press at The City University of New York, 1994), pp. 19–24. © 1994 by Wakako Yamauchi.

Index

Alexander, P. W., "Christmas at Home," 342

"Alice Walker's 'Father': A Process of Understanding and Acceptance" (Fan Lee), 146

"And the Soul Shall Dance" (Yamauchi), 171

Angelou, Maya, "Cotton Pickers," 317

Argument, 31–32

"Art of Healing, The" (Moyers), 276

Ashe, Arthur, "Can a New 'Army' Save Our Cities'," 347

Asimov, Isaac, "What Is Intelligence Anyway?," 40

Audience, 7–8

Austin, Nancy K., "Workable Ethics," 299

Bambara, Toni Cade, "My Man Bovanne," 364

"Battle between Men and Women, The" (Tran), 163

Becker, Robin, "Medical Science," 261

"Being a Boy" (Lester), 184

Böll, Heinrich, "The Laugher," 313

Brainstorming, 17–18

"Call to Service, A" (Taylor), 354

"Can a New 'Army' Save Our Cities?" (Ashe), 347

Carrillo, Richard, "Surviving Adolescence," 92

Cary, Rick, "Coming Out," 179

Castro, Julian, "Politics . . . *Maybe,*" 351

Chan, Dickon, "The Health Care Plan I Favor," 255

"Charles" (Jackson), 58

"Christmas at Home" (Alexander), 342

Clustering, 18–19

"Cohousing and the American Dream" (McCamant & Durrett), 376

Collaboration, 32–33

Collins, Derek, "Responding to 'The Art of Healing,' " 286

"Coming Out" (Cary), 179

Comparison, 30

Computers and writing process, 26

Community, 340–441

Corbin, Nikki, "Why Workfare?," 331

"Corla Hawkins" (Kozol), 64

"Cotton Pickers" (Angelou), 317

Conclusions, 24–25

Curtis, Kimberly, "Modern America: Metropolis or Necropolis?," 394

Description, 28
Dictionary, use of, 10
Didion, Joan, "On Going Home," 132
Dillard, Annie, "Sojourner," 227
Discovery drafting, 21
"Do Dogs Have Thoughts and Feelings?" (Thomas), 231
"Doctor, Do You Care?" (Razum), 282
"Doctor's Case: A Physician Becomes a Cancer Patient, A" (Kurland), 251
Dogs and Empathetic Observation (Pascerella), 238
"Dogs in Transition" (Simon), 235
Drafting, 20–22
and discovery, 21–22

Education, 38–39
Ehrenreich, Barbara, "A Step Back to the Workhouse," 325
Evaluative responses to reading, 13, 31

Fairley, Cecilia, "Whatever Happened to the Neighborhood?," 389
Family, 100–101
"Family Friends: A Process of Growth" (Wu), 112
Fan Lee, Shu, "Alice Walker's Father: A Process of Understanding and Acceptance," 146
"Father" (Walker), 136
Freewriting, 19–20

Gallagher, Tess, "The Hug," 361
Gender, 152–153
Goodman, Ellen, "Our Kids Are Not Just Copies of Us," 102

Headnotes, 7
"He Couldn't Get Off the Ground" (Plunckett), 52
Health, 244
"Health Care Plan I Favor, The" (Chan), 255

Hogan, Linda, "Walking," 203
Holmes, Jennifer, "The Work Ethic and Me," 305
Holt, John, "How Teachers Make Children Hate Reading," 43
"How Male and Female Students Use Language Differently" (Tannen), 70
"How Teachers Make Children Hate Reading" (Holt), 43
"Hug, The" (Gallagher), 361
Hunze, Jeff, "Lessons from the Earth," 211

"I Just Wanna Be Average" (Rose) 77
"I Just Wanna Be Challenged" (Schwartz), 88
"I Stand Here Ironing" (Olsen), 119
"Immigrant in a New School, An" (Le), 49
"Indiscriminate Discrimination" (Matthews), 166
Interpretation, 29–30
Introductions, 24

Jackson, Shirley, "Charles," 58
Journal, 34

Kaus, Mickey, "Yes, Something Will Work: Work," 321
Kerr, David, "Strawberry Creek: A Search for Origins," 207
Klass, Perri, "Learning the Language," 268
Kozol, Jonathan, "Corla Hawkins," 64
Kurland, Geoffrey, "A Doctor's Case: A Physician Becomes a Cancer Patient," 251

"Labor" (Rodriguez), 294
"Laugher, The" (Böll), 313
Le, Tin, "An Immigrant in a New School," 49

"Learning the Language" (Klass), 268
"Lessons from the Earth" (Hunze), 211
Lester, Julius, "Being a Boy," 184

Manuscript form, 27
Mapping, 11–12
Mar, Laureen, "My Mother Who Came from China Where She Never Saw Snow," 311
Marking the text, 10
Marx, Amy, "My Grandfather's Memories," 109
"Massage-Message" (Simon), 258
Matthews, Greg, "Indiscriminate Discrimination," 166
McCamant, Kathryn, and Durrett, Charles, "Cohousing and the American Dream," 376
McKenzie, Evan, "Trouble in Privatopia," 382
"Medical Science," (Becker), 261
"Men We Carry in Our Minds . . . and How They Differ from the Real Lives of Most Men, The" (Sanders), 158
Mena, Deirdre, "Welfare versus Workfare," 334
"Modern America: Metropolis or Necropolis?" (Curtis), 394
Morris, David, "Rootlessness Undermines Our Economy as Well as the Quality of Our Lives," 371
Moyers, Bill, "The Art of Healing," 276
Murray, Donald M., "Reflections from a Sick Bed," 246
"My Dad and Walker's Father" (Skinner), 143
My Grandfather's Memories (Marx), 109
"My Man Bovanne" (Bambara), 364
"My Mother Who Came from China Where She Never Saw Snow" (Mar), 311

Nani (Rios), 116
Narration, 28–29
Nature, 198–199
Nichols, John T., "What Is a Naturalist, Anyway?," 221
Notation, in reading, 8

"Olsen, Tillie, "I Stand Here Ironing," 119
"On Being Female" (Woodle), 189
"On Embryology" (Thomas), 200
"On Going Home" (Didion), 132
"Our Kids Are Not Just Copies of Us" (Goodman), 102
Outlining, of readings, 11
scratch, 20–21

Paraphrasing and summarizing, 10–11
Pascerella, Lori, "Dogs and Empathetic Observation," 238
Peer sharing, 33
Persuasive argument, 31–32
Piercy, Marge, "A Work of Artifice," 169
Plunckett, Jayme, "He Couldn't Get Off the Ground," 52
"Poem for the Creative Writing Class, Spring 1982" (Woo), 55
"Politics . . . Maybe" (Castro), 351
Purposes and Strategies for Writing, 27–32
Post-reading response, 12
Pre-reading, 6
Pre-writing, 17–20
Process, of writing, 16–17
Proofreading, 26–27
Punctuation, 25–26
Purpose, of an author, 7

Quindlen, Anna, "The War on Drinks," 273

Razum, Katherine, "Doctor, Do You Care?," 282
Reading, 3

Reading (*continued*)
  aloud, 10
  interest in, 5
  journal, 3
  pleasure in, 5
  relationship with, 4
  stages of, 6–13
Reading/writing journal, 3
"Reflections from a Sick Bed" (Murray), 246
Responding as a reader, 3–14
Responding as a writer, 15–35
"Responding to 'The Art of Healing' " (Collins), 286
"Reunion" (Wright), 105
Rios, Alberto Alvaro, "Nani," 116
Revising, 22–24
  fine-tuning, 25
  of paragraphs, 23–24
  of punctuation, 25
  of sentences, 25
  of whole essay, 23
Rodriguez, Richard, "Labor," 294
"Rootlessness Undermines Our Economy as Well as the Quality of Our Lives" (Morris), 371
Rose, Mike, "I Just Wanna Be Average," 77

Sanders, Scott Russell, "The Men We Carry in Our Minds and How They Differ from the Real Lives of Most Men," 158
Schwartz, Rainbow, "I Just Wanna Be Challenged," 88
Sentences, 25
Simon, Kirsten, "Massage-Message," 258
Simon, Kirsten, "Dogs in Transition," 235
Skimming, 7, 8–9
Skinner, Beverly, "My Dad and Walker's Father," 143

"Snapshot of Lost Lives of Women" (Tan), 128
"Sojourner" (Dillard), 227
Spelling, 27
Stafford, William, "Traveling through the Dark," 214
Stanton, Elizabeth Cady, "You Should Have Been a Boy," 154
"Step Back to the Workhouse, A" (Ehrenreich), 325
Strategies for writing, 27–32
"Strawberry Creek: A Search for Origins" (Kerr), 207
Studying (stage in reading), 7, 9–10
"Surviving Adolescence" (Carrillo), 92

Tan, Amy, "Snapshot of Lost Lives of Women," 128
Tannen, Deborah, "How Male and Female Students Use Language Differently," 70
Taylor, Jeremy, "A Call to Service," 354
Taylor, Peter, "A Walled Garden," 216
Tentative thesis, 20–21
Thomas, Elizabeth Marshall, "Do Dogs Have Thoughts and Feelings?," 231
Thomas, Lewis, "On Embryology," 200
Tran, Quynhchau, "The Battle between Men and Women," 163
"Traveling through the Dark" (Stafford), 214
Tse, Magnolia, "What About Being a Girl?," 192

Ueland, Brenda, "If You Want to Write," 33–34
"Use of Force, The" (Williams), 263

Walker, Alice, "Father," 136
"Walking" (Hogan), 203
"Walled Garden, A" (Taylor), 216

"War on Drinks, The" (Quindlen), 273

"Welfare versus Workfare" (Mena), 334

"What About Being a Girl?" (Tse), 192

"What Is a Naturalist, Anyway?" (Nichols), 221

"What Is Intelligence Anyway?" (Asimov), 40

"Whatever Happened to the Neighborhood?" (Fairley), 389

"Why I Hate Work" (Hip), 308

"Why Workfare?" (Corbin), 331

Williams, William Carlos, "The Use of Force," 263

Wing Kuen Hip, Kevin, "Why I Hate Work," 308

Woo, Merle, "Poem for the Creative Writing Class, Spring 1982," 55

Woodle, Nina, "On Being Female," 189

Words, 26

Work, 292–293

"Work Ethic and Me, The" (Holmes), 305

"Work of Artifice, A" (Piercy), 163

"Workable Ethics" (Austin), 199

Wright, Lawrence, "Reunion," 105

Wu, Charlie, "Family Friends: A Process of Growth," 112

Yamauchi, Wakako, "And the Soul Shall Dance," 171

"Yes, Something Will Work: Work" (Kaus), 321

"You Should Have Been a Boy" (Stanton), 154